D0204066

State Building
and Democratization
in Africa

State Building
and Democratization
in Africa

Faith, Hope, and Realities

EDITED BY
Kidane Mengisteab
and Cyril Daddieh

Westport, Connecticut
London

Library of Congress Cataloging-in-Publication Data

State building and democratization in Africa : faith, hope, and
    realities / edited by Kidane Mengisteab and Cyril Daddieh.
        p.   cm.
    Includes bibliographical references and index.
    ISBN 0–275–96353–5 (alk. paper)
        1. Africa, Sub-Saharan—Politics and government—1960–
    2. Democracy—Africa, Sub-Saharan.   3. Democratization—Africa, Sub-
    Saharan.   I. Kidane Mengisteab.   II. Daddieh, Cyril.
    JQ1875.S7   1999
    320.967—dc21   98–21642

British Library Cataloguing in Publication Data is available.

Library of Congress Catalog Card Number: 98–21642
ISBN: 0–275–96353–5

First published in 1999

Praeger Publishers, 88 Post Road West, Westport, CT 06881
An imprint of Greenwood Publishing Group, Inc.

Printed in the United States of America

The paper used in this book complies with the
Permanent Paper Standard issued by the National
Information Standards Organization (Z39.48–1984).

10 9 8 7 6 5 4 3 2 1

Contents

Acronyms

AAPO	All Amhara People's Organization
ABN	Association for a Better Nigeria
ACC	Anti-Corruption Commission
AFRC	Armed Forces Revolutionary Council
ANC	African National Congress
ASP	Afro-Shirazi Party
AST	*Action Socialiste Tchadienne*
ASUU	Academic Staff Union of Universities
AWEPA	European Parliamentarians for Southern Africa
BCMA	Black Consciousness Movement of Azania
BET	Biltine-Ennedi-Tibesti
CAN	Christian Association of Nigeria
CAR	Central African Republic
CBO	Community-Based Organization
CCM	Chama Cha Mapinduzi
CCT	Christian Council of Tanzania
CD	Campaign for Democracy
CDHR	Committee for the Defense of Human Rights
CDS	Center for Democratic Studies
CEAN	*Centre d'Etude d'Afrique Noire*
CENI	National Electoral Commission
CFA	*Communauté Financière Africaine*

CHADEMA	*Chama Cha Demokrasia na Maendeleo*
CLO	Civil Liberties Organization
COSATU	Congress of South African Trade Unions
CPK	Church of the Province of Kenya
CPP	Convention People's Party
CSC	*Confédération Syndicale du Congo*
CSC	*Conseil Superieur de Communication*
CSSPPA	*Caisse de Stabilisation et de Soutien des Prix des Produits Agricoles*
CST	*Conseil Superieur de Transition*
CUF	Civic United Front
EPRDF	Ethiopian People's Revolutionary Democratic Forces
EPRDP	Ethiopian Peoples' Revolutionary Democratic Party
FDC	*Front Démocratique Congolais*
FORD—Kenya	Forum for the Restoration of Democracy—Kenya
FPI	*Front Populaire Ivoirien*
FROLINAT	National Liberation Front
GDP	Gross Domestic Product
GEAR	Growth, Employment and Redistribution Strategy
GIRT	*Groupement des Indépendants et Ruraux Tchadiens*
GNU	Government of National Unity
GPRTU	Ghana Private Road Transport Union
GUNT	*Gouvernement d'Union Nationale Tchadinne*
HDI	Human Development Index
ICWU	Industrial and Commercial Workers' Union
IFDS	International Forum for Democratic Studies
IFES	International Foundation for Election Systems
IFIs	International Financial Institutions
IFLO	Islamic Front for the Liberation of Oromia
IFP	Inkatha Freedom Party
IGADD	Intergovernmental Authority on Drought and Development
IMF	International Monetary Fund
INGOs	International Nongovernmental Organizations
IPK	Islamic Party of Kenya
KADU	Kenya African Democratic Union
KANU	Kenya African National Union
KPU	Kenya People's Union

MCDDI	*Mouvement Congolais pour la Démocratie et le Développement Integrat*
MCP	Malawi Congress Party
MEECI	*Mouvement des Élèves et Étudiants de Côte d'Ivoire*
MESAN	*Mouvement d'Emancipation Sociale de l'Afrique*
MNCs	Multinational corporations
MNR	*Mouvement National de la Révolution*
MNRCS	*Mouvement National pour la Révolution Culturelle et Sociale*
MOSOP	Movement for the Survival of the Ogoni People
MPs	Members of Parliament
MSA	*Mouvement Socialiste Africain*
NADL	National Association of Democratic Lawyers
NAL	National Alliance of Liberals
NANS	National Association of Nigerian Students
NBA	Nigerian Bar Association
NCCK	National Council of Churches of Kenya
NCCR—Mageuzi	National Convention for Construction and Reform—Mageuzi
NDC	National Democratic Congress
NDSC	National Defense and Security Council
NEC	National Electoral Commission
NEC	National Executive Committee
NEMG	Nigerian Election Monitoring Group
NFD	Northern Frontier District
NGOs	Nongovernmental organizations
NICs	Newly Industrializing Countries
NLM	National Liberation Movement
NP	National Party
NPP	New Patriotic Party
NPP	Northern Peoples Party
NRC	National Republican Convention
NRM	National Resistance Movement
NUPENG	National Union of Petroleum and Natural Gas Workers
OALF	Oromo ABO Liberation Front
OAU	Organization of African Unity
OLF	Oromo Liberation Front
OPDO	Oromo Peoples Democratization Organization
ORH	Operation Restore Hope
PAC	Pan-Africanist Congress

PAGAD	People against Gangsterism and Drugs
PAMSCAD	Program of Actions to Mitigate the Social Costs of Adjustment
PCF	French Communist Party
PCT	*Party Congolais du Travail*
PDCI	*Parti Démocratique de Côte d'Ivoire*
PDOs	Peoples Democratic Organizations
PFI	*Front Populaire Ivorien*
PIP	Public Investment Program
PIT	*Parti Ivoirien des Travailleurs*
PNA	*Parti National Africain*
PNDC	Provisional National Defense Council
PP	Busia-Progress Party
PPC	*Parti Progressiste Congolais*
PPT	*Porti Progressiste Tchadien*
PS	*Parti Socialiste*
PSDC	*Parti Socialiste Démocratique Congolais*
RDH	*Rassemblement Démocratique Africain*
RDP	Reconstruction and Development Program
RENAMO	*Resistência Nacional Mozambicana*
RPF	*Rassemblement du Peuple Français*
SAA	*Syndicat Agricole Africain*
SACP	South African Communist Party
SADCC	Southern African Development Coordination Conference
SAFINA	The Ark
SAG	South African Government
SAIIA	South African Institute of International Affairs
SAMO	Somali African Muki Organization
SANDF	South African National Defense Force
SAP	Structural Adjustment Program
SATMACI	State Agricultural Service Agency for Export Crops
SDA	Somali Democratic Alliance
SDM	Somali Democratic Movement
SDP	Social Democratic Party
SFIO	*Section Française de l'Internationale Ouvrière*
SNA	Somali National Alliance
SNDU	Somali National Democratic Union
SNF	Somali National Front

SNL	Somali National League
SNM	Somali National Movement
SNU	Somali National Union
SPLM	Sudan People's Liberation Movement
SPM	Somali Patriotic Movement
SSDF	Somali Salvation Democratic Front
SSNM	Southern Somali National Movement
SSS	State Security Service
TANU	Tanganyika African National Union
TC	Transitional Council
TCP	Togoland Congress Party
TCRT	Transition to Civil Rule Tribunal
TGE	Transitional Government of Ethiopia
TNC	Transitional National Council
TPLF	Tigrai People's Liberation Front
TRC	Truth and Reconciliation Commission
UDDIA	*Union Démocratique Pour la Défense des Intérêts Africains*
UDF	United Democratic Front
UDIT	*Union Démocratique Indépendante du Tchad*
UDR	*Union pour la Démocratie et la République*
UDSR	*Union Démocratique et Socialiste de la Résistance*
UDT	*Union Démocratique Tchadienne*
UGTCI	*Union Générale des Travailleurs de Côte d'Ivoire*
UMD	Union for Multi-Party Democracy
UN	United Nations
UNDP	United Nations Development Program
UNF	United National Front
UNIR	*Union Nationale pour l'Indépendance et Révolution*
UNITA	*União Nacional para a Independência Total de Angola*
UNOSOM	United Nations Operations in Somalia
UOPLF	United Oromo People's Liberation Front
UP	United Party
UPADS	*Union Panafricaine pour la Démocratie Sociale*
URD	Union of Democratic Renewal
URD	*Union Pour la Démocracie et la République*
URT	*Union Républicaine du Tchad*
USC	United Somali Congress

USD	*Union des Sociaux-Démocrates*
USF	United Somali Front
USP	United Somali Party
UST	*Union des Syndicats du Tchad*
UST	*Union Socialiste Tchadienne*
VDOs	Voluntary Development Organizations
VORADEP	Volta Regional Development Corporation
WEREMUD	Western Region Movement for Unity and Development
WHAM	''Winning of Hearts and Minds'' Policy
ZANU-PF	Zimbabwe African National Union-Popular Front

State Building
and Democratization
in Africa

Chapter 1

Why State Building Is Still Relevant in Africa and How It Relates to Democratization

KIDANE MENGISTEAB AND CYRIL DADDIEH

INTRODUCTION

The end of the Cold War and the crisis of socialism (statism) have ushered in a new global power configuration and a ''new'' phase of capitalism, which is characterized by wide-ranging deregulation, privatization, and vigorous globalization of capital.[1] With this unfolding global order, the role of the state in economic activity, including its protection of the vulnerable segments of society either through direct redistributive welfare mechanisms or by encouraging poverty-reducing and labor-absorbing economic activities, has come under serious attack. An ideology of free market and open global competition has become the hallmark of this new global order, although the state still plays a critical role in the case of the big powers that form the oligarchies that shape the global system. In most developing countries, however, the role of the state has been downsized considerably, and its task in the economic sphere has essentially been reduced to coordinating the process of adjustment of national economies to the constantly changing global environment. In its efforts to promote liberalization, the World Bank has recently recognized the need for institutional capacity building in Africa. But this is largely aimed at insulating policymakers from popular pressure in order to enable the state to promote adjustment. The World Bank's notion of capacity building does not empower the state for charting autonomously its own development strategy.[2] There is also the danger that reforms that are insulated from public scrutiny are likely to contradict and even undermine the process of democratization.

In sharp contrast to the perspectives of the Cold War era, under the new global order development in Africa and in the rest of the countries of the South is believed to rest on integration with the global economy. Policy measures that

are intended to advance integration with the global economy, including promotion of exports, attraction of foreign investments, correction of macroeconomic imbalances, and extensive decontrols of prices, exchange rates, and
imports, are promoted in these countries. The following two statements by International Monetary Fund (IMF) managing director Michel Camdessus accen-
tuate the development perspective of the new global order.

In fact, open economic relations with the rest of the world provide one of the most
reliable generators of growth. The jury is no longer out on this issue: the verdict is
clear—the most open economies have been the most successful.[3]

In spite of all its risks, but also with all its potential for enhancing economic efficiency,
this international integration of financial markets is not only irreversible, but it can only
broaden and intensify in the future. Let us not make the mistake of believing that the
answer to financial crisis lies in reversing this globalization through exchange controls
and less open markets.[4]

Why, then, a book about state building in an era when the relevance of the
state is viewed to be declining and when an anti-state ideology that narrows the
scope of state intervention in economic activity has risen to prominence? There
are primarily two reasons for this. One is that the anti-state posture of the emerging global order grossly underestimates the positive roles of the state. Growing
disengagement of the state, and growing global policy convergence toward a
free market system in company with a rapid upsurge in the power of capital
have intensified polarization between rich and poor and between ethnic and
racial groups globally and can lead to serious destabilization if left unchecked.
With growing disengagement of the state, the narrowing of the scope of democracy also seems inevitable. Integrating national economies into the global
system by transforming marginalized sectors such as the subsistence sector is
also unlikely to succeed without an active state. Moreover, in African countries,
even the development of the market mechanism can be undermined by improper
downsizing of the role of the state. Second, in view of the tragedies that have
ensued from state disintegration in countries such as the former Yugoslavia, the
former Soviet Union, Somalia, Liberia, Sierra Leone, and Rwanda, state building, state transformation, and state preservation remain essential, although some
of the roles of the state may need to be modified or even transformed to better
serve the needs of societies in the new global order. The undifferentiating anti-
state ideology is thus unlikely to be sustained for long.

This book deals with the democratization efforts in Africa and how progress
or lack of it affects the process of state building in the continent. The phrase
"state building" is used in this book in two interrelated senses. One usage is
in lieu of "nation building" to avoid the confusion between state building and
the development of sub-state nationalism (ethnonationalism).[5] It refers to the

complex process of internally integrating countries by (1) improving relations among different ethnic and religious entities and uniting them under shared political and economic systems and (2) integrating different economic sectors into a complementary system by transforming the subsistent peasantry and integrating the fragmented dual economies. The second conception of the phrase is in terms of strengthening the state apparatus to make it more effective in advancing the welfare of its citizens and in managing society in line with its mandated authority.

The authors of the different chapters of the book do not share the same views on what the appropriate level of state intervention in economic activity is and on how feasible the development ideology that corresponds with the emerging global order is for the prevailing conditions in Africa. Yet there is a consensus among them that state building in Africa is still critical, despite all the state bashing that has accompanied the emergence of a new global order.

The objectives of this introductory chapter are threefold. Since the remaining chapters of the book are premised on the view that state building is still relevant, one objective is to outline some of the most important considerations that necessitate state building. A second objective is to briefly chart tentative relations between state building and democratization. Again, the views of the authors on what type of democratization is desirable and feasible for African realities are heterogeneous. However, they all agree that the two processes have become closely related. The last objective of this chapter is to briefly introduce the other chapters, which attempt to examine the intricate interplay between the processes of state building, democratization, and economic liberalization, at both the theoretical and empirical levels.

WHY STATE BUILDING IS ESSENTIAL IN AFRICA

There is little doubt that integration with the global economy under the right conditions can promote growth and development. However, there is no compelling empirical or theoretical evidence that openness without active state involvement achieves a successful transformation. Openness is not the same as integration, nor is it a sufficient condition for integration with the global system. Integration involves becoming an integral part of a system and being able to influence the system and to make a difference while being impacted by it. Openness is, at best, a necessary, but not a sufficient, condition for integration. By all indications African economies are already quite open relative to other regions.[6] However, they can hardly be considered to be integrated or to have any significant impact on the global system. Diversification of exports, which involves diversification of production and ability to attract foreign investment, to penetrate foreign markets, and to impact global production and distribution, is the real indicator of global integration rather than mere openness.

In these regards, the *New York Times* characterized Africa as follows:

Africa's share of world trade . . . is now closer to 2 percent. That is so marginal it is almost as if the continent has curled up and disappeared from the map of international shipping lanes and airline routes that rope together Europe, North America and the booming Far East. Direct foreign investment in Africa is so paltry it is not even measured in the latest World Bank study (20 June 1994).

A number of preconditions are required for openness to be successful in leading to integration and development. Among them is the ability to maintain favorable export prices and terms of trade, to involve significant portions of the general population in the production of tradables either directly or through linkages, and to exercise a reasonable degree of control over the national process of capital accumulation. African countries are among the least competitive in all these areas. Africa's access to foreign capital is negligible.[7] The concentration of its exports on a few primary products does not allow it to maintain favorable terms of trade. Consequently, terms of trade have generally been unfavorable for African states. With an average decline of 5.2 percent for the decade between 1986 and 1996, sub-Saharan Africa has faced the lowest terms of trade of any other region in the late 1980s and early 1990s.[8] The involvement of the African peasantry in the production of tradables such as cash crops and mineral exports has also been limited. From the time of its incorporation into the global system, Africa's exports have largely been produced in extroverted enclaves that have limited linkages with the large subsistence sector. The peasantry's ability to benefit from openness is thus marginal. All these weaknesses severely limit Africa's ability to control the process of accumulation.[9] Growing dependency on food imports, which is largely related to the marginalization of the peasantry from access to resources, has exacerbated this problem.

The North-centric export promotion strategy also appears to face the paradox that the more it succeeds initially, the more likely its eventual failure becomes. In other words, if some countries succeed, it becomes more difficult for others to follow suit, at least in the short to intermediate runs.[10] The more the newly industrializing countries (NICs) succeed in expanding and diversifying their exports, for example, the more the pressure for protectionism mounts in the North, and the less likely their markets would remain open for other developing countries. Moreover, the NICs have not left the labor-intensive, low-tech industries behind for less-developed countries. Not even the advanced industrial countries have abandoned such industries. It may be argued that the more countries diversify and industrialize, the more the global market expands, creating more opportunities for latecomers. However, mass consumption does not simultaneously expand with industrial production. As a result, a time lag hinders the realization of the potential of the export-propelled development strategy.

It thus remains highly doubtful that openness, by itself, creates the preconditions for successful integration, including the transformation of the subsistence sector into an active exchange economy and diversification of exports. The thrust of the new ideology that industrial development comes about through a free market system with minimal state involvement also runs counter to historical evidence.[11] The Dutch "Golden Age" of the seventeenth century was clearly perpetuated by strong state involvement in the importation of raw materials and exportation of manufactured goods.

During the eighteenth century also, Britain stimulated industrialization, especially in the area of textiles, not only by imposing tariffs on imports from India and China but also by illegalizing the wearing of some imports.[12] In the nineteenth century, countries like France, Germany, and the United States counteracted British hegemony through nationalist economic strategies that included protective tariffs and credit facilities from state banks in order to develop national industries.[13] Referring to the role of the state in Russia, Gerschenkron notes that despite the incompetence and corruption of the bureaucracy, the impact of the policies pursued is "undeniable."[14] In the twentieth century the state in Japan, South Korea, Singapore, and Taiwan promoted industrialization through a number of policy measures, including land reform, targeting of investments and credits to selected industries, protecting young industries, and providing extensive support in marketing and research facilities.[15]

That African countries would be better off under openness than under autarky or under the control of a self-serving state can be established relatively easily. However, the claim that unbridled openness is superior to an engagement with the global system on terms and conditions carefully selected and coordinated by a state committed to social interests and accountable to its citizens runs counter even to common sense. Unregulated openness can, for example, undermine the diversification efforts by destroying infant industries that are not ready to compete globally. Disengagement of the state can also easily lead to the continued marginalization of the peasantry and the neglect of domestic sources of growth instead of cultivating them and thereby expanding domestic markets. Furthermore, excessive reliance on external dynamics for growth generates fierce competition among the countries of the South for access to foreign investments and markets of the North, lowering their gains from openness. In tandem with the debt crisis, this intra-South competition has the potential to undermine further the ability of many less-developed countries to control the national process of capital accumulation.

The anti-state ideology may be partly explained by the widespread view that states are generally self-serving and cannot be expected to promote social interests. The failure of the African state in promoting social interest is abundantly clear.[16] Yet in view of the market-creating and developmentalist roles played by many states, including those of Japan and South Korea, such a generalization is not sustainable. Another reason for the rise of the anti-state ideology may be the shift in the balance of power between capital and labor in favor of capital. As capital gains the upper hand, it attempts to shape the nature of the state in line with its interests. The roles of the state that act as a check on the interests of capital would come under attack. The global system is facing a rapid surge in the relative power of capital. However, to the extent that democracy survives, such an imbalance is correctable through active, popular participation. Furthermore, as Barber aptly notes, unbridled capitalism self-destructs.[17] The surge in the relative power of capital over other economic classes tends to lead to growing inequality and declining purchasing power of the general population. These developments, in turn, by weakening capitalism, act as a built-in mechanism that reduces the dictatorship of capital.

As Rueschemeyer and Evans note, the state simultaneously expresses several contradictory tendencies.[18] It often serves the interests of the dominant interest groups or classes. At other times it becomes self-serving. It is, however, ultimately an organization of citizens and is capable, depending on the balance of power between the state and civil society and within civil society, to serve as a corporate actor or as an agency for promoting the common good. Under a genuinely democratic system where imbalances between social classes are mitigated, for example, the state can be expected to act on behalf of common social interest. It can, for example, protect society from the excesses of capital when capital becomes too dominant. It is inconceivable for such a state not to engage in the economic process to enhance the well-being of citizens, especially where development is the overwhelming concern. The appropriate question is thus not how to reduce the role of the state but rather how to transform it from one that is incompetent, self-serving, or serving the interests of dominant groups, to one that is effective and committed to advancing social interests.

Taking the state out of the development process can be very risky for the countries of the South, especially the least diversified ones, such as those of sub-Saharan Africa. For these countries, the new global order and its development ideology can (1) further undermine their ability to control the process of accumulation and development; (2) intensify polarization between rich and poor and among ethnic entities; (3) bring about a serious decline in the autonomy of the state and expose its citizens to more overt external domination; and (4) exacerbate the neglect of internal dynamics of development as emphasis is placed on the North's capital and markets as sources of growth. This, in turn, is likely to perpetuate the exiguity of their internal market and the fragmentation of their economies and make them more prone to sharp fluctuations and stagnation.

State Disintegration

Another factor that necessitates state building is the worrisome dangers associated with the state's collapse or disintegration. The civil wars and the shocking human tragedies of Somalia, Liberia, and Rwanda occurred with state collapse. Such tragedies can reoccur, since many African states are "verging on dissolution."[19] Many attribute the failure of state building in Africa to the nature of the state. Presently, the African state is generally considered to be highly centralized, authoritarian, and self-serving or serving the interests of what Keller calls "the state class,"[20] which includes the reigning political authorities, the central bureaucracy and its regional functionaries, the top echelons of the military, and members of, where it exists, the dominant political party. The capabilities of the African state in responding to social needs and interests, even when the political will is present, are also limited. Jackson and Rosberg have, in fact, described African states as states *de jure* but not *de facto*.[21] The failure of the state to advance social interest by providing health care, education, basic infrastructure, and so forth and the increasing surrender of its policy-making powers to external agencies have clearly weakened it and undermined its legitimacy among its constituents as well as in the eyes of the global community. Its chronic failure to provide minimum security and to correct the prevailing gross inequalities among ethnic groups has also led to an increase in interethnic conflicts, which, in turn, threaten to bring about the disintegration of the state.

As Shaw notes, there may be some cases where state disintegration may lead to more homogeneous and relatively more peaceful small states.[22] However, dividing states along ethnic lines is not feasible since ethnic groups often cohabit. Independence for the Oromo people in Ethiopia or creating independent states for Hutus and Tutsis in Rwanda and Burundi is, for example, unlikely to lead to peaceful coexistence. The decoupling of Eritrea from Ethiopia has ended in a peaceful settlement. Eritrea, however, is a special case that cannot be easily replicated. In the first place, the Eritrean conflict was not an ethnic conflict. Eritrea also had boundaries clearly demarcated by the colonial state. Although its self-declared independence has not received international recognition yet, Somaliland (the former British Somaliland) also has boundaries delineated by the colonial state.

The collapse of the Somali state also provides a useful lesson that, as long as the factors that lead to conflict, such as uneven access to resources and uneven distribution of power, are not carefully addressed, and mechanisms for economic, political, and social integration of different social entities are not developed, separation of ethnic groups does not prevent conflict. Even nation-states are likely to experience conflict along regional or even clan lines. Ethnic, religious, and cultural homogeneity did not prevent clan conflict in Somalia.

The Dangers of Fragmentation

State disintegration, even if it could be attained peacefully, would also have another problem. In most cases, African countries are already economic midgets. Fragmenting them further through disintegration is likely to worsen the prospects for their economic development. Fragmentation would further weaken their resource base. They are also likely to be too small to support any meaningful industrialization, to attract foreign investments, or to be of any consequence in the emerging global order, although, in the long run, state boundaries may gradually cease to be serious obstacles to economic development, if openness is fully attained.

To conclude this section of the chapter, then, the general crisis confronting

Africa has threatened the survival of African societies. It is highly unlikely that their survival and development would be assured without a strong organization locally, regionally, and at the level of the state. Multiethnic patriotic struggle liberated Africa from colonial rule. This kind of struggle, together with regional integration, is as essential now in liberating Africa from its present crisis in the emerging global order. However, the state cannot be strengthened without transforming its nature from self-serving to one that advances social interests. Strengthening the state also requires developing mechanisms for accommodating the interests of different ethnic groups and integrating them politically, economically, and socially. Such interethnic accommodation and integration are prerequisites for broad-based mobilization of resources to overcome Africa's general crisis.

RELATIONS BETWEEN DEMOCRACY AND STATE BUILDING

Given the anti-state ideology of the new global order, the inequalities globalization generates, the built-in economy of affection, nepotism, and corruption that characterize African countries, and the ethnic and religious tensions that are rampant throughout the continent, state building is certain to be a difficult process in Africa. Historically, state building preceded democratization and was generally accomplished by coercive means through conquests or resisting conquests. Referring to nationalism and state building in nineteenth-century Europe, Lewis Namier, for example, notes that "states are not created or destroyed, and frontiers redrawn or obliterated, by arguments and majority votes; nations are freed, united, or broken by blood and iron, and not by a generous application of liberty."[23] Economic interdependence, homogenization through educational and administrative institutions, and democratic arrangements have, however, consolidated state building. In the African case, the colonial state imposed the boundaries of states without creating the economic, political, and social conditions for the consolidation of the state or for homogenizing national entities. The postindependence state attempted, as former Zambian president Kenneth Kaunda notes, "to create nations from the sprawling artifacts the colonialists carved out."[24] It is clear that the postindependence state has failed in this objective. In countries such as the Sudan, the state is even proving to be too weak to maintain the colonial creations by means of coercion, although colonial boundaries have not yet changed.[25] The current global democratization and growing concerns about human rights violations and refugees have also made the option of state building by means of coercion less viable. As a result, state building has increasingly become fused with democratization.

This fusion has serious implications for the manner in which the process of state building can take place as well as for the nature of democracy. In regard to state building, it implies that integrating the disparate groups and determining the relations between them and the state can best be accomplished through consensual decisions by all the parties involved. Democracy entails empowering the general population to control decision making. As such, it implies that integration of ethnic groups with each other to form a state would need to be on a voluntary basis and on carefully negotiated terms that are acceptable to all of them. It also implies that if such agreements are not reached, the option of secession is available to ethnic groups. For this reason democratization may involve the risk of accelerating state disintegration, as Ottaway notes.[26] However, few ethnonationalist movements in Africa have made intractable demands to form their own states.[27] Even movements such as the Sudan People's Liberation Movement (SPLM) in the Sudan and the Oromo Liberation Front (OLF) in Ethiopia have not sought secession as the only solution to their cases. The Inkatha Freedom Party (IFP) in South Africa has also clearly rejected independence in favor of some form of federal arrangement. Thus, democratization appears to pose much less risk to state building than not democratizing.

The process of state building through the affirmation of the rights of nations may be viewed as reinforcement of ethnonational loyalties, which may undermine the effort toward building "nation-states."[28] However, the aim of building a nation-state out of a multination state is an unrealistic goal. The countries that were believed to have succeeded in this process have not been all that successful. The United Kingdom, France, and Spain, for example, can hardly be regarded as nation-states.[29] State building is much more likely to succeed if it adopts a realistic goal that integrates different nations to form a workable and peaceful multination state and minimizes conflict between the nation and the state than if it aims at transferring the loyalties of citizens from the nation to the state.

The fusion between state building and democracy also implies that the nature of democracy is subject to the outcomes of the agreements and negotiated compromises among the disparate groups. The levels of centralization/decentralization of power, the question of how to manage the relations between minority and majority ethnic groups, and what electoral systems to adopt are, for example, highly contentious issues that would be subject to the outcomes of the agreements and negotiated compromises among the disparate groups. The demarcation between the spheres of the private and public decisions or how much state intervention in economic activity is acceptable is also a difficult issue that has to be settled by agreement among the different parties to state building. This suggests that, given the fusion of democracy and state building, African countries may have to invent their own version of democracy, as Sklar notes.[30] The forms of democracy that exist in other countries, such as those of the West, are unlikely to be suitable for conditions prevailing in Africa. This does not suggest that democracy is to be reduced to power sharing among ethnic groups or establishing other mechanisms that govern relations among ethnic groups.

Democracy also establishes rules that govern relations among social classes. Although democracy does not equalize the influence of different social classes on the state, it mitigates the domination of the state by the elite by providing the lower classes a collective voice. Democracy also governs relations among individuals and protects citizens from excesses by the state, especially when it is not limited to the institution of periodic elections. In other words, democracy can be organized in such a way that rights of nations can be safeguarded without subjugating the rights of individuals and social classes, just as much as rights of states and those of individuals can be reasonably maintained simultaneously. The elections that are currently taking place in different African countries are important. However, if they do not quickly address the issues of state building and the type of democratization compatible with it, they are likely to advance neither state building nor democratization, especially in the countries where ethnic tensions are high.

The specific arrangements that deal with the contentious issues of democratization and state building are likely to vary from country to country since the balance of power among ethnic and social classes in African countries differs considerably. However, given the similarities of the ethnic problems and mal-integration of economic sectors that these countries face, the approaches that deal with these problems are likely to have many commonalities.

As noted earlier, the authors do not share, nor can they be expected to share, any firm position as to what type of democracy is the most suitable for African conditions. Some seem to be inclined to favor popular democracy, where the contentious issues are to be determined by popular choice, while others favor liberal democracy, where a number of issues are not entirely subject to popular choice. There are also some marked differences between country cases. Yet they all agree that democracy and state building have become closely intertwined. It is, for example, strongly shared that democratization makes the state more transparent and transforms its nature to become more suitable for advancing social interests. This transformation, in turn, strengthens the state both by enhancing its legitimacy and by integrating different national entities.

ORGANIZATION OF THIS BOOK

The book is divided into two parts. Part I presents theoretical explorations of the interrelated issues of democratization and state building. Chapter 2 by Kidane Mengisteab examines the simultaneous struggle for democratization and state building in Africa. He argues that the fusion of the two processes requires innovative democratic procedures and state-building arrangements that are quite different from those that prevail in most other regions of the world. Kidane argues that, given the chronic conflicts and tensions between state and civil society and among ethnic groups, African countries face the challenge of inventing a novel democratic arrangement that deals with these two types of conflicts. In his view, South Africa and Ethiopia have taken steps in this direction. In chapter 3, John S. Saul provides a powerful critique of the prevailing, narrow, neoliberal formulation of democracy. The chapter highlights the limitations of liberal democracy and how it can lead to undemocratic outcomes in the African context and explains why an alternative popular democracy has greater potential in facilitating state building as well as socioeconomic transformation in Africa. In chapter 4, Marina Ottaway strongly warns us that democratization that can, under certain conditions, promote state building can also lead to state disintegration by enhancing the importance of ethnic identities.

Part II consists of case studies that examine up close the experiences of several African countries. It presents a nice mix of Anglophone and Francophone African countries as well as broad regional coverage. The critical issues that emerge from a reading of these experiences revolve around the role and impact of civil society, political leadership, the international context or international political realities, and the nature of domestic political economies in promoting and nurturing or undermining democratization and state building.

Thus, in chapter 5 Julius O. Ihonvbere examines the demoralizing Nigerian experience where the military establishment had made a mockery of, and derailed as well as deformed, the democratization process and thereby unleashed class, regional, religious, and ethnic interests that have brought the country perilously close to national economic and political ruin. Ihonvbere leaves little doubt that, in large part, "the trouble with Nigeria is simply and squarely a failure of leadership," to borrow Chinua Achebe's poignant incantation. While civil society, ranging from the Nigerian Bar Association, human rights organizations, and independent newspapers and journalists, to university students and faculty staff associations, has been energized, the military leadership continues to subject it to various forms of harassment and brutalization, all the while trying to play the ethnic card in order to manufacture a tailor-made excuse for hanging on to power. In short, the military junta has endangered both democratization and state building in Nigeria.

The Nigerian experience with democratization and state building contrasts sharply with that of Côte d'Ivoire and Ghana, as examined by E. Gyimah-Boadi and Cyril Daddieh in chapter 6. The authors focus on a complex set of relationships between economic liberalization, democratization, and state building in the two countries. Their analysis reveals how, in both cases, reasonably competent governments had promoted state building through redistributive or allocational decisions that had kept ruling elites in power, especially in Côte d'Ivoire, and kept social groups relatively supportive or made them acquiesce to shrinking political arenas until serious economic downturns beginning in the late 1970s made distributional politics unviable. In both countries, governments had to turn to international financial institutions (IFIs) for help and, in return, embark upon adjustment policies. The painful impact of adjustment stimulated opposition to the governments and the revival of civil society, along with a modicum of ethno-regional associations and competition in both countries. The mounting pressure on the governments from such groups led to unexpected capitulation by both governments and the opening of the political systems to greater competition and democratic transitions, which the governments in both countries successfully controlled. As a result, unlike Nigeria, the ruling parties won the subsequent elections and did not have to resort to the dangerous tactic of annulling the elections.

Mario J. Azevedo tackles the issue of ethnicity raised by Ottaway even more frontally in his examination of the experiences of the Congo and Chad in chapter 7. While the Ghanaian, Ivoirian, and Nigerian cases do reveal some revival of ethnic nationalism, albeit subdued or contained in the Ghanaian and Ivoirian cases but stoked by the military leaders in Nigeria, the cases of Chad and the Congo suggest that ethnicity, even when reinforced by regionalism, need not present a mortal danger to democratization and state building. Azevedo posits complementarity between ethnicity and nation rather than irreconcilable antagonism. However, on the basis of the experiences of Chad and the Congo, he has to conclude that ethnic groups can present a major challenge to the development of Africa and the creation of a genuine democratic order, a point argued by Ottaway earlier.

The Chad case, which is a true ethnic polyglot, as opposed to the Congo with its more manageable three or five distinct groups, certainly reminds us that the more ethnic groups a country has, especially if the size of some are disproportionately larger compared to the others, the more likely it is to experience ethnic divisiveness and strife, making the democratic experiment extremely difficult. Here, too, the centrality of leadership has been underscored, with the relative success of democratization and state building attributable to the competence of a number of civilian and military leaders in the Congo and with the spectacular demise of similar processes in Chad equally laid at the doorstep of failed leadership. Like the Ivoirian case, the Congolese leadership was somewhat proactive in responding to internal pressures and civil society and seeking to stay one step ahead of the domestic opposition in order to ensure its eventual triumph in the democratic transition.

The contrast between Kenya and Tanzania on this issue is equally fascinating. Julius E. Nyang'oro's analysis in chapter 8 has revealed that civil society is particularly underdeveloped in Tanzania, a tribute to the successful "corporatist" project of state building pursued by Nyerere's government after independence. Relatedly, a Tanzanian political culture has developed that frowns upon the manipulation of ethno-regional divisions for political gain. The Tanzanian regime was also far-sighted enough to begin the process of transition from a one-party state to multipartyism and competitive elections, even when public sentiment did not favor such a move. By contrast, Kenyan civil society, consisting of business, women, and student organizations as well as the National Council of Churches of Kenya (NCCK), has had to play a much more pivotal role to bring an intransigent regime to the position of reluctant acceptance of political liberalization and multiparty elections. Lamentably, civil society and multiparty elections and hence state building and democratization suffer from excessive fragmentation and ethnic-based political mobilization, both of which have allowed the Moi regime to outmaneuver his opponents and remain in power. While the situation bears some resemblance to the experiences of Côte d'Ivoire and Ghana analyzed by Gyimah-Boadi and Daddieh, the fact that in the former there had been about a decade of gradual and controlled opening up of the political system, and the latter had experimented with a homespun democratic transition before jettisoning it in favor of multiparty elections mediated the more virulent forms of ethnic nationalism and minimized violence during the democratic transitions.

Among the more serious shortcomings of the democratic transitions in Africa has been their failure to pay close attention to the institutional dimensions of democratization. In pointing to the recrudescence of ethnic conflict alongside political pluralism, Ottaway lamented that the problem has been exacerbated by African politicians and well-meaning international advisers who have been oblivious to the special challenges democracy poses in multiethnic societies. As it happens, the three remaining chapters of this book respond in varying degrees to Ottaway's lament about the palpable tensions between ethnic nationalism and state building as well as to Mengisteab and Saul's search for the kind of democratization that could potentially facilitate ethno-regional reconciliation and entrenched minority rights and also enhance state capacity to embark on a developmental agenda focusing on poverty alleviation, skill formation, employment generation, and equitable access to such critical services as health care and education.

In a richly textured and far-ranging account of state building and democratization in South Africa, Larry A. Swatuk in chapter 9 reveals how the Government of National Unity (GNU) under the leadership of the ANC and Nelson Mandela has been attempting to transform an inherited state whose institutional structures were designed to marginalize and oppress the nonwhite majority. The task is a daunting one, in part because of the unenviable inheritance of an accumulation of development and social deficits. Yet, perhaps more than any other country, successful state building in the new South Africa hinges crucially on, as Swatuk suggests, "constructing and embarking on a developmental agenda whose central focus is the alleviation of poverty." The scale of human-made suffering is staggering, made all the more unacceptable by the opulence of the white minority. There is, thus, growing popular demand for democratization and development, involving state intervention and redistribution of resources. Simultaneously, state-makers face counterpressures from global and national capital to liberalize the economy, pursue market-oriented development, and practice fiscal responsibility. As these two pressures collide, the GNU must walk a political tightrope. While "elite-pacting" has resulted in the successful implementation of the forms of democracy, the development agenda is being increasingly contested. Swatuk's analysis of the strengths and weaknesses of state building in South Africa leaves him, on balance, to be cautiously optimistic, perhaps more so than Saul, about the future. Swatuk is impressed by the strength and diversity of civil society in South Africa. Here, unlike elsewhere in Africa, civil society has demonstrated skills, organizational capacity, and self-awareness.

The powerful trade union movement continues to be actively engaged. He points as well to an impressive demonstrated capacity for the spontaneous organization of social movements in response to the myriad problems facing South Africa's "less-conscientized marginal millions." Civil associations have been forging links with less well formed community-based organizations (CBOs) in the townships and rural areas in support of developmental activities, in contrast to civil society elsewhere in Africa. Furthermore, social forces in South Africa are predisposed toward "voice" rather than "exit" and "loyalty." As long as civil society remains robust and avoids being "captured" by the state, and as long as the African National Congress (ANC) leadership does not lose sight of its roots or of the double-edged nature of civil society as both a force for development and a force for social breakdown and maintains its current commitment to national reconciliation, internal party debate, and dialogue, and the new state can continue to strengthen its policy-making capacity, it stands a good chance of consolidating state building and the new democratic order.

The relative success of South Africa stands in sharp contrast to the failure of the state building and democratization projects in Ethiopia and Somalia. As an antidote to those failures, Mohammed Hassen in chapter 10 has turned into a forceful advocate of federalism, arguing that only a genuine federal arrangement can protect group rights and save the Ethiopian state from collapse or further disintegration. In Hassen's view, the attainment of this desired outcome hinges on the federal state-building project itself being a participatory or democratic one. Indeed, Hassen warns that a federal state project cannot work if it is designed and imposed by the leadership of a single party or group. Federal arrangements work best when they are designed by the people and their representatives and implemented with their freely expressed consent for its purpose and framework. Hassen laments the fact that Ethiopian leaders going back to 1941 have missed many opportunities to initiate such a federal and democratic state project. Instead, first the Amharic ruling elite and then the military regime of Mengistu sought to institutionalize a hegemonic state project that marginalized non-Amharic groups politically and economically as well as systematically trampled on their civic and cultural rights. Focusing particularly on the plight of the Oromo, Hassen demonstrates how a systematic attempt to deny their "national" identity led to their eventual politicization and the development of Oromo nationalism that threatens to dismember Ethiopia in the future. His fear is that the Tigrean-led Ethiopian People's Revolutionary Democratic Forces (EPRDF) government seems to be running the same risk of repeating past mistakes and missing another golden opportunity to establish a genuinely democratic federal system of governance. The chapter adumbrates what measures need to be taken to put the democratic state-building project back on track in Ethiopia.

Meanwhile, the viability of the federal system also hinges on the availability of economic resources that can be deployed to support both central and regional governments—in short, the view that a federal system should be not only politically desirable but also economically viable and affordable. The size of the component states or regions must strike some kind of reasonable balance in area, wealth, and population to make it possible for all levels of government to be independent within their specified spheres.

In the final chapter, Hussein M. Adam provides a fascinating analysis of the prospects for democratization in a country that had suffered implosion as a result of the spectacular failure of an earlier attempt at state building under highly authoritarian rule. This new democratic ethos stands in sharp contrast to the spectacular failure of past state-building efforts, a failure attributed to "greed, incompetence, and corruption among the emerging political elites," resulting in confusion and political paralysis. As Adam reveals, the state builders could not even agree on a script for the Somali language, let alone take resolute measures to transform rural life and create their own unique brand of consociational democracy based on local traditions. Interestingly, in the process, an anti-state political culture seems to be in the making, especially in the North, one that may well stimulate state building of a kind that is democratic because it is infused with mass or popular content. In Somaliland and northeast Somalia, there are embryonic manifestations of consociational democratic mechanisms involving consensus, proportionality, and a conscious effort to avoid winner-take-all solutions. According to Adam, with the complete collapse of the state, Somalis have been obliged to rely on local committees' utilizing traditional law, *xeer*, to maintain law and order. These areas are ready to embark on reconstruction, provided they get relevant assistance. "The priority is to turn swords into camel bells, to ensure peace and stability."

The issues of foreign involvement in Africa's democratization and state-building projects have intersected in the cases of Somalia and South Africa. It remains an intriguing issue that many of the cases suggest can be both a hindrance and an asset. In the Somali case, in the North and other areas that did not require the intervention of foreign troops, traditional elders have played visible and positive roles. It is worthy of note that women leaders have been active (this is equally true of South Africa), and women and children constitute a majority in demonstrations for disarmament and peace. Interestingly, Adam ties the revival of civil society to the revival of the private sector. While in Côte d'Ivoire, Ethiopia, Kenya, Nigeria, and elsewhere, the state continues to attempt to hamstring civil society and weaken its role in the democratic struggles, state collapse or the loss of "empirical statehood" has allowed a resurgent small private sector and a growing number of voluntary development organizations to spearhead the process of renewed state building and democratization. As Adam asserts, "There is a palpable spirit of anticentralism, an atmosphere favoring local autonomy, regionalism, and federalism, and in the North, self-determination and secession." It has also been suggested that there is an unabashed preference for locally controlled police forces over a large, standing, central army. In this connection, is Adam's prognosis that "Somalia's more democratic future will be better safeguarded if the present consensus not to establish a new central army is maintained'' prescient? Does it have relevance for other African countries embarking upon democratization and renewed state building?

NOTES

1. Robert W. Cox, "The Crisis in World Order and the Challenge to International Organization," *Cooperation and Conflict* 29, no. 2 (1994): 99–113.

2. For details, see Joan M. Nelson, "Labor and Business Roles in Dual Transitions: Building Blocks or Stumbling Blocks?" in J. M. Nelson, ed., *Intricate Links: Democratization and Market Reforms in Latin America and Eastern Europe* (New Brunswick, NJ, and Oxford: Transaction, 1994), 147–94.

3. IMF, "Camdessus Cites Ways to Ease Transition to Market Economies," *IMF Survey* 22, no. 13 (28 June 1993): 195.

4. IMF, "Closer Integration in Global Economy Vital for Africa," *IMF Survey* 24, no. 14 (17 July 1995): 217–20.

5. This usage is in order to distinguish state building from the development of substate nationalism. For details on the distinctions between the terms "state" and "nation" see Walker Connor, *Ethnonationalism: The Quest for Understanding* (Princeton, NJ: Princeton University Press, 1994).

6. Chandra Hardy, "The Prospects for Intra-Regional Trade Growth in Africa," in Frances Stewart, Sanjaya Lall, and Samuel Wangwe, eds., *Alternative Development Strategies in Sub-Saharan Africa* (New York: St. Martin's Press, 1992), 427.

7. United Nations, *World Economic and Social Survey 1996: Trends and Policies in the World Economy* (New York: United Nations, 1996), 325.

8. UNDP, *Human Development Report 1994* (New York: Oxford University Press, 1994); "Africa Strives to Move from Crisis Management to Strategic Thinking," *Africa Recovery* 9, no. 3 (November 1995): 1–7.

9. For details on the factors that limit the ability of African countries to control the national process of capital accumulation see Samir Amin, *Delinking: Towards a Polycentric World* (London: Zed Books, 1985).

10. Robin Broad and John Cavanagh, "No More NICs," in Gerald Epstein, Julie Graham, and Jessica Nembhard, eds., *Creating a New World Economy* (Philadelphia: Temple University Press, 1993), 376–90.

11. For details on the direct and indirect impacts of the state on economic development in particular and capitalist development in general, see Thomas Callaghy, "The State and Development of Capitalism in Africa: Theoretical, Historical, and Comparative Reflections," in Donald Rothchild and Naomi Chazan, eds., *The Precarious Balance: State and Society in Africa* (Boulder, CO: Westview Press, 1988), 67–99; Dietrich Rueschemeyer and Peter Evans, "The State and Economic Transformation: Toward an Analysis of the Conditions Underlying Effective Intervention," in P. B. Evans, D. Rueschemeyer, and T. Skoçpol, eds., *Bringing the State Back In* (New York: Cambridge University Press, 1985), 44–77.

12. Wim F. Wertheim, "The State and the Dialectics of Emancipation," *Development and Change* 23, no. 3 (July 1992): 257–81.

13. Wertheim, "The State and the Dialectics of Emancipation," 261–62. Also see

Robert B. Reich, *The Work of Nations: Preparing Ourselves for 21st-Century Capitalism* (New York: Vintage Books, 1992).

14. Alexander Gerschenkron, *Economic Backwardness in Historical Perspective* (New York: Praeger, 1962), 20.

15. Mrinal Datta-Chaudhuri, ''Market Failure and Government Failure,'' *Journal of Economic Perspectives* 4, no. 3 (Summer 1990): 25–39; Robert Wade, *Governing the Market: Economic Theory and the Role of Government in East Asian Industrialization* (Princeton, NJ: Princeton University Press, 1990); L. James Dietz, ''Overcoming Underdevelopment: What Has Been Learned from the East Asian and Latin American Experiences?'' *Journal of Economic Issues* 26, no. 2 (June 1992): 373–83; World Bank, *The East Asian Miracle: Economic Growth and Public Policy* (Oxford: Oxford University Press, 1993).

16. Robert H. Bates, *Markets and States in Tropical Africa* (Berkeley: University of California Press, 1981); John A. A. Ayoade, ''State without Citizens: An Emerging African Phenomenon,'' in Donald Rothchild and Naomi Chazan, eds., *The Precarious Balance: State and Society in Africa* (Boulder, CO: Westview Press, 1988), 100–118; Edmund J. Keller, ''The State in Contemporary Africa: A Critical Assessment of Theory and Practice,'' in Dankwart A. Rustow and Kenneth Paul Erikson, eds., *Comparative Political Dynamics: Global Research Perspectives* (New York: HarperCollins, 1991), 134–59; Crawford Young, *The African Colonial State in Comparative Perspective* (New Haven, CT, and London: Yale University Press, 1994).

17. Benjamin Barber, *Jihad vs. McWorld* (New York: Random House, 1995).

18. Rueschemeyer and Evans, ''The State and Economic Transformation,'' 47.

19. Aristide R. Zolberg, ''The Specter of Anarchy: African States Verging on Dissolution,'' *Dissent* 39 (Summer 1992): 303–11.

20. Keller, ''The State in Contemporary Africa,'' 142.

21. Robert H. Jackson and Carl G. Rosberg, Jr., ''Why Africa's Weak States Persist: The Empirical and Juridical in Statehood,'' *World Politics* 35 (October 1982): 1–24.

22. Timothy M. Shaw, ''The South in the 'New World (Dis)Order': Towards a Political Economy of Third World Foreign Policy in the 1990s,'' *Third World Quarterly* 15, no. 1 (1994): 17–30.

23. Quoted in Benjamin Schwarz, ''The Diversity Myth: America's Leading Export,'' *The Atlantic Monthly* 275, no. 5 (May 1995): 57–67.

24. Quoted in Benyamin Neuberger, ''State and Nation in African Thought,'' in John Hutchinson and Anthony D. Smith, eds., *Nationalism* (Oxford: Oxford University Press, 1994), 235.

25. Eritrea and even Somaliland can be regarded as returning to the colonial boundaries rather than changing them.

26. Marina Ottaway, ''Democratization in Collapsed States,'' in I. William Zartman, ed., *Collapsed States: The Disintegration and Restoration of Legitimate Authority* (Boulder, CO, and London: Lynne Rienner, 1995), 244.

27. James R. Scarritt, ''Communal Conflict and Contention for Power in Africa South of the Sahara,'' in Ted Robert Gurr, ed., *Minorities at Risk: A Global View of Ethnopolitical Conflicts* (Washington, DC: U.S. Institute of Peace Press, 1993), 252–89.

28. Neuberger, ''State and Nation in African Thought.''

29. Connor, *Ethnonationalism*.

30. Richard Sklar, ''Developmental Democracy,'' *Comparative Studies in Society and History* 23, no. 4 (1987): 686–714.

Part I

Relations between Democratization and State Building in Africa: Theoretical Analysis

Chapter 2

Democratization and State Building in Africa: How Compatible Are They?

KIDANE MENGISTEAB

INTRODUCTION

The pervasive problem of state building is one of the major factors that undermine the efforts for economic development of African countries. Widespread animosities among national (ethnic) groups and the weak links between the large subsistence sector and the extroverted modern sector are among the key aspects of the underdeveloped condition of state building in sub-Saharan Africa. The nature of the state and, more specifically, the self-serving and authoritarian characteristics of its functionaries are generally viewed as hindering state building and economic development. Many of these regimes represent ethnic domination and play ethnic groups against each other. They also foster the deprivation of the subsistence sector and the fragmentation of the economy by perpetuating reverse income redistribution. Manifested by the growing popularity of the pro-democracy movement in contemporary Africa, democratization is widely viewed as a necessary condition for the solution to many of Africa's ills, including the crisis of state building.

Democracy cannot be a sufficient condition to overcome all the internal and external factors that fragment African economies. It is also unlikely to bring about successful resolution of all conflicts among national groups. However, state building, which involves internally integrating national economies and accommodating the interests of all national identities, is unlikely to progress, at least in the African context, without some form of democratization. States are no longer likely, in this era of democratization and ethnonationalism, to bring about successful state building and economic development without creating conditions for the participation of different groups in decision making. There are, however, different types of democracies, and their impacts on state building are likely to vary considerably. The primary concerns of this chapter are to examine how democratization can help advance state building and what type of democratization is more suitable in overcoming the two identified aspects of the problem of state building, namely, transformation of the subsistence sector and resolution of ethnic strife.

VARIOUS NOTIONS OF DEMOCRACY

Democracy involves popular control over the public decision-making process on an ongoing basis.[1] Given the plurality of interests among the population, devising procedures of popular control that do not allow some interest groups to become permanent winners or permanent losers is important. As a result, many have paid more attention to the procedures than to the content of democracy. There is also a great deal of dispute over the demarcation of the domains of public and private decisions. This disagreement has been a critical source for the emergence of different varieties of democracy. Decisions on economic activity are, to a large extent, in the private domain in some societies. In other societies, public decisions infringe considerably on the economic sphere. One implication of these differences is a trade-off between property rights and individual liberty, on one hand, and social equality and the scope of popular control over decision making (popular sovereignty), on the other.[2]

Keeping economic decisions entirely private enhances property rights and individual liberty (at least for the propertied class). But it is likely to come into conflict with popular sovereignty, as the general population largely surrenders control over economic decisions to the propertied classes. The population may even give up broader social and political rights in order to obtain economic benefits, as Lindblom notes.[3] It also undermines equality and communal solidarity. Conversely, as Femia notes, the logical conclusion of the premise of popular sovereignty and equality infringes on property rights and on individual liberty. These choices are extremely difficult to make.[4] Bowles and Gintis note that ''a reasonable political philosophy does not choose between liberty and popular sovereignty.''[5] Most societies are likely to avoid the extremes. Yet due to their differences in culture, levels of socioeconomic development, and modes of production, it is highly likely that different societies would choose different mixes. Furthermore, some societies may choose to make decisions on the basis of the choice of the majority, while others may adopt a consensual decision-making formula that relies on negotiations and concessions. In any case, the different arrangements that societies choose would affect their socioeconomic development, including state building, differently.

In light of these conceptual differences, the relations between democracy and state building cannot be analyzed without distinguishing the different types of democracy. This chapter identifies three of the most important types of democracy and analyzes the impacts and prospects of each. This does not imply that there can be only three types of democracy. Rather, the three that are identified here are likely to capture the essence of most other varieties.

One type of democracy is liberal democracy, which is the predominant type in the industrialized world today. A second type is consensual democracy. It is claimed that this type has strong roots in most of Africa's traditional political cultures.[6] Lengthy debates aimed at blurring opposites and finding compromises characterize decision making in many traditional African political systems.[7] Some aspects of this type of democracy are also common in many other developing countries.[8] A third type is social democracy, which is predominant in the Scandinavian countries. It also appears that some of the Eastern European countries might be heading toward this type of democracy.[9] The three types are not mutually exclusive, although their differences are significant enough to justify such a classification. A brief identification of the most important distinguishing characteristics of these three types of democracy follows. An attempt is then made to examine how likely each of them is to foster state building and development in Africa by promoting internal integration through accommodation of the conflicting demands of different national identities and the transformation of the subsistence sector into a surplus-producing, active exchange economy.

LIBERAL DEMOCRACY

The crisis of socialism and the collapse of socialist regimes in many countries have been celebrated as the victory of capitalism and its twin, liberal democracy. For some, the crisis of socialism represents the end of ideology and of all forms of nonliberal democracy. The following claim by Sartori is a case in point.

As we enter the last decade of our century liberal democracy suddenly finds itself without an enemy. Whatever else had laid claim on the word democracy, or had been acclaimed as "real democracy," has fizzled out almost overnight.[10]

Sartori goes on to assert that "non-liberal systems also are, by the same token, non-democratic."[11] The crisis of socialism, however, does not necessarily bring about an end to the challenges that liberal democracy faces. Nor does it make liberal democracy the most appropriate for all countries. This section of the chapter attempts to point out the limitations of liberal democracy to conditions in much of the developing world in general and Africa in particular. It also attempts to refute the claim of the end of nonliberal democracy.

David Beetham provides a good summary of the essential principles of liberal democracy. They include:

1. the securing of democratic rights (individual rights) such as freedoms of expression, movement, association, and so on;

2. the institutional separation of powers between executive, legislature, and judiciary in order to ensure the rule of law;

3. the institution of representative assembly elected by popular vote through open competition;

4. the principle of limited state and a separation between the public and private sectors; and

5. the premise that there is no final truth about what is good for society.[12]

The most controversial distinguishing element of liberal democracy is the fourth principle, which partitions the spheres of private and public decisions. The line of demarcation is neither clear nor rigid, creating a condition that leads to the emergence of several variations along a continuum even within liberal democracy. As Bowles and Gintis note, liberals have both supported and opposed state intervention in economic activity as well as the welfare state.[13] At one extreme are the minimalists, who argue that only market economies create conditions for sustainable democracy.[14] At the other extreme are the maximalists, who view a laissez-faire market system as incompatible with democracy and thus incorporate a great deal of the economic sphere into public decisions.[15] This makes liberal democracy a moving target and makes it difficult to pin down what it can and cannot do. The maximalist version of liberal democracy is very similar to social democracy, and, therefore, it will be treated in that section. This section concentrates on the minimalist version and varieties close to it.

The economic sphere is placed outside the realm of public decisions in the minimalist liberal democracy, essentially for three reasons. One is because private property is viewed as an embodiment of the rights and freedoms of the individual that cannot be intruded upon by the state.[16] As Macpherson points out, liberal democracy is liberal first and democratic second.[17] In other words, democracy is coterminous with the desired goal of a free market system. The primary aim of the tradition of liberal democracy is restricting state power over private property and individual freedom; creating structures that would secure popular control over decision making is secondary. For Friedrich von Hayek, for example, liberalism—the doctrine about what the content of the laws ought to be—is more important than democracy, which is the manner by which the content of the law is determined.[18] In a 1982 interview in Chile, Hayek reasserted his position by stating that he prefers liberalism under dictatorship to democracy without liberalism.[19]

The second reason for restricting the role of the state (public decision) in economic activity is based on the claim by proponents of liberalism that private enterprises are more efficient than public enterprises. One such forceful claim is made by Sartori, who argues that the private sector (''possessive individualism'') has a built-in advantage of engendering caring and cost cutting, qualities that are regarded as essential for good economics, which, in turn, is a requisite for good government.[20] Sartori regards the public sector as a ''noneconomical economy'' because these qualities are largely absent from it. This argument may have some validity, considering the problem of incentives in socialist economies and in publicly owned enterprises. However, even if one concedes that the private sector is more efficient, good economics cannot be reduced to efficiency only. Other issues such as poverty alleviation, human resource development, and environmental protection are critical components of good economics, and the laissez-faire market mechanism is not known to have a good track record in these regards, especially in sub-Saharan Africa.

A third reason is that liberals view market allocation of resources as noncoercive, which can offset the state's coercive allocation.[21] There is, however, little doubt that the separation of capital from labor in a capitalist market constitutes coercion.[22] Moreover, as Macpherson notes, a regulatory welfare state can soothe this market coercion. Since the evidence on such roles of the state through promotion of development is plenty, there is little need to engage in this debate at this point. The experiences of Japan, South Korea, and Taiwan are among many examples.

Another controversial characteristic of liberal democracy is its majoritarian rule. Beetham does not identify this as an essential characteristic of liberal democracy. As Lijphart argues, it may also very well be exogenous to liberal democracy.[23] However, Lijphart also admits that it has become synonymous with liberal democracy.

Limitations of Liberal Democracy

With the end of the Cold War, liberal democracy of the minimalist persuasion appears to have risen to predominance in the emerging global order. Liberal democracy, despite its apparent victory over other contending forms, continues to face two major problems in its application to most countries of the developing world, especially those with deep societal divisions, less diversified economies, and a market mechanism that fails to coordinate available resources with social needs. Two of its controversial characteristics, namely, its restriction of public decisions from economic activity and its majority rule system, are the most important sources of its weakness. Furthermore, in countries where the market mechanism and an autonomous bourgeoisie are underdeveloped, liberal democracy lacks the social basis to sustain it.

Partition of Economic and Political Decisions

The economies of African countries are essentially fragmented into a large subsistence sector that is largely deprived of resources and a small, modern sector that monopolizes resources. Several outcomes are related to this condition of duality. Among them are disarticulation of the different economic sectors, underdevelopment of the domestic market, extroversion of the commercial sector, and the failure of the market to coordinate resources with social needs since the peasantry's purchasing power is too limited to influence resource-allocative decisions. Correcting these problems necessitates transforming the subsistence sector into a surplus-producing exchange economy. This, in turn, requires providing the peasantry with access to resources such as land, fertilizers, credits, appropriate technology, health care, and educational and communication facilities. A critical question that needs to be raised at this juncture is how liberal democracy's restriction of public decisions to the political arena affects the peasantry's access to resources.

Neoliberals make a strong case that the state in Africa has often been a self-serving predator that uses its allocative power to favor the politically more potent segments of society, thereby promoting a negative redistribution of income. There is a great deal of evidence to support this claim. Yet this is a problem that is expected to be mitigated by democratization and thus should not be generalized. If we have a "democratic" state stripped of its resource-allocative power, how is the existing deprivation of the peasantry to be corrected? How is a postapartheid, "democratic" South Africa to correct the deprivation of the victims of apartheid with a minimal involvement in economic activity? If the state gives up or reduces drastically its redistributive role, as neoliberal proponents argue, creating access to resources for the peasantry falls on the lap of the market mechanism. However, the market allocates resources on the basis of demand—need accompanied by purchasing power—and not on the basis of mere need. Thus, it is not a suitable mechanism for creating access to resources for the deprived, who possess little purchasing power.[24] In a strict market mechanism the benefits to the deprived are essentially limited to the trickles from the growth that the market's efficiency is expected to generate. The commercial sector that the market centers around in Africa is too small, too dependent on external sources, and too removed from the subsistence sector to be able to bring about meaningful transformation through a trickle-down process.

Under these conditions, restricting the redistributive role of the state may amount to perpetuation and even legitimization of the existing gross deprivation. Without the transformation of the peasantry the uneven dualism and fragmentation of African economies cannot be corrected. As a result, the domestic market would remain largely confined to the commercial sector. State building would also be unlikely to succeed since there is little dynamism for the development of exchange-based interdependence among the different geographical regions and ethnic groups and between rural and urban areas. The inability of the market to bring about the transformation of the subsistence sector, therefore, severely limits the impacts of the minimalist liberal democracy on state building in Africa.

Economic deprivation is generally accompanied by political marginalization. Different economic classes clearly differ considerably in their ability to organize and lobby policymakers to ensure representation of their interests. The peasantry is presently in no position to obtain real representation and influence policy. Its lack of education and of access to information is among the factors that severely limit its ability to articulate its interests and to meaningfully compete for attaining them. Under these conditions the minimalist liberal democracy can only lead to an exclusivist market system and an elitist democracy, or to what Owens calls "false democracy."[25] It is entirely possible that, under external or even internal pressure, many elitist regimes, including those of Zaire and Kenya, might liberalize political life relatively and allow elections without fundamentally changing the socioeconomic conditions of their populations. Following the fall of apartheid, South Africa has done this (see chapter 3). However, if the continued popular protests in post-Kaunda Zambia are any indications, liberal democratic regimes of the minimalist persuasion are unlikely to be stable. The stability that political liberalization is expected to engender is likely to be undermined by the failure to promote economic policies with redistributive impacts. The African condition suggests that the less diversified the economy and the greater the societal disparity, the less appropriate and more difficult it is to sustain minimal liberal democracy.

Majority Rule

The second problem of liberal democracy is perhaps less fundamental but important, nonetheless. Under conditions of gross uneven development and pervasive ethnic, regional, and religious strife, majority rule is likely to lead to the neglect of the interests and concerns of minority groups. In extreme cases, majority rule may even lead to civil wars and wars of secession. It is highly unlikely that a majoritarian system would function properly in countries such as the Sudan, Rwanda, and Burundi. In other words, the less advanced the process of state building is, the less suitable majority rule becomes. Sir Arthur Lewis was very perceptive when, almost three decades ago, he noted that majority rule may prove to be "immoral, inconsistent with the primary meaning of democracy, and destructive of any prospect of building a nation in which different peoples might live in harmony."[26]

There are arguments that, in practice, liberal democracy is hardly characterized by majority rule. Lijphart, for example, contends that coalition cabinets, multiparty systems, proportional representation, bicameral legislatures, judicial reviews, and federalism are factors that make it more consensual than majoritarian.[27] A combination of these factors can certainly reduce the potential dictatorship of the majority, although it does not make liberal democracy consensual. In an ethnically polarized society you can have all these and still marginalize minorities. Such a system can also marginalize a majority such as the peasantry even when ethnic division is not a major factor.

Relevance of Liberal Democracy

The identified limitations notwithstanding, liberal democracy "is worth struggling for," as Sandbrook and Saul in this volume note.[28] Compared to the existing self-serving, authoritarian regimes, it has the potential to free the producers from the "extra-economic coercion" by separating the market from the state.[29] It can also rationalize and set the rules of the game that would govern political relations among the bourgeois and petty bourgeois elites, who, despite their small size, are economically and politically the most potent groups in Africa. It can, for example, bring about a smooth transfer of power. The transfer of power in Zambia is a good example. It may also reduce human rights violations. The "protodemocratic" states of Botswana, Mauritius, Senegal, and the Gambia (before the 1994 coup) are, for example, said to have a vastly superior record on human rights.[30] The limited stability gained, in turn, is likely to have some economic repercussions. To the extent that liberal democracy engenders some competition within the elite for the votes of the masses, it may also have some trickle-down concessions to the general population by way of reforms. However, the magnitude of the reforms and their impacts on the standard of living of the peasantry are likely to be limited, although they would vary from country to country. It is unlikely that competition among themselves would lead the elite to surrender significant portions of their privileges to the masses. More importantly, to the extent that the ideals of liberal democracy are incompatible with the predominant ideals of the general population, it may not be sustainable. We come back to this point in the section on social democracy.

CONSENSUS DEMOCRACY

The limitations of liberal democracy do not necessarily imply that more successful alternative forms of democracy presently exist. However, there is no compelling reason that other forms cannot be developed. One possible alternative to liberal democracy is consensus democracy. Among the general characteristics of this type of democracy are that decisions are reached through compromises and concessions rather than through the majoritarian "winner-takes-all" election formula. This implies that power is shared among different social groups along some criteria. Some argue that this form of democracy is indispensable in developing societies that suffer from serious internal cleavages and face more sensitive and divisive issues.[31]

Others regard consensual democracy as unworkable. Nzouankeu, for example, contends that "consensual democracy does not recognize the conflict between private and public interests and as a result, can only exist in a society of gods or among slaves."[32] Moreover, he claims that it has already failed in Africa. There are two problems with these contentions. First, contrary to Nzouankeu's claim, no postindependence African state seriously adopted a genuine consensus democracy. In fact, failure to embrace it beyond the level of rhetoric is regarded by some as Africa's neglect of its cultural heritage.[33] Second, consensus democracy does not require negation of self-interest in favor of that of the community in an unfree and submissive manner as Nzouankeu claims. On the contrary, it implies negotiations and concessions between different social groups with competing interests in order to obtain consensus. In many African villages decisions are still made along these lines, with minorities enjoying a veto power. Those communities do not have police forces and jails to enforce majority decisions. The only means available to them for ensuring general observance of village decisions is by basing them on consensus. This makes the villagers neither gods nor slaves.[34]

Nevertheless, Nzouankeu's concerns are not altogether invalid. Consensus democracy in traditional Africa operated essentially within relatively small and homogeneous communities where direct participation in decision making (village assemblies) was possible and where class divisions were not fully developed. In other words, it operated in conditions where precapitalist communalism was predominant.[35] Consensus democracy may also be appropriate under conditions of ethnic or religious diversity, as Arthur Lewis notes.[36] Ethnic groups with competing interests can enter into compromises with others without violence as long as the system protects the weaker ones from domination by the more powerful.

Postapartheid South Africa is one country that has begun implementing some form of consensual (consociational) democracy. According to Lijphart, one of the architects of consociational democracy, postapartheid South Africa has already put in place the four essential characteristics of consociational democracy, namely, grand coalitions, mutual veto among ethnic and race groups, proportional representation, and segmental group autonomy. Political parties representing different races, ethnic groups, and social classes are represented in a coalition government with cabinet positions. Proportional representation is prescribed for elections for the National Assembly and the provincial legislatures. A two-thirds majority requirement for adopting the Constitution also gives some degree of veto for minorities. Decentralization and autonomy in areas such as education are also provided, although some groups, including the Inkatha Freedom Party (IFP), find these levels of decentralization insufficient.[37]

Ethiopia has also initiated a political system that largely meets Lijphart's conditions for a consociational system. After coming to power in May 1991, the Ethiopian People's Revolutionary Democratic Front (EPRDF) formed a transitional government on the basis of a grand coalition among many political organizations with some degree of mutual veto. It established a system of proportional representation by allotting seats in the legislature to different ethnic groups. It has also begun a process of decentralization by instituting a federal arrangement among the largely ethnic-based, newly crafted zones (states). Such arrangements have largely continued after the end of the transitional period. The new Constitution also recognizes that union within the federal framework is voluntary and that ethnic groups (nations) have the right to secede if they choose to do so.[38]

Both the Ethiopian and South African experiments have generated a great deal of criticism. One notable concern is that democracy can function in severely divided societies only when incentives are created to encourage elites from one group to cater to the interests of grassroots members of other groups. By contrast, ethnic-and race-based pacts tend to preserve communal differences and lead to risks of disintegration in the long run.[39] The Ethiopian experiment in particular has generated a great deal of concern from two opposing sides. One side charges that the new ethnic policy may lead to the disintegration of the country along ethnic lines.[40] The other side accuses the government of the Ethiopian Peoples' Revolutionary Democratic Front (EPRDF) of failing, in sharp contrast to its bold policy declarations, to allow ethnic groups to organize freely. This group of critics alleges that the government is engaged in manufacturing ethnic parties that march to its own orders and suppressing independent parties. Mohammed Hassen's chapter in this volume is among the most eloquent of these critics. The first charge is unconvincing since ethnic relations in the country were already poisoned by the previous two regimes. Given the situation that existed in the country in 1991, measures such as those implemented by the EPRDF government were essential, although risky, in averting the country's total disintegration. The second charge is more convincing as the government seems to be following a two-track strategy, one recognizing the rights of nations up to secession and the other imposing some restrictions on political organizations to prevent the likelihood of disintegration and also to thwart effective challenges to its own power. Unfortunately for Ethiopia, the withdrawal of the OLF from the coalition of the transitional government and its ill-fated decision to pursue an armed struggle complicated matters. Despite these complications and shortcomings, the ethnic policy outlined by the transitional government in 1991 and the country's 1994 Constitution has contributed in preventing the country's disintegration.

In the case of South Africa also, given apartheid's impact on race relations in the country, it was difficult to conceive an end to the country's chronic violence and a beginning of a peaceful state-building process without some consociational arrangement. Negotiated pacts are generally credited for making a peaceful transition possible in the country by giving minorities assurances that their interests would not be totally dominated by majorities. In both countries, then, it was clear that rapid consociational measures were critical, at least, in the short run. It is also hard to envision solutions to the conflicts in Somalia, Sudan, Rwanda, and Burundi without some sort of consensual arrangement.

Another concern with consociationalism is that power sharing is essentially a pact among the elite, and it does not address the class-based problems of state building. It is uncertain if and how consociationalism applies to the economic sphere. In traditional agrarian African societies, where land was essentially communally owned, consensual democracy was not restricted to the political arena, although it did not subject all economic matters to public decisions. Individuals decided what to grow in their fields, the size of their livestock, and so on. From the perspective of nationalist leaders like Nyerere also, consensual democracy was not restricted to the political arena. However, under conditions of severe ethnic strife, consensus democracy, if implemented, is likely to concentrate on ethnic relations and neglect class conflicts. Federal arrangements such as the Ethiopian case are unlikely to create consensus among different social classes. Yet it is not an insignificant achievement if consociationalism mitigates ethnic and religious conflicts. Consensus democracy that tries to "share, disperse, restrain, and limit power in a variety of ways,"[41] even if only within the elite and between ethnic and religious groups, would be more conducive to peaceful state building than majoritarian democracy. As Ake notes, ethnic cleavages are, after all, essentially instigated by the elite in their quest for power and political support as well as to justify authoritarianism after they have incited the conflicts or threats of them.[42] Moreover, peaceful coexistence and transfer of power among the elite would have some positive economic implications. There are, however, some potential drawbacks to intraelite consensus. If competition among the elite is mitigated by consensual democracy, then the economically deprived segments of society, such as the peasantry, may continue to be neglected, as they may become even more irrelevant.

SOCIAL DEMOCRACY

Marxism provides a theory of democracy that does not partition the political and economic spheres. Like the minimalist liberal democracy, Marxist democracy, at least in the Leninist vanguard form, ties democracy to certain outcomes, in this case, proletarian dictatorship and social equality. Whatever the theoretical merits of Marxist democracy, its applicability in Africa at this time of socialist crisis is rather limited. From the experiences of Afro-Marxist states as well as those of other socialist attempts, socialism has proved to be extremely difficult in less advanced countries where structures of democracy are unavailable, and productivity is low. Socialization of the means of production was essentially replaced by state ownership in these countries. In the absence of democracy, state ownership largely became a means of advancing the interests of those that controlled state power. As a result, the basic objective of socialism—the elimination of all forms of exclusion of any segments of the population from access to decisions on the application of the means of production or access to their fruits—remained unattained.[43]

Lack of democratization and the continued deprivation of large segments of the population in company with intensive conflict between private and social incentive systems during the transition also made the social-based incentive systems of socialism unworkable, resulting in lack of dynamism and economic stagnation.[44] Some have attributed the socialist crisis in general and socialist democracy in particular to its theoretical foundations. Bowles and Gintis, for example, point out that because of its emphasis on class and social groups, Marxism neglects individual liberty, hides nonclass and noneconomic forms of domination, and, therefore, cannot address fully the problems of despotism.[45] The socialist experience clearly shows that nationalization of the means of production does not necessarily end domination and exploitation or ensure democracy. Lack of ownership of the means of production did not prevent the political elite in actually existing socialist states from becoming despotic. However, it is unclear if despotism can arise in a classless society in which equality not only among individuals within a community but also between communities prevails. Actually existing socialist states could hardly be regarded as classless.

In any case, the crisis of socialism has almost rendered capitalist development the only game in town, at least for now. Yet democratization and humanization of capitalism as well as its adaptation to transitional societies are surely possible. There is little doubt that present-day capitalism and democracy represent considerable improvements over those of the last two centuries. Social democracy that has built-in elements of corporatism can provide a compromise by balancing conflicting demands between different classes such as unions and the organized private sector.[46] Unlike the minimalist liberal democracy, social democracy does not restrict democracy to the political sphere. At the same time, unlike Marxism, it does not attempt to socialize all of the means of production and, consequently, does not rely on the presently tenuous socialist incentive system for its dynamism.

Social democracy that is a variant of the maximalist liberal democracy is by no means revolutionary. There is little doubt about its commitment to preserving the capitalist socioeconomic system. However, it is relatively more flexible in the demarcation of the boundaries of the private and public decisions. In other words, social democracy does not rigidly fix a priori the confines of democracy. As a result, it allows for the possibility of a welfare state to attempt to satisfy the essential human needs by providing basic resources for all citizens by means of government-operated or government-financed services. This flexibility also enables a developmentalist state to more vigorously create access to resources to the peasantry and thereby to facilitate its transformation. More importantly, the compromise of social democracy may be essential in societies such as those in most of Africa, where the transition from precapitalist communalism to capitalist possessive individualism is incomplete and where state building is often hindered by gross interethnic inequalities. The social compromises of social democracy are much more compatible with the ideals of consensus, equality, and ''cooperative caretaking'' widely held among African societies.[47]

The most likely candidate for social democracy in Africa is postapartheid South Africa. The African National Congress (ANC) over the last few years has significantly moderated its radical economic program. Nevertheless, from its election platform, the Reconstruction and Development Program, it maintains that the magnitude of deprivation of the African people is unlikely to be corrected by a market mechanism alone. Mandela continues to express a concern that South African businessmen could not be trusted to develop a postapartheid economy without state intervention.[48] Although the process of their democratization is (perhaps with the exception of Zimbabwe) at a rudimentary stage, Ethiopia, Mozambique, Angola, and Zimbabwe are also poised in the direction of social democracy.

Weaknesses of Social Democracy

Social democracy, however, faces two problems. One is that, although it is rooted in the principle of class compromise, in its present formulation it is largely based on majoritarian decision making. Social democracy in Africa could be more appropriate if it adopts the consensual decision-making formula, for reasons already discussed. The second problem is more fundamental. Considering the power disparity between the elite and the peasant masses and the anti-state thrust of the unfolding global order, how do the compromises that social democracy entails come about? How is consensual social democracy to be implemented? Here we have to rely on Cabral's theory of social change. The recent alliances and coalitions of social classes in Africa's pro-democracy movements also provide some hint in overcoming this riddle.

Cabral regards the radical petty bourgeois, especially the intelligentsia, as a potential agent of social change, capable of adopting the cause of the masses and organizing them.[49] Cabral expects that this class would sacrifice its own short-term interests (''commit class suicide'') in order to bring about societal transformation, which would also bring about its own development as a class in the longer run. Such selflessness has not been widely visible among the African petty bourgeoisie.

In view of the failure of such saviors to emerge during the last three decades, one can hardly be confident about the role of the petty bourgeoisie. It remains to be seen if the ANC proves to be an exception or turns out to be another case of betrayal. The role that different segments of the petty bourgeoisie is playing in the current democratization struggle, however, gives reason for optimism. A new coalition of middle-class professionals, student organizations, women's movements, the media, church groups, and other nongovernmental organizations has joined industrial unions and the urban dispossessed in this struggle.[50] It also appears that the pro-democracy movement favors development programs that protect the poor and the peasantry.[51] Thus, it is still possible that segments of the petty bourgeoisie can champion the struggle for social democracy and provide farsighted leadership that relates the plight of the peasantry to the predicament of the national economy.

Undoubtedly, the likelihood for successful implementation of consensual social democracy will vary from country to country depending on specific conditions, especially in terms of ethnic relations. However, in the present era of democratization and growing concern for human rights, African countries are unlikely to succeed in their state-building efforts by means of force. African countries have to innovate a strategy that builds on their traditional values of negotiated consensus, equality, and collective security. As Sklar notes, it is clear that there is no ready-made and transferable formula of democratic process that is suitable for African conditions.[52] Despite their shortcomings, the Ethiopian and South African cases represent a beginning toward innovative experiments that transcend the reliance on force as a means of state building. If state building is to be attained by means of negotiated compromises and consensus, it is also likely that the demarcation between the private and public decisions in democracy is subject to negotiated outcomes. Thus, the ideals behind the institutions of democracy are unlikely to be successfully transplanted from other cultures.

To conclude this section of the chapter, then, our analysis shows that any form of democracy is preferable to the existing, self-serving, authoritarian regimes that dominate Africa's political landscape. However, some form of social democracy that adopts the consensual decision-making formula would seem to be more conducive to enhancing state building as well as socioeconomic development in the continent. Because of its greater ability to redistribute resources in favor of the poor, this combination has greater potential to promote the transformation of the subsistence sector. Its consensus-building mechanism through extensive decentralization and proportional representation is also better equipped to lead to a more legitimate system of governance that is conducive to state building. This is clearly a difficult combination that restrains the state. But in countries where class, ethnic, and religious tensions are very high, anything less may not be sufficient to bring about peaceful state building and transition. Moreover, its closeness to the ideals of consensus, equality, and solidarity that still are widely held among African societies is likely to make it more sustainable in Africa.

PROSPECTS FOR SUSTAINABLE DEMOCRACY

Relative to the era of decolonization in the 1960s, the conditions for democratization are now better: awareness of the relevance of democracy is greater, and the pro-democracy social classes are stronger. The post–Cold War global climate is also more conducive for democratization than that of the Cold War era.

The causes for the recent wave of pro-democracy movement help to shed some light on the improved conditions for democratization. Over the last 30 years some changes, such as a higher degree of urbanization, greater access to education, some degree of industrialization, and a relative expansion of the middle class, have taken place, albeit at a much slower pace than in much of the developing world. These changes have been accompanied by a deepening economic crisis and widespread dissatisfaction, especially since the late 1970s. The African state has also surrendered a great deal of its sovereignty in economic policy making to the multilateral financial institutions and other aid donors since the early 1980s. The economic crisis, in tandem with the growing loss of national sovereignty, has made many social groups seek greater accountability and transparency in the management of economic as well as political affairs. The elite that had little organized opposition at the time of decolonization is now facing a greater demand for rights and social justice, as well as multiparty democratic political systems.

External factors have also contributed to the current democratization drive. The democratization movement, which has engulfed much of the world, has likely impacted the pro-democracy movement in Africa. The end of the Cold War is another important external factor. Many regimes such as those of South Africa and Zaire milked their anticommunist position to obtain Western support in sustaining themselves in power while regimes such as Mengistu of Ethiopia used socialist rhetoric to solicit support from the Soviet Union. With the end of the Cold War many regimes have lost an important tool of diversion.

OBSTACLES TO DEMOCRATIZATION

Despite the relatively improved conditions, democratization in Africa still faces a number of formidable obstacles. Africa's socioeconomic distortions, which require democracy to overcome, constitute a major impediment to the democratization process itself. As noted earlier, lack of access to education, information, and resources largely marginalizes the peasantry from the democratization struggle. As Yusuf Bangura notes, these low levels of national integration restrict democratization to an urban phenomenon.[53] In other words, the pro-democracy forces are stronger now than they were at the period of decolonization. Yet it is uncertain that they are strong enough to win the struggle and to sustain democracy. Poor economic performance, which is likely to persist, given the existing internal and external socioeconomic structures, is also likely to be a threat to sustained democratization.

Ethnic conflicts and the impact of democratization on mobilization of ethnonationalism are other obstacles to democratization. Oppressed nations can clearly benefit from democratic rights in promoting their national struggle, which may include secession. Authoritarian regimes are also likely to use ethnic strife and the fear of state disintegration to curtail democratization.

Another obstacle to the success of democracy is the marketization drive, which is largely imposed from above by the state in concert with the IMF, the World Bank, and donor countries. From the liberal point of view, the two processes are compatible. From the perspective of social democracy, however, the two are not always compatible. The marketization drive strengthens the position of the economic elite and those with the potential to become an economic elite, while it squeezes further the lower economic classes, including the workers and the peasantry. In many countries this has driven the lower classes, especially those in the urban areas, to engage, from time to time, in riots and other measures that intensify political instability. Intervention by a reformed state to implement income redistribution and agrarian reform is, thus, indispensable not only for empowering the masses but also for bringing about stability. The marketization drive aims at reducing intervention by the state. Only from this point of view can we understand why the same social forces that are active in the pro-democracy movement in Africa are opposed to the structural adjustment programs.[54]

External influence is another potential impediment to the democratization process in Africa. According to some, external impact may be positively decisive.[55] Claude Ake also argues that political conditionality for aid by the multilateral financial institutions and donor governments can promote democracy in Africa by strengthening pro-democracy forces and weakening authoritarian regimes.[56] Clearly, the potential positive impacts of external influence cannot be denied. However, aid and economic conditionality have not promoted economic development in Africa. Political conditionality is not likely to have different results. Moreover, the Western powers and most of the democratic forces in Africa have different notions of democracy. By attempting to shape the process in their own image, the Western powers may, in fact, obstruct democratization in Africa. Furthermore, the stark global inequality, the hegemony of the North, and the undue influences by the multilateral financial institutions, such as the World Bank and IMF conditionalities, may impede democratization.

In conclusion, our analysis suggests that consensual social democracy is likely to be more effective than the other types of democracy in transforming the subsistence peasantry and in mitigating ethnic conflicts and thereby enhancing state building and general socioeconomic development. Given the magnitude of the deprivation of the peasantry and the consequent internal fragmentation of African societies, a democratic state that is active in promoting market-creating and redistributive measures is likely to have more significant impact in advancing human resource development and state building than a majoritarian democratic system in which the state largely disengages from redistributive activities. Consensual social democracy may, however, be of a transitory nature. Once state building and internal economic integration through the transformation of the subsistence peasantry are achieved, a different type of democracy may be more suitable.

NOTES

1. David Beetham, "Liberal Democracy and the Limits of Democratization," *Political Studies* 40 (Special Issue 1992): 40–53.

2. There is a great deal of disagreement on the relationships between property rights and individual liberty. As Macpherson notes, democracy in its original sense of government in accordance with the will of the common people was regarded as a leveling doctrine and "fatal to individual freedom" by the elite until about a century ago: Crawford B. Macpherson, *The Real World of Democracy* (Oxford: Oxford University Press, 1966). Economic democracy is still viewed as bad for individual freedom mostly by the economic elite. There is no compelling reason that individual liberty for the common people would be enhanced more if economic decisions are private.

3. Charles E. Lindblom, "The Market as Prison," *Journal of Politics* 44, no. 2 (May 1982): 324–36.

4. Joseph V. Femia, *Marxism and Democracy* (Oxford: Clarendon Press, 1993), 10.

5. Samuel Bowles and Herbert Gintis, "Democracy and Capitalism," in Philip

Green, ed., *Democracy: Key Concepts in Critical Theory* (Atlantic Highlands, NJ: Humanities Press, 1993), 172.

6. Jacques-Mariel Nzouankeu, "The African Attitude to Democracy," *International Social Science Journal* 128 (May 1991): 373–85.

7. Naomi Chazan, "Between Liberalism and Statism: Africa Political Cultures and Democracy," in Larry Diamond, ed., *Political Culture and Democracy in Developing Countries* (Boulder, CO: Lynne Rienner, 1993), 67–105.

8. Raul S. Manglapus, *Will of the People: Original Democracy in Non-Western Societies* (Westport, CT: Greenwood Press, 1987).

9. Social democracy, as we see later in this chapter, involves compromises between classes, for example, the bourgeoisie and the working class. The nature of the compromises depends on the relative balance of power between the contending classes. Whether Eastern European social democracy will differ significantly from the Western European version would likely depend on the ability of the Eastern European working class to assert its interests, given the communist experience.

10. Giovanni Sartori, "Rethinking Democracy: Bad Polity and Bad Politics," *International Social Science Journal* 129 (August 1991): 437.

11. Sartori, "Rethinking Democracy," 448.

12. Beetham, "Liberal Democracy and the Limits of Democratization."

13. Samuel Bowles and Herbert Gintis, *Democracy and Capitalism* (New York: Basic Books, 1986).

14. F. A. Hayek, *The Constitution of Liberty* (London and Henley: Routledge and Kegan Paul, 1960); Milton Friedman, *Capitalism and Freedom* (Chicago: University of Chicago Press, 1962); Larry Diamond, "Promoting Democracy," *Foreign Policy* 87 (Summer 1992): 25–46.

15. Lindblom, "The Market as Prison"; Robert Dahl, "Why All Democratic Countries Have Mixed Economies," in John W. Chapman and Ian Shapiro, eds., *Democratic Community* (New York: New York University Press, 1993), 259–82. The flexibility of liberal democracy in terms of drawing the demarcation line between the private and public decisions is another point that creates a problem in terms of isolating the characteristics of liberal democracy. This vagueness may allow consensual and social democracies to be regarded as simply variants of liberal democracy. This, however, would outstretch liberalism and shift the debate from different types of democracy to different types of liberal democracy.

16. Individuals by living under the state and by obeying its laws, have already submitted to limitations of their freedom. Why the economic decisions would be particularly intrusive on their freedom is not very clear. More importantly, it is unclear why enslavement of society is more tolerable than the enslavement of the individual.

17. Macpherson, *The Real World of Democracy*, 6.

18. Hayek, *The Constitution of Liberty*.

19. Bowles and Gintis, *Democracy and Capitalism*, 11–12.

20. Sartori, "Rethinking Democracy." It is doubtful that Sartori's "possessive individualism" applies to all types of private enterprises. In the era of large corporations there is considerable distinction between ownership and management.

21. Friedman, *Capitalism and Freedom*.

22. Crawford B. Macpherson, *Democratic Theory* (Oxford: Clarendon Press, 1973).

23. Arend Lijphart, "Majority Rule in Theory and Practice: The Tenacity of a Flawed Paradigm," *International Social Science Journal* 129 (August 1991): 483–93.

24. Charles Edward Lindblom, *Politics and Markets: The World's Political Economic Systems* (New York: Basic Books, 1977); Edgar Owens, *The Future of Freedom in the Developing World* (New York: Pergamon Press, 1987).

25. Owens, *The Future of Freedom*.

26. Arthur Lewis, *Politics in West Africa* (London: Allen and Unwin, 1965), 64–66. Unlike for Hayek, for Arthur Lewis the primary objective of democracy is "that all who are affected by a decision should have a chance to participate in making that decision, either directly or through chosen representatives" (64).

27. Lijphart, "Majority Rule in Theory and Practice."

28. Richard Sandbrook, "Liberal Democracy in Africa: A Socialist-Revisionist Perspective," *Canadian Journal of African Studies* 22, no. 2 (1988): 250.

29. Mahmood Mamdani, "Peasants and Democracy," *New Left Review* 156 (March/April 1986): 48. This is not to suggest that the market is not coercive, as Friedman claims (Friedman, *Capitalism and Freedom*). The coercion of the market has already been discussed. It simply means that if the state is self-serving, promoting a negative income redistribution, retrenching its involvement in economic matters, to the extent that it is possible, would reduce the magnitude of coercion to that of the market.

30. Sandbrook, "Liberal Democracy in Africa," 243.

31. Lewis, *Politics in West Africa*; Lijphart, "Majority Rule in Theory and Practice."

32. Jacques-Mariel Nzouankeu, "The African Attitude to Democracy," *International Social Science Journal* 128 (May 1991): 373–85.

33. Maxwell Owusu, "Democracy and Africa—A View from the Village," *The Journal of Modern African Studies* 30, no. 3 (1992): 369–96.

34. Such negotiations also take place in countries of liberal democracy, especially when no political party wins a clear majority, and coalition governments are formed.

35. Not all African states were characterized by precapitalist communalism. The Abyssinian empire, for example, is known for its feudal hierarchical social relations. Consensus democracy was little known in feudal Abyssinia.

36. Lewis, *Politics in West Africa*.

37. Arend Lijphart, "Prospects for Power-Sharing in the New South Africa," in Andrew Reynolds, ed., *Election '94 South Africa: The Campaigns, Results, and Future Prospects* (New York: St. Martin's Press, 1994), 219–31.

38. For details see Articles 39 and 47 of the 1994 Constitution of the Federal Democratic Republic of Ethiopia.

39. Donald Horowitz, "Democracy in Divided Societies," *Journal of Democracy* 4, no. 4 (1993): 18–38.

40. Marina Ottaway, *Democratization and Ethnic Nationalism: African and Eastern European Experiences* (Washington, DC: Overseas Development Council, 1994); Walle Engedayehn, "Ethiopia: Democracy and the Politics of Ethnicity," *Africa Today* 40, no. 2 (2d quarter 1993): 29–52.

41. Arend Lijphart, "Majority Rule in Theory and Practice: The Tenacity of a Flawed Paradigm," *International Social Science Journal* 129 (August 1991): 483–93.

42. Claude Ake, "Rethinking African Democracy," in Larry Diamond and Marc F. Plattner, eds., *The Global Resurgence of Democracy* (Baltimore: Johns Hopkins University Press, 1993), 70–82.

43. Kidane Mengisteab, "Responses of Afro-Marxist States to the Crisis of Socialism: A Preliminary Assessment," *Third World Quarterly* 13, no. 1 (1992): 78.

44. The social incentive system is the realization by individuals that their well-being is enhanced only when that of the society is advanced.

45. Bowles and Gintis, *Democracy and Capitalism*, 17–20.

46. Yusuf Bangura, "Authoritarian Rule and Democracy in Africa: A Theoretical Discourse," in P. Gibbon, Y. Bangura, and Arve Ofstad, eds., *Authoritarianism, Democracy, and Adjustment* (Uppsala: Scandinavian Institute of African Studies, 1992), 39–82; A. Cawson, "Is There a Corporate Theory of the State?" in G. Duncan, ed., *Democracy and the Capitalist State* (London: Cambridge University Press, 1989); A. Carter, "Industrial Democracy and the Capitalist State," in Duncan, *Democracy and the Capitalist State*.

47. Frederic C. Schaffer, "The Cultural Transformation of Democracy in Senegal," paper presented at the 38th Annual Meeting of the African Studies Association, Orlando, FL, 3–6 November 1995.

48. John S. Saul, "Globalism, Socialism and Democracy in the South African Transition," in Ralph Miliband and Leo Panitch, eds., *Socialist Register 1994* (London: Merlin Press, 1994), 191.

49. Amilcar Cabral, *Revolution in Guinea: Selected Texts* (London: Monthly Review Press, 1969).

50. Bangura, "Authoritarian Rule and Democracy in Africa"; Thandika Mkandawire, "The Political Economy of Development with a Democratic Face," in Giovanni Andrea Cornia, Rolph van der Hoeven, and Thandika Mkandawire, eds., *Africa's Recovery in the 1990s* (New York: St. Martin's Press, 1992).

51. Bangura, "Authoritarian Rule and Democracy in Africa."

52. Richard Sklar, "Developmental Democracy," *Comparative Studies in Society and History* 23, no. 4 (1987): 686–714.

53. Bangura, "Authoritarian Rule and Democracy in Africa," 51.

54. Bangura, "Authoritarian Rule and Democracy in Africa."

55. Samuel Huntington, "Will More Countries Become Democratic?" *Political Science Quarterly* 99, no. 2 (1984): 205.

56. Ake, "Rethinking African Democracy."

Chapter 3

"For Fear of Being Condemned as Old Fashioned": Liberal Democracy versus Popular Democracy in Sub-Saharan Africa

JOHN S. SAUL

The Tanzanian scholar Issa Shivji is among those who are currently writing most eloquently on the question of democracy in Africa, and Shivji argues most vigorously for a distinction between "liberal democracy" and "popular democracy," one that is central to the argument of this chapter.[1] Note, however, the difficulties Shivji himself has experienced in defending this distinction in recent African debates. He speaks, for example, of an important conference in Harare several years ago at which "the liberal perspective seemed to be dominant."

In my keynote address I attempted to address the key issue of constitutionalism within the larger question of democracy and situate it in a popular democratic perspective. Understandably it was not particularly well received. Former radicals trying to find a niche in the rising tide of liberalism felt a bit embarrassed; liberals were irritated and the statists saw in it their traditional *bête noire*. Liberalism held such sway that even revolutionaries got defined as *consistent liberalism*! Be that as it may. It is clear to me that in the current debate on democracy, the divide between the liberal, in whatever variant including radical, and the popular perspective—thoroughly anti-imperialist—from the standpoint of popular classes ought to set the term of debate. If not, we are likely to get a celebration of the liberal triumph; jump indiscriminately on compradorial (for that is what liberalism degenerates into in most of our imperialist-dominated countries) bandwagons and confuse the long human struggle for democracy (equality) with its particular historical form—western liberalism (individualism).[2]

Yet, as Shivji further states, much that "would clearly distinguish the popular perspective—[its] position on imperialism, state and class, class struggle, etc.—remains unsaid by its intellectual proponents for fear of being condemned as old-fashioned or demagogic."[3]

The main reasons for the prevalence of such an intellectual atmosphere are not hard to find. In part, as Shivji suggests, this atmosphere is defined by the difficulties even radicals have in defining what the alternative model—"popular democracy"—might actually be expected to look like, concretely, under African conditions; this is, self-evidently, a point to which we will have to return. But another element in the present milieu is even more central. Thus, in the kind of circles Shivji describes, the discussion of democratization has tended to be elided with, even subordinated to, a parallel discussion of the related process of economic liberalization that has swept the continent so dramatically in recent years. Too often these processes—political democratization and economic liberalization—are seen to be merely two sides of the same coin. Moreover, this approach tends, in turn, to proceed as if the debate regarding the wisdom (and/or inevitability) of "neoliberalism" as the essential framing premise for both economic policy and democratic possibility were pretty much settled—and settled, overwhelmingly, in neoliberalism's favor. True, one of the best of recent books on the impact of neoliberalism/structural adjustment on Africa counsels some measure of caution with regard to such premises. "[T]here may be more tension," its editors write, "between fostering individual freedoms and good governance on the one hand and creating rapidly growing marketing economies on the other than many people might like to admit."[4] But even these authors seem hostage to a liberal perspective on "market economies" that, in its own way, blunts the possibility of having the kind of root-and-branch discussion of African alternatives counseled by Shivji.

In short, the ubiquitousness of the liberal/"neoliberal" perspective tends, crucially, to frame the scientific discussion of democratization in Africa. One other distinction might help us to think through the impact of such a narrowing of the terms of the recent discussion of democracy. For, within this intellectual milieu, such discussion has come to focus all too exclusively on what might be termed the "political science of democratization"—with any simultaneous consideration of the "political economy of democratization" assumed to be foreclosed (as being "old-fashioned" perhaps!). I will attempt to elaborate this distinction—between the "political science" and the "political economy" of democratization—later (while also noting the importance of this distinction for the manner in which we conceive the linkages between "democratization" and "state-" and "nation-building" in Africa). However, in order to offset the temptation to operate at too high a level of abstraction in doing so, I will also draw briefly in this chapter on the experience of the two recent "transitions to democracy" that I had the opportunity in 1994 to study firsthand, those that centered on the national elections held in South Africa and in Mozambique.

THE "POLITICAL ECONOMY" OF DEMOCRATIZATION

Much of the literature on Third World democratization has come to turn on a very narrow reading, indeed, of democratic possibility, one rooted in the political elitism of Schumpeter and of the American theorists of "polyarchy." As I have noted elsewhere,[5] the most baldly stated variation on the theme is probably the best known, that advanced by the ubiquitous Larry Diamond in his various writings. As he puts the point:

Perhaps the basic tension in democracy is between conflict and consensus. Democracy implies dissent and division, but on the basis of consent and cohesion. It requires that the citizens assert themselves, but also that they accept the government's authority. *It demands that citizens care about politics, but not too much* (emphasis added).[6]

As he further warns,

if reform is to be adopted without provoking a crisis that might destroy democracy, the costs to privileged economic interests of overturning democracy must be kept greater than the costs of the reforms themselves. This requires realism and incrementalism on the part of those groups pressing for reform. It also requires sufficient overall effectiveness, stability and guarantees for capital on the part of the democratic regime so that privileged economic actors will have a lot to lose by turning against it.[7]

Moreover, this concern for the sensibilities of capital, phrased here, commonsensically enough, in tactical terms, is merely one dimension of a much more fundamental conceptual slide—expressed in its most unabashed form in Diamond's influential work but present in the bulk of the transition literature—from "democracy," *through* "liberal democracy," to (Diamond's own phrase) "liberal capitalist democracy." Fortunately, he writes,

the past four decades of Third World economic development have furnished invaluable lessons for distinguishing the policies that work from those that do not. Broadly speaking, market-oriented economies develop while state-socialist economies fall behind. Internationally open and competitive economies work; closed (or at least rigidly and persistently closed) economies do not. Economies grow when they foster savings, investment and innovation and when they reward individual effort and initiative. Economies stagnate and regress when bloated, mercantilist, hyperinterventionist states build a structure of inflexible favoritisms for different groups, curtailing change, experimentation, competition, innovation and social mobility.[8]

This, then, is the loaded way in which Diamond and his colleagues lay the foundations of the case for their brand of "democracy."

Small wonder, then, that for Diamond the effort to create "a balanced [democratic] political culture—in which people care about politics but not too much" requires, "in Eastern Europe and much of the developing world, restraining the partisan battle [by] deflating the state and invigorating the private economy."[9] Beyond that—at the conclusion of his text we have the customary invocation of polyarchy and of "democratic elitism"—there lies, precisely, the crucial role of "political elites" and of the pacts they create among themselves:

[E]lite actions, choices and postures can have a formative impact in shaping the way their followers approach political discourse and conflict. Opposing party leaders must take a lead in crafting understandings and working relationships that bridge historic differences, restrain expectations and establish longer, more realistic time horizons for their agendas. . . . [C]ompeting party elites must set an accommodating and civil tone for political life.[10]

The thrust of much recent literature is, then, to define the terms of any transition of democracy ever more narrowly and cautiously.[11] One more example may be to the point: the much cited work of Giuseppe di Palma, in which he emphasizes the importance to the "crafting" of democracies—defined as the "setting up [of] government in diversity as a way of defusing conflict"—of accepting certain stern limitations upon such efforts.[12] As he argues, "one factor that reconciles to democracy reluctant political actors tied to the previous regime is that in the inaugural phase coexistence usually takes precedence over any radical social and economic programs."

Such precedence [di Palma continues] stems from understanding the limits of democratic (and other politics) as natural harbingers of material progress. It stems as well from a fuller appreciation that willfully using democracy as a Jacobin tool of progress not only is ingenuous but may also raise intolerable political risks; namely, authoritarian backlashes and, in anticipation, escalation into a virtuous "guided" democracy. Past democracies—the most instructive example from the 1930s being the second Spanish republic—have foundered on such Jacobin instincts. By giving reform precedence over coexistence and making support for reform the test of legitimacy, they have unintentionally fulfilled a prophecy: the losers would be unwilling to reconcile themselves to a nascent democracy. The example looms large among political practitioners in Europe and Latin America. Indeed, the importance of coexistence has not gone unnoticed, despite its significant policy sacrifices, by those who still sympathize ideally with a more Jacobin democracy.

There is some bluff "good sense" in this, of course. A preoccupation with the way in which a would-be democratic society develops norms of tolerance and due process is not an irrelevant one. Yet how easy it is for such an approach to emphasize this issue at the expense of any real concern about socioeconomic outcomes and to underwrite, conservatively, a tendency to "blame the (willfully unrealistic) victims" rather than their oppressors for any transitions that fail. Thus, di Palma is quick, quite specifically, to identify "mobilizational models for the Third World" based on *dependencia* paradigms and undue popular suspicion regarding the role played by the "advanced industrial democracies" in the "global economic order" as representing a particularly clear danger to "democratic crafting." Not surprising, then, his comfortable conclusion that, currently, "democracy's *disengagement from the idea of social progress* [is] a silver lining because it has actually given democracy more realistic, more sturdily conscious grounds for claiming superiority in the eyes of public opinion

and political practitioners'' (emphasis added). It is no wonder that Perry Anderson can write of such tendencies that

what is missing [in contemporary political thought] is any conception of the state as a
structure of collective self expression deeper than the electoral systems of today. Democracy is indeed more widespread than ever before. But it is also thinner—as if the
more universally available, the less active meaning it retains.[13]

Put more sharply, Gills, Rocamora, and Wilson have presented the new or-
thodoxy as converging around a practice of ''low intensity democracy''—a
practice designed both to help legitimate the present global status quo *and* to
limit/contain possible challenges to it.[14] Nor, as noted before, is it difficult to
identify the tacit (and not-so-tacit) premises that lie behind such a narrowing of
the democratic optic. What is at stake are, quite simply, a dramatic abandonment
of the politics of public purpose and a fetishization of the market—the latter
premise part of a broader and now quite omnipresent worldview recently characterized by Colin Leys as follows:

Our leaders are currently directing a process of self-destruction of our societies in the
name of a utopia no less irrational than the beliefs of the Solar Temple. . . . This utopia
is the idea of a world-wide market in which the people of the world relate to each other
directly as individuals, and only as individuals: and ''globalization'' [linked in turn to
acceptance of the unchecked ''freedom of capital to move across national boundaries'']
is the process of trying to realize this idea.[15]

What about ''democracy'' under such conditions? Manfred Bienefeld continues
the argument:

Unfortunately genuine democracy is hard to reconcile with neoliberalism's mystical belief
in the magic of disembodied markets, its fierce hostility to the notion of state and society
as organic entities capable of defining and pursuing a common interest, and its insistence
on pervasive deregulation. Under such conditions, the state loses the capacity to manage
economies in accordance with democratically determined social, ethical or political priorities. Only the shallowest and most meaningless democracy will survive in a ''cowboy
capitalism'' where property rights become virtually absolute because states and electorates are disempowered by the mobility of capital.[16]

In Africa, Leys suggests, the result of such globalization—with its attendant
processes of structural adjustment and the like

has *not* been a market-based social and economic recovery based on individuals and their
initiatives in the marketplace. It has been, instead, an ethnic-based regression, as people
have been pushed back into reliance on precolonial social bonds for survival; and in
some cases it has resulted in economic and social catastrophe.[17]

In short, if the realities of Africa's present-day political economy qualify the democratic prospect on the continent, they also create conditions that undermine the prospects for any smooth consolidation of domestic peace and "state-building." This latter is a point to which we return in the following section. Note here, however, that even Larry Diamond is sufficiently nervous about this kind of argument to qualify somewhat his celebration of "low intensity democracy," stating that "democracy cannot endure if massive inequality and exclusion go unchallenged" and that "getting reform on the agenda requires that the disadvantaged and excluded economic groups organize and mobilize politically."[18] But such qualifications remain, by and large, to the side of his ideological exertions in defense of "liberal capitalist democracy."[19]

Even for those who have rather sharper doubts than does Diamond regarding the capacity of neoliberalism to be the universal solvent of the development problem and the guarantor of democracy in the Third World (including Africa), the challenges ahead are still pretty daunting, of course. Some seem prepared to choose a posture of resignation. In this respect, Adam Przeworski, one of the more astute students of the global "transition to democracy," might be taken to exemplify the tone of a defeated Left most starkly: "Capitalism is irrational, socialism is unfeasible, in the real world people starve—the conclusions we have reached are not encouraging."[20] In such a context, Przeworski asserts, transitions from authoritarian to more democratic politics will tend to find their transformative content constrained by the continuing strength of the holders of socioeconomic power: "[A] stable democracy requires that governments be strong enough to govern effectively but weak enough not to be able to govern against important interests. . . . [D]emocratic institutions must remain within narrow limits to be successful."[21]

Under such circumstances, Przeworski concludes, the best-case scenario for a "successful" transition is one in which "Reformers" within the erstwhile power structure distance themselves from their own "Hardliners" and agree to negotiate a form of democratic outcome with "Moderates" within the democratic camp—those who, in turn, are prepared to distance themselves from the "Radicals" who occupy a position farther over on the ideological spectrum. True, this probably implies acceptance by such Moderates (Przeworski terms theirs to be "the traditional dilemma of the Left")

that even a procedurally perfect democracy may remain an oligarchy: the rule of the rich over the poor. As historical experience demonstrates, democracy is compatible with misery and inequality in the social realm and with oppression in factories, schools, prisons, and families.[22]

Self-evidently, the tone here is very different from anything the Diamonds and di Palmas might adopt. Yet, in the end, there is little more that Przeworski can offer us, given his premises ("socialism is unfeasible"): a Left bending over backward to avoid "chaos"; a Left propitiating the powers-that-be; a Left that is nothing if not "prudent." Such is the shrunken vision of the transition to democracy that the "realism" of the epoch would seek to fashion for us.

Nor is Przeworski alone in his realism/pessimism. Thus, even so committed a socialist as Ralph Miliband also felt forced, in a book (*Socialism for a Sceptical Age*) written just before his death in 1994, to acknowledge that "in the 'third world,' it is quite clear that where economic development occurs, it will be under capitalist auspices, with Western capital much involved in the process." Of course, Miliband is as convinced as Przeworski that capitalism is "irrational" and is therefore not sanguine about the prospects for much "economic development" occurring under such capitalist auspices in many parts of the world. Nonetheless, for him the fact remains that virtually all "governments in the 'third world' have accepted the hegemonic role of the West and adapted their economic and social policies to it. *The price for not doing so is beyond their capacity and their will.*"[23]

But what if this means, in turn, that the vast majority in the Third World are merely doomed, by the present il/logic of imperialism, to underdevelopment and to ever more severe versions of social distemper, unless dramatic structural changes, both global and national, begin to occur? There is certainly one stream of authors on Africa who attest as much, focusing on the "stranglehold" presently exerted on Africa by international forces (and their local agents) and, in particular, on the policies of the international financial institutions (IFIs) in further promoting such a situation. Thus, John Loxley and David Seddon, in introducing a valuable recent issue of the *Review of African Political Economy* on the subject, comment as follows:

Where the IFIs identify failure they blame the domestic policies of African governments, but many observers . . . would insist that Africa's problems today are predominantly "external" in origin and that the IFIs in particular have played a significant role in reducing Africa's capacity and prospects for development. We share this view and suggest that the strategy adopted and the lending policies and conditions imposed by the IFIs are heavily to blame for the dismal performance of most African economies over the last decade or more—although there are also "internal" factors which should not be discounted and "external" factors which precede the interventions of the IFIs.[24]

Adopt such a premise for a moment—that capitalism really is irrational and destructive in its workings in Africa—and the otherwise cozy and "reasonable" world of the new democratic theorists turns very sour, very quickly. Take di Palma's image of "Jacobins" willfully wielding democratic claims in order to realize "progress," for example. In practical terms, isn't he actually evoking the "danger" that the vast mass of the Third World will begin to demand a different, more rational world order than the present process of globalization can be expected readily to provide? Others, even some professing to approach these matters from the Left, attempt to shuffle such difficulties aside in other ways: by implying that global capitalism (now in its "postimperialist" phase, according to Becker and Sklar[25]) is, in the end, profoundly developmental—although, to be sure, in need of somewhat greater (if rather unspecified) pressure from below in order to operate equitably. In such a context, it is argued, "capitalism versus socialism is no longer the prime issue of class analysis; it yields pride of place to the question of liberty versus dictatorship."[26] But if, to repeat, global capitalism is, cumulatively, making the situation of African countries *worse*, how sanguine can one really be about proclamations as to the probable "unfeasibility" of the socialist alternative?

There is, to be sure, one other alternative, exemplifying, in the recent literature on Africa, a kind of "postmodern turn." This approach also suggests an abandonment of the "grand narratives" of "socialism" and of "capitalism," of the developmental/predatory state and of the world market—and proposes instead an embrace of the village and the locality:

Africa's potential for democracy is more convincingly revealed by the creation of small collectives established and controlled by rural or urban groups (such as local associations) than by parliaments and parties, instruments of the state, of accumulation and of alienation.[27]

But this is only partly helpful. True, Africans must strengthen their capacities to act from the bottom up. But the negative impulses that spring from an irrational (global) capitalism and/or from the typically predatory state will not merely leave them alone to do so. The sources of these impulses must be transformed as well; we simply must not make things easier for ourselves by pretending this is not so, however difficult/impossible the task of doing so may seem. As Leys (reviewing Bayart's work) suggests:

I would say that the African state, for all its record of abuse, remains a potential line of defense for Africans against the depredations of the world economic and political system: part of the solution, if there is one, and not necessarily part of the problem, as the drive of the IMF and the World Bank to weaken the African state in the name of market efficiency implicitly acknowledges.[28]

Yet how is any such state to come to act consistently in this way if not in response to pressures from below? Clearly, analysts who see capitalism as part of the problem and not part of the solution and who insist on taking "imperialism" seriously have pressing reasons of their own for valuing democracy—would it not be a "popular democracy"?—highly.[29]

THE "POLITICAL SCIENCE" OF DEMOCRATIZATION

"Popular democracy?" We will return to a consideration of this concept. However, what will be apparent is that, precisely because it does *not* take the question of imperialism seriously, much of the current literature on democratization in Africa finds itself limiting the conception of democracy with which it works—the better, as noted, both to legitimate the neoliberal project *and* to insulate it against any unmediated claims by popular classes from below. This implies a firm step away from any consideration of an alternative economic project, prompting the suspicion that, from such a perspective, "democracy" is valued more as a plausible narcotic than as the route to any kind of genuine popular empowerment. With "political economy" (concerns about imperialism, class struggle, and the like) now bracketed off, the democratization debate can proceed on other fronts without bad conscience. The result: whether it is because they feel the Left/socialist alternative to be irrelevant (Diamond), dangerous (di Palma), or impossible (Przeworski), these and other theorists are prepared to shift quite sharply the center of gravity of the debate about democracy, toward what I have called, for want of a better term, "the political science of development."

We must avoid caricature, however. The emphasis upon "the political" within democratization theory can take different forms, and they are worth distinguishing. Only at its most crass—as in much of the literature on "governance," for example—does the narrowing of the democratic optic take an overtly manipulative turn, with "democracy" viewed as being as much problem as opportunity, its claims hedged in accordingly. As Susan George and Fabrizio Sabelli have recently documented, the World Bank has been a particularly important reference point for generating this discourse: its earlier efforts to downgrade the claims of the state to a developmental role are now qualified by a clearer recognition that some kind of viable, statelike structure be in place in order to maintain a minimum of both order and legitimacy.[30] In order to put "governments . . . on notice to get their acts together" and in order to specify "this process and this requirement" the bank "has chosen the rather archaic word governance." (" 'Government,' " George and Sabelli add, "would have been a bit too blatant since the Bank, according to its Articles, is not allowed to intervene in politics at all!") They then document the cautious dance that World Bank authors weave around the notions of "transparency," "public choice," "responsiveness," and "accountability" in their texts on governance. In fact, George and Sabelli's conclusions do not differ from Gerald Schmitz's recent summary of much the same literature:

[I]n contrast to *self*-empowerment and grass-roots democratic action, it is "we professionals," with access to our reams of paper, who know best how others should do participatory development. Extending the paradox, more "participation" ends up reinforcing the Bank's role, even though more real democracy in developing countries would quite likely reduce it![31]

The result: academic advocates of the bank approach find themselves saddled with the unenviable task of theorizing, in Joan Nelson's formulation, a working balance between the "contradictory pressures of political opening and economic management'' in situations of ''simultaneous dual transitions'' (i.e., situations witnessing both economic liberalization and some form of political democratization). Not surprisingly, they are forced to twist themselves almost out of shape in their efforts to do so. Thus, Nelson notes that

recent research on the politics of economic reform suggests a need to insulate key economic management functions from direct political pressures and at the same time to improve the channels for ongoing consultation between the government and concerned interest groups on other aspects of economic policy and reform.[32]

As an example, she argues that the question of

how to contain yet also integrate organized labour merits particular attention. . . . The process of economic liberalization inevitably hits labour hard. . . . Most Third World successes with sustained economic liberalization in the past two decades have entailed periodic or consistent repression of unions: among the obvious examples are Korea, Bolivia, Chile, Mexico, and Turkey. Some theorists have suggested that labour restraint is crucial not only for sustained economic development but also for consolidation of democratic openings, in order to encourage confidence and loyalty from business. Yet failure to integrate labor into democratic processes can also threaten democratic consolidation.[33]

It is difficult to know just where to add the emphases in such quotations, the tensions within them being so close to the surface. Small wonder that various ''hired guns'' from the academy have been working overtime to smooth down the rough edges of the ''governance'' approach. In African studies a key figure in attempting to do so has been Goran Hyden, whose essay ''Governance and the Study of Politics'' is widely cited. His work is also all too typical of this genre; seeking to give us an ''objective'' model of governance—one that, in its abstraction, only obliquely evokes the socioeconomic policy content such a model is designed to ensure—he nonetheless produces something readily available for use by neoliberals. For, within this model, ''democracy'' is, once again, a safely contingent and manipulable variable, not a defining requirement.

In its assumption that what matters now, and in the future, is whether politics is good or bad, the governance approach is cast in a postmaterialist and postpositivist vein. . . . This is where it departs from the literature trying to measure democracy or freedom. While that literature is important in its own right and obviously overlaps to some extent with the concerns of this approach, the study of governance is performance-oriented. It examines how well a polity is capable of mobilizing and managing social capital—both fixed and movable—so as to strengthen the civic public realm. In this respect it comes closer to the literature on business management[!]. In the same way as business management theory treats the organization as crucial to business success, the governance approach treats regime—the organization of political relations—as essential for social and economic progress.[34]

Meanwhile, in sharp contrast to the calculated blandness of such a way of presenting things, Schmitz feels able to conclude from his counterefforts to demystify the governance approach and to evoke "a more truly democratic . . . praxis" that "manufacturing 'democratic consent' is (fortunately, I believe) proving to be more difficult at the mass than the elite level."[35] Time alone will tell.

But if "governance" encapsulates one currently fashionable and highly suspect "political science" approach to democratization, it must be emphasized there are other, much better reasons for a preoccupation with the political interactions that mark an attempted transition to democracy. In taking seriously such approaches, we will see that the main charge against them is not that they are wrong-headed but rather that, in their tendency to ignore or downplay the political economy of democratization, they are one-sided. Two emphases in particular are worth noting in this respect. First, practicing democrats in Africa, as well as those who theorize their activities, stress the importance of establishing democratic institutions in order both to discipline entrenched autocrats and to help preempt the authoritarian tendencies that have become so much a part of African political life. Second, both practitioners and theorists also stress the possible importance of democratic institutions to the reconciling of "differences"—especially those that are "communally defined": by ethnicity, by religion, and by race—and the facilitating of "order" and (a central preoccupation of the present volume) "state/nation-building."

Take the first point: the demand to democratize the "predatory state" in Africa. This demand is quite understandable in light of recent African history and, indeed, has a rich history of its own. As the editors of a special issue (on "Surviving Democracy?") of the *Review of African Political Economy/ROAPE* remind us,

the present struggles form part of the long African struggle for democratic politics and systems, visible in the radical nationalist movements of the postwar decade in South and West Africa, in the populist revolts of the early 1980s in Ghana and Burkina Faso (and the related victory of the National Resistance Movement [NRM] in Uganda), and in the continued record of opposition, dissent, and resistance to authoritarian and repressive regimes of the last 20 years.[36]

Of course, it is this upsurge that Shivji found so often to be presented in exclusively "liberal democratic" terms (as at the Harare conference that he cites): some African writers have been so preoccupied—for very good reasons—with breaking the elision long central to continental political discourse between "democracy" and "the single-party system" that they have tended, themselves, to embrace alternative notions of "pluralistic democracy" (and its "most manifest criterion . . . a multi-party system") quite uncritically.[37] True, such authors have thrown up a variety of relevant considerations about the constitutional means by which the promise of a more open society might be more permanently and effectively realized in Africa.[38] At the same time, they tend to be not nearly so alert to the kind of nagging questions that the *ROAPE* editors—from a more "political economy"-driven perspective—permit themselves as they conclude the editorial cited earlier:

Multi-partyism and the rule of law, indeed even the codification of basic human rights, do not of themselves imply participation, representativeness, accountability or transparency. They may be essential to the possibility of reducing inequalities and of removing oppression, but do not accomplish this of their own accord. Much more commonly democracy serves as a system through which class dominance and various forms of systematic inequalities are perpetuated and legitimated. The challenge of those African nations undergoing a process of democratization is to use the space it opens to press for greater justice for the mass of the population.[39]

Some African commentators do, of course, recognize the danger that the democratization process in Africa may merely halt "at the level of periodic decorative elections."[40] Sidgi Kaballo is a case in point, arguing forcefully the need to establish, alongside electoral mechanisms, a much deeper culture (and attendant institutionalization) of "universal human rights" than has heretofore existed in postcolonial Africa. Kaballo even notes in passing the possible class determinants of such a culture, in his case lamenting the weakness in this regard of the class on which he might otherwise pin his hopes, the African bourgeoisie.[41] Even more suggestively, Peter Anyang'Nyongo, an influential Kenyan advocate of democratic processes and human rights, notes the existence of diverse cases of democratization in Africa. In some he finds that "profligate bureaucrats and politicians came under severe attack for corruption and mismanagement" from the "vocal middle classes" (who found their "standard of living . . . threatened by a tight economic atmosphere"). In others—he highlights the case of Zaire, mentioning the writings of Nzongola-Ntalaja—he finds democratization to be driven by the yearnings of "the popular masses" for a "second independence."[42] This is suggestive—yet in the end, Shivji might argue, too little is made of the possible implications of such distinctive social bases for the substance of diverse democratization processes.[43] True, some—like Claude Ake—are prepared to expand Nzongola's point evocatively to the rest of the continent:

The ordinary people of Africa are supporting democracy as "a second independence." This time they want independence not from the colonial masters, but from indigenous leaders. They want independence from leaders whose misrule has intensified their poverty and exploitation to the point of being life threatening. And they are convinced that they cannot now get material improvement without securing political empowerment and being better placed to bring public policy closer to social needs.

[Nonetheless] democracy is being interpreted and supported in ways that defeat these aspirations and manifest no sensitivity to the social conditions of the ordinary people of Africa. Generally the political elites who support democratization are those with no access to power, and they invariably have no feeling for democratic values. They support democratization largely as a strategy of power. . . . The people can [only] choose between oppressors and by the appearance of choice legitimise what is really their disempowerment.[44]

By and large, however, the class analysis of Africa's democratization boom remains to be done.

As for Kaballo, he also acknowledges that "the prevailing economic crisis and the harsh austerity measures required by the international financial institutions and donors decrease [the bourgeoisie's] chances of reaching compromises on the demands for better living conditions of the masses" (quite possibly creating conditions within which "the way to authoritarian politics opens up again"). His conclusion:

it is not enough to include the respect of human rights and the establishment of multiparty democracy as a new political conditionality in international and bilateral relations: the democratization process . . . needs [international] backing by relaxing the austerity measures and the provision of more economic assistance.[45]

Interestingly, he quotes, in support of this conclusion, Larry Diamond. But Kaballo gives no more reason than does Diamond (cited before) to anticipate the kind of global turnaround that guaranteeing such a benign context for democratization would require. He is, in short, as unsuccessful in carrying the contradictions of the global economy into the center of his analysis as he is the contradictions of Africa's domestic class structures.

Second, what of the question of order and of "nation building" (as evoked in the title of the present volume)? In a world and a continent scarred by the extreme tearing of the social fabric that has occurred in such settings as (the former) Yugoslavia, Rwanda, and Somalia, it would be unwise to trivialize the preoccupation of political scientists with this issue. This is, in fact, the other side of the coin of Przeworski's pessimism, cited earlier, regarding the (unlikely) radical/socialist dimension of any transition from authoritarian rule. For he also argues passionately for the possibility that, under certain circumstances, protagonists to such transitions will agree (if it proves possible for them to agree at all)

to terminate conflicts over institutions because they fear that a continuation of conflict may lead to [or perpetuate] a civil war that will be both collectively and individually threatening. The pressure to stabilize the situation is tremendous, since governance must somehow continue. *Chaos is the worst alternative for all* (emphasis added).[46]

In a parallel manner, James Dunkerley—in examining the "resolution of civil wars in Nicaragua (1981–90) and El Salvador (1980–91) where laborious and intricate negotiations terminated conflicts of great brutality and bitterness"— writes of the collapse of communism and the outbreak of other civil wars, the terrifying images of which should serve to remind us of the merits of what Cromwell called "settling and healing," even if this is achieved in unheroic manner, at the cost of dreams, and through the concession of often vital interests.[47]

As it happens, Przeworski and Dunkerley both cast their concerns primarily in terms of the compromises among classes and contending power blocs that might be necessary to facilitate a transition. In the African literature, with its own distinctive tilt toward the political science of transition, far greater attention has been paid to another possible route toward "chaos," that threatened by the uncontrolled escalation of "identity politics"—particularly as driven by an extreme expression of the politicization of ethnicity (although regionalism, race, and religion have also been mentioned as other possible modalities of such hyperpoliticized identity). From this angle, too, "settling and healing" have seemed an important goal, with "democracy" then assessed primarily in terms of its projected contribution to the underwriting of an effective level of societal order (di Palma's "setting up [of] government in diversity as a way of defusing conflict").

In the two case studies—of South Africa and Mozambique—that follow in this chapter, we see the way in which the introduction of electoral and other, related constitutional solutions to outstanding situations of deep-seated social conflict has, recently, helped to produce far more stable societies and polities than had previously existed. Of course, as scholars have also warned, the implications of "democracy" for the securing of order in fragile societies may sometimes be far more negative, the competitive aspects of democratic processes serving to exacerbate the claims and counterclaims of different communal interests rather than to assuage and domesticate them (see chapter 4 in this volume). Still, we would be unwise to ignore the contribution that the exercise of political imagination, of "statecraft," can and must make—both during the period of constitution making and the period before the initial elections and after them—to the ongoing reconciling of such claims and the creation of some greater sense of enlarged community and shared citizenship.

There is one major limitation to this way of formulating things, however. It is a limitation anticipated earlier when we noted the roots in Africa's contemporary political economy of the intensity of many such "claims and counterclaims." The fact remains that any sense of "enlarged community and shared citizenship" or of national institutional consolidation (of "state building," in the language of the present volume) that is won, momentarily, by statecraft may already be in the process of being lost, once again, to the fragmenting logic of "underdevelopment" and of peripheral capitalism. True, the specific tensions that mark the various fragile societies we study are the product of quite specific histories and circumstances. But such weaknesses are exacerbated—make no mistake—by the current global capitalist disorder (and by such corollaries as the undermining of any sense of a possible developmental role for the presently existing nation-state). Sapped of confidence in socialist and other related projects, "modern," collective, and humane, people turn for social meaning to more immediate identities, often to grasp them with quite fundamentalist fervor (as we have seen Leys, quoted earlier, to suggest). Here is Ralph Miliband's "extremely fertile terrain" for the kind of "pathological deformations"—predatory authoritarianisms and those "demagogues and charlatans peddling their poisonous wares . . . of ethnic and religious exclusion and hatred"—that now scar the landscape in Africa and elsewhere.[48] For, as Nancy Fraser has effectively argued, it seems extremely unlikely that tensions rooted in struggles for "recognition" can be resolved, in the long term, in any very effective and healing manner unless tensions rooted in struggles for "redistribution" (broadly defined) are also being addressed.[49] We are drawn back, in other words, to a consideration of the necessary simultaneity of the moments of "political economy" and of "political science" in the discussion of Africa's transition to democracy and of the links of that process to "nation building." The brief case studies in the following two sections are designed to put further flesh on the bones of this approach.

SOUTH AFRICA: A "LIBERAL DEMOCRACY"?

The South African election of 1994 was a crucial event, so overwhelmingly significant as a "liberation election" from white minority rule that it is, indeed, rather difficult to view it in any other terms: the drive for democratic rights in that country by and for the vast majority of its population is a well-known story that has captured the imagination of the world. At the same time, South Africa also has seemed to provide an almost classic case of the kind of transition Przeworski had in mind when he writes of transitions that involve the "extrication" (his term) of democracy from authoritarian regimes in which "political forces that control the apparatus of repression, most often the armed forces" remain strongly positioned.[50] Joe Slovo, South African Communist Party (SACP) leader and one of the major protagonists of the South African transition, writing in the midst of the negotiations stage in that country, characterized the South African situation in much these terms:

We are negotiating because towards the end of the 80s we concluded that, as a result of its escalating crisis, the apartheid power bloc was no longer able to continue ruling in the old way and was genuinely seeking some break with the past. At the same time, we were clearly *not dealing with a defeated enemy* and an early revolutionary seizure of power by the liberation movement could not be realistically posed. This conjuncture of the balance of forces (*which continues to reflect current reality*) provided a classic scenario which placed the possibility of negotiations on the agenda. And we correctly initiated the whole process in which the ANC was accepted as the major negotiating adversary.[51]

Moreover, this military stalemate was itself seen as merely the tip of the iceberg of other conflicts within the society, conflicts driven by the realities of "difference" (as defined by racial, cultural, and political party/movement identifications) that have been so visible, close to the surface, and dangerous in South Africa.[52] For example, one informed observer, assessing the racial dimensions of the situation, suggested that

the balance of power and the potentially catastrophic effects of a descent into civil war dictate that negotiated transition rather than revolutionary transformation is the order of the day—and that a settlement . . . require significant compromises to allay the concerns of the white elite.[53]

As the negotiations unfolded, the ANC was prepared to make a number of such compromises to meet white concerns and also prepared, on occasion, to make them toward Gatsha Buthelezi and his Inkatha Freedom Party (despite this latter's own sustained posture of intransigence and provocation).

Under the circumstances of a divided South Africa, the realization in April 1994 of a nationwide election that witnessed the transfer of power from a racial oligarchy to a new, panracial majority was a dramatic achievement.[54] Small wonder that the negotiations that served to realize such democratic possibilities and to hold in check such dangerous contradictions have been a magnet for the attention of students of the "political science" of transition. Here was a case, if ever there was one, of the "setting up [of] government in diversity as a way of defusing conflict"; accordingly, the temptation has been irresistible for political practitioners and political observers alike to draw the ebb and flow of political infighting, of intraelite trade-offs, and of constitutional compromise to the center of their analyses. Thus, a recent book by Alaister Sparks has usefully documented the manner in which the relevant negotiations had actually begun well before the release of Nelson Mandela from prison in 1990 and traced their continuation right up to the 1994 election.[55] Even more impressive in this regard have been the two important volumes on the South African transition prepared by Steven Friedman and his colleagues: *The Long Journey: South Africa's Quest for a Negotiated Settlement* and *The Small Miracle: South Africa's Negotiated Settlement*.[56] In these books one finds painstaking analyses of the intense interactions that took place, over the four-year period 1990–1994, among political elites regarding transitional political and bureaucratic arrangements, long-term constitutional dispensations, and the proposed workings of the electoral system that would eventually come into play in 1994.

There is even some discussion, in such works, of the moments at which political actors outside the formal negotiating framework broke into the process: the mass action campaign, spearheaded by the trade unions in August 1992, and the more chaotic events at Bisho that same month are cited in this regard. Of course, on the Left, there was concern that such mass action had come to be treated merely as a "tap," to be turned on and off at the ANC leadership's whim as short-term calculation of advantage at the bargaining table might dictate:

We must not confine or inhibit mass struggle. . . . Instead we need to encourage, facilitate and indeed build the kind of fighting grass-roots organizations that can lead and sustain a thousand and one local struggles against the numerous injustices our people suffer.[57]

But most academic analysts seemed to accept both as inevitable and as benign the fact that, on balance, the negotiations process had tended to sideline many of the bearers of popular resistance who had done so much to place negotiations on the table in the first place. "Elite coalescence has been the hallmark of South Africa's transition," writes Timothy Sisk approvingly, adding that "elite-concluded accords do not work unless elites are able to demobilize their own constituencies!"[58] The election itself was hailed, in effect, as locking the results of such "coalescence"—and such judicious "demobilization"—into place.

Some of the celebration by political scientists of the South African negotiations process that culminated in the 1994 election has been more qualified. The actual electoral process was an often chaotic one, for example. Given the heroic scope of the overall undertaking, most observers were inclined to be tolerant of many of the flaws in the process, but some flaws did seem to demand special attention. Most controversial was the manner in which the outcome of the election was itself a "negotiated" one, notably, in Kwazulu/Natal, where, in the context of considerable fraud and malfeasance and in the interest of safeguarding a peaceful outcome, the ANC and Inkatha leaderships merely agreed to the outcome in secret.[59] There could be no guarantee that so sanctioning Inkatha's victory in its "home province" would actually discipline its rogue tendencies, of course; the electoral process could prove to be merely one more avenue along which it will choose to advance its disruptive project. (Indeed, some observers have argued that additional constitutional concessions—an even more decentralized form of federalism, for example—are necessary so as to meet, in the interests of further guaranteeing order, Buthelezi's apparently insatiable demands.[60])

A handful of other authors have queried the actual scope of the democratic outcome in South Africa in quite other terms, notably, Hermann Giliomee, who fears that the elections may merely have produced "a one-party-dominant system" ("along Mexican and Taiwanese lines"!).[61] There are precedents in the region that might feed such concerns, notably, that of Zimbabwe, where the Zimbabwe African National Union-Popular Front's (ZANU-PF) continuing electoral successes can be traced, paradoxically, to "the grim model of multi-party democracy which Zimbabwe's ruling party has moulded and refined since coming to power in 1980":

It is a model which has mixed western-style liberal democratic political constructs with ZANU-FP's increasing partisan domination of state and civil society, to produce a *pro forma* democracy that evokes little popular enthusiasm and diminishes active participation from ordinary Zimbabweans.[62]

But if "the gradual depopularization of the formal political process"[63] is also a risk in South Africa, it might be mistaken to seek its roots primarily in any authoritarian proclivities the ANC may have.[64] Pace Giliomee, some left observers have seen a more serious risk of such an outcome to lie in the very fact that the ANC has committed itself so comfortably to the *liberal* nature of the democratization process in South Africa, rather than in not having committed itself to it enough.[65] Giliomee seems to have only two points to his political compass: authoritarianism versus liberalism—with no space for "popular democracy." However, we cannot make sense of South Africa in these terms: to understand why this is so, it becomes necessary for us to expand the scope of our inquiry beyond the confines of much of the currently fashionable discussion of the South African transition.

For the weakness of such discussion springs, once again, from that severing of "political economy" from "political science," the dangers of which we have emphasized throughout this chapter. Here one dramatic citation may suffice, although a more sustained canvassing of the literature would bear additional witness to much the same point. This citation takes us back to the two Friedman books previously singled out for praise for their handling of the intricacies of the political horsetrading that characterized the negotiations process. The special significance of this citation bears emphasizing. Note that it is the *only* moment in all the 543 pages of these books when it is acknowledged that there existed, in effect, a second level of "negotiations" in South Africa, albeit one clearly visible only within the optic of the political economy approach. Thus, on pages 290–91 of the second of these volumes, Chris Landsberg—writing a chapter entitled "Directing from the Stalls? The International Community and the South African Negotiation Forum"—notes the following:

But the SAG [South African government] was not the only target for persistent pressure from abroad. The ANC also came in for its share of the pressure. Since 1990, when the democratization process began, some foreign governments, notably the U.S. and some of its allies—Britain, Germany, Italy and Japan—successfully induced the ANC to move away from its socialist economic policies, including that of nationalization. Instead, they succeeded in persuading the movement to embrace Western-style free market principles which the ANC increasingly, albeit reluctantly, adopted. It is interesting to note, for example, that Mandela's evolving position on fiscal responsibility was a direct response to pressures from foreign investors and governments.[66]

This dimension, involving the moderation of the ANC's aspirations for socioeconomic transformation and the movement's consequent increasing acceptability to powerful vested interests, worldwide and local, was at least as crucial as any constitutional compromise to guaranteeing the smoothness of the transition to "democracy" in South Africa. Yet even in the context of Landsberg's own chapter it is noted only in passing, and certainly it is never presented—as it should have been—in such a way as to be integrated into these books' overall interpretive framework.

Permit me one other citation, in order to cap the point: it is drawn from another book that painstakingly traces the South African negotiations process, Timothy Sisk's previously mentioned *Democratization in South Africa: The Elusive Social Contract*. Sisk's priorities are established on his very first page and in no uncertain terms: "Determining how conflicts driven by identity politics are reoriented from the battlefield to the conflict-regulating institutions of an inclusive democratic state is *the* critical challenge of our era" (emphasis added).[67] True, Sisk does acknowledge at various points later in his book that critical questions of "redistribution" have also been at stake in a deeply unegalitarian South Africa[68]; he even suggests that such questions must now be dealt with, or the consequences might be disastrous. But his discussion of such issues is prisoner of his starting point: his framework literally does not allow him to see that the very nature of the negotiations process that centered on "identity politics" also shaped, in crucial ways, the terrain for any ongoing struggle over redistributional politics. As the ANC has become more "liberal"—adapting itself to the seeming imperatives of the global capitalist economy and, through "elite-pacting" and the prioritizing electoral models of political contestation (which, some feel, has encouraged a further demobilization of its constituency)—has it also become less able to champion effectively the struggle for "redistribution"?[69]

There is certainly evidence that the ANC has adopted a broadly "neoliberal" economic agenda, although there is not space here to pursue the point.[70] We can, however, speculate further as to what will happen if the movement's gamble on free-market capitalism—expected to provide both a sustainable solution to South Africa's economic problems and also sufficient surpluses to permit at least some redistribution of resources—does not work. The growing indifference of the black population, and its transformation into mere spectators at the political-cum-electoral game were earlier suggested to be one possible outcome. That there were already indications of this by early 1995 was apparent in the period preceding the local elections to be held later in the year:

Anxiety is starting to mount in provincial governments at the slow pace of voter registration, three weeks from the deadline. But registration has been slow in all parts of the country, and in some of the previously most politically active areas it has been slowest. . . . The 90-day voter registration exercise has met with a lukewarm response despite high-profile media campaigns. Last Saturday an ANC local government election rally at the Union Buildings in Pretoria attracted fewer than a hundred supporters. Rally organizers had been expecting up to 20,000. The lack of enthusiasm is being put down to disappointment about the failure yet to see material improvements after the last voting exercise, in April last year. An expectant black community has yet to see the houses, improved education and health facilities the ANC promised in its election campaign.[71]

Moreover, by September, the situation had not much improved, one high-profile study from the Center for Policy Studies warning that "large-scale apathy on election day could lead to local government based on a thin slice of popular support, which is not representative."[72] As Paul Graham of the Institute for Democracy in South Africa added, "In terms of internationally accepted criteria for free and fair elections, the forthcoming elections are getting to the point where it is sadly failing."[73]

Moreover—to build on the analysis developed in the previous section of this chapter—popular indifference may not be the worst thing that can occur under such circumstances. Might not any "demobilizing" of popular constituencies for purposes of consolidating "interelite accords" (à la Timothy Sisk) merely make such constituencies available for other forms of mobilization than developmental ones? Winnie Mandela's tendency to translate socioeconomic contradictions into starkly racial terms offers few solutions to South Africa's structural problems, but it has proven to be attractive in some of the popular circles in which she moves; and this kind of cultural nationalist politics could prove to be even more attractive in the future. In addition, if South African blacks are not effectively mobilized in terms of class interests and for purposes of national developmental goals and socioeconomic transformation, they may well fall back on more exclusively ethnic loyalties to ground their search for moorings in the unstable social universe that is the new South Africa. If these things were to occur, might not the "chaos" that negotiations are said to have preempted merely be found to be bubbling up again, within the electoral arena[74] and elsewhere, in new and even more dangerous forms?

This may be too bleak a picture, however. South Africa is also marked by other, much more progressive efforts to keep alive the popular term in the political equation and to strengthen initiatives that might qualify global capitalism's hold over policy making. Within the ANC coalition itself there are crosscutting tendencies, for example, leading some close observers to predict that "the 'broad church' of the ANC will eventually split into its component elements," largely along class lines, leading to new party-political alignments.[75] Others have argued that different class projects will continue, for the foreseeable future, to play themselves out within the ANC itself, suggesting that such contradictions are already visible within the movement's Reconstruction and Development Program (RDP)[76]—a key document developed through a process of internal debate and public consultation to serve as both election manifesto and policy guide for the ANC once in power. Thus, the RDP largely accepts the existing capitalist framework for purposes of macroeconomic policy making. Yet its dramatic first section locks into place a clear statement about the centrality of meeting "basic needs" as the chief performance standard against which to measure the success of the new South Africa, one to which all sectors, including the business community, can be held accountable. This is a powerful point of reference for challenging any easy slide into acceptance of a Brazilian-style "50 percent solution" (or worse) as "good enough" for South Africa. Even more importantly, later sections of the document affirm in dramatic terms the necessity that an ongoing process of popular empowerment from below keep the process of transformation alive. One is reminded, in this connection, of one of Nelson Mandela's more intriguing statements of the past few years: thus, speaking to the Congress of South African Trade Unions (COSATU) annual congress in 1993, he warned the assembled workers' representatives to be "vigilant." "How many times," he asked, "has a labour movement supported a liberation movement, only to find itself betrayed on the day of liberation? There are many examples of this in Africa. If the ANC does not deliver the goods you must do to it what you did to the apartheid regime."[77]

As it happens, this has not always been the message Mandela has delivered since assuming power. It is, however, the kind of language that continues to drive much of the Left in South Africa, as they have looked to the assertions of trade unions, civics, women's organizations, and the like—operating, from sites within "civil society," both inside and outside the ANC—to keep a progressive agenda alive:

The challenge is to engage with the democratic transition process, with a perspective and a movement that is more democratic, more far-reaching in its popular empowerment implications, a perspective that extends political democracy beyond the critically important institutions of representative democracy to embrace direct and participatory forms as well. And we need to extend democracy beyond political institutions, into the social and economic realms.[78]

Opinions differ as to how effectively popular demands can make themselves felt by such means, some observers already inclined to despair regarding the prospects for progressive endeavor in the near-to mid-future, others insisting that "the powerful grass-roots forces behind liberation can regain momentum," the current situation "compelling the still formidable—as well as many brand new—organizations of the poor and working class to demand that their representatives and leaders take an entirely different direction."[79] In any case, it is argued that only on this latter sort of path could the way lie open to a deepening of democracy and the retaining of a radical momentum in South Africa. As Adler and Webster argue (in their critique of the rightward pull of much of the transition literature, especially that of Przeworski), "disciplined and sophisticated social movements" may yet be able to

inject more progressive content into the democratization process and wrest important concessions from reformers and moderates alike [recall Przeworski's use of these terms, as cited earlier]. In other words a conservative outcome is in no way given in advance. . . . Rather than being a force to be restrained by the alliance between reformers and moderates, a mobilized civil society and powerful social movements—especially the labour movement—played a central and constructive role in creating the conditions for the transition, in shaping its character, and indeed in legitimizing the transition process itself. Whether the labour movement can continue to play this role is an open question. With the advent of parliamentary democracy and the creation of corporatist-type policy-making fora and institutions, as well as the emphasis on national reconciliation, pressures towards incorporation and demobilization have never been stronger. However, counter-vailing trends point towards the persistence of these movements and their democratic culture and toward a postapartheid politics of continued contestation within the new democratic institutions.[80]

THE MOZAMBICAN CASE: WHAT KIND OF TRANSITION?

We will return to the relative weight and merits of any such possibility in a subsequent section. Note, however, that certain ostensible alternatives to the liberal democratic framework have already been tried and found wanting in Africa. Mozambique is a case in point, much cited in South Africa as an example of what *not* to do. After all, didn't Mozambique attempt to mount a "socialist alternative" to the dictates of global capitalism—and that in the days when there at least existed an apparent global counterhegemonic force (the Eastern bloc) to link one's radical fortunes to? Look what happened.

There are those who will argue that Frelimo's activities in Mozambique did not actually constitute a genuinely socialist project even in its earliest days. I cannot agree with this reading. Elsewhere[81] I have argued the necessity to dis-tinguish "left developmental dictatorships" from "right developmental dicta-torships" and suggested that Mozambique under Frelimo leadership once fell within the former category: concerned precisely with those issues—"[a] position on imperialism, state and class, class struggle, etc."—that we have seen Shivji to identify with a "popular perspective." Moreover, in its early days, Frelimo quite self-consciously presented itself as embodying a "radical democratic" thrust: it both highlighted within the terms of its overall project the needs and interests of ordinary Mozambicans and sought to institutionalize in real ways the latter's active participation (through the formation of the "dynamizing groups" and of mass organizations of women, workers, and the like). But recall that Shivji also placed, alongside his models of liberal and popular democracy, a "statist" model, embracing regimes whose own distinctive "democratic" rhetoric (and authoritarian practice) Shivji sardonically epitomizes in the phrase "what-use-is-free-speech-to-a-starving-peasant"! Viewed in such terms, the in-itial Frelimo experiment was both "left developmentalist" ("socialist") *and*, ultimately, "statist" (authoritarian).

Interestingly, recent interviews I have had with the more committed of the first generation of Frelimo leaders find a number of them admitting ruefully that the undemocratic, "statist" nature of their undertaking contributed importantly to the failure of their initially progressive project—laying a dead hand over the very institutions of democratic activism that the movement was ostensibly will-ing into place. To be sure, Mozambique's inherited circumstances (the relative backwardness of Portuguese colonialism, the absence of trained cadres, the extreme vulnerability of the economy) were far from favorable for both radical endeavor and economic transformation. The ruthlessness of South Africa's policy of destabilization—concretized in Mozambique in the practices of the Renamo movement but part of a much broader regional strategy of defending apartheid—must still be considered the single most important factor in undermining Frelimo's efforts.[82] Yet the fact remains that, domestically, grievous errors in the sphere of economic policy making were twinned with highhanded political practices that undermined precisely the popular empowerment that might have set Frelimo's own project on far firmer foundations.

Empowerment? In principle, one might imagine such a "left developmental dictatorship" deepening its project in democratic terms—in line with its initially very real commitments to the popular classes—and moving toward a more genuinely (rather than notionally) "popular democracy." But the antidemocratic impact of a tendency toward militarist hierarchy, an embrace of the presumed centralizing imperatives of "developmentalism," and a fixation with quasi-Stalinist notions of socialist practice combined to negate any such trajectory in Mozambique.[83] Very soon, in any case, the effects of war and of the penetration of the country's faltering politicoeconomic structure by the IFIs and the aid community meant that little remained of Frelimo's initial left vocation. What Mozambique was experiencing under Frelimo leadership was something very like a "recolonization" (in the pungent formula suggested by economist David Plank[84]). Now, if the party's authoritarian instinct did remain in place, it was increasingly the instinct of a dictatorship ("developmental" or otherwise) of the Right!

There was to be no easy resting place for the Frelimo leadership at this point, however. The Frelimo state was in tatters—and the war ground on. Western interests, now ever more prominent (and unchallenged) actors in Mozambique, were increasingly insistent upon brokering a negotiated, "democratic" settlement to the country's "civil war." Moreover, Renamo, at first merely a vicious cat's-paw of external actors (Rhodesia, South Africa), had begun to root itself ever more indigenously in Mozambique's broken-backed society. Its sheer continuing presence in areas where it could not be driven out militarily increasingly allowed it to ground a certain "giveness" for itself within the emerging Mozambican political equation. It had also managed to carve out some space for itself by, for example, linking up with quasi-traditional structures and fanning regional resentments. Thus, even though much of its external backing (from such former sponsors as apartheid South Africa and Banda's Malawi) was beginning to evaporate, its political claims could not merely be wished away.

It was also the case that, in ideological terms, much less now separated Frelimo from Renamo than had once seemed possible: both had little choice but to embrace the conventional nostrums of "neoliberalism" (and, apparently, little desire not to do so). Add to this the fact that, at a certain point, the government's own morale seemed to snap, mounting corruption and the increasingly arbitrary use of power by both military and civilian authorities threatening to drag Frelimo's own project down to Renamo's level. Thus, by the time of the 1994 elections—with Renamo finally cajoled (by various international actors, most prominently) into taking up a more conventionally peaceful political role—a great deal of the distance separating the two movements-cum-parties had begun to disappear. As one South African journalist (Eddie Koch) commented of that election, it seemed to be marked by a kind of "moral amnesia," Frelimo's own high purposes at independence but a distant memory and Renamo's history as, first, Rhodesia's and then South Africa's brutal surrogate also obscured by time and changing circumstance.

In consequence, to observe closely Mozambique's first multiparty election in October 1994 was a very different experience from that of observing the South African election discussed in the previous section. For whatever the ambiguities that attached to the South African transition process, the overriding mood of most South Africans in April had been one of euphoria. Theirs was, as noted, a "liberation election," in which a large majority felt themselves to be voting, quite literally, for their freedom. We can see that Mozambique offered a far more somber context for exercise of the franchise. Indeed, large numbers of Mozambicans seemed to be voting, first and foremost, for the very idea of voting itself. Their apparent hope: that the election would prove to be an arena within which political differences might, at last, be resolved peacefully and the violence that has scarred their lives for so long might end. Was this not, then, a virtually archetypal case study in the "political science of democratization"?[85]

Moreover, in these terms the election did "work," albeit as part of a much broader peace process (one orchestrated to a signal degree from outside the country by interested players within the international community).[86] Both the United Nations and a number of Western countries (as well as various arms of the Catholic Church) placed strong pressure on Frelimo to cede a more pluralistic political structure, while also going to considerable expense to encourage the Renamo leadership to transform itself from guerrilla movement to more conventional political party. The result was, indeed, a smooth-running electoral process, financed, in large part, by substantial foreign subventions (notably, from the United Nations), although cleanly organized and run by the Mozambicans themselves.[87] Moreover, Renamo did surprisingly well in the election, even though Frelimo's Alberto Joaquim Chissano scored firmly over Renamo's Afonso Dhlakama in the presidential balloting, and Frelimo also scraped out a rather narrower majority in the National Assembly. Just before the election there had been much pressure on Frelimo to concede—the South African precedent was mentioned—Renamo participation in a postelectoral "Government of National Unity," which Frelimo refused to do. Moreover, despite the narrowness of its victory, the postelectoral Frelimo government seemed inclined to operate, rather high-handedly, on a "winner-take-all" basis.[88] Might this not, at best, produce a Mozambican version of the *de facto* one-party state or, at worst, be so provocative as merely to reactivate civil strife? In the event, Renamo was apparently reasonably reconciled to the new system.[89] It seemed, for the moment at least, that a democratic resolution had brought closure to one of the most horrific, chaos-producing wars in Africa: no small accomplishment.[90]

Yet, as hinted before, the kind of politics that was facilitated by the electoral process, if measured against the aspirations of advocates of "popular democracy," could not be considered to have been particularly empowering of the Mozambican populace. We have seen that the scope for national decision making had become quite narrowly defined by the global circumstances in which Mozambique found itself, the state eviscerated and any immediate prospect of political contestation over alternative socioeconomic visions sidelined. In the election, Frelimo—once the proponent of a clear (if controversial) socialist development alternative—ran a campaign centered on "showmicios" (a play on the Portuguese word *comicio*) and rallies in which show business (bands, parachutists, and the like), the trivialization of issues, and the glorification of the candidate took precedence over real substance. For its part, Renamo tended to fall back on the quite calculated manipulation of various regional, ethnic, religious, and (advanced in the name of "tradition") gender-oppressive particularisms and animosities in building its own electoral base—thereby setting a number of dangerous precedents for the texture of future political interactions in Mozambique.[91] The upshot, ironically, was that the introduction of the institutions of pluralist democracy has been, in some ways, *disempowering* for ordinary Mozambicans: rendering them less, not more, able to engage in meaningful debate about the nature of neocolonial structures in their country and about possible alternatives to them.

As with South Africa, this way of interpreting the situation does need qualification, of course. The liberalization/democratization of political space in Mozambique has had implications that stretch beyond both the opportunities and the mystifications of the electoral arena. As trade union and women's movement structures have been liberated from the deadening hand of monoparty control, for example, they have begun to assert themselves in new ways. Agricultural cooperatives, emerging in particular in the periurban green zones, are also felt to hold considerable promise in some areas, while the freeing up of space for a more creative brand of journalism has also had an often positive impact, albeit one felt primarily in the urban areas. If such varied initiatives can, indeed, root themselves firmly in Mozambique, the necessary sociopolitical underpinnings for pressing more powerful democratic demands upon governments, parties, and the electoral process itself may prove to be that much more firmly in place. Or take the recent observations regarding rural Mozambique by Ken Wilson, who finds—in present trends toward decentralization, in the mounting of the forthcoming local elections, in the new sensitivity of various governmental bureaucracies to grassroots demands and initiatives, and in the waning of politicians' high-handed devaluation of existing cultural sensibilities—the necessary context for a new and much stronger voice from the peasantry to be heard.[92]

Wilson may be overstating the positive side of the "opening to the villages" that he emphasizes; other observers have tended to stress more strongly the possible dangers (e.g., for the transformation of gender relations) of a compromise with "traditional" structures that such an opening might entail in practice.[93] Still, in reading his intervention, I was forcefully reminded of a conversation I had had a year earlier, during the time prior to the elections in Mozambique, with Graça Machel, former minister of education in the Mozambican government and widow of Samora Machel, who, as Frelimo leader, had been the country's first president. Saying that she would not herself be standing for the assembly this time around, she told me that she would, however, be voting for Frelimo. I was taken aback. This was an answer to a question it would not have dawned on me to ask.

Yes, she went on, Frelimo still represents more of a national project—Frelimo's most crucial historical accomplishment, in her view—than any other alternative currently on offer. But in terms of deepening democracy and ensuring the eventual revival of other, more progressive strands of Frelimo's original undertakings for the country and of building ever more secure foundations for a genuinely stable Mozambican national political system, she saw the chief hope to lie in the strengthening, in her phrase, of "the institutions of civil society." This is the sphere toward which, for the foreseeable future, she said she intended to direct her own considerable energies.

THE MISSING ALTERNATIVE: A "POPULAR DEMOCRACY"?

Are the seeds of alternative democratic possibilities to be found here, as in South Africa, in the building, from the ground up, of an invigorated "civil society"? This is the kind of question to which we turn in conclusion. One thing is clear, however: the refrain of "liberal democracy"—drawing, as Shivji says, "its inspiration from western liberalism centered around notions of limited government, individual rights, parliamentary and party institutions, the centrality of the economic and political entrepreneur of the market-place, etc."[94]—is currently hegemonic in South Africa and even (however much more tentatively) in Mozambique. As noted at the outset of the present chapter, this hegemony, the current "common-sensedness" of liberal democratic discourse, is one reason progressive political actors and analysts have difficulty in mounting the case for an alternative. But are such actors and analysts not also stymied by the difficulty of giving concrete form to their own ideal type, that of "popular democracy"? Are they able only to contrast glibly that model's abstract claims to the perceived imperfections of the real-life system of liberal-democracy—while incapable of specifying what it might mean to put their own imagined alternative firmly on the political agenda?

Of course, if "liberal democracy" is, indeed, likely to prove to be an oxymoron in southern Africa, that would be a point worth making—whether or not any more progressive alternatives to it and to the neoliberal economies with which it intersects were readily forthcoming. The "historically necessary" is not always the "historically possible," as Roger Murray wrote of the African condition many years ago. Nor is someone like Shivji prepared to apologize for the difficulty of evoking, for purposes of comparison, the experience of any "real-life" popular democracies in Africa—since, in fact, the attempt to build them has only just begun.

The popular [perspective on democracy] remains most undefined. It opposes both the statist and liberal in their typically top-down orientation by emphasizing popular struggles and mass movements from below. It challenges the universality of liberal values and the authoritarianism of statist positions.[95]

As an ideology of resistance and struggle . . . [its] exact contours and forms of existence can only be determined in actual social struggles in given, concrete social conditions. Yet, at the minimum, it has to be an ideology which articulates anti-imperialism and anti-compradore-state positions.[96]

Must we leave the case there, however? Have we not already begun to specify the ways in which the "concrete social conditions," the contradictions of peripheral capitalism in southern Africa are even now throwing up "resistance and struggle" of the kind necessary to ground increasingly "popular" expressions of democracy? Can we not also identify *existing* practices that begin to exemplify the promise of just such resistance and struggle? To these questions many observers would answer yes, looking to a range of organizations in "civil society" as exemplifying precisely the promise in question. Indeed, we have suggested this to be a key emphasis on the Left both in South Africa and in Mozambique.

True, "civil society" has become something of a buzzword in discussions about Africa, often masking as much as it reveals about the class content of struggles there (as elsewhere). As Ellen Wood has forcefully reminded us in a number of her writings, it is a deeply ambiguous concept, tilted in its origins toward the interests of emergent entrepreneurs, yet also used, more recently, to encapsulate the claims of broader publics and a wider range of interests.[97] It is noteworthy, in any case, just how central the notion has become to those who press the case for something considered to be more empowering of ordinary people than mere liberal democracy. A case in point, perhaps, is Benjamin Barber, one of a handful of Western political thinkers who have defied the hegemony of the theorists of "polyarchy" and "democratic elitism."[98] Writing in 1984, Barber anticipates the argument of the present chapter by arguing that "we suffer, in the face of our era's manifold crises, not from too much but from too little democracy."

From the time of de Tocqueville, it has been said that an excess of democracy can undo liberal institutions. I will try to show that an excess of liberalism has undone liberal institutions: for what little democracy we have had . . . has been repeatedly compromised by the liberal institutions with which it has been undergirded and the liberal philosophy from which its theory and practice have been derived. . . . Liberal democracy is . . . a "thin" theory of democracy, one whose democratic values are prudential . . . means to exclusively individualistic and private ends. From this precarious foundation, no firm theory of citizenship, participation, public goods, or civic virtue can be expected to arise.[99]

Barber's alternative? "Strong democracy . . . defined by politics in the participatory mode," a politics through which "active citizens govern themselves directly, not necessarily at every level and in every instance, but frequently enough and in particular when basic policies are being decided and when significant power is being deployed." Note that Barber, in arguing the case for "strong democracy," is careful to distinguish this from anything smacking of "unitary democracy," a quite different concept and one much closer to the kind of "statist" formulation of "authoritarian quasi-democracy" we have seen critiqued by Shivji.[100] A strong democracy is one in which consensus, community, and a sense of the "public realm" are won through political *interaction*, not imposed from above.

In more recent writing Barber worries about the arena within which such politics might best be pursued—asking where, in effect, meaningful citizenship must come to be defined. For he is well aware that the surge of globalization (his "McWorld") has grouped many of the forces that most deeply affect people's lives at that global level. But whether in the community, national, or worldwide arena, the challenge is "to make government our own" through a recasting of "our civic attitudes"; this, in turn, "is possible only in a vibrant civil society where responsibilities and rights are joined together in a seamless web of community self-government."[101] Barber is by no means sanguine about the prospects for so "making government our own," especially at the global level. Yet his very underscoring of the necessity to do so marks him as a genuine democrat:

How civil society can be forged in an international environment is an extraordinary challenge. Recognizing that it needs to be forged is, however, the first step towards salvaging a place for strong democracy in the world of McWorld.[102]

Here Barber's concerns intersect with the southern African progressives whose ongoing struggles we mentioned earlier: there is a shared sense that *genuine popular empowerment* must be struggled for in the name of democracy and that it, in addition, can alone undergird any meaningful project of "state/nation-building." There is something more: even those in South Africa who have already lived the intense history of popular activism that was so much a part of the antiapartheid struggle realize that the bases of such empowerment can never be taken for granted: they must continue to be built painstakingly—conceived, renewed, struggled for, given institutional form—from the bottom up. There is no shortcut to popular democracy or any elite-pact or refined constitutional dispensation that can guarantee it—however important these latter accomplishments can sometimes be in opening up space for the pursuit of a more deep-cutting process of democratization.

Identifying the goal of "strong democracy" can therefore make an important contribution to our understanding of democratic practice and of truly effective institution building. Measured against it the insensitivity, even brutality of the formulas of Diamond ("citizens [should] care about politics, but not too much") and Huntington (his fear of an "excess of democracy") are unmasked.[103] Here is the kind of "political science of democratization" that could really help us to get somewhere. Still, even Barber can take us only so far; in the end his writings run the risk of valuing democratic activity for its own sake and for the sake of producing a more meaningful "community"—but without really spelling out the concrete policy ends that a more effectively empowered citizenry might be expected to produce. Thus, while the global system churns on, he can satisfy himself with the bromide "that neither capitalism nor socialism has much to do with the economic realities of the modern world."[104] This is not an emphasis that the South African "strong democrats" whose concerns we have linked with those of Barber would be comfortable with, however. For they are much more inclined to be political economists than Barber is, their "strong democracy" having far more in common with Shivji's "popular democracy" in underscoring the fundamental importance of bringing capital under social control: the importance, in short, of a preoccupation with "imperialism, state and class, class struggle" in the grounding of democratic assertion!

Note, however, that an approach that is both realistic and long-term must be part and parcel of this aspect of the progressive agenda as well: in Africa, as hard experience has shown, the building of a socialist alternative in socioeconomic terms can be no more of an overnight enterprise than the building of a popular democracy can be on the political front. Few radicals in South Africa, for example, advocate any kind of ultraleft adventurism as the necessary antidote to the vaguely reformist neoliberalism that many within the ANC now seem tempted by. Elsewhere I have argued that the notion of "structural reform"— a measured, yet revolutionary, project of closing in on the prerogatives of capital and shifting the balance of power over the production process slowly but surely in the direction of the popular classes—epitomizes what the best of South African progressives still feel to be both necessary and possible.[105] Statements by such important socialist-minded South Africans as prominent trade union leader Enoch Godongwana and leading ANC activist Pallo Jordan may serve to document this point. Acknowledging that "if we want a socialist alternative in the absence of an insurrection, that poses a challenge for us," Godongwana suggests that

we argue a socialist alternative, but within the constraints of saying we cannot simply storm and seize power tomorrow. Therefore we should be creative—how do we make sure that, in the process of struggling for socialism, we assert ourselves as a class with the objective of having a class rule. . . . We must begin, while we assert a leading role in various areas of society, to build certain alternatives within the capitalist framework that will tend to undermine the capitalist logic.

Or, from the same debate, consider Jordan's similar interest in a kind of strategy

which doesn't necessarily imply grabbing hold of the state or nationalization of the commanding heights of the economy, but in a sense establishing a number of strategic bridgeheads which enable you to empower the working class and the oppressed, and from these bridgeheads you begin then to subordinate the capitalist classes to the interests of society in general.[106]

Of course, as it stands, much of this kind of argument remains at the level of mere metaphor, even in South Africa. Spelling out what it would have to look like in practice requires real imagination, with respect both to the concrete mechanisms of state activity to be employed (the use of tariffs, taxes, procurement policies, and the like) and to any complementary actions that might have to spring from civil society (e.g., via collective bargaining structures or through the full range of existing socioeconomic forums). Nor is a reliance on mere populist spontaneity likely to produce the subtle tactics and deft timing that we can see necessary to realize such ongoing struggles: clearly, effective leadership must come to complement the kind of mass energy and action that are so essential to radical undertakings. Nonetheless, the language in which the challenge now confronting South Africans is framed does make a difference.

For seeking to discipline capital to service socially defined priorities cannot be done merely by wielding the rhetoric of shared national purpose. Instead, real countervailing power—social power, class power—must be brought to bear upon it. This will not be easy. Yet it is precisely here that the goals of "popular democracy" and socialist assertion—of the political science and the political economy of democratization—come together. It is also true that any such efforts will be that much more difficult to realize in other African settings (e.g., Mozambique) where global capital (the IMF, the World Bank, the aid industry, the multinational corporations [MNCs]) has an even more unqualified run of the shop, where the instruments of possible popular empowerment within "civil society" are much less developed, and where parties and states that might begin to express a new set of progressive demands are far more distant on the horizon than is the case in South Africa. Yet there, too, the struggle continues.

Of course, the question of whether the popular forces-in-the-making can become strong enough to stem the logic of recolonization and the further underdevelopment of Africa that is occurring in the name of an ascendant neoliberalism remains a very open one. Should we not admit, in fact, that it is difficult to be sanguine regarding the prospects for democratic empowerment in

Africa—in large part, because it is difficult to be sanguine about the prospects for the social and economic transformation of Africa under the current regime of neoliberalism and global-market hegemony? This is a painful truth, but, unfortunately, it is one that is not as "old-fashioned" as it is sometimes made to appear. Nor should acceptance of this truth serve as an invitation to trivialize other concerns that drive the debate about democracy in Africa: the need to discipline abusive authority; the need to create fresh space for individual and collective self-expression; the need to institutionalize the possible means of reconciling communal (ethnic and racial) differences and of reviving and refocusing some more positive sense of national purpose. The "political science of democratization" must not be allowed to displace "the political economy of democratization," but it must never again be merely reduced to it either—as the Left has too often been tempted to do in the past.

Yet the fact remains: institutional ingenuity in the name of democracy (and of "state" and "nation building," for that matter) can do only so much to contain and humanize Africa's contradictions so long as the socioeconomic "terrain" remains so "fertile" for "pathological deformations" (to allude to Miliband's formulation, cited earlier). Indeed, under such circumstances, the tendency for "democracy" in Africa to exacerbate, rather than resolve, the difficulties of "nation building" may well be the predominant one. Must we not conclude, in short (and pace the likes of Becker and Sklar, quoted earlier), that the twin issues of "capitalism versus socialism" *and* "liberty versus dictatorship" are inextricably linked in Africa? But if this is true, are we not also left with a mere counsel of despair (socialism being "unfeasible," after all)? Certainly, as Colin Leys has recently put the point so tellingly, ideas that might begin effectively to address the question of Africa's economic crisis

could come to seem rational only in a world that was in the process of rejecting the currently predominant ideology of the market. While this world must come, it is not yet in sight, and meantime the African tragedy will unfold.[107]

"While this world must come"—would that it were so. Still, his sentiment parallels that of Miliband: "Such a situation cannot endure." As the latter concludes his final book:

[C]hange in the political system and the advent of "democracy" do not change the social order; but the demand that it too should be radically changed is certain to come into focus.... The specific demands and forms of struggle which [are generated] will vary from country to country: there is no single "model" of progressive or revolutionary change. But everywhere, there are common goals and aspirations—for democratic forms where they are denied, and for more democratic forms where they are a screen for oligarchic rule; for the achievement of social order in which improvements in the condition of the most deprived—often a majority of the population—is the prime concern of governments; for the subordination of the economy to meeting social needs. In all countries, there are people, in numbers large or small, who are moved by the vision of a new social order in which democracy, egalitarianism and cooperation—the essential values of socialism—would be the prevailing principles of social organization. It is in the growth in their numbers and in the success of their struggle that lies the best hope for humankind.[108]

Not least in Africa.

NOTES

1. Issa Shivji, ed., *State and Constitutionalism: An African Debate on Democracy* (Harare: SAPES, 1991). See his chapters "State and Constitutionalism: A New Democratic Perspective" (chapter 2) and "Contradictory Class Perspectives in the Debate on Democracy" (editor's Epilogue). Shivji also identifies a third, "statist" perspective on democracy, which we will also have to return to later.

2. Shivji, *State and Constitutionalism*, 255.

3. Shivji, *State and Constitutionalism*, 255.

4. Thomas M. Callaghy and John Ravenhill, eds., *Hemmed In: Responses to Africa's Economic Decline* (New York: Columbia University Press, 1993), 17.

5. See John S. Saul, "Globalism, Socialism and Democracy in the South African Transition," in Ralph Miliband and Leo Panitch, eds., *Socialist Register 1994: Between Globalism and Nationalism* (London: Merlin Press, 1994), which I have drawn on in writing the next several paragraphs.

6. Larry Diamond, "Three Paradoxes of Democracy," in Larry Diamond and Marc F. Plattner, eds., *The Global Resurgence of Democracy* (Baltimore: Johns Hopkins University Press, 1993), 103; see also Larry Diamond, "The Globalization of Democracy," in Robert O. Slater, Barry M. Schutz, and Steven R. Dorr, eds., *Global Transformation and the Third World* (Boulder, CO: Lynne Rienner, 1993), 31–69.

7. Diamond, "Three Paradoxes of Democracy," 105. Note the parallel with a much earlier formulation by one of the gurus of the current democratization literature, Samuel Huntington: "Problems of governance in the United States today stem from an 'excess of democracy.' . . . [T]he effective operation of a democratic political system usually requires some measure of apathy and non-involvement on the part of some individuals and groups." This is quoted from an article by Huntington entitled "The Democratic Distemper," *The Public Interest 41* (Fall 1975), in Benjamin Barber, *Strong Democracy: Participatory Politics for a New Age* (Berkeley and Los Angeles: University of California Press, 1984), 95, n.2.

8. Diamond, "Three Paradoxes of Democracy," 98. This is an extremely one-sided way in which to present the development record in Africa—to go no further afield; Diamond's formulations ignore the catastrophic outcomes of most capitalist development strategies on the continent, as well as the crucial role the state (authoritarian, interventionist) has played in settings (e.g., the Asian NICs) where capitalism has been more successful. Here, as so often in their "scientific" writings, Diamond and his colleagues in the democracy business are marketing almost pure ideology.

9. Diamond, "Three Paradoxes of Democracy," 106.

10. Diamond, "Three Paradoxes of Democracy," 106.

11. Not that this is a novel tendency: note, also Claude Ake's pungent comment that "the history of democracy is a history of resistance to its essence, popular power" in

his essay "The New World Order: A View from Africa," in Hans-Henrik Holm and George Sorenson, eds., *Whose World Order? Uneven Globalization and the End of the Cold War* (Boulder, CO: Westview Press, 1995), 36.

12. Giuseppe di Palma, *To Craft Democracies: An Essay on Democratic Transitions* (Berkeley and Los Angeles: University of California Press, 1990), 22–24, from which pages the quotations from de Palma in the present paragraph are drawn.

13. Perry Anderson, *A Zone of Engagement* (London: Verso, 1992), 355–56; for an earlier discussion highlighting the distinction between "thin" and "strong" democracy see Benjamin Barber, *Strong Democracy: Participatory Politics for a New Age* (Berkeley and Los Angeles: University of California Press, 1984), to whose writing we will return later.

14. Barry Gills, Joel Rocamora, and Richard Wilson, eds., *Low Intensity Democracy* (London: Pluto Press, 1993).

15. Colin Leys, "The World, Society and the Individual," unpublished paper, November 1994. The reference to the Solar Temple is to an incident that occurred on 5 October 1994, when "25 people, members of the Church of the Solar Temple, killed themselves, or were killed by their leaders, in a house belonging to the Church in Switzerland. . . . A community of people had destroyed itself, or had been destroyed by its leaders, in the name of some far-out utopian ideal. . . . Yet I believe that the self-destruction of the Church of the Solar Temple *is* a symbol (for) what is happening on the world's stage."

16. Manfred Bienefeld, "Structural Adjustment and the Prospects for Democracy in Southern Africa," in David B. Moore and Gerald G. Schmitz, *Debating Development Discourse: Institutional and Popular Perspectives* (forthcoming), 52. In Bienefeld's words, the

new enthusiasm for democracy is conditional. . . . Democracy will lead to good governance, as defined by the IFIs, only if electorates "choose" to support their neo-liberal policies. Just as Henry Ford once declared his Model-T to be available "in any colour so long as it is black," bemused electorates now find they can choose "any policy regime, so long as it was the neoliberal one." In fact they can only choose how to deal with the consequences of that regime and those who demand a wider choice are dismissed as naive, foolish or subversive, on the grounds that "reasonable" people understand that this regime is good for them and that there is no alternative in any event.

17. Colin Leys, "The World, Society and the Individual," 7.

18. Diamond, "Three Paradoxes of Democracy," 104–5.

19. Is Diamond also being disingenuous when he extends such qualifications of his arguments to the global level—significantly enough, as a kind of unproblematic aside—with the thought that "the new democracies will also need economic assistance, access to Western markets, and debt relief if they are to show that democracy can work to solve the staggering economic and social problems they face? The international system can play a crucial role in creating the economic space for struggling democracies to undertake badly needed economic transformation with a social safety net and a human face, thereby making them politically sustainable" (in his "The Globalization of Democracy," 61). These kinds of qualifications, if further problematized and shifted from the margins toward the center of his analysis, would, of course, totally transform that analysis.

20. Adam Przeworski, *Democracy and the Market* (Cambridge: Cambridge University Press, 1991), 122.

21. Przeworski, *Democracy and the Market*, 37.

22. Przeworski, *Democracy and the Market*, 34. Bracket for the moment the fact that Przeworski seems here to be working with a concept of democracy that Philip Green (see his *Retrieving Democracy: In Search of Civil Equality* ([London: Methuen, 1989]) would probably label mere "pseudodemocracy."

23. Ralph Miliband, *Socialism for a Sceptical Age* (London: Verso, 1994), 190–91.

24. John Loxley and David Seddon, "Stranglehold on Africa," *Review of African Political Economy (ROAPE)* 62 (1994): 485–93.

25. See David G. Becker and Richard L. Sklar, "Why Postimperialism?" in David G. Becker, Jeff Frieden, Sayre P. Schatz, and Richard L. Sklar, *Postimperialism: International Capitalism and Development in the Late Twentieth Century* (Boulder, CO, and London: Lynne Rienner, 1987).

26. Becker and Sklar, "Preface," to Becker et al., *Postimperialism*, ix. The narrow economic determinism that underlies this approach can sometimes be quite breathtaking. Offered up in the name of "realism" and as evidence of the virtues of "analyzing capitalism holistically, as postimperialism does," Sklar's collaborator David Becker concludes his essay "Postimperialism: A First Quarterly Report" in the same volume by suggesting: "The implication is that socialism in the 'third world' may be achieved after a considerable prior experience of capitalist experience" (219). But what instructions follow from this kind of sub-Second International Marxism for progressives in the many Third World countries (not least in Africa) where capitalism merely fails to "develop" their countries to any significant degree?

27. Jean-François Bayart, "Civil Society in Africa," in Patrick Chabal, ed., *Political Domination in Africa: Reflections on the Limits of Power* (Cambridge: Cambridge University Press, 1986), 125.

28. Colin Leys, "Confronting the African Tragedy," *New Left Review* 204 (March–April 1994): 46.

29. Note, for example, the final sentence of Loxley and Seddon's overview article on the IFI's "stranglehold on Africa," cited earlier: echoing Leys' point that African governments must have a "bigger voice in their own futures," they nonetheless conclude their (largely economically driven) argument with the following challenge to the democratic theorists of Africa: "As to how these governments may be rendered more representative of, and accountable to, the broad mass of their citizens, [that] is another matter" (Loxley and Seddon, "Stranglehold on Africa," 493).

30. See Susan George and Fabrizio Sabelli, *Faith and Credit: The World Bank's Secular Empire* (London: Penguin Books, 1994), especially their chapter 7, "Governance: The Last Refuge?" from which my quotations in this paragraph are drawn.

31. Gerald Schmitz, "Democratization and Demystification: Deconstructing 'Governance' as Development Discourse," in Moore and Schmitz, *Debating Development Discourse*, 32.

32. Joan Nelson, "The Politics of Economic Transformation: Is Third World Experience Relevant in Eastern Europe?" *World Politics* 45, no. 3 (April 1993): 459–60. For a relevant and suggestive African case study, see Marcia Burdette, "Democracy vs. Economic Liberalization: The Zambian Dilemma," *Southern Africa Report* (SAR) (Toronto) 8, no. 1 (July 1992).

33. Nelson, "The Politics of Economic Transformation," 461.

34. Goran Hyden, "Governance and the Study of Politics," in Goran Hyden and Michael Bratton, eds., *Governance and Politics in Africa* (Boulder, CO: Lynne Rienner, 1992), 22.

35. As Schmitz ("Democratization and Demystification," 41) adds in capping his point (he also refers to Hyden, among numerous others): "the 'vision' of governance tries to evade the implications of this because at bottom, even when it speaks of popular participation and 'empowerment of the poor,' it is really not a democratic approach which respects peoples' rights to freely choose their own modes of development and to decide their own public policies. Participation—which has an obvious appeal for purposes of fund-raising and building public support for development—is seen more restrictively as instrumentally valuable to the success of development projects."

36. Chris Allen, Carolyn Baylies, and Morris Szeftel, "Surviving Democracy?" *ROAPE* 54 (1992): 6.

37. Jacques-Mariel Nzouankeu, "The African Attitude to Democracy," *International Social Science Journal* 128 (May 1991): 373–85. Not that one can easily escape the conclusion that an embracing of the legitimacy of multipartyism is a necessary condition for the kind of societal openness necessary to the building of a democratic culture and practice; the point is that it is very far from being a sufficient one. Nonetheless, the fact remains that those who once argued for the possibility of a "democratic one-party state" (the literature on the Tanzanian experience in the 1960s and early 1970s under the leadership of Julius Nyerere provides numerous examples of writers tempted by such a formula, including the present author) have had good reasons to rethink their position.

38. See the various chapters in Shivji, ed., *State and Constitutionalism*.

39. Allen, Baylies, and Szeftel, "Surviving Democracy?" 10.

40. Sidgi Kaballo, "Human Rights and Democratization in Africa," *Political Studies* 43 (1995): 203.

41. This failure is further defined, Kaballo suggests, by the inability of the African bourgeoisie "to generate an ideological and intellectual discourse that would rally the masses under its leadership" ("Human Rights and Democratization in Africa," 203). Compare Shivji's emphasis on the need for "*reconceptualizing* the dominant human rights and constitutionalist ideologies into ideologies of resistance of the oppressed," in Shivji, *State and Constitutionalism*, 257.

42. Peter Anyang' Nyong'o, "Democratization Processes in Africa," *ROAPE* 54 (1992): 97.

43. Kaballo ("Human Rights and Democratization in Africa"), in Shivji, *State and Constitutionalism*, 257.

44. Ake, "The New World Order," 39–40.

45. Kaballo, "Human Rights and Democratization in Africa," 203.

46. Przeworski, *Democracy and the Market*, 85.

47. James Dunkerley, *The Pacification of Central America: Political Change in the Isthmus, 1987–1993* (London: Verso, 1994), 3.

48. Miliband, *Socialism for a Sceptical Age*, 192. See also, in this connection, Benjamin Barber, *Jihad vs. McWorld* (New York and Toronto: Random House, 1995). Barber sees fundamentalism, or "jihad" (a word he seeks to use generically), as a comprehensible, if inevitably unhealthy, reaction—"it identifies the self by contrasting it with an alien 'other,' and makes politics an exercise in exclusion and resentment" (222)—against the raw and radically desocializing individualism that has been so central a feature of the globalization process ("McWorld"). As Barber summarizes his argument, "In a future world where the only available identity is that of blood brother or solitary consumer, and where these two paltry dispositions engage in a battle for the human soul, democracy does not seem well placed to share in the victory, to whomsoever it is deliv-

ered. Neither the politics of the commodity nor the politics of resentment promise real liberty'' (224).

49. Nancy Fraser, "From Redistribution to Recognition? Dilemmas of Justice in a 'Post-Socialist' Age," *New Left Review* 212 (July–August 1995): 68–93. Fraser so argues even while noting that "the struggle for recognition is fast becoming the paradigmatic political conflict of the late twentieth century" (68). As she continues, "Demands for 'recognition of difference' fuel struggles of groups mobilized under the banners of nationality, ethnicity, 'race,' gender, and sexuality. In these 'post-socialist' conflicts, group identity supplants class interest as the chief medium of political mobilization. And cultural recognition displaces socioeconomic redistribution as the remedy for injustice and the goal of political struggle." Her aim, she suggests, "is to connect two political problematics that are currently dissociated from one another" (69)!

50. Przeworski, *Democracy and the Market*, 67.

51. Joe Slovo, "Negotiations: What Room for Compromise?" *The African Communist* 130 (3d quarter 1992): 36–37. As Slovo added, "But what could we expect to achieve in the light of the balance of forces and the historical truism that no ruling class ever gives up all its power voluntarily? There was certainly never any prospect of forcing the regime's unconditional surrender across the table."

52. Gender difference might also be mentioned here, although, unfortunately and despite considerable efforts (and some accomplishments) to the contrary, these were rather less prominent among the "differences" seen to demand reconciliation/resolution during the transition than they should have been.

53. Steven Friedman, "South Africa's Reluctant Transition," *Journal of Democracy* 4, no. 2 (April 1993): 57.

54. See, for example, Andrew Reynolds, ed., *Election '94 South Africa: The Campaign, Results and Future Prospects* (London: James Currey, 1994).

55. Alaister Sparks, *Tomorrow Is Another Country: The Inside Story of South Africa's Road to Change* (New York: Hill and Wang, 1995).

56. Steven Friedman, ed., *The Long Journey: South Africa's Quest for a Negotiated Settlement* (Braamfontein: Ravan Press, 1993); Steven Friedman and Doreen Atkinson, eds., *The Small Miracle: South Africa's Negotiated Settlement* (Braamfontein: Ravan Press, 1994).

57. Jeremy Cronin, "The Boat, the Tap and the Leipzig Way," *The African Communist* 130 (3d quarter 1992): 182–83. As Cronin continues his argument: "Democracy is self-empowerment of the people. Unless the broad masses are actively and continually engaged in struggle, we will achieve only the empty shell of a limited democracy."

58. Timothy D. Sisk, *Democratization in South Africa: The Elusive Social Contract* (Princeton, NJ: Princeton University Press, 1995), 123.

59. See, for example, Joseph Hanlon, "Acceptable—But Was It Fair?" *African Agenda* 1, no. 4 (1995); Morris Szeftel, " 'Negotiated Elections' in South Africa: 1994," *ROAPE* 61 (1994).

60. See, for example, Frederick Johnstone, "Quebeckers, Mohawks and Zulus: Liberal Federalism and Free Trade," and "New World Disorder: Fear, Freud and Federalism," in *Telos* 93 (Fall 1992) and *Telos* 100 (Summer 1994), respectively.

61. Hermann Giliomee, "Democratization in South Africa," *Political Science Quarterly* 110, no. 1 (1995): 83–104. Giliomee, in support of his misgivings, also cites Marina Ottaway, who from quite early on in the transition had raised doubts about the actual depth of the ANC's democratic commitment (see her "Liberation Movements and Tran-

sition to Democracy," *Journal of Modern African Studies* (*JMAS*) 29, no. 1 (March 1991): 61–82. See, in addition, Roger Southall, "The South African Elections of 1994: The Remaking of the Dominant-Party State," *JMAS* 32, no. 4 (1994).

62. Richard Saunders, "Not by Votes Alone," *African Agenda* 1, no. 4 (1995): 6. See also Saunders, "A Hollow Shell: Democracy in Zimbabwe," *Southern Africa Report/ SAR* (Toronto) 10, no. 4 (May 1995).

63. Saunders, "A Hollow Shell," 3.

64. This is not to say that the ANC's historical record suggests it to be innocent of such tendencies within its ranks—although it is also true the ANC would be hard-pressed to match the kind of overweening and self-conscious arrogance of power that has driven Robert Mugabe and his colleagues in Zimbabwe.

65. Giliomee ("Democratization in South Africa"), sensibly enough, sees the absence of broad-based economic development and the continuing existence of deep-seated cultural divisions as, in their own right, qualifying South Africa's democratic prospects. He is less sensitive to the possibility that even a relatively achieved liberal-democratic system may, under African circumstances and in the long run, merely exacerbate such problems.

66. Chris Landsberg, "Directing from the Stalls? The International Community and the South African Negotiation Forum," in Steven Friedman and Doreen Atkinson, eds., *The Small Miracle: South Africa's Negotiated Settlement* (Braamfontein: Ravan Press, 1994), 290–91.

67. Sisk, *Democratization in South Africa*, 3.

68. Thus, Sisk cites in apparent agreement (albeit in a footnote) the notion that, in defining its own negotiation strategies, one of the key things the National Party learned from the transitions in Zimbabwe and Namibia was that "the opposition [i.e., the ANC] will be hamstrung by world pressures in its attempts to redistribute wealth." Sisk, *Democratization in South Africa*, 180.

69. There are, of course, those who have always been deeply skeptical of the suggestion that the ANC, qua liberation movement, was ever actually the bearer of a radical/ socialist project. Such analysts are therefore not surprised when they find evidence of the ANC's leadership failing to press for transformative policies or aggrandizing itself in individual terms. See, for example, Baruch Hirson, "The Election of a Government," and "South Africa: The State of a Nation," in the final issue of *Searchlight South Africa* 12 (June 1995).

70. Note, for example, a recent intervention by South African poet and activist Dennis Brutus, who argues "that the struggle within the ANC between TINA and THEMBA— There Is No Alternative, and There Must Be an Alternative—seems to have been won by those who want to push into the world economy at all cost, even gutting the RDP via the White Paper, accepting IMF conditionality, destroying once protected industries, and encouraging arms exports." Quoted in Patrick Bond, "Under the Microscope: The ANC in Power," *SAR* 10, no. 3 (March 1995): 3.

71. "SA: Concern Grows at Apathy over Voter Registration," *Southscan* 10, no. 15 (14 April 1995): 113–14; see also Judith Matleff, "South African Blacks Ask Why They Should Vote," *Christian Science Monitor*, 17 February 1995.

72. As cited in an article entitled "Widespread Voter Registration Manipulation Alleged," *Southscan* 10, no. 34 (15 September 1995): 263.

73. "Widespread Voter Registration Manipulation Alleged."

74. Thus, another recent report on the upcoming local elections in South Africa ("Eth-

nic Electioneering as IFP Makes Coloured Pact,'' *Southscan* 10, no. 35 (22 September 1995), suggests that "racial politics is starting to become the dominant theme in party electioneering for the upcoming local government poll,'' adding that "the IFP and the Pan-Africanist Congress (PAC) are seeking to whip up support on ethnic lines, estimating that this will be the main way in which they can glean votes and undercut the African National Congress and National Party (NP)'' (270).

75. Sparks, *Tomorrow Is Another Country*, 238–39, where he predicts—however belatedly in terms of the silences in his earlier discussion of the politics of transition, cited earlier—the growing centrality "of a new class stratification gradually beginning to overlay South Africa's old racial strata, never completely eliminating the old divisions but blurring them and adding a different dimension.''

76. African National Congress, *The Reconstruction and Development Programme* (Johannesburg: Umanyano, 1994); see also Patrick Bond, "The RDP—A Site for Socialist Struggle,'' *The African Communist* 137 (2d quarter 1994); SACP, "Defending and Deepening a Clear Left Strategic Perspective on the RDP,'' *The African Communist* 138 (3d quarter 1994).

77. Nelson Mandela, quoted in Karl von Holdt, "COSATU Special Congress: The Uncertain New Era,'' *South African Labour Bulletin (SALB)* 17, no. 5 (September–October 1993): 19.

78. Jeremy Cronin, "Sell-Out, or the Culminating Moment? Trying to Make Sense of the Transition,'' paper presented at the History Workshop Conference on "Democracy: Popular Precedents, Practice, Culture,'' University of the Witwatersrand, Johannesburg, July 1994.

79. Bond, "Under the Microscope,'' 7. Note also a recent news story that suggests that "the ANC will use the new session of parliament . . . to assert its control and seek to restore a sense of direction to its members and supporters.'' The story ("ANC Will Reassert Self in New Session of Parliament,'' *Southscan* 10, no. 30 [18 August 1995], 229) also quotes veteran academic observer David Welsh as saying, "I sense in the African National Congress something akin to desperation. They feel that they must take a grip on the country that they believe is rightfully theirs and begin to pass those laws that will alter it. . . . There is mounting evidence of impatience amongst their own people. . . . They have got to come to grips with the legislation that will affect the lives of the people . . . who voted for them.''

80. Glenn Adler and Eddie Webster, "Challenging Transition Theory: The Labour Movement Radical Reform, and the Transition to Democracy in South Africa,'' *Politics and Society* 23, no. 1 (March 1995): 76–77.

81. See "The Frelimo State: From Revolution to Recolonization,'' in Saul, *Recolonization and Resistance in Southern Africa in the 1990s* (Trenton, NJ: African World Press, 1993), chapter 3.

82. See, on this subject, the judicious account of William Minter, *Apartheid's Contras: An Inquiry into the Roots of War in Angola and Mozambique* (London: Zed Books, 1994).

83. For a related and instructive case study see Carollee Bengelsdorf, *The Problem of Democracy in Cuba: Between Vision and Reality* (New York and Oxford: Oxford University Press, 1994).

84. David Plank, "Aid, Debt, and the End of Sovereignty: Mozambique and Its Donors,'' *JMAS* 31, no. 3 (1993). See also Merle Bowen, "Beyond Reform: Adjustment and Political Power in Contemporary Mozambique,'' *JMAS* 30, no. 2 (1992); Judith

Marshall, *War, Debt and Structural Adjustment in Mozambique* (Ottawa: North-South Institute, 1992). Bowen analyzes the headlong process of class formation now afoot in Mozambique, while Marshall discusses the sapping, under the tutelage of the IFIs, of the various social programs that were once Frelimo's proudest accomplishment. The work of Anne Pitcher of Colgate University on the quasi-colonial role of new joint venture companies in northern Mozambique is also extremely revealing of present trends.

85. For detailed analyses of the actual carrying out of the Mozambican elections see the various papers presented to the seminar on "Eleiçøes, Democracia e Desenvolvimento" held in Maputo, 13–15 June 1995, notably, the contributions from Brazao Mazula (the head of the National Elections Commission during the electoral process), "As Eleiçøes Moçambicanas: A Trajectória da Paz e Democracia" and Luis de Brito, "O Comportamento Eleitoral nas Primeiras Eleiçøes Multipartidárias em Moçambique"; see also the special issue on the Mozambican election of *SAR* 10, no. 2 (December 1994), "Mozambique: The Peace Election." On the implications of the elections for women, see Ruth Jacobson, *Dancing toward a Better Future? Gender and the 1994 Mozambican Elections*, a report prepared for the Norwegian Agency for Development Cooperation, November 1994.

86. On this subject, see, inter alia, Alex Vines, *"No Democracy without Money": The Road to Peace in Mozambique (1982–1992)* (London: Catholic Institute for International Relations, 1994); Cameron Hume, *Ending Mozambique's War: The Role of Mediation and Good Offices* (Washington, DC: U.S. Institute for Peace, 1994); John S. Saul, "Inside from the Outside: The Roots and Resolution of Mozambique's Un/civil War," in Taisier Ali and Robert Mathews, eds., *Civil Wars in Africa* (Kingston and Montreal: McGill-Queen's University Press, 1996).

87. For a documentary history, from a United Nations perspective, of the latter stages of the overall transition process up to and including the elections, see United Nations, *The United Nations and Mozambique, 1992–1995*, United Nations Blue Books Series, vol. 5 (New York: United Nations, 1995).

88. See the cover story—entitled, quite specifically, "Winner Takes All"—to *Mozambique Peace Process Bulletin* 14 (February 1995), a periodical published over the course of the Mozambican electoral process by AWEPA, the European Parliamentarians for Southern Africa. See also Joseph Hanlon, "A Democratic One-Party State," *African Agenda* 1, no. 4 (1995), who argues (controversially) that "Frelimo has used the multiparty electoral system imposed by the West to reinstate the one-party state" (11), adding that "the industrialized world has been trying to sell [Africa] a very narrow concept: namely, that democracy is simply holding multi-party elections" regardless of whether or not such a process actually "involves everyone, without significant exclusions, in discussion, policy formulation and decision making."

89. Its military capacity had tended to melt away, in any case, as soldiers in their thousands (from both sides, as it happens) voted with their feet for civilian life—while availing themselves of United Nations (UN)-sponsored demobilization buyouts.

90. Of course, the legacy of the war has continued to make itself felt negatively across a wide range of related fronts, the markedly high level of criminality, for example, being as much a reflection of the wholesale availability of arms and of war-induced lack of moral scruple (on the part of many of the recently demobilized former combatants, among others) as it is of the desperate economic situation in which the country finds itself. Land mines, widely and cavalierly sown across the country during the war, continue to take a deadly toll.

91. It is also true that Frelimo had often been tempted, in its initial modernizing arrogance, to ride roughshod over such sensibilities, thus providing fertile ground for the particular brand of the "politics of recognition" that Renamo has now exploited for its own purposes.

92. Wilson's intervention, in response to an earlier article in *SAR* 10, no. 4 (May 1995) by a "Special Correspondent" and entitled "After the Count Is Over: Mozambique Now," appears in *SAR* 11, no. 1 (October 1995).

93. Compare, for example, the approach taken several years earlier by the late Otto Roesch in an article entitled "Mozambique Unravels? The Retreat to Tradition," in *SAR* 7, no. 5 (May 1992). See also Bridget O'Laughlin, "Interpretations Matter: Debating the War in Mozambique," *SAR* 7, no. 3 (January 1992).

94. Shivji, *State and Constitutionalism*, 255; note, too, Shivji's additional observation to the effect that "democracy from a liberal perspective, I argue, is part of the ideology of domination—in Africa essentially a moment in the rationalization and justification of compradorial rule"!

95. Issa Shivji, "The Democracy Debate in Africa: Tanzania," *ROAPE* 50 (March 1991): 82.

96. Shivji, *State and Constitutionalism*, 255.

97. Ellen Meiksins Wood, "The Uses and Abuses of 'Civil Society,' " in Ralph Miliband and Leo Panitch, eds., *The Socialist Register 1990: The Retreat of the Intellectuals* (London: Merlin Press, 1990).

98. Another such thinker is Philip Green. As noted earlier, Green—in his important book, *Retrieving Democracy: In Search of Civil Equality*—labels the vision of this latter group of theorists as "pseudodemocracy," defined as "representative government, ultimately accountable to 'the people' but not really under their control, combined with a fundamentally capitalist economy." As he adds, this kind of democracy is "preferable to most of the immediately available alternative ways of life of the contemporary nation-state. But it is not democracy; not really" (3). Colin Leys and I have summarized the relevant point elsewhere (in chapter 10, "The Legacy: An Afterword," of Saul, *Namibia's Liberation Struggle: The Two-Edged Sword* (London: James Currey, 1994)) as follows: "In reality, . . . liberal democracy does not imply that citizens rule themselves, but that rule by elites is made legitimate by periodic elections, and—very importantly—by various ancillary mechanisms, above all the mediation of political parties." Along these lines we discuss the limitations of the "transition to democracy" in Namibia in the wake of that country's recent liberation from South African colonialism.

99. Barber, *Strong Democracy*, xi, 4.

100. Barber writes (*Strong Democracy*, 149): "Democracy in the unitary mode resolves conflict . . . through community consensus as defined by the identification of individuals and their interests with a symbolic community and its interests." But this, in turn, throws up "all the grave risks of monism, conformism and coercive consensualism. No wonder that liberal democrats cringe at the prospect of 'benevolent' direct democratic alternatives." He adds that "the central question for the future of democracy thus becomes: is there an alternative to liberal democracy that does not resort to the subterfuges of unitary democracy?" His answer, as we see, is "strong democracy."

101. Barber, *Jihad vs. McWorld*, 276.

102. Barber, *Jihad vs. McWorld*, 288. For a related analysis that specifies, quite concretely, some of the global political strategies that might help "reverse the race to the

bottom," see Jeremy Brecher and Tim Costello, *Global Village or Global Pillage: Economic Reconstruction from the Bottom Up* (Boston: South End Press, 1994).

103. The comparison between Barber and his South African counterparts, on one hand, and the likes of Diamond, Huntington, and Timothy Sisk (whose book on the South African transition, cited earlier, never rises above a rather crude rational choice model in explaining political interactions), on the other, is reminiscent of a comparison C. B. Macpherson (in his important essay "Politics: Post-Liberal Democracy," reprinted in Robin Blackburn, ed., *Ideology in Social Science* [London: Fontana, 1972]) once made between Jeremy Bentham and John Stuart Mill. "Mill must be counted more of a democrat," he wrote. "For he took people not as they were but as he thought them capable of becoming. He revolted against Bentham's material maximizing criterion of the social good . . . and put in its place the maximum development and use of human capacities. . . . This was, we may say, an act of democratic faith" (21). Unfortunately, there is far too little of such faith in most currently fashionable democratic theory.

104. Barber, *Strong Democracy*, 252.

105. See Saul, *Recolonization and Resistance*, chapters 4 ("South Africa: Between 'Barbarism' and 'Structural Reform' ") and 5 ("Structural Reform: A Model for the Revolutionary Transformation of South Africa"). Note, too, that Adler and Webster, "Challenging Transition Theory," link their emphasis on the important ongoing role of "civil society" and "social movements" in South Africa's transition to a project for progressive socioeconomic transformation (albeit a somewhat more modest version of that transformation, which they label "radical reform").

106. As presented in contributions by Godongwana and Jordan (at pages 86 and 92, respectively) to the debate entitled "Social Democracy or Democratic Socialism," featured in *SALB* 17, no. 6 (November–December 1993).

107. Leys, "Confronting the African Tragedy," 46.

108. Miliband, *Socialism for a Sceptical Age*, 194–95.

Chapter 4

Nation Building and State Disintegration

MARINA OTTAWAY

After three decades of independence, the future of the African postcolonial states appears more uncertain than at any time before. The probability that all African states will survive intact within the borders established by the colonial powers now appears remote. Ethiopia has already divided with the secession of Eritrea and could split again. The Sudan, Nigeria, and Zaire are threatened. Rwanda and Burundi have been shaken by a new round of ethnic slaughter. Many more countries are experiencing heightened ethnic tensions and even episodes of ethnic cleansing.

The major threat to the integrity of existing states does not come from the outside, from neighboring countries aspiring to more territory and seeking to modify existing borders. Rather, it is coming from the inside, from the growing force of ethnic conflict and ethnic nationalism.

This rise of ethnic nationalism, with its destructive potential, has been triggered, in many cases, by a promising development, namely, the opening up of authoritarian political systems and the beginning of a democratic transition. Under pressure from their citizens and from aid donors, a majority of African governments are at least formally moving toward greater democracy. The two developments are linked: ethnic nationalism is increasing, at least in part, because of the greater openness of the political systems.

Thus, two processes are under way in Africa simultaneously: a process of state building, aiming at the development of more democratic political systems, characterized by greater transparency and accountability; and a process of nation building, which threatens the integrity of existing multiethnic states as ethnic nationalist movements increase in militancy and make a bid for their own state. State building and nation building, which in the early postcolonial period were seen as synonymous, are turning into conflicting forces. The nations that are asserting their independence forcefully are nct the new, multiethnic nations embracing the entire population of the country envisioned by Africa's founding fathers but ethnic nations that predate the state (at least claim to predate it) and challenge its legitimacy. The outcome of this tension between the attempts to build more democratic states and the attempts by the groups that constitute their populations to assert their rights to self-determination may well be the disintegration of some states and a new wave of nationalist authoritarian regimes.

THE MYTH OF NATION BUILDING

All African leaders at independence were aware of the fragility of their countries. Most of the new states had no common history other than the one provided by the colonial powers. They had heterogeneous populations, which had not been together in one state long enough to begin to amalgamate and assimilate. They had weak administrative systems with which to hold the countries together and few resources to help generate the material improvements that might increase the allegiance of the citizens. As Jackson and Rosberg have aptly concluded, they were states *de jure* but not *de facto*.[1]

A response to this weakness was the idea of "nation building."[2] The priority task for newly independent African states was the creation of a common identity and the fostering of a strong allegiance to the new country among the disparate groups that made up the population. Citizens heterogeneous in culture, language, religion, social structures, and political traditions were expected to acquire a new national identity overriding all the others. Ideologies, the charisma of leaders, popular mobilization, and the single party were the tools most often employed in this endeavor. In the enthusiasm of the newly gained independence, the goal of "nation building" appeared within easy reach. "In three or four years," Sekou Toure of Guinea declared in 1959, "no one will remember the tribal, ethnic or religious rivalries which, in the recent past, caused so much damage to the country and its population."[3]

Only a small minority of African politicians dared raise the question whether the despised "tribes" African governments wanted to obliterate from memory were in reality "nations" with a legitimate identity and deserving recognition. In Uganda, Kabaka Mutesa II ruefully observed:

We are invariably accused by our detractors of being tribalist in a sense of the word that it is a wickedly retrogressive thing to be. But I have never been able to pin down precisely the difference between a tribe and a nation and see why one is thought so despicable and the other is so admired. Whichever we are, the Baganda have a common language, tradition, history and cast of mind.[4]

But such voices were rare. Optimistically taking for granted the success of the "nation-building" project, Africans and outsiders alike started referring to African countries as nation-states, something they definitely were not at independence, and, indeed, never became. In no African country did the nations within the state give way to a nation embracing the whole state.

Mobilization efforts could not be sustained. After the initial enthusiasm for independence, ordinary citizens quickly tired of attending party meetings and mass rallies, of volunteering their time on weekends to build schools or plant trees, of donating funds to projects that never appeared to accomplish anything. The voluntary efforts continued over the long run were not the ones that aimed at building the nation but the more parochial ones, such as the *harambee* projects in Kenya, that mobilized people for local, rather than "nation-building," projects.[5]

The structures originally set up to promote "nation building" nevertheless persisted, turning from instruments of mobilization into instruments of domination. "Nation building" turned into state building—the building of authoritarian states, at that. The new countries were kept together not by a new common identity among their citizens and their voluntarily chosen allegiance to a new emerging "nation" but by the force of authoritarian regimes.

The international institutions developed by the new African states, above all, the Organization of African Unity (OAU), reflected the same concern with the preservation of the states and the disregard for their populations. The most famous principle of the OAU, that of the inviolability of colonial borders, showed this clearly. On one hand, the principle aimed at safeguarding peace among states by preventing the reciprocal territorial revendications that could lead to war. On the other hand, the principle denied African populations the possibility of self-determination: people born within the boundaries of a particular state were to remain part of it, whether or not they liked it. Thus, according to the OAU, the Somali state had no right to claim the Ogaden region of Ethiopia as its own, but neither did the Ogadenis have the right to choose whether they wanted to be Somali or Ethiopian citizens.

The OAU concern with the rights and privileges of states, to the detriment of those of people, was also confirmed by the fact that the organization, contrary to the United Nations, did not include among its principles a charter of human rights. Such a document, the Banjul Charter, was adopted only in 1981, coming into force in 1986. In the history of independent Africa, the state has been much better protected than its citizens.

"Nation building," which failed in most African countries, was a difficult, but not unprecedented, task. European countries during the nineteenth century had to tackle the same problem. Even purported nation-states where the political borders of the country supposedly coincide with the "natural" borders of a preexisting, homogeneous nation in reality did not acquire their cultural homogeneity until well into the nineteenth century, after the state had consolidated its control over territory. The French nation, Eugen Weber has argued, was really consolidated only in the late nineteenth century, in large part, as the consequence of the development of a homogeneous system of compulsory education.[6]

The African states failed at nation building, in large part, because they were weak. They lacked the resources to foster a common identity among their people through universal, homogeneous education and a well-developed administrative system that made the state a real, but not an oppressive, presence. They also lacked the resources to promote rapid economic development, thus giving their citizens a vested interest in feeling part of the new country.[7]

But authoritarian state building was not a success either. By and large, African governments failed to set up a strong system of control over the country, let alone good government, and to forge political institutions with authority and staying power that went beyond those of individual leaders. The African state, many writers have concluded, was authoritarian but soft or, in Thomas Callaghy's felicitous expression, a "lame Leviathan."[8]

STATE REFORM: THE DEMOCRACY MOVEMENT

Despite their weaknesses, African countries managed to muddle through the first two decades of independence. The 1980s, however, brought economic collapse and, with it, the need for political reform. Economic conditions deteriorated sharply, due to a combination of unfavorable external circumstances and unsuccessful domestic policies. Even countries such as Kenya and the Ivory Coast, previously considered success stories, faced a critical downturn of their economies. Bankrupt, most African governments lost much of their ability to dispense patronage or curb urban discontent by providing cheap staple food, overemployment in the civil service and parastatals, or free schooling and medical care. The economic reforms mandated by the IMF and the World Bank as the price of structural adjustment loans increased discontent while further limiting the governments' ability to buy off opponents. The fall of the socialist regimes in Europe and the Soviet Union deprived several governments of an important external source of support. More broadly, the international climate turned against a central role for the state and toward democratic reform and free enterprise. The authoritarian, "developmental" state taken for granted in the 1960s and 1970s became definitely unfashionable, even with erstwhile supporters.[9]

The combined result of all these factors was that many African governments, unable to crush or co-opt the opposition, were forced to open up their political systems to some degree—prematurely, such political openings have often been represented as transitions to democracy. The bare facts are simple. After 1990, the majority of African countries amended their constitutions to make possible multiparty elections. The significance of the step should not be overestimated— constitutions have most often not been respected in African countries. Nevertheless, the abrogation of the clauses prohibiting the formation of multiple political parties made it more difficult for incumbent regimes to continue prohibiting all overt opposition activity.

The move toward multipartyism was not smooth. It was initially resisted by the incumbent leaders and their parties and accepted only when the internal or external pressure to change could no longer be resisted. It took an unprecedented seizure of power by a national conference taking the bankrupt government by surprise to effectuate the change in Benin. It took a lot of international pressure and evidence of the great strength of a united opposition movement for Kaunda to abandon the single-party system in Zambia. Eventually, a mixture of internal pressure and fear that foreign aid would be suspended coaxed most governments into undertaking the formal steps of a transition to democracy: constitutional reform to allow a multiparty system, followed by elections, usually in the presence of foreign observers. In some cases, the strength of the domestic opposition forced the change—this was particularly true in the earliest cases, such as Zambia and Benin. In others, the pressure of the international community, including the suspension of aid or the threat to suspend it, played a major part in the government's eventual acceptance of the change to multipartyism.

On paper, the scope of the change was impressive. Between 1990 and 1994, some 30 African countries held multiparty elections. In many countries, however, the election process was "widely criticized," and in others, such as Nigeria and Angola, the results were promptly overturned.[10] Nevertheless, according to an evaluation by the Carter Center, by late 1994 only three African countries—the Sudan, Libya, and Nigeria—could be considered outright authoritarian. In four other cases—Algeria, Angola, Somalia, and Liberia—sovereignty was "contested." But a dozen countries were judged to be democratic, while the rest were considered to be in transition to democracy, although with varying degrees of commitment to completing the process. Democracy appeared to be a growing force in Africa.[11]

Although the form of democracy triumphed through the holding of multiparty elections, the content remained extremely fragile. The holding of multiparty elections was not always a sign of democratization. Part of the problem was that in many countries elections were held at the very beginning of the process of transformation, rather than at a more advanced stage, as was the case elsewhere.[12] Some elections were held despite the fact that the conditions for meaningful political competition did not exist, with barely formed, underfunded opposition political parties on one side and ruling parties drawing on state resources on the other. Everywhere, governments controlled the mass media, and rarely were effective mechanisms put into place to ensure that all competitors would have equal chance to communicate their message. Indeed, in many countries, elections were held even as the basic rights of opposition parties' leaders and members were substantially violated. Far from being plain, the field on which the election game has been played in Africa was severely tilted and quite bumpy.

Even when elections were reasonably free and fair, the future of democracy remained uncertain. In many countries, the victory of one party, either the incumbent or the opposition, was too complete, leaving the country with a weak and disorganized opposition. Organizations of civil society—the voluntary associations that make the citizens part of the political process even between elections through their lobbying efforts and watchdog activities—were weak everywhere. It was thus unclear in many cases whether elections were the beginning of a democratic transition or simply a device to promote the circulation of elites.

The fragility of the new, more democratic state institutions in most African countries is not surprising and by itself would not be a reason for alarm. Given the speed of the change, it would be unrealistic to expect democracy to be consolidated anywhere after only a few years. It is possible to adopt the forms of democracy relatively fast, but the content is a different issue, because it requires both the growth of countervailing centers of power—the network of political and civic voluntary associations often referred to as civil society—and the emergence of a new political culture that accepts both the inevitability of conflict over political goals and the possibility of regulating them without authoritarianism or violence.

If the fragility of the new democratic systems were the only problem, one could well conclude that the glass of democracy in Africa is half full and likely to be filled some more, despite the occasional spill. Unfortunately, the situation is more problematic. Democratization has also triggered processes that risk destroying the gains made so far. Foremost among them are the increase in ethnic conflict in virtually all countries and the rise of ethnic nationalism—that is, of movements advocating independence or autonomy for a particular group—in some. Left unchecked, these developments could bring the process of democratic change to a quick halt, increasing instead the level of civil strife, possibly causing other states to collapse, and ushering in a new period of authoritarianism.

DEMOCRACY AND ETHNICITY

Thirty years ago many African leaders predicted that Western-style, multiparty democracy would divide their countries along ethnic lines, encouraging "tribalism" and undermining the building of the "nation." The fear of ethnic division was one of the major justifications provided for the adoption of more authoritarian styles of government. As the now-discredited single-party systems give way to more competitive ones, the prediction that open political systems would increase ethnic conflict appears to be vindicated. In virtually all countries, rival political parties appeal to different ethnic constituencies. In many, ethnic violence has escalated. In a few, ethnic nationalism has arisen.

Ethnic politics did not suddenly make its appearance with multiparty elections. The single party never put an end to the politicization of ethnic identities—this is amply documented. Leaders played on ethnic divisions and relied on ethnic support when it was in their interest or tried to co-opt or forge alliances with powerful representatives of rival ethnic groups in order to maintain the peace. The variety of devices to settle the ever-present conflict of "state versus ethnic claims" was vast, but in no country did a new national identity override the importance of politicized ethnicity.[13] Most countries, nevertheless, managed to establish a balance and learned to live with their ethnic pluralism and rivalries.

Political openings upset this balance. By calling into question who would govern the country, they also challenged the balance of power among ethnic groups as well as their relations to the central government. Uncertainty increased competition and conflict.

Any major regime change would have created increased ethnic conflict. The fact that the change was in the direction of democracy paradoxically made the situation worse. Democratic systems, as the historical experience of European countries suggests, create the need for a redefinition of the political community. In an authoritarian system, the polity is defined from the top down, and it is passive. It is composed of "subjects" of the monarch or, in the African case, of the particular group of "subjects" of a colonial power that found themselves living within borders established by London or Paris for their own administrative convenience. In a democratic system, however, the political community is composed not of passive subjects but of active citizens who need to define their own boundaries. "We, the people" necessitates a definition of the "we."

This need to define the political community from below made the idea of the nation and the nation-state central to the political process of Europe during the nineteenth century and drastically changed its map. The "nations" that became the basis of the states were, in the words of Benedict Anderson, "imagined communities," but the imagination was powerful enough to make the nations real, to provide them with a history and traditions that were often of very recent invention.[14] Democratic ideals thus contributed to define the concept of the nation-state.

In Africa, too, the demise or weakening of authoritarian regimes is encouraging a redefinition of the political community from a passive conglomerate of subjects to an active citizenship. But the multiethnic nations that the authoritarian regimes had tried to forge did not command the allegiance of the population and provided a weak common identity on which to build the democratic political community.

A question often raised about these ethnic identities and the ensuing conflict is whether they are genuine and primordial, rooted in age-old identities and rivalries, or whether they are instrumental and artificial, the result of manipulation by ambitious politicians seeking to increase their power. The question is as moot in Africa as it was in Europe. It is true that most ethnic identities in Africa are of recent, postcolonial origin. A vast literature has documented well the extent to which African tribalism as we know it has been created in this century, sometimes surprisingly recently.[15] But even if detached analysis suggests that contemporary ethnic conflict is rooted in contemporary problems, this is not necessarily the way the situation appears to most participants. Even ethnic conflict deliberately promoted in the pursuit of contemporary political goals can acquire the highly emotional connotations of primordial conflict. The ethnic slaughter in Rwanda was not a spontaneous outburst, but it was promoted for instrumental purposes. The extent of the massacres that ensued cannot be explained as simply the result of an instrumental, cold-blooded policy.

Democratization also probably contributed to the strengthening of ethnic identities by increasing the importance of rural constituencies in the political process. In the past, African politics was largely a game played by urban elites, for whom the country as a whole had a reality and a meaning. These educated urban elites were, to a large extent, national in their outlook. They had been pulled away from their local communities in order to attend schools and universities. They knew, and shared experiences with, their contemporaries drawn from other regions. For this elite, the country was a single entity, and while ethnic ties were important and convenient for getting jobs and maintaining support, the political arena was the country. This political elite was probably out of tune with the mass of the rural population, which had not been subjected to this process of nationalization. But the rural population carried little political weight, as shown by the urban bias of the policies enacted by most African governments. The urban masses received more consideration, because discontent could lead to unrest threatening to the government. But even the urban masses were, at best, sporadic participants in the political process.

The political openings of the 1990s, no matter how imperfect, enhanced the political role of the mass of the population and of the rural population in particular. Voting made numbers important, and the majority of Africans remain rural. Identities of rural groups are more likely to be local and regional, thus often ethnic, than national. Democracy thus enhanced the importance of these identities.

A final factor that explains the increased importance of ethnicity in African politics is the changed political climate in the world. Ethnic nationalism, which appeared a spent force after World War II, has reappeared with tragic consequences all over the former socialist world. It has resulted in the splitting apart of three countries—the Soviet Union, Yugoslavia, and Czechoslovakia—and it continues to rack the successor states. As a result, the hopes for a consolidation of democracy have dimmed in many countries, victims of conflicts that make the imperatives of state survival or national self-determination much more important than the respect for human rights and the observance of democratic rules.[16]

In Central Europe, the Balkans, and Central Asia, nationalism has emerged as a dominant ideology and political force. In the 1990s, nationalism means again ethnic nationalism, the struggle for self-determination of a group defined in ethnic, linguistic, and cultural terms. It is the brand of nationalism that destroyed the Hapsburg and Ottoman empires, rather than the multiethnic nationalism that destroyed the British and French colonial ones. Between the end of World War II and the beginning of the current wave of ethnic nationalism, the creation of states based on ethnic or religious identification has been a rare occurrence. Pakistan and, later, Bangladesh became the major exceptions in a

world where borders were increasingly dissociated from ethnic or religious identity and expected to remain that way. In Africa, the short-lived independence of
Biafra remains to this day the sole and unsuccessful example—Eritrean nationalism belonged to the anticolonial, not the ethnic, variety.[17]

This new, worldwide wave of ethnic nationalism inevitably affects African
countries. Not only does the domestic process of transformation increase the
importance of ethnicity, as we argued earlier, but the international context con-
tributes to legitimating ethnic politics. The norm of the post–World War II
period was the sanctity of the state and its duty to build the nation within. The
norm of the 1990s is becoming, as it was in an earlier period, the sanctity of
the nation and its right to build its own state.

While both the internal and international situation predisposed African countries to an increase in the level of ethnic conflict, the problem was exacerbated
by African politicians and often well-intentioned international advisers who did
not consider that democracy in multiethnic countries presents special challenges.
With very few exceptions, notably in Nigeria and Ethiopia, the constitutions and
the electoral systems were not tailored to handle the complex problems presented
by multiethnic and multireligious societies. Instead, African countries formally
ignored the complications created by the diversity of their societies, gave no
thought to the management of the inevitable problems such diversity poses, and
opted instead for an ethnic-blind approach. Officially, African leaders continued,
as they had done since independence, to deny any legitimacy to expressions of
ethnic identity and demands based on it, condemning them as primitive ''tribalism.''

Ignoring the importance of ethnicity was problematic in itself. The situation
was made much worse by the fact that most politicians exploited ethnic allegiances and, in some cases, deliberately stirred ethnic conflict in order to gain
support. In other words, democratic openings changed neither the official attitude toward ethnicity nor the practice of exploiting it.

In the past, this approach to ethnicity served most African countries quite
well. However, there were some major exceptions. In 40 years of independence,
the Sudan never succeeded in reconciling the Arab north and the African south,
except for a 10-year period following the signing of the Addis Ababa Accord
of 1972. With time, the divisions between the two parts of the country sharp-
ened, driven by the growing importance of politicized Islam in the north. As a
result, the history of independent Sudan has been one of civil war based on
ethnicity and religion.

A second major exception was Nigeria. With its huge population and hundreds of ethnic groups, Nigeria confronted a seemingly insoluble problem. Balance among the larger population groups was difficult to maintain because of
the complex equation that involved population size, representation in the military, levels of education, and degree of economic development. Population size
gave the advantage to the Hausa-Fulani from the north; presence in the high
echelons of the military also favored the northern groups; education and rep-

resentation in the civil service were on the side of the Ibos of the eastern region; and economic development gave the advantage to the Yorubas of the western part of the country. The problem was complicated by the myriad of smaller ethnic groups, which could not aspire to a dominant role in governing Nigeria but nevertheless demanded a piece of the revenue pie and a state of their own in the federal system.

The early outcome of the conflict was the secession of the eastern region— Biafra—in 1967 and the bloody war that racked the country for two years before the insurgents were defeated. But the overall problem of ethnic relations was never solved. Decades of revising the federal system, creating an ever-greater number of states, did not help. In 1994 Nigeria remained an unstable country, ruled by a military government, racked by resurgent ethnic conflict, and further than ever from attaining any kind of stability, let alone democracy, as Ihonvbere's chapter shows.

Another country where the government failed to contain ethnic conflict was Ethiopia. Beginning with the overthrow of Emperor Haile Selassie, a master at managing ethnic and regional tensions by co-opting potential leaders and working out informal deals, ethnic liberation movements quickly sprung up around the country. By the end of the decade, virtually all opposition groups had an openly ethnic base, except for the Eritrean nationalist organizations, which invoked the sanctity of colonial borders to legitimate their struggle for independence. To an extent, this resurgence of centrifugal forces was a replica of the phenomenon that manifested itself whenever the emperor died or became weak. But there was a new twist. Resistance to central control was led not by regional potentates trying to reassert their autonomy but by ethnic leaders proclaiming the right of their nation to self-determination. The revolt of feudal lords tired of paying fealty to the emperor had turned into modern nationalism.

The openness of ethnic conflict forced all three countries to start exploring institutional solutions. Nigeria, a federal country since independence, sought ways of redesigning the states so as to both provide more space for ethnic groups seeking a degree of self-government and decrease the possibility that any one group would control the country. All attempts failed, due in part to the concentration of oil revenue in the hands of the federal government. This concentration of revenue made a mockery of federalism and decentralization.

Under the terms of the Addis Ababa Accord the Sudan experimented between 1972 and 1982 with a form of asymmetric federalism—the south had its own government and a degree of autonomy, but the north controlled the central government. The system worked for almost ten years, but it was eventually destroyed by pressure from the Islamist element opposed to southern autonomy, the discovery of oil in the southern part of the country that encouraged the resumption of fighting, and the southerners' growing fear of political Islam. Civil war resumed in 1983 and continues unabated.

Ethiopia went through two distinct phases in its managing of ethnic nationalism. Under the Mengistu regime, most efforts were directed at defeating the nationalist movements militarily. A plan to redesign the regions along ethnic lines and give them more autonomy, adopted in 1987, came too late and offered too little to appease the nationalist movements.

After the overthrow of Mengistu in 1991, the new government, dominated by the Tigrean People's Liberation Front and its army, undertook to reorganize the country into a federation of ethnic regions, recognizing the right of any of them to secede. Decentralized in theory, the new system was glued together by the Tigrai People's Liberation Front (TPLF), the broader alliance of ethnic movements it controlled (the Ethiopian People's Revolutionary Democratic Party), and the TPLF army, which served as the national army after the defeat of Mengistu. Clearly inspired by the former Soviet approach to the problem of the nationalities, the new system risked leading to the disintegration of Ethiopia if the TPLF lost control. This is what happened in the Soviet Union, Yugoslavia, and Czechoslovakia with the weakening of the Communist Party.

The three countries that had recognized openly that ethnic divisions required special institutional arrangements lagged behind the rest of the continent in terms of democratization. Countries experiencing democratic openings continued to ignore the challenge of ethnicity. But all elections in Africa were deeply influenced by ethnic conflicts, and many were the occasion for the outbreak of open conflict. Burundi provided the most dramatic case of elections triggering renewed ethnic conflict. But there are few examples of countries where tensions were not heightened by a political opening.

THE NATION VERSUS THE STATE

The long-term consequences of the increase in ethnic conflict that has accompanied political openings remain difficult to predict, and, in any case, they will certainly not be the same for all countries. At present, it is possible to envisage three broad scenarios, presenting different degrees of challenge to the existing states, different implications for democracy, and different potential for creating acute conflict in African countries.

The first scenario comprises benign outcomes, which allow the process of democratization to proceed within the boundaries of the existing states. These are cases where ethnic competition continues, but the ethnic parties realize that none of them can win elections and, even less, govern the country on their own. The result, thus, is the forming of interethnic coalitions, before or after the elections, or the formation of multiethnic parties. South Africa appears to be moving in this direction, although a reversal is still possible. In the transitional elections of 1994, three major parties competed: the largely white National Party (which also drew some Indian and colored support), the overwhelmingly Zulu Inkatha Freedom Party, and the multiethnic African National Congress. This panoply of parties gave voters the choice of voting an ethnic ticket or a multiethnic one. The agreement to form a government of national reconciliation further reduced the potential for immediate conflict. The result was a relatively peaceful transition, despite the ethnic violence that marred the preceding months.

The second scenario involves a continued increase in the level of ethnic conflict, with a resulting pattern of ethnic cleansing, retaliatory measures taken by the victims, and eventually the collapse of the state as power gets endlessly fractioned. An extreme example of this is provided by Somalia, although the divisions there are based on clan rather than more broadly ethnic identities (see chapter 11). What characterizes this scenario is the unbridled use of subnational identities for political gain. Since any group that gains power on the basis of its capacity to mobilize ethnic allegiances is bound to be seen as an enemy by members of other groups, stability is very difficult to reestablish. Democratization is the first victim of such chaos.

The third scenario envisages the breakup of existing states. Increased ethnic conflict fuels ethnic nationalism—that is, the demand of some groups for their own state—with boundaries supposedly coterminous with those of the "nation." At present, Ethiopia is the country where this outcome is most likely, given the nationalism that characterizes both the ruling TPLF and many opposition groups.

Nationalism has coexisted with democracy in some periods.[18] Unfortunately, the nationalism of the 1990s, in Africa and elsewhere, is characterized by a narrow, intolerant, and thus antidemocratic ethnic approach. Narrow ethnic nationalism is a threat not only to democracy but also to long-term stability. The problem here is the impossibility of carving out pure ethnic states—nowhere in the world does population distribution allow a neat separation of ethnic groups without massive population transfers or extermination. The logic of narrow ethnic nationalism is continued strife among the dominant population and ethnic minorities, in the original states or in their successors, as the former Soviet Union shows.

RECONCILING STATE AND NATION—THE TASK AHEAD

During the 1960s, the dominant assumption in Africa was that the state was a given, and the nation could be formed. Increasingly, the opposite assumption is gaining acceptance: what is given is the nation, and what can be formed is the state. Neither assumption is realistic. Ethnic identities cannot be made to disappear easily, but, at the same time, it is impossible to form homogeneous ethnic states except by forcing major population migrations. This leads to the conclusion that African states can achieve stability and continue to democratize only if they learn to live with their multiethnicity.

Achieving democracy in a multiethnic state is a difficult task because it is based on contradictory requirements. Democracy is a political system that puts the individual at the center. All individuals are assumed to be equal: thus, all individuals are assumed to have equal rights. Ideally, the democratic state can draw no distinctions among its citizens.

Nationalists, however, demand recognition of, and respect for, difference. They demand recognition of the rights of an entire group to self-determination—through independence or at least autonomy—and this group is, by definition, different from all others. Balancing democracy and nationalism thus requires balancing individual and group rights, defending minorities against discrimination without, at the same time, imposing on them an assimilation that they do not necessarily want.

Democracy in multiethnic societies is made possible by recognition of equal rights for all in the realm of basic civil and political rights but also of separate rights for members of each group in the realm of culture and education. More importantly, democracy in multiethnic societies also usually requires some form of special representation for members of minority groups, to make sure that they will not be outvoted in all situations and thus not deprived of their rights by members of the majority.

Such balance between seemingly contradictory requirements has proven difficult to maintain in any country. But some have succeeded, as we pointed out earlier, although tensions always remain. Democratic systems in multiethnic societies are conflict management systems, not conflict resolution ones. The balance is not achieved once and for all, as the United States is discovering at present, when the demand for equality and integration that characterized the civil rights movement of the 1960s is being replaced increasingly by the refusal of minorities to be assimilated and their demand for special treatment. Ideas such as Afrocentric education for the inner cities, Spanish-language education in some areas, or the creation of gerrymandered voting districts for minorities all stem from a common assumption that equality with the majority does not satisfy the rights and needs of minorities.

African countries, as seen earlier, have not even begun the process of thinking how to tailor democratic systems to the ethnic diversity of their population. Despite their multiethnic character, Africans cling to the fiction that the nation-state can be achieved in Africa, if not by creating the nation, then at least by redesigning the state. But it is quite clear that in the foreseeable future African states, old or even new, will remain multiethnic. Only if this reality is accepted can African countries stop the present slide into increasing ethnic conflict and resume the process of creating democratic states, capable of living with their diversity and stable enough to resume the process of economic development. The task ahead for African democrats is to recognize the reality of ethnic diversity and devise conflict management institutions.

NOTES

1. Robert H. Jackson and Carl G. Rosberg, ''Why Africa's Weak States Persist: The Empirical and Juridical in Statehood,'' *World Politics* 35 (October 1982): 1–24. See also Robert Jackson's more extensive recent discussion of the issue in *Quasi-States: Sover-*

eignty, International Relations and the Third World (Cambridge: Cambridge University Press, 1990).

2. For a discussion of the confusion surrounding the concept of nation building, see Walker Connor, *Ethnonationalism: The Quest for Understanding* (Princeton, NJ: Princeton University Press, 1994), especially "Nation-Building or Nation-Destroying?" and "A Nation Is a Nation, Is a State, Is an Ethnic Group, Is a . . .".

3. Cited in Crawford Young, ed., *The Rising Tide of Cultural Pluralism* (Madison: University of Wisconsin Press, 1993), 13.

4. Cited in Crawford Young, *The Politics of Cultural Pluralism* (Madison: University of Wisconsin Press, 1976), 226.

5. See Joel Barkan, "The Rise and Fall of a Governance Realm in Kenya," in Goran Hyden and Michael Bratton, eds., *Governance and Politics in Africa* (Boulder, CO: Lynne Rienner, 1992), 167–92.

6. Eugen Weber, *Peasants into Frenchmen: The Modernization of Rural France* (Stanford, CA: Stanford University Press, 1976).

7. The importance of these factors in forging a common identity in an ethnically different population is shown in Seymour Martin Lipset, *The First New Nation: The United States in Comparative Perspective* (New York: Basic Books, 1963).

8. Thomas Callaghy, "The State as Lame Leviathan: The Patrimonial Administrative State in Africa," in Zaki Ergas, ed., *The African State in Transition* (New York: St. Martin's Press, 1987), 87–116.

9. An example is provided by Richard Sklar, "Democracy in Africa," in Patrick Chabal, ed., *Political Domination in Africa* (Cambridge: Cambridge University Press, 1986).

10. *Africa Confidential* 36, no. 1 (6 January 1994): 2.

11. "Africa 1994: Ecstasy and Agony," *Africa Demos* 3, no. 3 (September 1994).

12. See Guillermo O'Donnell and Philippe Schmitter, *Transitions from Authoritarian Rule, Tentative Conclusions about Uncertain Democracies* (Baltimore: Johns Hopkins University Press, 1986). In this concluding volume to the seminal study of democratization they directed, the authors show how the founding of elections in most countries has come after a lengthy and complex period of transformation. By contrast, in most African countries, external pressure has led to the holding of elections very early in the process of transformation.

13. Donald Rothchild and Victor A. Olorunsola, *State vs. Ethnic Claims* (Boulder, CO: Westview Press, 1983).

14. Benedict Anderson, *Imagined Communities: Reflections on the Origins and Spread of Nationalism* (London: Verso Editions, 1983).

15. See, for example, Leroy Vail, ed., *The Creation of Tribalism in Southern Africa* (Berkeley: University of California Press, 1989).

16. See Marina Ottaway, *Democratization and Ethnic Nationalism: African and Eastern European Experiences* (Washington, DC: Overseas Development Council, 1994).

17. Eritrean nationalists claimed that they had a right to independence from Ethiopia because Eritrea had been an Italian colony, colonies had a right to self-determination, and the OAU principles imposed that colonial borders be recognized. Eritrean nationalists never claimed that their country was an ethnically homogeneous nation. Indeed, one of the many challenges that Eritrea faced after independence in 1992 was that posed by its

ethnic and religious heterogeneity. See ''The Cultural Construction of Eritrean Nationalist Movements,'' in Young, *The Rising Tide of Cultural Pluralism*, 179–99.

18. For a discussion of the different forms of nationalism in various periods, see Eric Hobsbawm, *Nations and Nationalism since 1780* (Cambridge: Cambridge University Press, 1990).

Part II

Democratization and State Building: Country Experiences

Chapter 5

Militarization and Democratization: Nigeria's Stalled March to Democracy

JULIUS O. IHONVBERE

Nigeria is certainly one African nation that has had very serious problems with building and sustaining democracy. As well, it has never succeeded, in spite of the introduction of new institutions, symbols, constitutions, and so on, in laying an effective foundation for nation building. A national identity has never been constructed in Nigeria, as the vast majority remain attached to their religious, regional, and ethnic bases. To be sure, this is largely a precipitate of the failure of the peripheral state to create the necessary environment for mediating the power and influence of primordial considerations in national politics. Moreover, the crisis of the nation-building project is a reflection of the ability of primordial associations to more effectively respond to the existential needs of the people. This does not in any way mean that issues of class and gender no longer impact on the nature and construction of political and social alignment and realignments. Yet, each day that passes, in spite of abundant natural resources (including oil) and the complex interplay of class and ethnic interests, Nigeria finds itself more bifurcated along primordial, gender, and class lines. This bifurcation, which takes place alongside the fragmentation of sociopolitical constituencies, has weakened all classes and constituencies. Today, there is hardly a political or social constituency in Nigeria that speaks with one voice: students are divided between university and nonuniversity as well as between northern and southern members of the proscribed national students' association. Workers are divided along professional, religious, regional, and ethnic lines. Intellectuals are divided along generational, ideological, and religious lines. Christians and Muslims are divided along regional lines as well as along affiliations to particular sects. Women are divided between the urban and rural, professional and nonprofessional, literate and "illiterate." The list could go on. Added to these fragmentations are the steady suffocation of civil society, the disintegration of the state, and the delegitimization of its institutions and custodians. Without doubt, these factors work directly against democratization and nation building, however conceived.

In the context of a highly fragmented and suffocated civil society, the military has come to occupy *the* dominant place in the country's political equation. This is not to say the military is not divided. It is divided along ethnic, religious, and authority lines. As well, the Nigerian army, in spite of increasing professionalism, has disintegrated into an assemblage of "camps" organized around the power of generals: the so-called boys. Yet, it enjoys the advantages of commandism, location on specified sites, legal monopoly of the means of coercion, domination of power structures and institutions, access to resources with which to mediate contradictions and challenges, and a pervasively conservative ideology. Thus, it is impossible to discuss or comprehend the Nigerian reality without a proper appreciation of the place and role of the military in the political process. In the country's 37 years of political independence, the military has ruled for about 27 of those years. Thus, it has left its imprint not just on the consciousness of the people but also on the content and context of politics, the nature of institutions, and the character of political and social alignments in the country.

In this chapter, we focus on the recently aborted march to a third civilian republic in order to demonstrate the pressures for democratization, the actors in the process, the role of the military and the power elite, and the responses to the annulment of the election from several constituencies. The Nigerian experience described in this chapter is a clear example of the ways in which the democratization process can unleash negative political interests that culminate in the erosion of the quest for nationhood and in the consolidation of narrow and divisive interests. Unlike in some African states like Kenya, where democratization unleashed severe ethnic violence sponsored by the state, the Nigerian democratization agenda had to contend with the powerful military constituency, which believes, rightly or wrongly, that it has a right to control political power. Of course, the political and economic history of Nigeria is well known and well documented.[1] As well, there is agreement among scholars of Nigeria, that contemporary crises and contradictions cannot be separated from the country's historical experience and the impact of that experience. The neocolonial economy, an unsteady and nonhegemonic state, largely unproductive and factionalized classes, the survival of ethnic and regional inequalities and suspicions implanted by the British, and the conditions of vulnerability, underdevelopment, domination, and dependence certainly play a major role in the reproduction of the contemporary problems and contradictions. Yet, the postcolonial era has witnessed the alignment and realignment of social forces to give domestic constituencies enough room for maneuver. Even at this level, the Nigerian state and its custodians have failed to employ available resources and opportunities to dismantle inherited institutions and to construct *national*, viable, and legitimate alternatives.

While in several African countries there were efforts at some sort of ideological reconstruction of the African personality (and society) like humanism in Zambia, *Ujamaa* in Tanzania, and authenticity in Zaire, no such thing has ever been attempted in Nigeria. The closest was the bogus "war against indiscipline," which featured illiterate and semiliterate soldiers flogging civilians in public for some misdemeanors or forcing people to queue at bus stops for buses that never came. In short, the postcolonial project in Nigeria has never succeeded in weaning the people away from reliance on their ethnic and religious leaders, communities, self-help associations, and other organizations in civil society toward the state. It is not an exaggeration to say that after 37 years of *political* independence there is really no Nigerian nation to speak of. Nigeria is one country that has no *national* heroes and certainly no *national* institution that serves to pull the people together and give them a sense of vision and unity. Under the conditions described thus far, democracy and nation building can hardly survive. In fact, such efforts are constantly interpreted in the context of complex patron–client relations as opportunities to loot the treasury and facilitate private accumulation and to advance the interests of particular constituencies. The nation's democratic agenda has frequently been derailed by a combination of the preceding factors and forces above though the military, which, given its monopoly of the means of coercion, has always found it easy to hijack popular contestations for power.

BACKGROUND TO THE NEGATION OF THE POPULAR WILL

We can identify ten major reasons that democracy and nation building have never succeeded in Nigeria. To be sure, these explanations are not exhaustive and have meaning only within the overall historical context of the Nigerian experience as well as the specificities of the social formation:

1. The impact and implication of the distortions, disarticulations, and dislocations of the colonial experience. Like other African nations, Nigeria has not recovered from this experience.

2. The postcolonial alignment and realignment of forces along primordial, conservative, and opportunistic lines. These realignments have never been directed at liberating the people, promoting development, or establishing a platform for self-reliance. The alignments have tended to consolidate inherited coalitions, contradictions, and conflicts.

3. The salience of ethnic particularities and loyalties. Modernization, no matter how it is defined, has not wiped out ethnicity as a major aspect of Nigerian politics. In several ways, the state has encouraged it through its undue bias in favor of the three major ethnic groups (Yoruba, Igbo, Hausa/Fulani) and the neglect of the minorities. The fate of the Ogoni people in the oil-producing area of Rivers State is a typical

example of the fact that those from whose territory the wealth of the nation comes from the territory of the most denigrated, marginalized, and impoverished.

4. The inability of the state to build hegemony and legitimacy. Irrespective of new political systems, constitutions, a new anthem, new federal capital, several state and local government creation exercises, and so on, very few Nigerians give a damn about the state and country. The regions (states) have remained points of attraction and power. Though the civil war (1967–1970) did fragment and weaken the regions, political actors who go to the center still see themselves as representing ethnic interests and, at best, state interests. Even their appointments are often reflective not of merit but of ethnic, religious, and regional balancing. Politics still has one purpose: to penetrate the state and loot its resources as much as possible. After all, very few Nigerians can count on the state for justice and support, and very few have ever been censured for corruption, and such censures are often very temporary.

5. The weakness and fragmentation of civil society. Not only are the constituencies divided along primordial lines, but they are weak and often under the control and manipulation of elites who lack vision, ideological principles, class agenda, and sense of mission. Thus, quite often, representatives and community leaders remain in power forever or simply privatize public institutions to promote private accumulation at the expense of growth and development.

6. The continuing complex interplay of ethnicity and religion, an interplay that reflects, in large measure, the weaknesses of the dominant classes, their inability to construct a national agenda, and the weakness of the center vis-à-vis the regions in spite of several political engineering acts by several governments since 1960.

7. The domination, manipulation, exploitation, and marginalization of the Nigerian economy by foreign capital. Since political independence, the Nigerian capitalist class has remained largely subservient to foreign capital, and several efforts to "displace" or "replace" foreign capital have actually been very clever efforts at rationalizing and legitimatizing unequal relations with foreign capital and defining the spheres of accumulation. The introduction of an orthodox stabilization and adjustment regime has shifted the economic balance once again in the favor of foreign capital.

8. The unbridled corruption, ineptitude, and mismanagement of the ruling factions of the Nigerian bourgeoisie. This class has squandered resources, subverted the goals of development and growth, and enshrined a tradition of national disrespect and disregard of the public sphere. Consequently, an oil-rich nation, with a very hardworking population, the largest market in Africa, and potentials for industrialization, remains a backward, nonindustrialized, confused, crisis-ridden, debt-ridden, poverty-stricken, and marginal actor in the global system.

9. The continuing divide and conflict between social constituencies: gender, rural–urban, military–civilian, traditional and modern, imported and indigenous religions, bureaucrats and technocrats, oil and non-oil-producing states, and so on. These have weakened the entire national project and splintered people into constituencies that cooperate and engage in conflict without rules and without viable mediating institutions and processes.

10. The frequent intervention of the military into the public sphere with very disastrous consequences for national unity, regional cooperation, accountability, the solidifi-

cation of institutions, and democratization. More than any other predicament, the military has remained the most formidable challenge to nation building and democratization. Not only has it prevented the political elites from establishing traditions and institutions, but it has also prevented them from forging alliances, learning from experience and mistakes, and developing leadership patterns that rely on civil society rather than on decrees and commandist political structures. The military in Nigeria has completely militarized politics, enthroned corruption and waste, decapitated political institutions, and negated possibilities for consensual and rational politics as it has arrogated to itself the right to dictate and determine which government is good, which constitution is good, how many states, political parties, and so on are appropriate for the nation. In this process, the military has been very well aided by scholars and factions of the political class.

In spite of its vast human and natural resources, in spite of its potential for leverage in the global system, Nigeria has not succeeded in creating structures capable of pulling the citizenry together and developing a national identity. The sites of politics and power continue to be influenced and reconstructed to reflect the interests of political elites and interests with limited or no location within civil society. As well, probably more than any other African state, the democratic project remains completely without direction, confused, suffocated, and under the control of disgraced politicians, retired generals, traditional rulers, opportunistic professionals, and ''emergency'' or ''born-again'' democrats.

NIGERIA'S TRANSITION TO DEMOCRACY, 1987–1993

Since the transition program was formally launched in 1987, Nigerians have generally suspected General Ibrahim Babangida and the military top brass of having a ''hidden agenda.'' It was felt that the regime loved power so much that it would not let it go voluntarily. More importantly, top military officers and their friends had so abused their power and mismanaged the economy that only the control of power could guarantee their safety and security. Still, others had grown so used to the privatization of public resources and power and the numerous perks of office that they could not imagine life without power.[2] For Babangida personally, he had stepped on so many toes and generated so many scandals that the only way he could feel safe was to remain in power, in control of the national purse and the means of coercion and thus the ability to eliminate, contain, or intimidate the opposition. Such thoughts, we must point out, were possible because the general had carefully calculated that, with the opportunism of the political elites, the fragmentation and weakness of civil society, and the military's control of the means of coercion, the military could intimidate the country into accepting permanent military rule or a sort of arrangement that would include civilians but be dominated and controlled by the army. Thus, in spite of several amendments, changes, and interferences by the military in the transition process; in spite of forming and imposing its own two political parties (the Social Democratic Party [SDP], a ''little to the left'' and the National

Republican Convention [NRC], a "little to the right"); in spite of unilaterally banning former politicians, including those who had not been found guilty of any offense; and in spite of the tight control the regime exercised over the transition, some Nigerians somehow felt that a transition to participatory democracy was still possible: "All we could do was hold out some hope that deep down in his heart, Babangida would realize that Nigeria was not his private company and would eventually allow Nigerians to elect their own leaders."[3] To many, it was "uncomfortable, in fact, impossible to imagine that one man could hold a nation like Nigeria to ransom, and refuse to leave power after becoming so wealthy and staying in power for so long."[4] As well, when the government ousted the jurisdiction of the regular courts to adjudicate disputes relating to the transition program and transferred these powers to the National Electoral Commission (NEC), the president, and the Transition to Civil Rule Tribunal (TCRT), it was felt that the process was now fully under the control of the president. After all, the president appointed the chairmen of NEC and the TCRT.

After the government had spent billions of naira in nurturing a so-called new breed of politicians and earlier banning former politicians whom he vilified in several speeches, President Babangida turned around in 1991 and revoked the ban. The old politicians had sponsored several younger politicians and had controlled the political parties from the background. The process of their reentry into the political arena threw the parties into a lot of confusion as the old tried to reestablish control, and the new, having tasted power, resisted such moves. This weakened the parties considerably. What this experience showed was that Nigerian politics had not moved away, in any manner, from the decadent political traditions of the first republic, which was terminated in a military coup in January 1966. The actors, political methods, goals, and issues were still the same: politics was still an investment, and the goal was to capture power in order to accumulate wealth through the institutions of the state. In fact, the "new breed" politicians of the third republic were more corrupt, vicious, intolerant, and very impatient with democracy. They bribed the electorate, forged unreliable alliances, pandered to the military, refused to discuss critical national issues, employed thugs, and relied heavily on discredited politicians and the widespread use of money to get elected.[5] The important issue, however, is that the military was addressing the manifestations of the Nigerian crisis and completely ignored the nature of class alliances and civil society when it thought that it could nurture a so-called new breed of politicians without structurally transforming the relations of power, politics, production, and exchange.[6]

General Babangida disbanded the Armed Forces Revolutionary Council (AFRC) in January 1993 and set up a Transitional Council (TC) under the leadership of Chief Ernest Shonekan and others handpicked by him. He then set up a National Defense and Security Council (NDSC) with himself as head. As usual, the TC was powerless and fully under the control of the chairman of the NDSC, General Babangida. Though these changes were ostensibly to prepare the country for the transition to civilian rule in August 1993, in reality they were part of the general's grand strategy of domesticating the democratic process, civilianizing himself, and retaining political power. That such an agenda was conceived at all in contemporary Nigeria gives a direct insight into the fractionalization and factionalization of the dominant class, the nature of civil society, the weaknesses of political institutions, the absence of a political culture or tradition that respects the popular will, and the total absence of a national project capable of mediating efforts to appropriate the state.

Ironically, just as constituencies campaigned to terminate military rule in order to embark on a democratic project in Nigeria, also powerful constituencies openly campaigned for a continuation of military dictatorship. The government was widely suspected of being behind several shadow organizations and "patriots" who took pages of paid advertisements in the newspapers urging Nigerians to reject a "premature" transition to democracy and allow Babangida to remain in power. The most sinister of these organizations, which operated in the open with a lot of funding from undeclared sources, was the Association for a Better Nigeria (ABN), which claimed to have 25 million supporters and whose declared objectives, quite in contravention of the Transition Decree No. 9 of 1987, were to thwart the transition program and give General Babangida at least "four more years" as president of the country. Led by Chief Arthur Nzeribe, a well-known and wealthy politician with very limited credibility in the country, the ABN did not hide the fact that it had strong support from the presidency, and its ability to subvert the democratic process was to attest to this (see later).

Following the annulment of the 1992 primaries of both political parties, the government introduced a new system for selecting presidential candidates: Option A4. Since the argument was that the original contenders lacked grassroots support, Option A4 required the parties to organize and conduct primaries at ward, local, and state government levels for the selection of candidates, who would ultimately be elected at the national primaries as the final candidates. It was assumed that this would reduce the influence of money and force the candidates to identify with the local communities. This prescription was widely criticized because there were no guarantees that money would not play a role in the primaries irrespective of where they were conducted. More importantly, it was felt that this was one more effort to delay and divert the transition program, that the new decision was the result of dissatisfaction with the sort of candidates in both parties who were not Babangida's favorites, and that the new process would simply provide the general with more excuses as to why the politicians were not fit to rule. It was clear at this point that the military government was stuck on the issue of money in politics. It never concerned itself with why it was so important for people to capture political power to the extent that they would spend all their savings and get into debt just to win elections. More importantly, it was convenient to overlook the fact that the ultimate guarantee that elections would be free and fair and that the elected would be responsible and accountable was a strengthening of civil society. Rather, the military was busy suffocating civil society and harassing popular groups while claiming to be organizing a transition to democracy.

The Campaign for Democracy (CD), an umbrella organization for about 35 popular organizations and movements (see later), attacked Option A4 as a diversionary tactic:

rather than admit courageously that his political experiments with the country have failed disastrously, and allow Nigerians to seek their own salvation, General Babangida has decided to impose yet another "419" process on the nation. He calls the process Option A4 which is a recipe for even greater confusion and more far-reaching stalemate than the failed staggered primaries system. . . . Babangida did not and still does not intend to hand over power at all be it in October, 1990 or 1992, January 2, 1993 or August 27, 1993. The so-called Option A4 is a dangerous booby trap designed to make it even more difficult for the parties to reach a consensus on their presidential candidates, a situation that would give Babangida the excuse to extend his rule indefinitely.[7]

According to the CD, going by the Option A4 strategy, primaries at the ward level will produce 14,000 presidential candidates, 1,120 at the local government level, and 62 at the national level. It contended that "if 23 aspirants proved unmanageable in the two failed primaries of August and September (1992) only a miracle will prevent a disaster this time around."[8] The CD called on Nigerians to refuse to participate in the "racket" called Option A4.

Somehow, the CD and other groups that were opposed to Option A4 were saved from the task of having to worry about the possible negative consequences of Option A4. The parties were ready to be hijacked by the rich and powerful: people with sufficient money to run through the four levels at such speed that the government would not have sufficient time for a new delay tactic. This condition facilitated the emergence of Chief Moshood K. O. Abiola as the flag-bearer of the SDP and Alhaji Bashir Tofa as the flag-bearer of the NRC. Both men were multimillionaires, and both were very good friends of General Babangida. In fact, a year earlier, Tofa had taken paid advertisements in Nigerian newspapers urging General Babangida to remain in power till A.D. 2000 because no one in Nigeria could run the country as he had done. It was an incredible development, as all the predictions of confusion were proved wrong, and two very new members to both parties, very wealthy, with little or no political experience, found it so easy to take over the leadership of both parties. The big question was, What happened to the over 100 aspirants who had consistently showed that they were interested in the presidency? What happened to those who were founding members of both parties? What happened to those who had not been banned and who had spent a lot of money on setting up campaign organizations, printing posters and programs, and so on? Once again, we saw the power of money, especially foreign exchange, and the weaknesses and gullibility of the Nigerian political class. As Paul Adams has rightly observed,

Option A4, . . . produced two presidential candidates whose main achievement has been to make large fortunes, but who have no record of public service. Tofa emerged from almost complete anonymity outside his native Kano to win the nomination of the NRC in Port Harcourt. Abiola has never suffered from obscurity and won nomination of the SDP in spite of his reputation for excelling at the business methods for which Nigeria is notorious.[9]

In spite of the efforts of the politicians to operate by the very constraining rules set by the military, the government was determined to ensure that democracy remained suppressed in Nigeria. It was, without doubt, committed to ensuring that it found some excuse to cling to power. Ironically, it never occurred to the military that by suppressing the democratic option, the government was negating possibilities for creating a platform for constructing a viable national agenda by providing the populace with something they could all identify with. The opposite would be to encourage the people to return to the regional, religious, and ethnic bases.

DEMOCRACY WITHOUT BASIC FREEDOMS

One of the hallmarks of a democratic system is the constitutional and legal protection and guarantee of basic rights and freedoms. One of the hallmarks of a transition from authoritarianism to democracy is not just the opening up of the political system to pluralist ideas and pluralist politics but also the evidence that the state is willing to protect the liberties and rights of the citizenry. The latter was not the case in Nigeria, and this shortcoming cast an early doubt on the democratic enterprise. The preelection period was characterized by unprecedented attacks on the media, militant associations and unions, and human rights organizations. In March, the government promulgated Decree No. 21 of 1993, signed on 18 February and made retroactive to 31 July 1992, practically taking over the militant Nigerian Bar Association (NBA). This was one association that the government had found difficult to domesticate. The new decree empowered the government to take over the NBA and empowered the conservative fringe of the association, the Body of Benchers, made up of older lawyers, to set up a caretaker committee to run the organization for at least twelve months. The Body of Benchers was also empowered to set up a disciplinary committee for misbehavior, apparently to contain the more militant and radical younger lawyers who had little regard for the politics and political positions of the older lawyers. This way, the government expected to force the lawyers to fight among themselves and thus have little time to confront the state. The decree also stipulated that anyone who challenged it in a court of law would be subject to a very stiff fine or one-year imprisonment or both. Section 23A (3) of Decree 21 prescribed a fine of N10,000 or imprisonment for a term of one year or both for anyone who contravened its provisions.[10]

In addition, virtually every legal practitioner in Nigeria who was active in the human rights movement and in the pro-democracy organizations or who had the courage to speak out against the corruption, repression, and abuse of the rule of law by the government was subjected to one form of harassment or another. These acts of harassment did not deter the lawyers and their associations from instituting cases against the government and from remaining active in the opposition to military rule and extrajudicial behavior by government.[11] Of course, the government's decree itself violated the Legal Practitioners Act of 1975, which gave only one function to the Body of Benchers: to call persons seeking to practice law to the bar. It was clear, therefore, that the march to democracy was to be carried out in a purely undemocratic environment, with lawyers, judges, and the courts being manipulated and intimidated by the military junta. The government never made secret of the fact that it did not intend to play by its own rules and that it had no regard whatsoever for the judiciary and the law courts. Of the 22 court orders issued between 26 May 1992 and 1 July 1992, the government disobeyed 19, while 3 were overtaken by events.[12]

Universities had been closed for months for several reasons, but more evidently to keep the students away from the campuses. As the Committee for the Defense of Human Rights (CDHR) has rightly noted, "Anti-intellectualism is an essential element of fascist dispositions. Thus, fascists tend to undermine the growth of education among the teeming populace so as to ensure an uncritical attitude towards their policies." In the case of General Babangida, he

gave expression to this element. The regime could afford to close down schools at its whims and caprices. For the most part of the year under review (1993), higher institutions were closed down, to the extent that students had to forfeit one academic session. . . . In the same vein, many were either rusticated or expelled outright by university administrators.[13]

At the same time, in the brief periods in which schools were open, the children of the rich and powerful formed dangerous secret cults and "unleashed cult war in most campuses."[14] Between 1985 and 1994, there was no leader of the National Association of Nigerian Students (NANS) who was not arrested and detained by the police or the State Security Service (SSS). This strategy of frequent harassment enabled the state to weaken that constituency as an effective opposition to its zigzag transition to democracy.

This way, the government could ensure that students did not mount any collective response to its agenda whenever it became known and was unacceptable to the public. Earlier, it had reneged on a previous agreement with the Academic Staff Union of Universities (ASUU) on conditions of service, claiming it was a mere "gentleman's agreement" and therefore not binding. When the professors went on strike, the government simply dismissed all of them from their jobs and ordered the universities to recruit new faculty from within and outside the country. So, it had gotten rid of the students, the radical teachers' union, which had been banned, and the professors, who were all now dismissed and ordered to vacate the campuses or be forced out at gunpoint. It also felt it had contained the radical NBA. On 5 May 1993 it followed up its actions by announcing a new decree that classified teaching as an essential service and prohibited strike actions in that sector. Though it suspended the decree on 21 May, following outcries from within and beyond Nigeria, it had demonstrated the extent it was willing to go to maintain "order." Of course, the actions against the universities and faculty failed, as the institutions found it impossible to recruit new staff. They lacked money, and, unlike in the 1970s, very few foreigners wanted to come to such a politically unstable country with a terribly devalued currency.

The government now directed its attention at the media, the non-government-owned media. Since the murder of Dele Giwa of *Newswatch* by a parcel bomb suspected to have been sent by the government because of Giwa's investigation of the drug-trafficking business and the role of Nigeria's top military elite in the trade, Nigerian journalists have had to be very careful. In spite of intimidation, draconian laws, and detentions, the press remained comparatively very free in the African context. This freedom was not granted or guaranteed by the state. Rather, it was acquired through sacrifice and commitment to the ideals of a responsible and pro-people journalism. Many journalists were prepared to go to jail, and the more experienced ones easily left government-owned media to support the independent press or set up rival newspapers and magazines. Two of Nigeria's most militant and most courageous magazines, *TELL* and *The News*, were set up by young journalists who abandoned the larger ones that were privately owned by conservative establishments.

The military government did not believe that a free, enlightened, independent, and active press was required for democracy. It would not tolerate any discussion or write-ups on its corruption, manipulation, human rights abuses, and strategies to remain in power and frustrate the politicians. The first six months of 1993 witnessed the detention of Haliyu Hayatu of *The Reporter*, largely to silence its owner, retired major general Shehu Yar'adua, who had been banned as a presidential candidate after he won the primaries of the SDP twice. The newspaper was proscribed for six months in May 1993 by decree. In March, Dapo Olorunyomi, Akin Adesokan, Seye Kehinde, and Chiedu Ezeanah of *The News*, a magazine set up by young journalists who refused to be intimidated by the military, were detained for publishing articles considered unfavorable to the government. When they eventually met the stiff bail requirement, High Court judge Justice Moshood Olugbani extrajudiciously raised the bail conditions. Only following a successful appeal at the Court of Appeal in Lagos were the journalists eventually released. A month later, several copies of *The News* were confiscated by security forces, who also occupied the premises and prevented normal functioning. When the magazine obtained a court injunction ordering the police to vacate the premises, the police simply ignored the injunction. For publishing a very critical interview given by former head of state, retired general Olusegun Obasanjo, *TELL*, another Lagos-based magazine, drew the wrath of the military government. Two thousand copies of the issue were seized and in

May 70,000 copies were confiscated by security forces because the issue had identified 21 reasons that the transition to civil rule might ''hit a roadblock'' set by the government. Martin Oloja and Bukar Zarma of *Abuja Newsday* were detained by security forces for publishing an article on the illegal campaign launched by the ABN. This was the illegal campaign to derail the transition program, discredit the politicians, and ''encourage'' Babangida to remain in power for ''at least'' four more years beyond 1993. Several newspaper and magazine journalists, except those who worked for the government, were subjected to one form of harassment or another. This was to increase tremendously after the annulment of the results of the 12 June election (see later). With these acts of intimidation, the government felt it had contained the media.

Human rights activists were the next object of government attack. The government was aware of their roles in Kenya, Zambia, Malawi, Ghana, and other parts of Africa. It therefore sought to divide, weaken, and discredit the human rights organizations before the elections. This way, the government hoped, they would be in no position to mount any effective opposition following developments after 12 June. This was not new, for, as Africa Watch has rightly noted,

For years, Nigeria's active human rights groups and activists have suffered harassment and threats by the government. As the groups have become more involved in pro-democracy activities and more vocal in their calls for a hand-over of power, the government has become more harsh in response.[15]

In its 1993 annual report, the Committee for the Defense of Human Rights noted:

Harassment of Human Rights activists in the year under review was particularly remarkable. Although the phenomenon has been a continuous one, which widened in scope and dimension under the regime of General Ibrahim Babangida, the exertions of the activists rose to a climax during the year. In spite of incessant harassment, incarceration and other forms of human degradation, they persisted in their resistance against military misrule while clamouring for the enthronement of a democratic government.[16]

These acts of ''resistance'' and ''persistence'' attracted the wrath of the military government. The government tried to blackmail them by announcing that the human rights and pro-democracy groups were being funded from abroad to derail the transition to democracy! No one in Nigeria took this seriously. There is virtually no form of punishment, harassment, intimidation, and abuse that the government did not direct at the activists and their organizations. Activists like Dr. Beko Ransome-Kuti, chairman of the Campaign for Democracy; Titilayo Olusoga, a printer for the Civil Liberties Organization (CLO); Panaf Olakunmi, a printer for the CD and the Committee for the Defense of Human Rights; Femi Falana, president of the National Association of Democratic Lawyers (NADL); Shina Loremikan and Segun Jegede of the CDHR; Henry Onwubiko, a lecturer and member of the CD; Gambo Danjuma, speaker of the University of Nigeria Students' Union; and Silas Moneke, an activist from the University of Nigeria, suffered various acts of arrest, detention, harassment, prolonged and illegal questioning, and searches. Properties belonging to the printers and organizations had been seized, members of their families had been arrested and detained when they could not find those they wanted, documents had been confiscated, and properties had been looted and destroyed by security forces as part of a grand program of domesticating these organizations.[17]

Finally, following the religious/ethnic riots in Kaduna state in the Zango-Kantaf area, the government not only accommodated a very unfair and biased trial that sentenced fifteen Nigerians, including a former military governor, retired major general Zamani Lekwot, to death with several others detained under the obnoxious Decree No. 2 but moved on 20 May to proscribe by decree all ethnic, religious, and regional associations that had supported political candidates. This move, according to Africa Watch, "further heightened tensions between the Hausas and the minority groups in Kaduna by forcing underground their political goals."[18] While this crisis was brewing in the northern part of the country, the Ogonis in the Rivers State, an oil-producing community that for several years had been pillaged and devastated by transnational oil corporations in alliance with the Nigerian state, were being shot, harassed, detained, and displaced by Nigerian soldiers sent to put down their resistance to continued exploitation and land degradation. Their struggle, led by the Movement for the Survival of the Ogoni People (MOSOP) and Ken Saro Wiwa, a radical poet and writer, was described as treasonable. On 5 May, the government promulgated the Treasonable Offences Decree, which, according to justice secretary Clement Akpamgbo, prescribed the death sentence for those found guilty. Specifically, the decree was so broad in scope that, like the Transition to Civil Rule Decree, it could be employed against anyone: "Anybody who acts alone or conspires with anybody in Nigeria or outside, either by word or publication of any material capable of disrupting the general fabric of the country or any part of it, is guilty of an offence under the decree."[19] Ken Saro-Wiwa and eight other colleagues were later arrested and executed by hanging following a clearly flawed trial in November 1995.

Against this background of intimidation and heightened suffocation of personal liberties by the government, Nigerians approached the 12 June 1993 presidential elections. On the side of popular forces, relations were characterized by uncertainty, poverty, alienation, fear, and deepening contradictions arising from heightened ethnic, religious, and regional conflicts mostly encouraged by the state, its agents, and agencies. Unlike in many African countries (Kenya, Zaire, and Ghana), the pro-democracy forces could not form a political party. This gave them only an indirect access to the political process, as they were forced to support the SDP with its conservative and opportunistic leadership and agenda. This support meant that they had no constituency of their own, and their agenda was not part of the political discourses that were going on. As well, their members who supported the NRC felt that the movements did not reflect their particular interests. This inability to come together and set up a political platform to articulate the agenda of the pro-democracy community made the political process vulnerable to military manipulation throughout the transition era.

THE PRESIDENTIAL ELECTIONS: THE HIDDEN AGENDA IS OPENED UP

The 12 June election was unprecedented in the history of Nigeria. It was the only election in which the two candidates did not accuse each other of election malpractices and that received passing marks from popular organizations, international observers, and practically everyone except the military government elite and its handful of supporters. To be sure, the two presidential candidates, who had used their vast wealth to hijack the presidential candidacy of both parties, used a lot of money, misled the public with vain promises, and did not lift political debates to any new heights. They did not display any outstanding vision and played up the politics of religion, region, and ethnicity. As well, they struggled hard to forge linkages with conservative elements like religious leaders and traditional rulers. But before, during, and after the elections, violent acts were few and far between. They were readily pronounced the most free and fair elections in the history of Nigeria. The predominant impression was that, given all the visible indicators that Babangida was bent on finding excuses to cling to power, and given the widespread desire to see him go, Nigerians for once suppressed their differences and proceeded to vote in an orderly manner without the usual antagonism, rigging, threats, manipulation, and subversion of democratic traditions. Omo Omoruyi, director of the government-sponsored Center for Democratic Studies (CDS), had actually described the elections as the "best the nation ever had."[20] The Nigerian Election Monitoring Group (NEMG), led by Okon Asuquo Osung, commended Nigerians for the "visible, high degree of political maturity and patience in the conduct of the presidential election."[21]

This is interesting for several reasons. Ethnicity and religion had always been a problem with politics in Nigeria. Why did Nigerians vote en masse for the SDP? Among other reasons, it is possible to argue that, in the face of economic adversity and uncertainty, people will tend to support platforms rather than individuals and primordial considerations. Though these primordial issues were played up by the leaders of the parties, the electorate paid less attention to them than the two candidates and their leading supporters. This showed that the people were not just fed up with Babangida and military rule but willing to try out a system that allowed them to decide on their own rulers. At this stage, we can argue, democracy held out hopes for a more harmonious, stable, accountable society that could have been put on the path to nation building. We are not contending that ethnicity has disappeared as a viable factor in Nigerian politics. Rather, we are contending that the nature of the country's political predicaments and the rapid delegitimization of the military junta propelled the people to consider an alternative form of governance and to choose between two candidates: the one, Abiola, flamboyant, well known, heavily philanthropic, with known businesses and extensive international connections; the other, Tofa, unknown, lackluster, almost colorless, and with no widely known involvement in national affairs.

The SDP candidate, Chief Abiola, had chosen another Muslim from the north, Baba Kingibe, as his running mate. The NRC candidate, Alhaji Tofa, had chosen a southern Christian from the East, Sylvester Ugoh, as his running mate. The NRC and agents of the government, especially members of the ABN, played up the so-called Muslim-Muslim SDP ticket as a strategy for discrediting it. It was argued that the SDP ticket did not reflect the realities of Nigeria and would eventually lead to the imposition of Islam on Nigeria. This argument failed to do any damage to the Abiola ticket, as the militant and very influential Christian Association of Nigeria (CAN), led by the Catholic archbishop of Lagos, Olubumi Okojie, endorsed the SDP ticket. As Femi Falana, president of the NADL, noted,

when the battle started it was on Muslim-Muslim, Muslim-Christian ticket. But Nigerians showed on June 12 that the politics of the country had transcended ethnicity, religion and primordial sentiments to a large extent. Hence Abiola and Kingibe who are both Muslims won overwhelmingly.[22]

From all unofficial published results, the SDP ticket won the June election. Thirty percent of registered voters turned out on election day.

Through all sorts of underhanded and underground manipulation of the judicial system, the ABN, working on behalf of General Babangida, succeeded in getting the courts to declare the 12 June election illegal, thus precipitating one of the most dangerous political stalemates in Nigeria's history. Though the military tried to give the action a judicial coloration, the political interests involved were too obvious to be ignored by Nigerians, especially members of the SDP.[23] In contravention of Decree No. 13, the Campaign for Democracy, on behalf of its constituent groups and under threat of a five-year jail term, published an unauthenticated election result on 18 June. This publication showed that Abiola of the SDP had won a majority of the votes cast in 19 of the country's 30 states. Abiola had scored a total of 58.4 percent of the vote, while Tofa received 41.66 percent. This publication infuriated many Nigerians, and calls came from scholars, traditional rulers, trade unionists, politicians, and persons from all walks of life to NEC to release the official results and declare Abiola of the SDP winner of the elections. Chief Abiola himself moved to claim victory and urged NEC to officially declare him winner. A government that had earlier contended that its decrees were superior to court rulings now decided to obey the ruling of the courts, declaring the election illegal following a court injunction obtained by the notorious ABN. The NEC was disbanded, and Decrees 52 of 1992 and 13 of 1993 were abrogated. The president's press secretary threatened the nation with all sorts of violent responses if anyone dared to oppose the government's decision. In fact, Nduka Irabor warned Nigerians that a state of emergency would be declared if there were protests against a decision that had been taken in the interest of the nation. The hitherto hidden agenda had come into the open: it was now clear to all that all along, Babangida had no plans of handing power over to elected politicians. The narrow interests of a clique within and outside the military had taken precedence over an agenda that had been originally designed to lay the foundation for national cohesion, peace, and democracy.

HOW TO DERAIL A MARCH TOWARD DEMOCRACY: THE NIGERIAN EXAMPLE

The willingness of incumbent elites to make concessions to the opposition is directly related to (1) the power and effectiveness of the opposition; (2) the power and vibrancy of civil society; (3) the extent of local and international sanctions as perceived by incumbent regimes; (4) the interests at stake in the transition; (5) the importance of political power to the contending elites, which influences whether to give it up or not, once it is captured; (6) the existence of outlets for rationalizing the derailment or containment of the democratic process; and (7) the willingness of the incumbent leader to take the risk of negating the popular will. The Nigerian case was a combination of all seven reasons. Explaining why he canceled the elections, Babangida came up with spurious explanations that made sense only to very few. According to the general:

lasting democracy is not a temporary show of excitement and manipulation of an over-articulate section of the elite and its caption [sic] audience. Lasting democracy is a permanent diet to nurture the soul of the whole nation and the political process. Therefore, . . . lasting democracy must be equated with political stability.

. . . you would recall that it was precisely because the presidential primaries of last year (1992) did not meet the basic requirements of free and fair elections that the Armed Forces Ruling Council then had good reason to cancel those primaries. The recently annulled presidential election was primarily afflicted by these problems. Even before the presidential election and, indeed, at the party conventions, we had full knowledge of the bad signals pertaining to the enormous breaches of the rules and regulations of democratic elections. . . . Unfortunately, these breaches continued into the presidential election of June 12, 1993, on an even greater proportion.[24]

The "irregularities" identified by Babangida included "allegations of irregularities," "acts of bad conduct," "proofs and documented evidence of the widespread use of money during party primaries," "expenditure of over two billion, one hundred thousand naira" by the candidates, "moral issues . . . cases of documented and confirmed conflict of interest between the government and both presidential aspirants which would compromise their positions and responsibilities were they to become president," and a "huge array of election malpractices virtually in all the states of the federation before the actual voting began.'' General Babangida also accused party officials, members of NEC, and ''some members of the electorate'' of having been influenced by money. Perhaps the most bizarre allegation made by Babangida was when he claimed that his administration ''became highly concerned when these political conflicts and breaches were carried to the courts'' because the ''performance of the judiciary . . . was less than satisfactory . . . the courts have become intimidated and subjected to manipulation of the political process and vested interest,'' and the ''entire political system was in clear danger.''[25] This was the same government that had sacked judges, disregarded hundreds of court orders, detained hundreds of innocent Nigerians without cause, closed media houses and schools at the slightest cause, and demonstrated that it valued corruption more than honesty and service. Finally, Babangida claimed that he canceled the elections because the emerging results would have culminated in the election of someone who had encouraged ''a campaign of divide and rule amongst our various ethnic groups.''

This decision shocked the vast majority of Nigerians. The address, according to TELL, was a ''farrago of quibbles and inconsistencies. After much diversion into an irrelevant and unnecessary self-serving review of his administration's achievements, the General went into the heart of the matter.''[26] According to Abubakar Sadiq Umar, a Kano-based lawyer, ''if that speech is a true reflection of the collective wisdom and intelligence of the NDSC members, then it is a historical disaster that such people are the ones charting the destiny of Nigerians.''[27] A leading leftist scholar in Nigeria wondered how

such a pedestrian and terribly crafted address could have come from a government that harbored several leading scholars and political scientists. It was clear evidence of the confusion, lack of direction, and irresponsibility that had characterized this junta since it grabbed power in 1985.[28]

The issues raised in the address showed very clearly that General Babangida was looking for excuses to create diversions, confusion, and uncertainty so as to postpone the hand-over date and retain power. This was unfortunate because, rather than breed a rational political culture, harmony, stability, unity, and a sense of nation, this blatant derailment of the political process threw up countless contradictions, negative alignment and realignment of political interests, tensions, violence, and the alienation of regions and ethnic groups, especially those in the Yoruba west who felt very aggrieved.

The strategy of derailing the democratic process was quite simple: create numerous ''transition'' institutions, draft a new Constitution, sponsor a new breed of politicians, create government-backed parties and finance them, constantly declare your commitment to the transition process, allow elections at all levels except the presidency, play around with that final seat of power, and allow presidential elections. Then, on the basis of imaginary and sometimes government-sponsored irregularities, annul the elections and terminate the transition process. With this singular act of annulling the June presidential election, the Nigerian military destroyed all possibilities for nation building and for democracy. It alienated whole communities, curtailed the popular enthusiasm for democracy, and pushed back the effort to mediate the influence and importance of religion, ethnicity, and region in Nigerian politics as had been demonstrated in the national spread of the voting for the SDP.

It is clear, therefore, that Babangida had deliberately derailed the transition to democracy only because it was not accompanied by violence as was expected, and this deprived him of the opportunity of putting his plan into action: disqualifying the candidates, disbanding the two parties, appointing a prime minister from outside the military, and retaining a permanent hold on power. He had already created the National Guards to quell any opposition to his plan and had surrounded himself with enough sycophants to sing his praises and divert attention from the steady march toward fascism. His rationalizations lacked meaning in a political economy dominated by foreign capital and a corrupt elite, where there were no legal limits on election expenses, and where the state, though aware of irregularities, tolerated, and even encouraged them right from the beginning. But he had no support from the political class; he had no support from the rank and file of the army; he lacked support from his service chiefs, who began to insist that he resign to make way for peace; and he had no support from the general population. As well, Babangida lacked support from major Western powers, especially the European Community, the United States, and the United Kingdom. Military field commanders made it very clear to him at several meetings that he had no support within the army, and they were unwilling to risk their lives in pushing a ''Babangida project.'' They advised him to release the election results and declare a winner. He also failed to get the support of the National Assembly in spite of an arranged impeachment of the SDP Senate president and widespread bribery of legislators. With no support from his own ''people,'' General Babangida began to realize that this time he had not only miscalculated but stretched his capability to manipulate and intimidate Nigerians too far. The final push to get the general out of power was to be provided by the Campaign for Democracy.

POPULAR RESPONSES AND THE NEGATION OF PROSPECTS FOR NATION BUILDING

Our contention in this section is that the task of nation building in terribly distorted and disarticulated social formations can take place only in a democratic environment. Forced integration and the veneer of nationhood often projected under dictatorships hardly stand the test of time and primordial changes. The slightest cracks in the system often lead to violent confrontations and the emergence of separatist and secessionist movements. The Nigerian experience is clearly one in which the prospects for democracy in the next decade can be described as very dim. This is for three main reasons. First, the annulment seriously bifurcated political interests in the country with far-reaching implications for political cooperation. More than any other ethnic group, the Yoruba of the west felt victimized by the Hausa/Fulani group of the north, which controlled the reins of power. The north clearly does not support a revisitation of 12 June since Tofa, a northerner, clearly lost the election. Of course, the NRC was a northern-dominated political party. The east is in a similar position. It wants to see the north and west fight it out, and, if they succeeded in exhausting themselves, it would take advantage of it by projecting itself into the forefront of Nigerian politics. Hence, there are very few pro-12 June voices from that region. The Yoruba have been splintered into several groups for and against 12 June. Several prominent Yoruba elements helped Abacha to solidify his government. Even Chief Abiola was initially in support of the Abacha coup. The three leading pro-democracy activists who openly invited the military and Abacha in particular were, ironically, Yoruba. As well, many of the leaders of the pro-democracy (and pro-12 June) community also come from the west. Sections of the Yoruba community have passed declarations stating that they no longer have confidence in Nigeria as presently constituted. It is fair to say that Nigeria has never been closer to a civil war or breakup than it is today since the war that ended in 1970. The march toward democracy has clearly taken Nigeria to the precipice of disintegration and disaster. As the International Forum for Democratic Studies has accurately summarized:

Nigeria today is in the throes of an unprecedented political and economic crisis. In the political realm, an intensely unpopular military junta rules, the man elected president a year and a half ago languishes in jail, almost all opposition to the regime has been repressed, political conflict is on the rise, and there are growing threats of large-scale violence or even civil war . . . underlying and shaping these relatively recent developments are a number of highly divisive regional, ethnic, religious, political, and social issues that have vexed Nigeria for decades. As a result *the annulment of the June 12 election has provoked a crisis not merely of democracy but of nationhood.*[29]

Second, the pro-democracy groups that mobilized against the military succeeded in getting Babangida out of power through mass action and extreme sacrifice. However, since they lacked a constituency, they failed to replace Babangida and the military and actually enabled the military to return to power. This was because there was a tendency to personalize the struggle for democracy, which revolved around the exit of Babangida. The exit of Babangida did not mean the exit of the military. The groups were factionalized, lacked resources, were effective mostly in the southwest with very limited showing in the east and north (confirming the return to ethnicity and regionalism), and lacked an effective working relationship with the political class. Ironically, though members of the political class had invited Abacha and enabled him to actualize a long-held dream of becoming president of the republic, Abacha has turned against them and has refused to give meaning to their overt and covert objectives: mainly, the restoration of the 12 June mandate.

As soon as General Sani Abacha, on 17 November 1993, ousted the illegal interim government installed by General Babangida, he remilitarized the political terrain and completely dismantled all democratic institutions in the country. This action has wasted scarce resources, set the political clock back by decades, and subverted the only real opening for building some form of national consensus. The reaction to the Abacha coup by its supporters and opponents, supporters and opponents of Chief Abiola and the SDP, pro-military rule and antimilitary rule constituencies, and the international community has further complicated the efforts at democratization and national harmony.

Finally, given the political stalemate in the country following the annulment, the imposition of an interim government, the military coup, the role of pro-democracy forces in helping the military to consolidate its rule, and the refusal of General Abacha to reach accommodation with pro-12 June forces, it is doubtful if a genuine and widely accepted redemocratization agenda can be initiated or implemented in the near future. In fact, without resolving the 12 June issue to the relative satisfaction of the SDP and the West, there is no way in which a government, military or civilian, can count on the loyalty and support of those who feel they have been cheated out of a legitimately won election. The politics of 12 June exposed hundreds of political opportunists within the SDP and the pro-democracy constituency. Many of them joined the military in various capacities to dismantle the institutions of the third republic and push back the march toward democracy. Even Chief Abiola's running mate, who would have become vice president if the election had not been annulled, joined the military as minister for foreign affairs! As well, the annulment and opposition to Abacha by popular constituencies have hardened the political positions of ethnic, religious, and regional groups as well as those of conservative political constituencies. This development will make the process of national reconciliation even more difficult in the future. Strikes organized by the trade unions led by the National Union of Petroleum and Natural Gas Workers (NUPENG) in mid-1994 were contained with limited achievement. Following the arrest of the union leader, Chief Frank Kokori, the oil workers returned to work, as did other unions. General Abacha had succeeded in exhausting the pro-democracy constituency, containing the labor movement, and actually reaching some accommodation with lenders and donors. As well, he had succeeded in creating some diversion through the Constitutional Conference, which ruled in May 1995 that he could remain in power for as long as he wished. The introduction of a transition agenda following the execution of nine Ogoni activists and environmentalists in 1995 has succeeded in buying support from politicians (including those in Abiola's Yoruba base) and in splitting the opposition to the regime. Yet the net effect is that divisions within and between political constituencies remain very deep.

The November 1995 execution of Ogoni activists has further eroded the quest for nationhood. Not only has it alienated most of the small, but strategically located, Ogoni community, but it has frightened popular groups, minority communities, and opposition elements. The imposition of sanctions on Nigeria by the Commonwealth, the Western nations, and some African states, including South Africa, has diverted resources and focused on the construction of a national project to critical issues of regime survival, polishing the national image abroad, and containing internal and external opposition. For the regime, survival and manipulating the dynamics of global responses to its violent responses to community agitations now seem primary. The emergence of numerous opposition groups, some with openly violent agendas, has also eroded the basis of national unity and cohesion, especially as some of the groups identify with particular regional and religious interests. Whether the military successfully disengages from politics in October 1998 or not, nothing has changed in the bifurcated, corrupt, unstable, and conflict-ridden context of politics in Nigeria. A new regime or government will have to deal with the negative coalitions and primordial interests that erode national cohesion and the development of national consciousness. The ongoing transition program involves the same actors, objectives, tactics of competition, and institutions that ruined previous experiments at democratic governance and subverted the goals of nation building. On the government side, its total focus is on the superficial levels of power and politics: democracy equates political parties and elections. On the side of the political elite, politics remains a business and an opportunity to capture power to facilitate private primitive accumulation. The national question at the root of the Nigerian predicament and the inability to construct a national project are not being addressed in Abacha's "transition."

CONCLUSION

At one level, one could argue that what is going on in Nigeria is not a process of nation building but one of national disintegration: the programmed and deliberate effort of a faction within the military, aided by a faction of the political elite and international capital to negate the process of nation building and precipitate a major political crisis in the country. The state is at war with civil society, minorities feel intimidated and marginalized, the disadvantaged feel terribly alienated and dominated, and national institutions continue to be inefficient, ineffective, and irrelevant to the living conditions of the people. With hundreds of pro-democracy and trade union leaders in jail and with the military junta carefully plotting complex strategies to civilianize itself, nation building is last on the regime's agenda.[30] Given the disposition of the junta and its seeming ability to domesticate and incorporate large sections of the political class, the only road open for the future will be one of increasing violence. The recent spate of bombings at airports, military barracks, and other strategic locations, assassinations, and the construction of parallel sites of power and politics all point in this direction. On the other hand, we can argue that, out of the present generalized conditions of violence, intolerance, crises, coalitions, contradictions, and delegitimation of the state and its custodians, a true national project will emerge, and the process of harmonizing community and constituency interests will emerge. This process will be hastened only if the military successfully disengages, civil society is strengthened, and democratic politics is reintroduced.

Unfortunately, the chances for the second option at the moment are rather slim. The initial opposition to the junta from the international arena has quietly died down. Even the sanctions imposed on the junta, especially following the execution of the "Ogoni Nine," have not been fully implemented. Shell continues to do business in Nigeria, as do transnational corporations and Western governments.[31] The political class is abandoning its stance on 12 June and joining Abacha's transition program in spite of all the flaws and fears. The pro-democracy groups have no base within the country, as their leaders have either been jailed or been forced into exile. The opposition abroad is yet to gain the required clout to raise money, attract committed cadres, and work out a holistic agenda for post-Abacha and postmilitary reconstruction. Many of the foreign-based opposition movements are not just short of funds but led by inexperienced activists. While the foreign-based opposition has demonstrated commitment to change, it has not produced a serious document to address the national question, redress existing inequalities and fears, contain tensions and conflicts, and guide the country into the twenty-first century.[32] The internal and external opposition is challenging a junta that collects about $45 million daily from the sale of oil and is willing to expend that money on the domestication, containment, and, if necessary, elimination of its opponents. These conditions show that the road to democracy is still paved with a lot of uncertainties and dangers. As well, the inability of Western governments (except Canada) to take decisive actions or, at the very least, stick to imposed limited sanctions has tended to strengthen the intolerance and arrogance of the military junta.

Yet, five major issues need to be addressed for democracy or nation building to become part of the agenda for recovery: first, the release of Chief Abiola and other political detainees and the reopening of shut media houses and schools; second, the restoration of all dismantled democratic institutions and the completion of the 12 June process through some sort of negotiation with the affected communities and constituencies; third, the effective withdrawal of the military from politics and power and the restoration of the Constitution and the rule of law; fourth, the establishment of critical national institutions capable of generating a national consciousness and promoting the processes of nation building through a democratic interplay of contending interests; and fifth, respect for minority and group rights as well as personal and collective liberties and freedoms. A national project cannot be initiated when leading pro-democracy and opposition leaders are harassed and jailed or executed; minority communities are invaded, occupied, and intimidated; and the already established institutions and ideological platforms are eroded through regime intolerance, corruption, and mismanagement. Whether Nigeria will survive the next decade as a nation remains a relevant question, as political interests with vast resources and strong foreign connections and support are retreating into their ethnic and regional bases. At the moment, it would appear that only democratic forces, learning from their mistakes and drawing lessons from experiences in other societies, are capable of providing a new basis for democratic politics and nation building.

NOTES

Research in Nigeria for this project was sponsored by the Aspen Institute, the American Philosophical Society, and the National Endowment for the Humanities.

1. See Toyin Falola, ed., *Nigeria and Britain: Exploitation or Development?* (London: Zed Press, 1987); Claude Ake, ed., *Political Economy of Nigeria* (London: Longman, 1985); Okoi Arikpo, *The Development of Modern Nigeria* (Harmondsworth: Penguin, 1968); R. O. Ekundare, *An Economic History of Nigeria* (London: Methuen, 1973).

2. See Julius O. Ihonvbere, *Nigeria: The Politics of Adjustment and Democracy* (New Brunswick, NJ: Transaction, 1994).

3. Interview with a member of the Campaign for Democracy (CD), CD Secretariat, Imaria Street, Lagos, Nigeria, November 1993.

4. Interview, Lagos, Nigeria, July 1993.

5. See Julius O. Ihonvbere, "The Military and Political Engineering under Structural Adjustment: The Nigerian Experience since 1985," *Journal of Political and Military Sociology* 20 (Summer 1990).

6. See Pita O. Agbese, "Sanitizing Democracy in Nigeria," *TransAfrica Forum* 9, no. 1 (Spring 1992); Babafemi Ojudu, "As in the Beginning . . . Money and Ethnic Loyalties Manifest in Third Republic Politicking," *African Concord* (Lagos), 6 August 1990.

7. Campaign for Democracy, "Breaking a Vicious Circle," text of press statement, Nigerian Union of Journalists Lighthouse, Victoria Island, Lagos, 24 November 1992. "419" refers to section 419 of the Nigerian Criminal Code, which deals with obtaining money from others under false pretenses.

8. Campaign for Democracy, "Breaking a Vicious Circle."

9. Paul Adams, "Babangida's Boondoggle," *Africa Report* (July–August 1993): 28.

10. The lawyers were usually able to challenge the state because they were mostly self-employed in private practice. This contrasts with public employees, including academics who could be sacked at any time for merely expressing an opinion anywhere. As well, because the lawyers usually worked together, getting a colleague to represent a fellow lawyer for no fee was relatively easy, unlike other public servants, who would have to retain the services of a lawyer to fight the state.

11. Nigerian Bar Association, Ikeja Branch, Press Release, 20 May 1992.

12. See Ayo Olarenwaji, *The Bar and the Bench in Defence of Rule of Law in Nigeria* (Lagos: Nigerian Law Publications, 1992).

13. Committee for the Defense of Human Rights, *1993 Annual Report: Human Rights Situation in Nigeria* (Lagos: CDHR Secretariat, 1993), 17.

14. Committee for the Defense of Human Rights, *1993 Annual Report*, 17.

15. Africa Watch, *Nigeria: Threats to a New Democracy—Human Rights Concerns at Election Time* 5, no. 9 (June 1993): 7.

16. Committee for the Defense of Human Rights, *1993 Annual Report*, 13.

17. For details see Julius O. Ihonvbere, *Nigeria*; Africa Watch, *Nigeria*; Africa Watch, *Campaign of Silence: Human Rights Concerns on the Eve of Elections* (New York: Africa Watch, June 1993).

18. Africa Watch, *Nigeria*, 15.

19. Clement Akpamgbo, quoted in Africa Watch, *Nigeria*, 22. Following massive opposition, the government was forced to announce that it had suspended (not revoked) the decree on 21 May 1993.

20. This was part of a speech he had drafted for General Babangida without realizing the general's hidden agenda. He discussed this version on the BBC, and, when he knew of the general's true position, he went into hiding. See Onome Osifo-Whiskey and Ayodele Akinkuotu, "A Dance on the Precipice," *TELL*, 19 July 1993.

21. Okon Asuquo Osung, *West Africa*, 28 June 1993.

22. Femi Falana, "The Struggle Has Just Started," interview with *TELL*, 13 September 1993, 25.

23. Details of this development can be found in Julius O. Ihonvbere, *Democratization and Civil Society in Nigeria* (forthcoming); Mobolaji Aluko, "Re-Visiting June 12 1993 Nigerian Presidential Election," unpublished paper, Burtonsville, MD, October 1994.

24. General Ibrahim Badamasi Babangida, "Laying the Foundation for a Viable Democracy and Path of Honour," Address to the Nation, 26 June 1993. Reproduced in *Newswatch*, 5 July 1993.

25. Babangida, "Laying the Foundation."

26. Osifo-Whiskey and Akinkuotu, "A Dance on the Precipice."

27. "On June 12 We Stand," *TELL*, 19 July 1993.

28. Interview, Lagos, Nigeria, November 1993.

29. International Forum for Democratic Studies, *Nigeria's Political Crisis: Which Way Forward? Conference Report* (Washington, DC: IFDS, February 1995), 3.

30. See Julius O. Ihonvbere, "Will Abacha's Transition Lead to the Restoration of Democracy in Nigeria?" unpublished paper, Department of Government, University of Texas at Austin, December 1996.

31. See Julius O. Ihonvbere, "The Nigerian State, the Ogoni Crisis, and the Struggle for Democracy in Nigeria," paper presented at the Annual Meeting of the African Studies Association, San Francisco, 23–25 November 1996.

32. See Pita Ogaba Agbese, "Containing the Military: Strategies for Pro-Democratic Forces," paper presented at the Annual Meeting of the African Studies Association, San Francisco, 23–25 November 1996.

Chapter 6

Economic Reform and Political Liberalization in Ghana and Côte d'Ivoire: A Preliminary Assessment of Implications for Nation Building

E. GYIMAH-BOADI AND CYRIL DADDIEH

INTRODUCTION

Recent events in Africa (e.g., in Liberia, where armed rebellion against the autocratic regime of Samuel Doe degenerated into a three-way ethnic genocide, the recurrent cycle of violence between Hutus and Tutsis in Rwanda and, to lesser degree, in Burundi, and the protracted civil wars in the Sudan and Somalia) provide poignant reminders that the passage of time has not muted intergroup conflicts on the continent. Ethno-regional, religious, and other forms of social conflicts persist and have escalated in some instances. This reflects the failure of postcolonial political and economic development; clearly, the project of nation building, energetically embarked upon after African decolonization, is far from completed and has backfired in some cases.

Two major developments in recent years call for a revisiting of the issue of nation building in Africa. First is the severe economic crisis that ravaged the continent in the late 1970s and early 1980s, especially the fiscal crises that accompanied it and the subsequent preoccupation of African governments with the resuscitation of their economics within the framework of the neoliberal Structural Adjustment Programs (SAPs) inspired by the IMF-World Bank. By the latest count, over 30 African countries had adopted one version or another of SAP. These programs (featuring, e.g., economic stabilization and rehabilitation of infrastructure) emphasize economic rationality and production at the expense of social and political goals. In essence, they constitute an attempt to execute a retreat from purportedly politically and socially expedient, but economically unproductive and ultimately unsustainable, patterns. SAPs are therefore distributive in impact, though not necessarily by design. The potential effect of such wide-ranging economic reforms with allocative and distributive implications for social and ethno-regional groups in multiethnic and increasingly class-divided states is of more than passing academic interest.

Second is the wave of political liberalization and democratization occurring concurrently with economic restructuring in the 1990s. Influenced by external developments such as the fall of the Berlin Wall and communism, the collapse of the former Soviet Union, the end of the Cold War, dramatic pro-democracy movements in Eastern Europe, and pressure from Western donor countries and IFIs and pushed by domestic civil society, many African countries have embarked on the democratization of their political systems. A degree of political liberalization has been achieved in many countries, and a few have gone through successful democratic transitions between 1989 and 1994. Military and single- or no-party authoritarian political systems and rule by decree are giving way, albeit grudgingly and haltingly, to elected, constitution-based governments. Political parties have once again been legalized and are fashionable, new, liberal democratic constitutions with all the usual guarantees of personal freedoms and liberties have been promulgated, independent newspapers are flourishing, and so on.

What are the implications of these fundamental economic and political changes for the uncompleted project of nation building in Africa? How are African governments managing the problems and tensions arising from these changes in their political economies? These are some of the issues addressed in this chapter. As multiethnic and multireligious societies that are attempting to liberalize both their economic and political systems simultaneously, Ghana and Côte d'Ivoire provide an opportunity to analyze the implications of economic and political liberalization on nation building, albeit in a preliminary fashion.

The first part of the chapter provides a broad outline of the political and economic strategies adopted for nation building by governments of the two countries in the first 25 years of independence. The remaining sections look at the economic and political liberalization processes in both countries within the last decade and analyze their country-specific implications for nation building.

THE POLITICAL ECONOMY OF NATION BUILDING IN GHANA AND CÔTE D'IVOIRE: THE PRELIBERALIZATION YEARS

Ghana is a country of about 16 million people made up of a variety of sociocultural groups, of which the most important are the Akan (subdivided into Ashanti, Fante, Akwapim, Brong, Akim, Nzema, and other smaller units), constituting about 44.1 percent of the population; the Mole-Dagbani, 15.9 percent; the Ewe, 13 percent; the Ga-Adangbe, 8.3 percent; the Guan, 3.7 percent; the Gurma, 3.5 percent; and other groups, 11.4 percent.

There is a rough coincidence of ethnicity and administrative region, with each region also serving as home to a sizable number of ''strangers'' and others who might not have migrated from their ''home'' regions. The Ashanti, Brong Ahafo,

Eastern, Central, and Western regions are generally peopled by Akans and the Mole-Dagbani and Gurma are in the Northern, Upper West, and Upper East regions, while the Volta region is home to mainly the Ewe. The southern half of Ghana in general and the Akan groups in particular have enjoyed relative economic and political dominance in both colonial and postcolonial times.

As in other African countries, nation building, construed largely as national integration, has been high on the agenda of postcolonial Ghana. This preoccupation with nation building arose from a general recognition by the nationalist elite that as an entity put together by the colonial authorities without regard to ethnic affinities, national unity rested on shaky grounds. But the ethno-regional (and class) animosities that surfaced in the immediate preindependence period gave much urgency to the project. Having been largely neglected and left relatively undeveloped under colonial rule, the Northern region declared a social and economic distance from the rest of the country, and its leaders argued that their people were not ready to be governed as part of independent Ghana without special protections. In the southeast, having been colonized by Germany and governed later on as part of the UN Trusteeship Territories together with Togoland, Ewe exerted irredentist pressures toward their cousins in Togoland. The Ashanti demanded special protections for their cocoa and mineral wealth as well as their culture.[1]

Postcolonial governments, especially that of the first republic under Dr. Kwame Nkrumah, took energetic steps to promote national unity and integration. Arguing that economic development required maximum political and social peace and that a degree of "totalitarianism" was necessary to contain the otherwise fissiparous tendencies in ethno-regionally and culturally divided Ghana, the Nkrumah-Convention People's Party (CPP) government embarked on a process of democratic closure and the institution of authoritarianism. The process began innocuously enough with the passage of laws forbidding the formation of political parties along ethnic, religious, and regional lines and others that weakened the provisions in the independence Constitution for decentralized local government. It continued with the expansion of presidential powers, the elimination of constitutional checks on executive power, and the formalization of single-party rule in the Republican era between 1960 and 1966. Democratic closure in Ghana reached its apogee under the military regimes that ruled the country from 1966 to 1992. Under the National Liberation Council (1966–1969), the National Redemption Council/Supreme Military Council (1972–1979), the Armed Forced Revolutionary Council (1979), and the Provisional National Defense Council (1982–1993), constitutional rule was replaced by decree, parliaments disbanded, political parties banned, and citizens detained without trial or tried in extrajudicial tribunals.

However, distribution and redistribution of economic and symbolic goods as well as bureaucratic and political appointments appear to have been the chief strategies used in the fight for national integration. Thus, efforts were made under both civilian and military and authoritarian and democratic regimes in

Ghana to spread the provision of economic infrastructure (especially roads, bridges, and post offices) and social services (clinics and health posts, schools, etc.) in all regions. Special attention was paid to the historically disadvantaged Northern region. For example, in the field of education, in addition to the system of fee-free primary and middle school for all Ghanaians, special facilities were given to children from the North for secondary and university education. Even in the location of state-owned enterprises, ethno-regional considerations were tolerated, sometimes in violation of economic rationality, with predictable financial losses. For instance, a tomato factory was located in Tamale in the North, even though it was far away from the main tomato-producing and-consuming markets in the southern parts of Ghana.[2] Ghanaian governments pursued a policy of full employment in the state enterprises in particular and the expanding public sector in general—a policy that led to the creation of over 300 state-owned enterprises and a bloated civil service by the 1970s and made the government the leading employer in the formal sector[3]; they also maintained controls on the market, especially on the prices of popular consumer items, and provided direct and indirect subsidies on various consumer items and social services—to keep ethno-regional conflicts in check and to keep the urban middle and nascent working classes, and especially the growing number of new graduates from the country's educational institutions politically quiescent. In addition, ministerial, bureaucratic, and technocratic positions in government and the public service, as well as membership of ruling military councils, were informally balanced to reflect the cultural and ethnic diversity of the country.

Paradoxically, notwithstanding these measures, ethno-regional tensions persisted under all regimes and seemed to escalate during the short-lived episodes of democratic rule. For instance, the first competitive electoral contests in the 1950s witnessed the emergence of ethno-regionally based political parties—the Ashanti-based National Liberation Movement (NLM), the Ewe-based Togoland Congress Party (TCP), and the Mole-Dagbani-Gurma-based Northern Peoples Party (NPP). There was a resurgence in tensions between Akan and Ewe in the late 1960s around the multiparty elections of that period and during the Busia-Progress Party (PP) administration when the ruling party and its opposition, the National Alliance of Liberals (NAL), were widely regarded as Akan- and Ewe-based, respectively. Indeed, tensions have persisted also between Ewe and Akan, between Brongs and Ashanti, between the Kokombas and Nanumbas in the Northern region, between Akan settler farmers and their hosts in the predominantly Akan cocoa-growing areas in the Eastern region, and between Ashanti settler farmers and their hosts in the Western region. An Ewe irredentist movement also surfaced in the late 1970s. In addition to considerable ethnic rivalry, there have been conflicts between the populist and elitist strands in the Ghanaian society and polity. In the late 1970s and early 1980s, class conflicts appeared to emerge as a leading form of intergroup conflict—with the popular classes (urban workers, the lumpen-proletariat, and, to some extent, the rural poor) cohering around the person of Flight Lieutenant Jerry John Rawlings and a group of left-wing intelligentsia to attack the Ghanaian political, social, and economic establishment.[4] The attempted coup of 15 May 1979, the successful coup of 4 June 1979, and the three-month populist interregnum, as well as the 31 December 1981 coup and its immediate aftermath, represent the highest point reached in overt class conflict in postcolonial Ghana. During that "revolutionary" period, there was an attempt to pursue economic remedies and to institute new political arrangements that responded to the needs of the subordinate classes as opposed to those of the middle and professional classes as well as the traditional rulers.[5]

On the whole, however, the system of rough equity in the distribution of government-controlled resources and of high-level bureaucratic positions, complemented by centralization of political power, worked reasonably well in the first 30 years of independence. At least, relative to other countries in the subregion such as Nigeria (see chapter 5), Ghana did not experience any major eruptions of ethno-regional conflicts, and relations between the social classes and religious groups remained relatively cordial. The preeconomic recovery (i.e., before 1983) strategies of economic distribution[6] (in the form of either Nkrumah's "state socialism" in the late 1950s and early 1960s, General Acheampong's "capturing the commanding heights of the Ghanaian economy"[7] in the 1970s, or Rawlings' "populist economics" of 1979 and the early 1980s) have been at the core of the efforts made by postcolonial governments to manage ethno-regional, generational, and nascent class conflicts and to promote national unity. Thus, the failure to develop an efficient internal market during that period[8] and the consequent economic, social, and political distortions could, at least in part, be viewed as the price paid for the equally pressing imperative of nation building in an unformed nation.[9]

The problem, however, is that this mode of nation building through distribution of the national product in Ghana worked best under conditions of relative economic buoyancy. Unfortunately, there were severe limitations on the ability of the Ghanaian economy, which was never strong in the first place, to sustain such distribution-driven programs. By the early 1980s, the strategy had become untenable as the Ghanaian economy had hit rock bottom, with export production precipitously dropped, foreign exchange acutely scarce, the country's international credit rating very low, and chronic shortage of spare parts, consumer goods, and other supplies, along with decaying economic and social infrastructure.

Moreover, the strategy of centralized control and distribution of the national economic product fostered neopatrimonialism and its accompanying political and economic logic, one in which Ghanaian regimes and their leaders raided their own treasuries, engaged in reckless fiscal behavior, and brutally exploited the most productive socioeconomic sectors—especially the export crop producers—in order to secure their hold on political power.[10]

CÔTE D'IVOIRE: STATE AND NATION BUILDING DURING THE GOOD TIMES, 1960–1979

Côte d'Ivoire shares a number of sociocultural, religious, and ecologic characteristics and fault lines with its neighbor, Ghana. The two countries not only are ethnically heterogeneous but comprise some of the same indigenous groups. Territorially larger than Ghana, Côte d'Ivoire's population has always been much smaller, currently only 11 million, a fact that lies at the heart of the country's search very early on for labor and markets in the region and elsewhere. The 60 or so ethnic groups that make up this population can be categorized into seven clusters or roughly four or five main regional and language (cultural) clusters, namely, Akan (made up of Baoulé, Abron, Anyi, Nzema), Krou (West Atlantic), Malinké (or North Mandé), South Mandé, and Voltaic. As in neighboring Ghana, the Akan are numerically superior, constituting about 42 percent of the population. Another significant similarity is that, on the whole, ecology, economy, and polity have interacted since colonial times in such a powerful way as to (re)produce relative southern affluence and political dominance and relative underdevelopment and marginalization of the north in both cases.

It is important to note that some 3 million (28 percent) of the Ivorian population are considered ''foreigners,'' or people who have immigrated from elsewhere in the subregion. This figure is a bone of contention because it appears to include persons born in the country to immigrant parents. While a majority of these ''foreigners'' are Mossi from Upper Volta (now Burkina Faso), a country that was once attached to Côte d'Ivoire as a labor reservoir from 5 September 1932 to 4 September 1947, many are from Mali, Guinée, Ghana, Bénin, Nigeria, and elsewhere. These foreign Africans fill both rural and urban unskilled and semiskilled jobs and, together with the estimated 100,000 Syrians and Lebanese living in the country, also dominate medium and petty trade. There is also a substantial European (mostly French) presence, which has dwindled in recent years largely because of the fiscal crisis of the state but still numbers slightly more than 32,000, down from the peak figure of 50,000 during the good times.

The immigration situation aside, the most important dissimilarity between the two countries, with profound implications for their nation-building projects, is to be found in the trajectory of their postcolonial political systems. First, Ivorian politics has been dominated by a single party, the *Parti Démocratique de Côte d'Ivoire* (PDCI), and one man, Félix Houphouët-Boigny, from the mid-1940s until his death was officially announced at 1:30 P.M. on 7 December 1993, a timing that was pregnant with symbolism that served only to elevate him to the Pantheon and to mythicize his already considerable hold over the political system and the national imagination. It might be recalled that December 7 is the anniversary date of independence, and each year the celebrations were punctuated by a presidential address to the nation.[11]

Second, the nation-building project was intimately linked to a kind of ''creation-myth'' that revered Houphouët-Boigny as a savior sent down by the Creator (or is it the African ancestors?) to deliver his people from the hated corvée or forced labor and discriminatory agricultural labor and pricing policies. This mission was successfully accomplished, first, through the creation of the *Syndicat Agricole Africain* (SAA) on 10 July 1994 by Houphouët, by then a medical doctor and wealthy planter, and seven of his colleagues. The goal of this agricultural union by Africans for Africans was purely economic: to seek parity in official treatment with French cocoa and coffee farmers with respect to pricing, access to labor, credit facilities, and so on. Members of this emerging planter class enjoyed the exalted advantage of being either traditional chiefs in their own right or being linked to households with a chief. Moreover, the union quickly caught popular imagination, and its membership grew to 20,000, of mostly southern and Baoule planters. The SAA roster became the basis for a new political party, the PDCI, a year later. After surviving a concerted effort by the colonial administration to crush it through repression, imprisonment of its leaders, and other forms of intimidation, the party forged a tactical alliance with the French Communist Party (PCF) for a brief period. The leadership subsequently came to terms with the colonial authorities and in 1950 renounced its flirtation with communism, along with any illusions of "radicalism" it might have harbored, and began gradually to define as well as reinforce the central "bourgeois" tenets of the emerging postcolonial state, tenets that have guided its policies to this day.[12] As Samir Amin had noted, these guiding principles include (1) cooperation with France in all fields; (2) the path of evolution, not revolution, and the rejection of the ideology of class struggle as a means of resolving the outstanding contradictions in the emerging postcolony, on the grounds that classes "do not exist in the Ivory Coast"; (3) unrestricted reliance on foreign and local private initiative to help improve its economic prospects; and (4) consolidation of national sovereignty while vigorously resisting any attempts to form larger African groupings, deemed illusory.[13] Thus, from its inception, the SAA was reformist in its ideology, southern-oriented, and predominantly ethnic in composition, with important implications for postcolonial state formation and the nation-building project. Its subsequent conversion into a political party did not alter its fundamental essence as a conservative organization. These attributes had prompted Alex Rondos to conclude that "with this class at its head, the party became a highly structured political means by which the planters were able to come to favourable agreements with the colonial authorities. They were able to acquire land for their private use and negotiate with northern chiefs for the supply of labor."[14]

At independence in 1960, Houphouët-Boigny and the PDCI appeared to enjoy unprecedented popular support that cut across ethno-regional and linguistic lines, having been credited with delivering the country from bondage by the popular masses. Although the preindependence era was characterized by multipartyism, the PDCI emerged virtually without a political peer. The country had become a *de facto* one-party state from the start of independence. Consequently, the prospects were comparatively better for a successful nation-building project.

However, here, as in Ghana, the nation-building project was complicated as well as given greater urgency by the ethno-regional and generational cracks that appeared in the veneer of national unity shortly before and after independence. In 1959, the emerging state had to contend with the revolt and secessionist struggles of the Anyi of Sanwi (an Akan subgroup). The Sanwi king claimed that his kingdom had been incorporated into Côte d'Ivoire illegally by the colonial state without the consent of his people.

Also, generational battles that had been waged prior to independence were apparently rejoined in 1962, when a group of young radicals from the party who were disenchanted with the regime's conservative policies allegedly planned to abduct Houphouët-Boigny and other party leaders.[15] More than 125 people were reportedly arrested and secretly tried in a kangaroo court in Ya-moussoukro, the president's hometown. The president was apparently able to get convictions for 44 of the alleged plotters. In 1963 another alleged plot with ethno-regional and generational/ideological overtones was uncovered. This time the plotters apparently consisted of a motley coalition of opposition groups, including left-wing youth, disgruntled politicians, and northerners, that resented southern domination of the government. The president himself apparently diagnosed the plot as "ideological" in nature and communist-inspired. It was even suggested that the PCF had a hand in instigating the trouble, apparently peeved by Houphouët's severed relations with his former associates.[16] In mid-1964, Houphouët-Boigny used these threats, real or imagined, to purge the party hierarchy, including six members of the Executive Committee of the Party's Youth Wing, who had been implicated in the alleged plot.

Worse yet, in December 1969, the Sanwi king again advocated secession for his kingdom. Government troops swiftly suppressed the ensuing revolt. In November 1970, in an apparent bid for political recognition and power, a Bété leader by the name of Gnagbe Niabe proclaimed himself grand chancellor of Côte d'Ivoire. He made an attempt to contest the presidential election, but his candidacy was rejected. When President Houphouët-Boigny also refused to grant his wish for a cabinet post, Gnagbe mobilized a large group of supporters and marched on Gagnoa, the Bété capital. Again, government troops were dispatched to confront the threat. They succeeded in capturing the rebel leader and crushed this rebellion as well.[17] To this day, the bitter memories of the military campaign against Gnagbe and his followers linger in the Bété region and have had a negative impact on the PDCI's electoral fortunes there. The region appears to have permanently realigned politically so that the PDCI has had trouble carrying the region, while the opposition has had some of its best results during the recent era of multipartyism.

Toward the end of the decade of the 1960s, a number of politicoeconomic issues bubbled to the surface. Witness the protest demonstrations organized by the *sans-travail*, or unemployed Ivorians, in Abidjan in 1969 to pressure the government to institute the Ivorianization of low-level jobs. The government responded by arresting some 1,600 demonstrators in Abidjan on 30 September

1969, provoking widespread resentment. In turn, in October, the *sans-travail* vented their anger and frustration against foreign workers. These were the first palpable signs of xenophobia toward the hundreds of thousands of unskilled and cheaply paid labor, mostly Mossi from Upper Volta, who had flocked into the country with Ivorian government encouragement to work on cocoa and coffee plantations in large agroindustrial estates and served as "houseboys" for the urban elites, thus reinforcing the good feeling of embourgeoisement of this class. To its credit, the state refused to be stampeded into a mass expulsion of foreign workers, arguing that they performed jobs that Ivorians themselves were loath to do. Meanwhile, a potentially more damaging conflict began to brew as well. It pitted the nascent educated class against the state over the suffocating presence of the French in all facets of Ivorian life, including the cabinet, education, army, civil service, and, in particular, their control over the "national" economy.[18] The government was understandably reluctant to undertake large-scale Ivorianization of the civil service and economy for fear of undermining administrative effectiveness or state building as well as jeopardizing the close economic ties it continued to cultivate with France. Again, bear in mind that close collaboration with France or dependent capitalism was at the very core of the development strategy the PDCI leadership had chosen.[19] However, from their foggy positions on the periphery of the state and economy, many Ivorians perceived Houphouët as preferring Europeans to Ivorians. The calls for increased Ivorianization were to become more strident and insistent as the 1970s wore on, most especially as a critical mass of educated Ivorians earned diplomas from the nation's institutions of higher learning or returned home from their studies in France, only to face a very tight job market and doors seemingly barred to them because of the presence of "foreigners."

However, in the 1960s, the issue was not jobs: there seemed to be enough of those around for the educated—hence, privileged—few. The key problem was that many of the Ivorian students who had studied in France or had come into contact with students from other African countries had had their political consciousness sufficiently raised as to reject the PDCI's ideological departures from socialism to unabashed capitalism that had begun in 1950. They rejected as well the state's neocolonial policies vis-à-vis France. Many students also objected to the government's attempt to co-opt the *Mouvement des Élèves et Étudiants de Côte d'Ivoire* (MEECI), the leading student organization at the time, and bring it under tighter PDCI and presidential control. A student crisis erupted in May 1969, when MEECI attempted to force the government to initiate specific reforms at the National University in Abidjan. Following a strike action by students, the government moved swiftly to crack down: Ivorian student protesters were arrested, foreign students expelled, and the university closed down for two weeks.[20]

The Ivorian political elite had concluded much earlier on that an atmosphere of peace and stability was an absolute prerequisite for attracting foreign capital investments and expertise for economic development. Thus, the government passed laws restricting the freedom of the press, tightly controlled the dissemination of information, and imposed severe sanctions on individuals who published or reproduced documents that caused dissent or discredited political institutions. Moreover, the government not only prohibited the creation of competing parties but sought to achieve monopoly control over civil society by insisting that all interest groups and associations be affiliated with government-controlled federation of Ivorian workers, the *Union Générale des Travailleurs de Côte d'Ivoire* (UGTCI). All civil servants became, willy-nilly, card-carrying party members. Farmers, fishermen, bakers, transporters, doctors, lawyers, women's movement, teachers, students, you name it; all came under intense pressure to join the UGTCI.

Revealingly, the UGTCI saw itself as a participant in development rather than as an advocate of working-class interests. It supported the government's efforts to promote unity and development. It did not object to the state's development policies; indeed, its leaders participated in government policy debates and thus became instruments of economic development. It is hardly surprising that the UGTCI exercised little political or economic clout. Strikes were legal, but groups contemplating strike action first had to complete lengthy negotiations with the government, during which any work stoppage was illegal. Only the teachers' unions managed to maintain their autonomy, despite strenuous efforts to incorporate them or, at the very least, to influence their governance structures.[21] The president's intention was quite clear: to channel associational demands through quasi-corporatist structures and to transform most interest group associations into semiofficial organs of the party.[22]

After the first decade of independence, during which the president strenuously resisted all pressures to implement too rapid an Ivorianization policy, the president began creating government positions for younger intellectuals and highly trained technocrats in the 1970s. Following the 1970 party congress, the president also began appointing younger members to the political bureau and endorsing their candidacy to the National Assembly. This patronage system proved quite effective in the 1970s in securing the compliance of the emergent elite. The robustness of the economy during the first two decades enabled the state to co-opt real or potential opposition through expanding job opportunities and widespread distribution of economic gains among politically salient social and economic interests. Individuals and representatives of corporate groups as well as dissident politicians were often brought into the fold with offers of prime land, lucrative licenses, scholarships, forestry rights, and well-paid positions in government and party. While the formation of ethnic-based associations was discouraged, such associations were invariably inducted into the government and party hierarchy, especially as they became too large and too well organized to be ignored. The system could be sustained for as long as the economy produced sufficient largesse for the state to dispense, and the output of the national university and technical institutes together with the number returning home after their studies in France was kept sufficiently small to ensure that graduates found lucrative jobs in the government, parastatal industries, and the private sector.

The state let the apparent success of its chosen path to development, based on dependent capitalism, which produced an "economic miracle" characterized by consistently high growth rates averaging 7–8 percent a year for nearly two decades, speak for itself. The record of achievement was all the more impressive because it was based principally on the export of primary products, especially cocoa and coffee. Using surpluses generated from cocoa, coffee, and timber and captured by the *Caisse de Stabilisation et de Soutien des Prix des Produits Agricoles* (CSSPPA, hereafter, the Caisse), the state embarked on an aggressive interventionist program of crop diversification, which was tied to the creation of an array of state-owned import-substitution industries involving palm oil, cotton, rubber, sugar, rice, pineapples, bananas, coconuts, and so on.

The success of the development strategy reflected growing state capacity building: the ability of the state to provide credit facilities and inputs to farmers in a timely fashion through SATMACI (the state agricultural service agency for export crops); the ability to support a dizzying array of urban and rural roads throughout the country; the establishment of a functionally efficient and effective marketing system in which buyers showed up at appointed times, made proper use of advances, paid promptly for crop deliveries, and so on; the ability to formulate and enforce a unique approach, by African standards, to land that favors cultivators (anybody who puts land to productive use) over original owners, even though it implies a permanent alienation of communally owned land. Together, this set of policies has drawn Ivorian peasants and even many elites, albeit as "weekend farmers," into the circuits of production and reinforced their loyalty toward the state. For a time, there appeared to be something in the "economic miracle" for everyone. So spectacular have the peasants' response and subsequent production results been that a historic policy decision was taken by the state in April 1988 to curtail cocoa production because of fears of over-production and accompanying market glut.[23]

All the same, the president used each successive crisis episode or perceived threat to the new and fragile state to further tighten his grip on power and the political system, to demand and receive pledges of unflinching loyalty from colleagues and other state officials, to respond concretely as well as creatively to some calls for reform, and to deflect and postpone other demands, all the while using a style of leadership that was at once a mixture of neotraditional paternalism and philosophical moralizing. The "first peasant of the country" could connect with the masses as few politicians could because he understood the traditional political culture and because he "personified the nation in the process of creation."[24] In these and other ways he was able to make himself even more indispensable to the ultimate success of the twin projects of state and nation building.

Perhaps even more importantly, the fact that the political elite of Côte d'Ivoire has been the longest-serving and most stable in Africa, dating from the early 1950s, when the PDCI, led by Houphouët-Boigny, took a share of power under French colonial tutelage, has been enormously helpful in this regard. Elite longevity and stability can be measured in terms of not only the long and distinguished career of Houphouët himself but the fact that a political and administrative core elite dominates the system through multiple officeholdings in the key institutions of the party and government: the president's office, PDCI Political Bureau, National Assembly, and the Economic and Social Council. Tessy Bakary has shown that only 320 individuals have held the 1,040 positions available in these institutions (excluding the presidency) between 1957 and 1980. He has also shown that half of the officeholders were university graduates, and 40 percent had completed their secondary education. Among government ministers, however, the percentage of graduates had grown to 68. Furthermore, these graduates were mainly from science and technical backgrounds, making the political elite of Côte d'Ivoire much more technocratic than Ghana's. Those who held office between 1960 and 1980 were also much more likely to have come through the ranks of the civil service. Indeed, 75 percent were middle-or high-ranking civil servants. For instance, 88 percent of those appointed to the Political Bureau in 1980 were from the public sector, and 95 percent of the government ministers were ex–civil servants. Thus, Bakary aptly described Côte d'Ivoire as "the civil servant republic" par excellence.[25]

The uniqueness of the Ivorian political system relative to that of Ghana and many other African countries is that even with the 1980 "opening up" of the system, the generation born between 1920 and 1934 accounted for 63 percent of the political elite. The average age of the ministers and Political Bureau members was 42 and 47, respectively. Just as significantly, the average term of office of a minister was 7.5 years, and 25 percent of ministers in 1981 had been in office for more than a decade. Astonishingly, 50 of the 84 people who held office in the 1954–1959 period continued to exercise power among the 1960–1981 cohorts.[26] Elite longevity, stability, growing competence, and relative cohesion are also crucial factors in Ivorian state building or state capacity, that is, the state's political and administrative effectiveness or its ability to implement and sustain its policies.[27]

Meanwhile, the trouble with the nation-building project was that it hinged on a growth-oriented development strategy centered around the exploitation of those critical sectors that could produce quick results. As a consequence, it engendered the concentration of social services, jobs, and wealth in major centers in the south. In the absence of state mediation to correct imbalances, this strategy naturally produced or exacerbated regional economic disparities, increased the gap between the rich and the poor, between rural and urban areas, and, even more significantly, between the north and the south. Over time, the accumulation of these inequalities became intolerable and began to threaten ethnic harmony. The president then responded by exploring alternative strategies.

To defuse the tensions arising from the perceived disparities in the levels of development between the north and the south and to induce ethno-regional harmony, especially from about the mid-1970s, the president made highly publicized visits upcountry in which he proclaimed "the unity and especially the equality of all Ivorians, north, south, east and west" and promised that "the Savanna will have its revenge . . . [and that] each peasant . . . will attain equality with his southern brothers within five years."[28] The president made good on his pledge by initiating politically expedient development programs, notably, the cotton, rice, and sugar schemes. The sugar schemes in particular have proved to be overly ambitious and financially catastrophic for the state.

One creative solution to the problem of ethno-regional imbalances in the distribution of social services was a decision to alternate Ivorian independence festivities between Abidjan and the different prefecture capitals. Although this strategy amounted to trickle-down, it produced the kind of visible and tangible results that the masses could appreciate. Capitals hosting the festivities underwent massive face-lifts, which included jobs in construction of new government buildings, paved streets and roads, provision of water and electricity, new housing, and so on. To appease the emergent postindependence elites of younger intellectuals and technocrats, the president dropped his decade-long resistance to rapid Ivorianization and began to actively absorb them into the parastatal sector and into the government and political party in the 1970s. Of course, cabinet appointments were carefully calibrated to give all major ethnic groups some representation.

Also in the early 1970s the president began experimenting with a new model of conflict management and decision making. Beginning with the first *journées des dialogues* in January 1974, in which 2,000 party workers were invited to critique and recommend solutions, the president has institutionalized this method of dealing with socially explosive issues. He would bring together a certain number of Ivorians from various walks of life, including representatives of different corporatist groups (2,000 seems to be the magic number), to engage in intensive dialogue about a problem over the course of several days. These "dialogue days" often provided an opportunity for scathing public criticism of the shortcomings of institutions and for castigating individual government and party officials for their lack of probity and dereliction of civic responsibility. The president himself often weighed in, transforming himself into a leading critic of the very elites he had nurtured and thereby ingratiating himself with the common Ivorian. He would then appoint various committees to study the recommended reforms.[29] The significance of these "dialogues" was that "by allowing public criticism, albeit in a tightly controlled environment, the president remained informed about popular dissatisfaction. Subsequently he could take steps either to remedy or to suppress problems while maintaining his firm grip over Ivorian politics."[30]

While President Houphouët-Boigny's conflict management style inclined him toward dialogue, reconciliation, and even rehabilitation (of discredited politicians), he was uncompromising about the need to maintain order and stability as a sine qua non of national economic development. This attitude was summed up by his insistence that, if forced to choose between disorder and injustice, he would not hesitate to choose injustice. He added that "when there is disorder, the lives of people and a regime are at stake, but an injustice can always be corrected."

We highlight all of this to demonstrate that while the prospects for nation building may have been far more promising in Côte d'Ivoire, the new state spent its first decade putting out ethno-regional and generational brushfires as well. While the state met each challenge or opposition with firmness, using all its coercive apparatus, in contrast to its counterparts elsewhere in Africa, force was used rather sparingly, kept in reserve for the rare occasions when it was really needed. Instead, the state relied on economic incentives to secure political acquiescence and national support for its twin projects.

However, the abrupt downturn in the economy from 1979 tarnished the much-vaunted "Ivorian economic miracle." The accompanying fiscal crisis of the state severely compromised state capacity and nation building. One impact of *tonton conjoncture*, as the recession was popularly nicknamed, was a growing popular awareness that their country could go the way of other basket cases in the region. This sense of déjà vu contributed to the surge in radical political activism by students and teachers in the early 1980s.[31] Unfortunately, "radical" measures by the regime to secure improvements in international terms of trade by withholding Ivorian cocoa from the international market and to confront international finance capital by repudiating external debts could not stop the economic downward slide. Ultimately, the Ivorian government, as Ghana was to do later on, was forced to turn to the World Bank and the IMF for assistance and to embark on an IFI-dictated economic restructuring.

But how have these major changes in the direction of economic policy in the two countries impacted national unity in general and, in particular the postcolonial model of nation building through economic distribution? What opportunities and constraints did neoliberal economic reforms present to the process of nation building and national integration in the two multiethnic and multicultural societies? The following sections examine the nature of the new policies and analyze their impact on nation building.

ECONOMIC LIBERALIZATION: PROBLEMS IN THE TRANSITION FROM DISTRIBUTION TO RATIONALIZATION

In Ghana, the Provisional National Defense Council (PNDC) led by Jerry Rawlings embarked on an economic recovery program along World Bank, IMF lines in 1983. The focus of this program, at least initially, was on economic stabilization, rationalization, and the rehabilitation of infrastructure. However, with the strong emphasis on economic principles and goals (such as quick return on investment and comparative advantage), initial SAP investments went into the rehabilitation of Ghana's export sector and the supporting infrastructural base of roads, railways, and harbors. Thus, the cocoa-, timber-, and mineral-producing areas/regions of Ashanti, Brong Ahafo, and Western regions, the port cities of Tema and Takoradi, Accra (the national capital and home of most of the country's manufacturing establishments), and Kumasi (the Ashanti capital) have been showered with attention in the SAP reconstruction exercise. By contrast, the historically disadvantaged and the extant economically depressed areas, especially the Northern regions (Northern, Upper East, and Upper West regions) appear to have suffered benign neglect during most of this period.[32]

SAP-induced austerities affected all segments of the Ghanaian population and socioeconomic groups, but partial evidence suggests that the urban low-wage earner and unemployed, as well as the poor in the historically disadvantaged and the extant economically depressed areas/regions, were among the most negatively affected groups. The urban working class suffered job losses under the labor retrenchment exercise in which at least 36,000 persons were laid off from the lower ranks of the Ghana Education and Civil Service between 1987 and 1990. In addition, their real incomes stagnated as the government imposed restraints on wages and allowed the cost of living to skyrocket through massive currency devaluations, price decontrol, and the withdrawal of subsidies on health, education, and potable water. Some analysts suggested that they could see a link between the outbreak of the guinea worm epidemic in Northern Ghana in the mid-to late 1980s and the introduction of ''user fees'' on potable water under SAP within the same period. Other studies documented a drop-off in hospital attendance and enrollment in primary and middle schools in some of Ghana's historically disadvantaged (Northern) and economically depressed (Central and Volta) regions.[33]

THE POLITICAL MANAGEMENT OF NEOLIBERAL ECONOMIC REFORM

As in many other countries in Africa, Ghana's SAP provoked widespread negative public reactions. While ethno-regional reactions to SAP were muted and largely indirect, class reactions were sharp and direct. The strongest opposition came from working-class elements and labor unions—notably, the Industrial and Commercial Workers' Union (ICWU), students, and radical intelligentsia. Workers and their unions protested wage restraints, removal of subsidies, adoption of cost recovery measures, the threatened cancellation of leave allowances, and labor retrenchment. Student agitations arose over the reduction in student allowances and the threat to impose charges on student services, while the radical intelligentsia charged that the PNDC had betrayed its anti-imperialist and populist ideology by consorting with World Bank/IMF neo-orthodoxy.

The adjusting regime in Ghana appeared to recognize the uneven impact of the programs across social and ethno-regional groups and attempted to compensate losers directly and indirectly. The most direct attempt to compensate SAP losers came under the Program of Actions to Mitigate the Social Costs of Adjustment (PAMSCAD). Under the program, an amount of $84 million was earmarked for spending on community-initiated projects in health, education, housing, and sanitation; and impoverished farmers in the Northern and Upper regions and those who lost their jobs in the labor retrenchment exercise were targeted for assistance. Additionally, the infrastructural rehabilitation activities undertaken by the Public Investment Program (PIP) from 1986 to 1988 had been designed to give special attention to job creation. Furthermore, the extension of the national electricity grid through Brong-Ahafo to the Northern regions of Ghana, as well as the general spillover from SAP such as improvements in roads, railways, telecommunications, and supplies, could be regarded as indirect compensations to SAP losers.[34]

However, it is important to note that these limited governmental concessions to social class and ethno-regional anti-SAP pressures constituted a deviation from SAP.[35] They did come only as an afterthought and were invariably perceived as "slippages" and intolerable breaches of "conditionalities" by the World Bank, IMF, and the other relevant international financial institutions and bilateral donors. The penalties for such offenses ranged from deliberate delays in disbursing pledged donor assistance and reduction in donor support, to outright suspension of structural adjustment program and accompanying aid. Fear of incurring the wrath of powerful IFIs and other external actors and provoking sanctions imposed severe constraints on the ability and inclination of the PNDC government to use economic redistribution to appease ethno-regional and class interests and/or to maintain ethno-regional and class coalitions.

Determined to stick with painful neoliberal economic reforms and afraid of measures that might incur the wrath of donors, the PNDC government became severely constrained in its ability to provide relief from austerities to affected social groups and ethno-regional interests. Thus, the regime resorted to a combination of authoritarianism and ethnic solidarity to undergird its political base.

The institutions and practices introduced earlier under the banner of revolutionary populism, such as the extralegal public tribunals and National Investigations Committees, arbitrary arrests, detention without trial, disregard for due process, cruel and unusual punishment, and retroactive decrees, were retained and readily used to suppress opponents of the regime. It maintained a tight control over the print and broadcast media and used them as tools for government propaganda. In addition, it established a pattern of political violence in which alleged subversionists were tortured, tried in kangaroo courts and, not infrequently, executed. It also kept a proliferating network of paramilitary and security organizations such as the Civil Defense Organizations, Commandos, and Panthers, which served as vigilantes and enforcers for the government.[36]

PNDC authoritarianism was complemented by quasi-corporatist arrangements that involved state-supported private and public organizations such as the 31st December Movement, the June Fourth Movement, Committees for the Defense of the Revolution, Mobisquads of the National Mobilization Program, the armed forces (through the office of the PNDC chief of staff and the Armed Forces Directorate), and the Ghana Private Road Transport Union (GPRTU).

This intense and prolonged political repression gave rise to the state of affairs in Ghana in the late 1980s aptly described by a PNDC official as the "the culture of silence." Repression had become necessary as an instrument for the political management of an unpopular economic program because state contraction had resulted in much-diminished opportunities for state patronage and clientele. It is instructive to note that, by the late 1980s, when robust autocrats in Africa and other parts of the world were in full retreat, PNDC authoritarianism was in full swing.

The adoption of neoliberal economic reform was, at least in part, a causal factor in the isolation of the Rawlings government into a narrow ethnic base. The reforms and their accompanying austerity and ideological implications caused a rift between the PNDC regime and its original support base of urban workers, students, and radical intelligentsia.[37] At least one major political outcome of this was the dislocation in the ruling coalition, and, at the level of the political leadership, it led to the ethno-regionally significant departure from the regime of the "northern radicals" (Chris Bukari Atim, Sergeant Alolga Akata Pore, and Zaya Yeebo), all of whom had been big supporters of radical populist policies, and a spate of attempted coups. But more significantly, it marked the beginning of the isolation of the Rawlings government and its inability to expand its social base beyond a narrow Ewe/Volta region core and a few old friends. A critic of the PNDC government drew attention to this fact in a public lecture in 1988 when he asked:

Is it not strange and rather unfortunate that the Head of State, the Head of National Security, the Head of the Police Service, the Head of the Army, the acting Governor of the Bank of Ghana and the head of the National Investment Bank, and I am sure there are others—all happen to belong to a single ethnic group or at least a single region of the country?[38]

It is instructive to note that, despite the unfavorable public commentary inspired by this perception and the obvious political embarrassment it caused, the PNDC government remained unable to overcome this problem throughout the remainder of its tenure.

Heightened ethno-regionalism may also be seen in the increase in the number and activities of ethno-regional and community-based voluntaristic cultural and economic development organizations in the PNDC era. They ranged from the usual "old boys/girls" and parent-teacher associations servicing schools at the elementary and secondary levels, to town and village development associations and ethnic-regional solidarity groups. The best examples of the latter kinds of associations in this period may be the Volta Region Social Development Association, whose activities were organized innocuously around a soccer team—

the Volta Regional Development Corporation (VORADEP) and the Western Region Movement for Unity and Development (WEREMUD). Interestingly, the formation of the latter organization sparked government interest and hostility. While these developments could be regarded in a positive sense as the healthy emergence of community self-responsibility and the flowering of civil society institutions, they also represented centrifugal forces in the malintegrated and unformed Ghanaian nation. In the PNDC era and under SAP, individuals appeared to have become inward rather than nationalistic in their outlook and expectations.

CÔTE D'IVOIRE: NATION BUILDING DURING LEAN YEARS, 1979–1990

As suggested earlier, Côte d'Ivoire fell on hard economic times in 1979 due to a dramatic fall in the price of its major export earners, cocoa and coffee, and the unwillingness of the government to reduce budget expenditures in line with the shortfall in revenue. By 1988, it was estimated that as a result of the slump in commodity prices, government revenues from cocoa and coffee were 25 percent less than what they had been in 1981. Combined with the rise in import prices, the balance of payments situation deteriorated. While total public and publicly guaranteed external debt in 1970 amounted to $255 million, by 1986 the figure had ballooned to $6.5 billion; private, nonguaranteed debt, which stood at $11 million in 1970, had also shot up to $2,955 million. Interest payments on the external public debt had climbed dangerously to $532 million, or 23.5 percent of the total value of exports of goods and services in 1986. Under pressure from the IFI, the government somewhat reluctantly agreed to tighten its economic belt. In return for rescheduling the Ivorian debts and for additional financial assistance, the Ivorian government undertook to implement a structural adjustment program in the 1980s. The program included the usual recipe of removal of state subsidies and introduction of, and increases in, user fees. But perhaps the most controversial of the measures demanded by the IFIs were the reduction of the producer prices for coffee and cocoa and the downsizing of the government and parastatal sector. In addition to lowering the producer prices of cocoa and coffee, efforts were made to improve tax and customs collection; strict regulations were passed to control the use of government vehicles; the cabinet was reorganized, and its size reduced; salaries of government ministers, civil servants, and other state officials were cut by as much as 40 percent; a "solidarity tax" was levied on incomes in the private sector; and a decision was made to privatize all but 7 of 35 state-owned enterprises. In addition, public works programs, including those intended to enable "the savanna to catch up with the forest," were abandoned in the midst of the SAP-induced state contraction.

The consequences of the neoliberal SAP reforms in Côte d'Ivoire were no less traumatic for that society, its economy, and politics. While SAP exacted a heavy financial toll on everybody, its impact was uneven; it affected social groups in Ivorian society differently. The hardest hit groups were the rural cash-crop producers, whose incomes were effectively cut by more than half, and the urban unemployed and working poor, including those who were self-employed or who worked in the informal sector, who now found their incomes further eroded by rising food, water, and electric bills and rising school fees and hospital charges, thus further limiting their access to the health system and resulting in deschooling.[39] Indeed, the cost of living was estimated in 1990 to have risen by 50 percent since 1980, while incomes had been effectively frozen.[40]

One important social consequence of the economic crisis was a wave of wanton lawlessness and Mafia-style banditry. Indeed, so serious was this problem that stricter security measures were announced in 1987 under which the armed forces were to be deployed along the country's borders in an attempt to stem the tide of smuggling and illegal immigration. They were also expected to assist the police in combating crime in the principal towns. In October 1989, a Security Fund (to which all residents of Côte d'Ivoire were asked to make contributions) was established for the modernization and reequipping of the country's security forces. It is interesting to note that the Levantine population in Côte d'Ivoire contributed generously to the fund and received widespread publicity for their contributions. Dramatization of the ''Lebanese contribution'' reflected another problem related to the SAP-era recession. Ivorian society, which had proved very hospitable to diverse groups of West African and non-African immigrants, turned sharply xenophobic in the period.

While the economic adjustment program in Côte d'Ivoire was not as far-reaching as that of Ghana, the political problems it presented were no less tricky for the government. The popular classes, especially students and teachers hit by the cutbacks in higher education associated with the neoliberal reforms, became increasingly radicalized and mounted sustained attacks on the state; middle-class ire grew as graduate unemployment, a phenomenon largely avoided in postcolonial Côte d'Ivoire, worsened.[41] SAP-related measures such as the lowering of producer prices for farmers and cuts in the salaries of state elites as well as increased taxation on the middle class in general and the private sector in particular implied a break in the postcolonial social contract between key socioeconomic groups and the Ivorian regime.

Even more nettlesome for the neopatrimonial Boigny-PDCI regime was the reduction in the ability of the state and regime to use co-optation as the main tool for nation and state building. Public sector retrenchment entailed the loss of jobs and the diminution of political sinecures that had characterized appointments to senior positions in the government and parastatal sectors. In the meantime, fissures began to appear in the hitherto fairly solid facade of elite cohesion. As the economy deteriorated, it exacerbated the rivalries between the members of the ruling class.

Compared to Ghana, the political management of the growing crisis in Côte d'Ivoire in the 1980s was more nuanced and generally benign, if of dubious effectiveness. The president sought to open up the political system in a limited and tentative way while maintaining a firm grip over Ivorian politics. First, the dialogue approach, which seems to have worked so well in the early 1970s, was revived in the 1980s. The president used those forums to launch a public repudiation of certain institutional practices and shortcomings and to initiate ad hoc committees to investigate public complaints.[42] An attempt was made to open up the Ivorian political system by making elections more competitive, albeit within the single-party structure. Thus, beginning with legislative elections in 1980 and then with legislative, local, and municipal elections in 1985, the president discarded his earlier practice of handpicking the candidates and allowed any qualified citizen to be a candidate.

The new system of competitive elections within the single-party framework in the mid-1980s was complemented by measures to strengthen the representation of key socioeconomic classes and the educated youth in the ruling party and in government. Thus, in 1985, the National Assembly was enlarged from 147 to 175 deputies, and the Political Bureau and the Committee Directorate, two of the more powerful institutions of the state, also went from 35 to 58 and 100 to 208 members, respectively. The latter served as an instrument for broadening the base of support for the party by expanding its representation as well as co-opting potential foci of dissident activity into the political process. For those reasons, it included members of the judicial, executive, and legislative branches of the government, current and former military officers, leaders of government-supported unions, women, business leaders, and members of the professions, including university professors. Its function was to advise the president on political matters through a series of ad hoc committees. In addition, the membership of the Political Bureau came to include the cabinet ministers and other members of the political, military, and business elite. It was headed by a thirteen-member Executive Committee. By the mid-1980s, the Executive Committee was composed almost exclusively of younger cabinet ministers. Local government also underwent further decentralization with the addition of 64 new *communes de plein exercise* to the existing 34. Administratively, the country was further subdivided into 49 *départements*.

POLITICAL LIBERALIZATION IN THE 1990S AND FURTHER COMPLICATIONS FOR NATION BUILDING

By contrast, in Ghana, with the increasing untenability of state distribution/state patronage and mass social welfare clearly exposed by economic decline, neoliberal reforms, and state contraction, the Rawlings-PNDC regime came to rely primarily on authoritarianism as the strategy of choice for controlling centrifugal pressures and promoting nation building. But growing internal and external pro-democracy pressures in the late 1980s and early 1990s necessitated a review of that strategy, too. Thus, the regime was compelled to prepare the country for a return to civilian constitutional rule, against its own protestations (and those of its supporters) that political liberalization would undermine economic reform and revive societal conflicts. A Constitutional Advisory Committee was appointed to draft proposals for a new Constitution. Its report went to a Consultative Assembly, and the final draft Constitution (providing for a president, a National Assembly elected on a multiparty basis, and a wide range of liberal democratic freedoms and checks on executive power) was approved by popular referendum in April 1992. Presidential elections were held in early November 1992, followed by parliamentary balloting in late December 1992. On 7 January 1993, Ghana launched its Fourth Republic under a liberal constitution, with Rawlings as the elected president and his National Democratic Congress (NDC) as the ruling party.[43]

Like its predecessors, the newly elected Rawlings-NDC government remains committed, at least officially, to nation building. It has been careful to maintain ethno-regional balance in appointments to the cabinet and to the constitutionally designated bodies such as the Council of State, Media Commission, Commission on Human Rights and Administrative Justice, and so on. But as has been the pattern in the past, political liberalization and multiparty electoral competition appeared to have brought ethno-regional, class, and ideological conflicts to the fore of Ghanaian society and economy. The relatively broad-based anti-Rawlings opposition and pro-democracy coalition centered around the Movement for Freedom and Justice splintered into the right-wing New Patriotic Party (NPP) and an assortment of parties claiming an Nkrumah-Convention People's Party heritage. The NPP was mainly regarded as an Akan/Ashanti party, while the NDC was seen as Volta region/Ewe party.

Perhaps the most poignant indication of an ethno-regional character in party political activity at this time is found in the pattern of voting in the presidential elections of 1992. The two leading presidential candidates scored heavily in the regions regarded as home bases. While Rawlings received 93.3 percent of the votes in the Volta region, Adu-Boahen, the candidate for NPP, received 60 percent of the votes in the Ashanti region (his highest score in the entire contest). Hilla Limann, the president from 1979 to 1981 and leader of the Nkrumahist People's National Convention, also received his highest votes in that election in his home area (Upper East and West regions). This pattern of voting, in which Ashanti generally voted anti-Rawlings, and Ewe/Volta region voted pro-Rawlings, was all the more remarkable in view of the fact that the latter region had benefited least from the neoliberal economic reforms and the gains derived therefrom, whereas the former counts among the regions that benefited the most from those reforms.[44]

Indeed, in the months immediately following the elections and installation of the Rawlings-NDC government, a spate of accusations of Ewe hijacking of key or sensitive bureaucratic and political appointments was publicly traded between Akan and Ewe in the state and private media. The atmosphere was further poisoned by the recriminations arising from an alleged Ewe conspiracy revealed in a book whose author, Dr. Kofi Awoonor, is an Ewe himself and a key insider of the regimes of Rawlings. It is instructive to note that this book, published abroad in the mid-1980s, had become widely noticed and discussed within Ghana only after the 1992 elections, the return to constitutional government, and, especially, the relaxation of press controls.[45]

But perhaps the most serious eruption of sectarian conflict in Ghana's young fourth republic was the intercommunal violence between Kokombas and Nanumbas in the Northern region of Ghana in February 1994. Within a few weeks of conflict revolving around Kokomba demands for land and cultural rights and Nanumba counterclaims of "power of eminent domain," over 2,000 lives were lost, several villages were razed to the ground, and thousands of the area's inhabitants were displaced. In March of the following year, the conflict flared up again, and over 100 people were reported to have been killed.

However, there are no indications that ethno-regional tensions and conflicts have continued in the fourth republic. In fact, they have subsided considerably after the short-lived public preoccupation with, and exhaustive discussion of, the ethnic composition of the military, public services, and ruling regime— without official censorship. In addition, the truce arranged between the Kokomba-Nanumba combatants appears to be holding. In general, the leaders of the various parties have been restrained in exploiting the conflict for political advantage, and support for the mediation efforts of the government appears to be genuinely bipartisan. Thus, contemporary Ghanaian experience hardly validates the contention of postcolonial governments, especially the Rawlings-PNDC government, that pluralistic democracy promotes national disintegration.

But if democratization/political liberalization has not necessarily undermined national unity, it has certainly complicated economic development in general and neoliberal economic reforms/structural adjustment in particular. It is true that the elected Rawlings government continues to express a commitment to economic reform. Indeed, it has announced plans to accelerate the privatization of state-owned enterprises, divesting half of its shares in the Ashanti Goldfields Corporation in 1993. But by most conventional measures, economic development in Ghana has suffered a setback since 1992 and since the process of political liberalization and democratization has been under way. Per capita gross domestic product (GDP) has fallen from $447.8 in 1991 to $322.7 in 1994[46]; real GDP (constant 1975 prices) declined from 5.3 percent in 1991 to 3.8 percent in 1994; inflation rose from 18 percent in 1991 to 22.8 percent in 1994; the value of the local currency, the cedi, has fallen from 375 to one U.S. dollar in 1991 to 956 to one U.S. dollar in 1994; and the budget balance has gone from a surplus of U.S. $170 million in 1991 to a deficit of U.S. $322.7 million in 1994. In addition, major public works and infrastructural rehabilitation programs initiated before the return to constitutional rule were suspended after that event for lack of funds.

To be sure, these apparent setbacks in economic renewal may reflect structural problems in the Ghanaian economy, unrelated to any political changes. They may also represent a temporary negative "blip" or, as government spokesmen put it, "a bad patch" in an otherwise upward trend in economic development. But they also reflect the loss of fiscal discipline in the period before the 1992 elections and after, as well as the growing ability of civil society to effectively challenge the austerities entailed in the neoliberal economic reforms. It appears as if political expediency has come to overtake economic management in the context of electoral competition, free expression, and free association. Thus, in response to union and student unrest and to secure the votes of urban workers in the 1992 elections, the Rawlings-PNDC government made across-the-board wage increases of between 70 and 100 percent and annulled a planned increase in petroleum taxes; in direct response to popular pressures, it suspended planned public-sector job retrenchments and increased student allowances in 1993 and 1994; and, more seriously, the value-added tax introduced in the annual budget in 1995 had been withdrawn as a concession to paralyzing labor strikes and violent demonstrations against the measure. Clearly, economic reform has suffered a setback under democratic pluralism. First, the government itself is unable to resist the temptation to raid the national treasury to secure its reelection. Second, the elected Rawlings-NDC government is unable to resort to strong-arm tactics to secure quiescence in the liberalized political setting. Third, civil society (trade unions, student organizations, professional bodies, traders' associations) has gained a greater ability to articulate an opposition to adjustment reforms and to mobilize constituencies in defense of the status quo welfarist/distributionist policies—notwithstanding the unsustainability of such policies.

CÔTE D'IVOIRE: THE BEGINNING OF THE END?

In Côte d'Ivoire, the moderation of authoritarian rule in the 1980s did not succeed in mollifying the opposition movement emerging out of the ranks of those alienated by continuing economic recession and increasing austerity. The Boigny-PDCI regime was compelled to make further concessions to political liberalization and finally to democratization in 1990. With their purchasing power eroded by a decade of structural adjustment and confidence in the regime at a low ebb, students and teachers and other groups in civil society, as well as elements within the ruling elite, were ready to take to the streets and take on the state. A series of strike actions virtually paralyzed the state in 1990, and it was not long before the political system itself started unraveling. A few of the significant actions included the mid-February boycott of classes by university students, ostensibly to protest interruptions to electricity supply that affected their preparations for examinations. On 2 March 1990 schoolchildren took to the streets in support of the university students and to protest alleged corruption by the ruling elite. Security forces dispersed the demonstrators with truncheons, tear gas, and stun grenades. Following several violent clashes, the university and schools in and around Abidjan were closed. Antigovernment demonstrations continued unabated in spite of the crackdown. Physicians and other health workers also withdrew their services but were subsequently ordered to return to work.

On 21 May, the 6,000-strong police force went on strike demanding higher pay and better working conditions. This appeared almost a copycat of the strike by hundreds of armed force conscripts who staged a series of protests nationwide during the previous week. Dozens of police went on joyrides through the streets of Abidjan and barricaded the streets, sealing off the center of the city for several hours. Not to be outdone, about 100 striking firemen drove into the grounds of the presidency and headed for the president's private residence on 22 May. Police apparently looked on unconcerned. Meanwhile, dock, customs, electricity, and post and telecommunications workers all threatened to go on strike unless wage and other demands were met by the end of May.

Worse yet for the president and his government, France, whose military and economic support had been a key factor in the country's long political stability, had come to join the other Western nations and IFI to press for democratization. This change in the attitude of key external patrons to status quo Ivorian domestic politics was signaled in a loud and clear manner on 16 May 1990, when France declined a request to help recapture the Abidjan airport (held for twelve hours by disgruntled air force conscripts) and to restore order elsewhere in the capital. The 1,000-strong French marine infantry based in the vicinity of the airport was placed on alert but refrained from intervening.[47]

Visibly shaken by the apparent repudiation of the system he had so carefully crafted, wanting very much to restore stability, peace, and unity to Côte d'Ivoire, and apparently failing in health, the octogenarian president Houphouët-Boigny began a process of capitulating to the demands of the various strikers that culminated in the surprise announcement of 3 May 1990 legalizing opposition parties and setting a date for multiparty elections. This was intended, in part, to catch the opposition napping and to ensure the reelection of the president and the PDCI.

Notwithstanding continued dominance of the Boigny-PDCI regime over Ivorian politics and public administration (winning the multiparty presidential elections of 1990 and 1995) and the marginal presence of opposition parties in the National Assembly, democratization has resulted in the opening up of the political system. Over 40 opposition parties have emerged (with the *Front Populaire Ivorien* [PFI], the *Parti Ivoirien des Travailleurs* [PIT], and the *Union des Sociaux-Democrates* [USD] as the main ones), and they have been boisterously vocal in their efforts to influence government policies through newspaper articles in the vibrant private media, their interventions in the National Assembly, street demonstrations to dramatize their concerns about particular political problems, and organizing and mobilizing women, the youth, and other interests to confront state power. In addition, there has been a flowering of civil society—as reflected in the disaffiliation of key unions from the PDCI-controlled federation of trade unions (UGTCI) and the formation of 63 associations in 1991 alone (constituting 32 percent of all associations).[48]

On the face of it, democratization in Côte d'Ivoire has brought at least a mild surge in ethnocultural sectarianism in the politics of that country. The leading contenders for political power have appeared to play an ethno-regional and religious card. Thus, Prime Minister Alasane Ouattara's attempts to succeed Houphouët-Boigny as president in late 1993 and to contest the presidential elections in 1995 were generally perceived and portrayed as a Northern-Muslim bid to challenge Southern-Akan dominance in Ivorian politics. His detractors have alleged that he was linked to the ''Northern Charter'' group of politicians who favored separation of the north from Côte d'Ivoire. As supporting evidence for his ethno-regional ambitions, they point to the promise he made to the Muslim community that he would release land in fashionable Plateau for the construction of a mosque as well as his decision to declare the period between the twenty-sixth and twenty-seventh days of the Islamic Ramadan as a public holiday.[49] Fearing his potential electoral draw, President Bédié has strongly disputed Ouattara's nationality on the ground that his father is originally from Burkina Faso; not wanting to take any chances, he crafted a controversial electoral law requiring five years of continuous residency, which served to disqualify Ouattara from the elections of October 1995. However, a commitment to national unity in the era of political liberalization, which is indicated by the continued practice of working a rough ethnic arithmetic into the composition of the cabinet, has also been maintained. Thus, the most recent post-Houphouët cabinet headed by Prime Minister Daniel Kablan Duncan reflected this ethnic balancing or ethnic arithmetic. This 24-member ''cabinet of continuity'' consisted of thirteen Akan, four Bété, and five Northerners, including three Muslims.

But the opening up of the Ivorian political system has posed a serious challenge to economic restructuring in that country. On one hand, the Bédié-PDCI regime remains committed to economic restructuring and to turning the country into a regional economic powerhouse.[50] The passage of a law opening up the telecommunication sector for competition in July 1994 and other measures to privatize state-owned enterprises and monopolies provide an indication of a commitment to pursue neoliberal strategies of economic reform. On the other hand, the proliferation of unions has led to an unprecedented increase in wildcat strikes,[51] which gives the appearance that political stability has gradually given way to the appearance of political disorder.

SOME INTRIGUING CONTINUITIES AND DISCONTINUITIES

In Côte d'Ivoire, the Akan, especially the Baoule, have been overrepresented among the political elite. The dominant political figure, Felix Houphouët-Boigny, who exercised uninterrupted political control until the formal announcement of his passing on 7 December 1993, was Baoule. Moreover, the baton of head of state has since been passed on to his dauphin, another Baoule, Henri Konan Bédié. By contrast, because of its comparatively unstable political situation, the Akan of Ghana have not enjoyed the same monopoly of power. Arguably, Akan dominance of the political system extends from Nkrumah to

Acheampong/Akuffo regimes, or roughly the first half of the postindependence period. Since then, power has been ceded to Flight Lieutenant J. J. Rawlings, who, in turn, has been perceived as ushering in Ewe predominance in government. In other words, whereas the Akan, or, more precisely the Baoule, are still in control of the political system in Côte d'Ivoire, the Akan or Ashanti have witnessed a diminution of their political fortunes in Ghana. Also in terms of ethno-regional rivalry or conflict, both countries have produced some surprises. The chief rivals of the Baoule and the Ashanti have been the Bété and the Ewe, respectively, rather than a coalition of northerners against southerners. Both the Bété and the Ewe have been accused of fomenting dissent right from the early days of independence. There is also an interesting recent twist in that with the Ewe in control in Ghana, the lightning rod of the opposition is an Ashanti, Professor Adu Boahen. In Abidjan, the chief opposition leader, Laurent Gbagbo, is a Bété. Curiously, both men are former history professors from their respective national universities.

The classic fault lines are ethno-regional-religious, between an underdeveloped north, which is Voltaic and Mandé and Muslim, and a relatively affluent south, which is Akan and Christian and social class, between a vast rural and agrarian rural population and a small, urban elite. The urban populations and the political systems of the two countries have been dominated by a politico-bureaucratic class that, at least in the case of Côte d'Ivoire, has used its privileged access to the state to accumulate wealth and to reinvest some of that wealth into business ventures, especially real estate and nontraditional, high-yield horticultural crops such as pineapples.

Thus, ethnic rivalry/competition is a potential source of conflict in both countries, although governments in both countries have been reasonably successful in managing it through a mixture of co-optation and balancing, with the occasional stick thrown in. Ethnic rivalry provides a persistent undercurrent of political gossip and factionalism, which is not officially acknowledged, particularly in Côte d'Ivoire, but nevertheless forms the basis of leadership calculations. In the case of Côte d'Ivoire, ethnic balancing is rather more formal. President Houphouët-Boigny was apparently determined not to appoint any ethnic "barons," anybody who might pose a threat by mobilizing a large ethnic following. Thus, ethnic mobilization was kept low, while the reality of its potential dangers was recognized.[52] Again, the principle of ethnic and regional balancing was even adhered to by President Bédié in his first post-Houphouët cabinet appointments. Of course, ethno-regional representativeness was not the only decision-making calculation. Some ministers were chosen for their loyalty or services rendered.

As indicated earlier, both countries share a rough coincidence of ethnicity and administrative region, though each region is also home to a sizable number of "strangers." For instance, there has been considerable movement of peoples from the savanna regions of the north to the forest zones of the south over the years in search of employment and a better standard of living. In both countries, the north-south migratory flows are emblematic of the ethno-regional inequities

that earlier colonial patterns of development nurtured by leaving the north relatively underdeveloped while concentrating most infrastructural and productive
projects in the south. In the south itself, Akan from Côte d'Ivoire have migrated
westward into Krou country in search of land to exploit for plantation agriculture, while northers have migrated southward to work in cocoa, coffee, oil palm,
rubber, banana, and pineapple plantations in the south and also in search of
factory and service jobs. There are pockets of Djuula and Akan in Senoufo
territory as well. In Ghana, the Ashanti, Brong Ahafo, Eastern, Central, and
Western regions are generally settled by Akan, with considerable intra-Akan
migration in search of land for cocoa farming and jobs in the gold mines. Similar
to the situation in Côte d'Ivoire, there is an important development gap between
the underdeveloped north and the more affluent southern half of the country.
Superimposed over the considerable ethnic rivalries in both countries, a by-
product of these historical developments, are additional conflicts between the
populist and elitist strands in the Ghanaian society and polity versus genera-
tional/ideological and succession conflicts in Côte d'Ivoire.

SUMMARY AND CONCLUSION

As multiethnic/multicultural countries, nation building has been very high on
the agenda of the governments of postcolonial Ghana and Côte d'Ivoire. It has
been a driving factor and/or provided an excuse for the adoption of statist strategies of economic development and authoritarian modes of governance. Statist
(socialist in the case of Ghana and capitalist in the case of Côte d'Ivoire) economic policies facilitated welfarist/distributionist programs that had been so important for securing the loyalties of, and political quiescence from, the diverse
ethno-regional and other politically salient societal groups; authoritarian rule
provided governments in both countries with the coercive instruments for keeping social conflicts under control.

This strategy of nation building via economic distribution worked reasonably
well in both Ghana and Côte d'Ivoire, especially in the periods of relative economic growth and steady expansion of the state sector (1960 to 1980). It had
become largely untenable in the late 1970s and early 1980s in the prevailing
conditions of economic decline, neoliberal economic reforms, and, especially,
the contraction of state. At the same time, the externally and internally driven
pressures for political liberalization and democratization in the early 1990s have
imposed restrictions on the use of authoritarian modes of political management.
These pressures have led to the liberalization of authoritarian rule and an end
to quasi-military and single-party rule in both countries.

In both Ghana and Côte d'Ivoire, there is at least superficial evidence of a
surge in ethno-regional and other social tensions in the new political era. The
competing political groups have found themselves unable to resist playing the
"sectarian card," and voting patterns have followed at least mildly ethno-
regional lines. However, in both countries, politicians have been sensitive to the

ethno-regional issues and have tried to balance the representation of the various societal groups in their cabinets and other key political and administrative positions.

While democratization and political liberalization do not appear to pose a direct threat to nation building in the two countries, they do present a challenge to economic reform, which, in turn, could undermine nation building. In both Ghana and Côte d'Ivoire, the opening up of the political systems and the relaxation of controls on civil society have brought opposition to economic reform into the open, though incumbent regimes remain committed to such reforms. Thus, Ghana and Côte d'Ivoire, like other African countries, continue to face the crucial challenge of how to combine sound and sustainable economic development with democratic governance and thereby build a solid basis for nation building.

NOTES

1. For details, see Dennis Austin, *Politics in Ghana, 1946–1960* (London: Oxford University Press, 1964).

2. A discussion of the distributionist and welfarist emphasis in the economic programs of successive Ghanaian regimes before the neoliberal reforms is found in M. M. Huq, *The Political Economy of Ghana, the First 25 Years* (London: Macmillan, 1989); see also Tony Killick, *Development Economics in Action* (London: Heinemann, 1978); David Rooney, *Kwame Nkrumah: The Political Kingdom and the Third World* (New York: St. Martin's Press, 1988); Roger Genoud, *Nationalism and Economic Development in Ghana* (New York: Praeger, 1969).

3. See Killick, *Development Economics in Action*.

4. The emergence of radical, urban-based opposition to the Ghanaian establishment in the late 1970s and early 1980s, giving rise to a wave of populism and populist coups in Ghana, is discussed in Eboe Hutchful, "New Elements in Militarism: Ethiopia, Ghana and Burkina," *International Journal* 1, no. 4 (1986): xi; also Donald Rothchild and E. Gyimah-Boadi, "Populism in Ghana and Burkina Faso," *Current History* 88, no. 538 (May 1989): 221–24, 241–46.

5. For details see Rothchild and Gyimah-Boadi, "Populism in Ghana and Burkina Faso"; Donald Ray, *Ghana: Politics, Economics and Society* (Boulder, CO: Lynne Rienner, 1986).

6. Huq, *The Political Economy of Ghana*.

7. For a detailed summary of statist economic development strategies in postcolonial Ghana, see J. Frimpong Ansah, *The Vampire State in Africa: The Political Economy of Decline* (Trenton, NJ: Africa World Press, 1992).

8. The political logic underlying the tendencies of African/Ghanaian governments to intervene in internal markets is analyzed in Robert Bates, *Markets and States in Tropical Africa* (Berkeley: University of California Press, 1981).

9. See Bates, *Markets and States in Tropical Africa*; Robert M. Price, "Neo-Colonialism and Ghana's Economic Decline: A Critical Assessment," *Canadian Journal of African Studies* 18, no. 1 (1984): 163–93; James Ahiakpor, "The Success and Failure

of Dependency Theory: The Experience of Ghana," *International Organization* 35 (1985): 532–55.

10. For an elaboration on this point, see Ansah, *The Vampire State in Africa.*

11. See C. Vidal, "Côte d'Ivoire: Funérailles Présidentielles et Dévaluation entre Décembre 1993 et Mars 1994," in Centre d'Etude d'Afrique Noire (CEAN), *L'Afrique politique 1995: Le Meilleur, Le Pire et L'Incertain* (Paris: Karthala, 1995), 31–46.

12. For more on this, see Cyril Kofie Daddieh, "Ivory Coast," in Timothy M. Shaw and Olajide Aluko, eds., *The Political Economy of African Foreign Policy: Comparative Analysis* (New York: St. Martin's Press, 1984), 122–44.

13. Samir Amin, *Neo-Colonialism in West Africa* (New York: Monthly Review Press, 1973), 50–51; see also his "Capitalism and Development in the Ivory Coast," in J. L. Markovitz, ed., *African Politics and Society* (New York: Free Press, 1970), 277–88.

14. Alex G. Rondos, "The Price of Development," *Africa Report* 24, no. 2 (March–April 1979): 4–9.

15. For more on generational conflicts in Côte d'Ivoire, see Aristide Zolberg, "Political Generations in Conflict: The Ivory Coast Case," in William J. Hanna et al., *University Students and African Politics* (New York and London: Africana, 1975, 103–33.

16. See John Barratt, "The Ivory Coast: A General Profile and Policy toward South Africa," *South African Institute of International Affairs (SAIIA) Newsletter* 8, no. 1 (April 1976): 18.

17. For more on this, see Robert E. Handloff, ed., *Côte d'Ivoire: A Country Study* (Washington, DC: Federal Research Division, Library of Congress, 1991).

18. For details, see Daddieh, "Ivory Coast."

19. For a testimonial, see Félix Houphouët-Boigny, "Black Africa and the French Union," *Foreign Affairs* 35, no. 4 (July 1957): 593–99.

20. Handloff, *Côte d'Ivoire*, 26.

21. See Handloff, *Côte d'Ivoire*, 168.

22. For more on this issue, see Dwayne Woods, "Ethnicity, Class and 'Hometown' Associations in the Côte d'Ivoire: A Critical Examination of State-Society Links in the Post-Colonial Period." Unpublished manuscript.

23. For more on Ivorian agricultural policies and peasant responsiveness, see Cyril K. Daddieh, "Food and Agricultural Strategies and Popular Responses in Côte d'Ivoire," in Naomi Chazan and Timothy M. Shaw, eds., *Coping with Africa's Food Crisis* (Boulder, CO, and London: Lynne Rienner, 1988), 119–43.

24. The leadership style and conflict management strategies of the president are elaborated in Cyril Kofie Daddieh, "The Management of Educational Crises in Côte d'Ivoire," *The Journal of Modern African Studies* 26, no. 4 (1988): 639–59.

25. For more on this, see Tessy Bakary, "Elite Transformation and Political Succession," in I. William Zartman and Christopher Delgado, eds., *The Political Economy of Ivory Coast* (New York: Praeger, 1984), 38–46; see also Richard C. Crook, "Patrimonialism, Administrative Effectiveness and Economic Development in Côte d'Ivoire," *African Affairs* 88, no. 351 (April 1989): 205–28.

26. Bakary, "Elite Transformation," 45.

27. Crook, "Patrimonialism, Administrative Effectiveness," 207–10.

28. For more on this, see Richard E. Stryker, "A Local Perspective on Developmental Strategy in the Ivory Coast," in Michael F. Lofchie, ed., *The State of the Nations: Constraints on Development in Independent Africa* (Berkeley: University of California Press, 1971), 130.

29. Daddieh, "The Management of Educational Crises."

30. Handloff, Côte d'Ivoire, 28.

31. For details, see Gerald Bourke, "A Tarnished Miracle," Africa Report 32, no. 6 (November–December 1987): 62–64; also George McFarlane, "Hard Times for an African Success Story," Africa Report 29, no. 2 (March–April 1984): 20–23.

32. This is the thrust of the arguments advanced by Jacob Songsore in "The Economic Recovery Program/Structural Adjustment and the 'Distant' Rural Poor in Northern Ghana," paper presented at the International Conference on Planning for Growth and Development in Africa, ISSER, University of Ghana, 13–17 March 1989 (mimeo).

33. See UNICEF, Ghana: Adjustment Policies and Programs to Protect Children and Other Vulnerable Groups (Accra: UNICEF, November 1986).

34. We are grateful to Kwasi Anyemadu of the Economics Department of the University of Ghana for pointing this out to us.

35. For a useful discussion of "slippages" and the penalties attached to them, see John Toye, "Ghana's Economic Reforms and World Bank Policy-Conditioned Lending, 1983–1988," paper presented at a conference on Politics and Structural Adjustment, Institute of Development Studies, Brighton, Sussex, 1989.

36. For details of PNDC-era repression and authoritarianism, see E. Gyimah-Boadi, "Economic Recovery and Politics in the PNDC's Ghana," Journal of Commonwealth and Comparative Politics 27, no. 3 (1990): 328–43; also Mike Oquaye, "Law, Justice and the Revolution," in E. Gyimah-Boadi, ed., Ghana under PNDC Rule (Dakar: Codesria Books, 1993), 154–75, and "The Ghanaian Elections—A Dissenting View," African Affairs 94 (1995): 259–75.

37. See E. Gyimah-Boadi, "Economic Recovery and Politics."

38. Albert Adu Boahen, The Ghanaian Sphinx: Reflections on the Contemporary History of Ghana, 1972–1987 (Accra: Ghana Academy of Arts and Sciences, 1989), 53.

39. Joseph Y. Yao, "Impact de l'Environment National et International sur le Processus de Prise de Decision et la democratisation en Côte d'Ivoire: Document Preparatoire sur le developpement humain en Côte d'Ivoire, 1992 PNUD" (Mimeograph, 1992).

40. African Economic Digest (1990): 6.

41. Cyril K. Daddieh, "The Political Economy of Student Political Activism in Côte d'Ivoire, 1980 and Beyond: A Decade like No Other Decade?" paper presented to the African Studies Association Annual Meeting, Seattle, 20–23 November 1992; also Daddieh, "The Management of Educational Crises in Côte d'Ivoire."

42. Handloff, Côte d'Ivoire; also Daddieh, "The Political Economy of Student Political Activism."

43. For details, see E. Gyimah-Boadi, "Ghana's Return to Civilian Rule," Africa Today 28 (1991): 3–16; also "Ghana's Uncertain Political Opening," Journal of Democracy 5, no. 2 (1994): 75–86.

44. Colonel Osei-Wusu, a minister in the Rawlings-NDC government, was to publicly accuse Ashanti of "ingratitude" for their display of defiance and for not voting for Rawlings.

45. See various issues of the state and private newspapers in the first half of 1993, especially "Anlo Tribalism, a Threat to the Heritage—A Rejoinder," Ghanaian Times, 17 and 18 June 1993; "Who Was Who and Who Is Who in the Armed Forces," Ghanaian Chronicle, 7–13 June 1993, in which contending claims of Ewe domination are discussed. Kofi Awoonor's book, The Ghana Revolution: Background Account from a

Personal Perspective (New York: Oases, 1984), had been a lightning rod for these public recriminations.

46. Macroeconomic data cited in this section are taken from Government of Ghana, Government of Ghana, *Ghana: The New Gateway to Africa* (Accra: Ministry of Information, 1995).

47. *African Economic Digest* (1990): 12.

48. For a useful discussion of this phenomenon in Côte d'Ivoire, see Jennifer A. Widner, "The Rise of Civic Associations among Farmers in Côte d'Ivoire," in John Harbeson, Donald Rothchild, and Naomi Chazan, eds., *Civil Society and the State in Africa* (Boulder, CO: Lynne Rienner, 1994), 191–215.

49. C. Vidal, "Côte d'Ivoire: Funérailles Présidentielles et Dévaluation entre Décembre 1993 et Mars 1994," in CEAN, *L'Afrique politique* 1995 (Paris: Karthala, 1995), 31–46.

50. See Howard French, "Africa's Ballet Box: Look for Sleight of Hand," *New York Times*, 24 October 1995, 3.

51. Yao, "Impact de l'Environment National et International," mimeo.

52. See Crook, "Patrimonialism, Administrative Effectiveness," 213.

Chapter 7

Ethnicity and Democratization in Congo and Chad (1945–1995)

MARIO J. AZEVEDO

INTRODUCTION

As the process toward multiparty democracy takes hold in Africa, many social scientists fear that ethnicity will pose a major threat to its success. They point out, often without much convincing evidence, that the multiparty elections that have been held in Africa during this decade, Kenya being a perfect example, have been primarily informed by strong ethnic loyalties that adequately explain why some candidates have lost and why some others have won. Although as a generalization this position appears credible on the surface, on close examination, it is untenable, as it is challenged by events in Cape Vert, Zambia, Malawi, and, to a large extent, Equatorial Africa, in such countries as Gabon, Cameroon, and Central African Republic. The problem here lies in the fact that, while democracy seems to be more definable, ethnicity is an elusive concept whose impact is extremely difficult to measure, particularly when it is intertwined with other factors such as regionalism, as is the case in the Congo, and religion-cum-regionalism, as the Chadian situation illustrates vividly.

This chapter analyzes the evolution of democratic institutions in the Congo, drawing parallels with Chad and paying particular attention to the role of ethnicity. It argues that, at present, ethnicity has not been the major obstacle to multiparty democracy. Regionalism, which has left many areas underdeveloped, unchecked personal ambitions, and economic insecurity have been much more important than ethnic loyalties in the Congo. In Chad, on the contrary, regionalism and religious differences, civil war, and a past of enslavement and raids have been so interwoven that it is difficult to sort out the major culprit preventing rapid changes and the establishment of democratic institutions. I argue that, unlike Chad, the Congo has been able to move forward toward multiparty institutions due, in part, to the army's cautious approach to politics and governance and to the prominent role played by the labor movement.

Essentially, democracy is a political construct through which people play an active role in those important decisions that affect their lives, guiding themselves "only by the rules they themselves freely chose."[1] As such, democracy can manifest itself in varying ways and degrees, although at present Africa is desperately attempting to emulate the democratic institutions now firmly established and entrenched in the traditions of the West. Taking inspiration from the West does not, however, negate that Africans had devised and followed some democratic institutions and processes in their distant past, nor does it mean that Western capitalist democracy is perfect, as Francis Fukuyama seems to imply.[2] It simply means that Africans have been unable to devise a better system and that they accept the premise that, for the present, the Western model seems to be working relatively well.

The phenomenon of ethnicity or "tribal affiliation," on the other hand, surfaces as a problem among social scientists primarily when dealing with the problems of developing societies, particularly Africa, and is seen as a major obstacle against the process toward democratization there. More recently, however, events in Eastern Europe have demonstrated that "tribalism," to use the now almost defunct term among Africanists, is not confined to Africa and has been dormant all along only in the so-called civilized nations of Europe. It would appear, however, that ethnicity is not necessarily the evil that has slowed down the advance of human rights and political participation in Africa. Indeed, ethnicity becomes a hindrance to statehood and mass political participation only when it is exclusivist and attempts to ascribe to one or more select ethnic groups the country's resources. In this sense, ethnicity becomes "ethnicism" or, to use the old term, "tribalism." Ethnicity is primarily a sense of belonging and loyalty to one's extended and remote kin, based on several factors such as shared territory, history, mythical origins, often religion, and, more importantly, language. Ethnicity can be channeled to build individual identity and pride as a foundation for an entity higher than the ethnic group itself, namely, the state (nation). Thus, the concepts of ethnicity and nation are not necessarily exclusive of each other but, if handled properly, can complement each other and enhance the democratic process. In the words of one expert, "The ethnic group constitutes a form of integration less advanced than that of the nation. . . . This perception does not, however, postulate a necessary evolution from one to the other. Yet, it indicates that ethnic identification and nation are not necessarily antithetic to one another."[3] In other words, it is possible to have a nation of only one ethnic group such as France and one made up of several ethnic groups such as Belgium and the United States.

Complementarity does not, however, imply that ethnic groups do not present a major challenge to nation building, economic development, and the success of true democratic reforms in Africa. Indeed, the more ethnic groups a country has, particularly if the size of some is disproportionately larger than that of others, the more likely it will be affected adversely by ethnic divisiveness and strife, making the democratic experiment problematic. When, for reasons of trade and imperial strategy,[4] the French entered Equatorial Africa during the 1880s, they encountered in Chad over 200 ethnic groups, while in the Congo, they faced essentially three or five clearly distinct ethnic groups. Both the Congo and Chad became part of French Equatorial Africa in 1910, along with Oubangui-Chari (now Central African Republic) and Gabon (and East Cameroon after 1916).

With a population of close to 2 million people at present, Congo's Kongo or Bakongo people account for 45 percent of the population, are the overwhelming majority, live in the south, as well as along the coast, and are subdivided into several classes such as the Vili, who inhabit most of Pointe-Noire on the coast, and the Lari, who dominate Brazzaville.[5] The Bakongo are said to be more homogeneous, enterprising, aggressive, like the Fang of Gabon, and assertive and have taken advantage of the opportunities offered by the French, although they never acquiesced to colonial rule. In fact, they consistently resisted by the force of arms and otherwise, as was the case with the religious and liberation Messianic movements of Andre Matsoua's *Société Amicale des Originaires de l'Afrique Equatoriale Française*, founded in Paris in 1926, and the Kimbanguism of Simon Kimbangou.

As a result of the opportunities offered by colonialism, the Bakongo became urbanized faster than the other ethnic groups (22 percent of them living in the cities by 1960), while the remainder lived in compact farming villages cultivating some cash crops, which included tobacco and palm oil, along with fruit and cassava. Their suspicion of Christianity notwithstanding, the Bakongo availed themselves of the education Catholic and Protestant missionaries (particularly Swedish evangelists) have offered in their areas since the 1880s. Because of their distrust of any colonial innovations and their attempt to preserve their own traditions and pride, they did not exert as much political influence as their numbers would have suggested during the 1940s and 1950s: they participated lukewarmly in the political reforms brought about by Charles de Gaulle that ended forced labor in the French empire in 1946 and by the *Loi Cadre* of 1956 abolishing the dual college.[6]

The Teke or Bateke, constituting about 26 percent of the population, live in the center, in Pool, along the Lefini rivers, north of Brazzaville, and in the region of Alima-Lefini, Lefini Prefecture. The third group, about 20 percent of the total Congolese population, is made up of the less homogeneous Mbochi-Kouyou, who live in the Alima region and are dispersed throughout the Likouala-Mossaka Prefecture. The Mbochi constitute the majority within this ethnic group. Small numbers of the Mbochi were Christianized as far back as 1900, but the majority strongly resented interference by the Europeans, but not to the extent of the Tubu in Chad. Strongly jealous of their traditions, they fought both colonizer and missionary and were therefore not as much affected by colonialism as the Bakongo, and their region remained less developed. This has prompted Virginia

Thompson and Richard Adloff to unfortunately label them, as recently as 1984, as "isolated and primitive" in their northern village habitat.[7] The last discernible group consists largely of the Mbeti and the Batoka, whose majority live in Gabon, sometimes classified as Pahouin, of whom the Fang of Gabon are an offshoot. Finally, one encounters perhaps the oldest inhabitants of the entire area, who are now dispersed in the five prefectures of Lefini, Alima, Likouala-Mossaka, Likouala, and Sanga—namely, the Babinga, pejoratively known in the past as Pygmies.

In Chad, the ethnic diversity is much greater. With a population of some 5.5 million, Chad comprises 200 ethnic groups, sharply divided by region, religion, and lifestyle and by an antagonist history that preceded the colonial era. While the north has for centuries been arid and poor in resources, except in livestock (camels, horses, donkeys, goats, sheep), the south is more naturally endowed (with crops such as millet, corn, cassava, and peanuts). Whereas northerners tend to be pastoral and semisedentary, southerners have for centuries remained sedentary farmers. The French, as a result, concentrated their attention on the south, *le Tchad-utile* (useful Chad), where they introduced cotton cultivation, rubber collection, and some timber cutting during the 1920s.

The seasonal slave raids and slavery carried out by the northern states, especially Kanem-Bornu, Baguirmi, and Wadai (inhabited by the Tubu, the Arabs, the Barma, the Maba, the Hadjerai, the Kotoko, the Massalit, and a myriad of others), most of which had embraced Islam by the sixteenth century, created a cleavage between them and the peoples of what became Southern Chad, namely, the Sara, Moundang, Massa, Tupuri, Mboum, Laka, Kabalaye, Gabri, Gam, Somrai, Moussa, Marba, Muluri, and many others.[8] In Chad, French presence and colonial policies reinforced, rather than mitigated, the differences between the *Dar-al-Abid* (the land of slaves) and the *Dar-al-Islam* (the land of Islam).[9] However, the contest for resources and power following the introduction of colonialism pitted mostly the Sara of Chad, who constitute about 30 percent of the population, against northerners, particularly the Tubu of Biltine-Ennedi-Tibesti (BET), the Arabs who are scattered throughout the Sahara and the Sahel and make up between 22 and 40 percent of the population, the Barmi of Baguirmi, and the various ethnic groups living in Wadai.

Although the Sara, in a sense, benefited from colonial education and infrastructural development, they suffered most because they served as the sole providers of military service, forced labor recruitment, porterage, concessionaires' manpower needs, and cotton cultivation only because the French considered them less "civilized," "more docile," and more suited to demanding physical tasks.[10] The north was left practically intact politically as long as it paid taxes and allowed free access to French colonial agents and the military. As a result, more disruption of family life and traditions as well as more resistance against the colonial presence occurred in the south than in the north once the colony had been pacified during the 1920s.[11]

The way these various populations interfaced with colonialism greatly affected their present status in the country, their political strength, and how they have viewed one another over the past century. Whereas the Bakongo rose prominently in the colony and were more literate than the rest of the ethnic groupings in the Congo, they faced a strong challenge for political control from the Mbochi and the rest of the Congolese population. Because their habitat was closer to the ocean and therefore more accessible and more productive, it received the bulk of the available developmental resources, making it the more industrialized and the more agriculturally productive region of the entire country. Had they, indeed, been more receptive to colonial overtures as the Sara of Chad, for example, the Bakongo would have easily controlled postcolonial Congo without paying much attention to the Mbochi and the Bateke. The Sara, on the contrary, came out as the natural inheritors of the colonial state, as the Muslim north rejected French education, which they saw more fit for their slaves than for their sons, calling it "cultural contamination"[12] by "Christian pigs."

Although French colonial policies were not specifically and intentionally designed to target the Bakongo as the favorite ethnic group, as the Northern Chadians were, the end result of the development of their region at the expense of the other regions, particularly the north, was, for a long time, the predominance of the Bakongo in the political and social life of colonial and postcolonial Congo. It would seem, therefore, that, in the Congo, as in Chad, resentment over disparity in regional development carried out by the French was as strong a factor in the polarization of the colony during the 1950s and later as traditional ethnic differentiations and antagonisms were. Yet, unlike in Chad, where the Sara remained practically the sole bearers of the colonial burden but nevertheless inherited the colonial state, in the Congo, the colonial yoke of forced labor, for example, was more evenly divided, and thus, when the end of colonialism was in sight, ethnic groups here were able to share more evenly the political spoils of colonial legacy.

COLONIAL POLITICAL REFORMS (1945–1960)

The political conditions in colonial Congo and Chad were shaped as much by the nature of the colonial reforms enacted after 1944 as by the traditional ethnic differences exploited by the colonial administration. Indeed, regionalism, which at times cut across ethnic boundaries, as was the case in Northern Congo, became one of the major obstacles to democratic institutions and governance in the Congo, as it did in Chad. In Chad, however, the intrusion of aggressive Islam and the memories of a painful past of slavery and enslavement complicated the situation. All these factors were reflected in local and territorial politics after 1945, particularly after 1956. Although unintended, the *Loi Cadre* of 1956 favored the major ethnic groups, as it instituted no measures to protect the minorities.

From 1945 to 1961, particularly after 1956, three parties dominated the Congolese political arena. The contest for party formation was fueled by colonial representation in the French Constituent Assemblies after World War II, the National Assembly in Paris, the French Senate, the Colonial Territorial Assembly, and the *Conseil de Gouvernement* (a protoexecutive colonial body). One of the first African political parties to emerge in the Congo in 1946 was the *Parti Progressiste Congolais* (PPC), a local affiliate of Félix Houphouët-Boigny's *Rassemblement Démocratique Africain* (RDA). One of the founders of the PPC was Jean-Félix Tchikaya, a Bakongo Vili (of Pointe-Noire and Niari regions), a leader from the extreme west of the colony but born in Libreville in 1903, who nevertheless exerted considerable influence in Brazzaville and Pointe-Noire. Educated at the *Ecole Supérieure* William Ponty at Dakar, Tchikaya was the first African to be elected to territorial and national legislative posts in the post-1945 period.[13]

The Mbochi forwarded their own rival candidate, Jacques Opangault, from Ikanga (Ewo District), described by Thompson and Adloff as ''a minor African official in the judicial service,'' representing the interests of the north and those of people living in the Brazzaville suburb of Poto Poto. With European support, he united in 1946 the local branches of the *Section Française de l'Internationale Ouvrière* (SFIO), known in 1957 as the *Mouvement Socialiste Africain* (MSA). Although the Europeans ran the *Union Démocratique et Socialiste de la Résistance* (UDSR) and the *Rassemblement du Peuple Français* (RPF), and the Africans created such other parties as the *Union Démocratique Pour la Defense des Intérêts Africains* (UDDIA) in 1956, the *Mouvement d'Emancipation Sociale de l'Afrique* (MESAN) in the early 1950s, the *Front Démocratique Congolais* (1955), the *Parti Socialiste Démocratique Congolais* (PSDC) (Mbochi-based), and the *Parti Démocratique de l'Indépendance* (1958), only the PPC (Bakongo-based), the MSA, and the UDDIA of Bakongo Père Fulbert Youlou influenced politics in Congo between 1956 and 1960.

Indeed, the most spectacular occurrence on the Congolese political scene prior to independence was the emergence of Youlou, a Balali or Lari Bakongo. Born in Libreville in 1917, Youlou studied at the Major Seminaries at Yaounde, Cameroon, and on the M'Bamou Island near Brazzaville and was ordained a Catholic priest on 9 June 1949. Despite his vows, Youlou entered politics in January 1956 and founded his UDDIA on 29 May 1956, becoming the most formidable rival of the PPC and the MSA. After losing the 2 January 1956 territorial assembly elections by a narrow margin—31 percent for Tchikaya, 29.1 percent for Opangault, and 27.6 percent for Youlou—Youlou rose to leadership faster than any other political leader in the colony.

At this point, the distribution of the vote gives little credence to the theories of overwhelming ethnic voting in Africa. In the 1946 National Assembly elections, the PPC received 46 percent of the vote, while the SFIO garnered 28 percent. The rest of the votes were shared by the other less influential parties. In the 1947 local assembly elections, the PPC won 15 seats, and the SFIO 9, while in the 1951 local assembly elections, Tchikaya's PPC captured 44 percent of the votes, and Opangault's SFIO took 25 percent. The 1952 contest, on the other hand, resulted in 34 percent of the vote going to the PPC, and 30 percent to the SFIO.[14] In 1956, following the appearance of Youlou, the municipal elections showed how strong the UDDIA had already become on the political landscape: the UDDIA: 20,907 votes (23 seats), the SFIO, 12,167 (11 seats), and the PPC, 2,478 (3 seats). In Pointe-Noire, for example, the stronghold of the PPC, Tchikaya secured only 8 seats, while the UDDIA and the SFIO, which had coalesced for the elections, gained 22 seats. On 18 November, Youlou became mayor of Brazzaville, the most important elective local office at the time, in a landslide victory, and Stephane Tchichelle, an independent Vili, about whose affiliation people were unsure, received support from the UDDIA to win the mayoral seat at Pointe-Noire.

Future contests continued to show the strength of the UDDIA and that of the MSA and the decline of the PPC and the European parties. In the 1957 elections for the 45 Territorial Assembly seats, for example, both the UDDIA and the MSA secured seventeen seats each, the SFIO two, and the PPC two, the remainder having gone to insignificant European parties. Although several of these parties coalesced, particularly the MSA and the PPC against the UDDIA, and Opangault's MSA formed a short-lived government in 1958, the earlier allies worked in greater harmony. Notwithstanding the coalitions, Youlou's party managed to overshadow every other political organization. Thus, in the June 1958 elections, the UDDIA received 64 percent of the vote and took 51 of the 61 assembly seats, indeed, transcending ethnic boundaries. This allowed Youlou to form his own government on 8 December 1958 and assume, in 1959, the presidency of the Republic of the Congo (within the French Community), proclaimed earlier in November 1958.

In Chad, a plethora of some 40 parties, some conservative, some progressive, some socialist, some militant, and others purely local and parochial in goals, appeared during the post-1945 period. However, just as in Congo, the most heated political contest occurred among three or four parties, ending with the uncontested, lopsided victory of one of them.[15] In Chad, the situation was complicated by the presence of an active and aggressive expatriate population that, until 1956, had been strengthened by the double college. During the 1940s and 1950s, the most influential parties in Chad were the *Union Démocratique Tchadienne* (UDT), founded in 1946 by prominent Muslims, including Moundang chief of Mayo-Kebbi, Gountchome Sahoulba. As the first African party, it appealed to traditional authorities and conservatives from both north and south and often allied itself with the European parties, the *Union Démocratique Indépendante du Tchad* (UDIT) (1953), the *Union Démocratique et Socialiste de Résistance* (UDSR), the *Union Républicaine du Tchad* (URT), and the *Rassemblement du Peuple Français* (RPF) (1947). From 1953 on, the UDT was superseded by its offshoot, the *Action Socialiste Tchadienne* (AST), and enjoyed the membership of well-known politicians beyond Sahoulba, such as Bechi Sow, Ahmed Koulamallah, and Ahmed Kotoko, and was popular in Logone, Mayo-Kebby, Wadai, Batha, and Chari-Baguirmi. (A southern-based party but with much support in the north was the *Parti Progressiste Tchadien* [PPT], founded in 1946.)

The (UDSR), founded in 1946, was the first European party in Chad and succeeded in sending the first (European) deputies—Malbrant and Borssoudi—to the French National Assembly. It later merged with the Gaullist (RPF) in 1947, enjoying much support from Sara veterans of the two world wars. The AST had its own offshoot in 1956, called the *Grouppement des Indépendants et Ruraux Tchadiens* (GIRT), headed by Sahoulba.

The PPT was founded in Logone by Gabriel Lisette in 1947 and attracted many southerners, particularly the Sara, and stood against the power and abuses of the traditional authorities, opposed cotton cultivation, and spoke against the power of the colonial agents and expatriates. At its zenith, the PPT was popular in Logone, Moyen-Chari, and even Abeche and Wadai. In Wadai, it was represented by neo-Marxist Abba Siddick, grandson of one of Rabah's generals. From 1956 on, the PPT became the dominant party, although at times its influence was threatened by a coalition of its opponents. In 1956, for example, it enjoyed a 79 percent voter participation in the south (Mayo-Kebbi, Logone, and Moyen-Chari) and won by a landslide, propelling Lisette, a few months later, to win the Fort-Lamy mayoral race, with the PPT taking 18 of the 33 seats in the Municipal Council.[16] In the 1959 National Assembly elections, the PPT secured 59 of the 85 seats, 16 having gone to the UDIT, 9 to the AST, 2 to the GIRT, and 1 to the UNT.

At this point, it was clear that the PPT would dominate Chad's future for some time. Following the collapse of three provisional governments, one led by Lisette (16 December 1958–30 January 1959), one by Sahoulba (11 February 1959–12 March 1959), and another by Koulamallah (12–14 March 1959), François Tombalbaye, assuming then greater prominence than Antillian-born Lisette, formed first a short-lived government (24 March–16 June 1959) and then a permanent one following constitutional changes he had engineered in the interim. His government, after forcing the opposition to coalesce into the *Parti National Africain* (PNA), ruled the country until 1973, when it was replaced by his *Movement National pour la Revolution Culturelle et Sociale* (MNRCS).

What is particularly remarkable about the pre-1960 parties in the colonies of Congo and Chad are their multiparty democratic character, at least in function if not in origin, and higher membership numbers. In fact, at the time, the ethnic element was rarely a cause of violent conflict; leaders cooperated with each other outside the electoral process; and rival parties formed coalitions that at times functioned just like the contemporary coalitions we have witnessed in Israel or elsewhere. In Chad, some deadly ethnic incidents involving the Sara and the northerners, the latter usually known to the former as the Djelabah (merchants, slave traders), occurred in Fort-Lamy in 1946 and 1947. On 5 November 1947, for example, "a group of Sara toughs, attacked the police station" and freed four of their kin from jail, and later that evening 500 of them, armed, assaulted the home of two prominent UDT politicians.[17]

It is true that ethnicity was an element in the violent conflicts of the 1940s and 1950s, in Fort-Lamy and elsewhere, as was the case of the April 1958 deadly encounters between the Fulani and Arabs in Koulamallah's district, which resulted in 31 deaths and 41 wounded people, and then, in the village of Am Tanabo, 100km east of Fort-Lamy, when a fight between the same ethnic groups resulted in 19 deaths.[18] However, disputes over land pasture and cattle were also part of the confrontations. Yet, both in Chad and in Congo, parties tended to attract voters from various districts, and none gained prominence without forming coalitions. All provisional governments (1958–1960) in Chad, for example, survived because of the strength of their coalition or fell because of a defection from the coalition, as happened to Lisette's government when the GIRT left the PPT alliance and joined the Union Socialiste Tchadienne (UST) *Entente*, or when the PPT in 1959 refused to join the Sahoulba government, forcing it to collapse after fewer than 30 days in office. Although ethnicity did influence the voting in the various districts, routinely leaders were able to transcend region, ethnicity, and religion to win prior to 1960.

One is therefore pressed to explain why this phenomenon evaporated as soon as Africans were left alone. Indeed, after independence, virtually everywhere in Africa, the rising strongman eliminates all opposition, and interethnic conflict flares up. Perhaps a strong expatriate presence and a colonial administration that still dictated politics had a sobering effect on the behavior of the African politician and his constituency. Yet because the colonial regime was despotic, political reforms notwithstanding, once the European autocrat was gone, the African head of state simply replaced him.

In the Congo, following independence, leaders addressed national issues and explicitly urged reconciliation and national unity. Moreover, the ideological differences, which amounted to little at that time, except perhaps for Youlou's obsession with communism due to his priestly Catholic training, did not translate into violence except on rare occasions, as was the case in 1956 and 1959, notwithstanding the fact that practically every year the Congolese and the Chadians had to go to the polls, sometimes twice in a single year. In January 1956, for example, following Youlou's losing bid for a Territorial Assembly seat, directly challenging Opangault and Tchikaya for the first time (a challenge that resulted in a marginal victory of the PPC and Tchikaya), Balali youth and supporters of Opangault attacked PPC members in Brazzaville. The incident resulted in one death and 46 wounded, while property damage was estimated at 25 million Central African Francs.[19]

Three years later, in February 1959, bloody riots erupted between northerners and southerners, particularly among members of the UDDIA and the MSA in Brazzaville. Although the riots were short-lived, the degree of violence was unprecedented. Between 16 and 20 February, Balali and Mbochi partisans turned against each other, causing 99 deaths, wounding 177 people seriously, and destroying more than 350 homes in the city of Brazzaville alone.[20] Interestingly, at times, in the Congo ethnic identification was heightened by the adoption of an ethnic totem as a party symbol. The UDDIA, for example, used the crocodile as its symbol, while the Mbochi-based PPC adopted a cock. In symbolic desecration designed to provoke their rivals, the Balali sacrificed cocks openly, whereas the Mbochi would throw "pepper in the eyes of baby crocodiles brandished aloft by the Balali."[21] This amounted to scorning the opponent's ethnic tradition, arousing at the same time one's ethnic loyalty to maximize the gain at the polls.

Furthermore, in 1959, for instance, of 122 candidates, only 11 chose to run outside their original districts. Yet, there were ways of transcending the ethnic group and guaranteeing nonethnic vote, namely, co-optation of traditional authorities or "barons." The barons would always bring an ethnically diversified clientele with them. Youlou turned out to be a master of this strategy regarding the north, which, in part, propelled him rapidly to political prominence. The smaller ethnic groups, such as the Bateke, were quite often brought this way into the political arena.

The fact that Youlou asked the north in 1958 whether or not it wished to secede from the rest of the republic should not be taken seriously as underscoring ethnic tension. His was a two-pronged strategy. First, it was designed to accuse the north of inciting ethnic regionalism and divisiveness; and second, it aimed at forcing the north to behave as part of a multiethnic nation under him. Youlou was aware that most prominent leaders in the region would oppose partition not just for the sake of national unity, notwithstanding the problems, but because the Mbochi and others could not survive without the naturally resourceful south, just as the impoverished north in Chad could not secede from *Chad-utile* (useful Chad).

Throughout the preindependence period, several other factors mitigated against the establishment of a truly democratic society in Congo and Chad, including the presence of the Europeans, who were free to form their own racist parties—often playing one African party against another—as well as the interference of the interterritorial RDA, which, at first, in Congo, formed an alliance with the PPC and then withdrew its support from Tchikaya and embraced Youlou's UDDIA in 1957. In Chad, the marriage between the PPT and the RDA did not break until 1956 because of alleged communist influence in the PPT. That the Congo did not disintegrate into separate territories when independence approached and that the Sara or the northern politicians did not attempt to secede from Chad in 1960 (although the latter made efforts to slow down the movement toward independence) attest to the fact that ethnicity, even when reinforced by regionalism, had never constituted a mortal enemy to the democratic experiment of the 1940–1960 era. We can, therefore, say that in most French colonies, the major obstacle and threat to true multiparty democratic reform and to the realization of African democratic aspirations were not ethnic loyalty but the autocratic colonial presence itself.

THE ROAD TO THE SINGLE PARTY AND A REQUIEM TO MULTIPARTY DEMOCRACY (1960–1990)

The Congo colony became independent on 15 August 1960, under the presidency of Abbe Fulbert Youlou, in a multiparty democratic regime dominated by two parties: Youlou's UDDIA, the majority party, and the *Parti Socialiste* (PS). Responding to Youlou's demands, the Constitution was amended on 2 March 1961 to introduce a presidential system that would, however, maintain a multiparty structure. Consequently, on 20 March 1961, Youlou ran as the sole candidate for the presidency, capturing 88.4 percent of the vote in a "landslide" victory very much stemming from his regional support. He received a considerable number of votes from the Bateke, who in three *sousprefectures*, for example, voted 100 percent for him, while in Mbochi territory, at the urging of Opangault, who had reconciled himself with Youlou, people gave the aspiring president 100 percent of their vote. According to the records, in Likouala-Mossaka (except the river region of Mossaka) and Likouala, a stronghold of the MSA, the vote for Youlou was still overwhelming—90 percent—with numbers exceeding the national average.[22]

Yet, alleging ethnic divisions, in August the president announced his intention to institute a single-party system in the country. Like many other African leaders, Opangault associated the strength of the country's unity with the establishment of the single-party system. Practically all party leaders, both within the UDDIA and the opposition, went along with the request as a means to unify and strengthen the nation.

A similar pattern occurred in Chad, which achieved its independence on 11 August 1960. After forcing all parties to join the PPT or disband, Tombalbaye had, by 1962, instituted an autocratic regime and made Chad a *de facto* single-party state. In 1963, he proceeded to arrest major opposition leaders, including Mahamat Abdelkerim, former speaker of the National Assembly, and Abbo Nassour, Ahmed Koulamallah, and Djebrine Ali Kerallah, both northerners and southerners, although the majority of the arrested leaders were Muslims and from the north. However, here the religious factor reinforced regional and ethnic differences. As Michael Kelley observes, "After 1963, perceptions of ethnic, religious, and regional differences gave new meaning for mustering support and decrying opposition," and "politicians from both the government and the opposition used these differences with their historical implications, to solidify popular support behind their opposition."[23]

On 4 June 1964, Tombalbaye's will prevailed over the National Assembly, which declared Chad a *de jure* one-party state. Subsequently, from 1964 to 1971, particularly as a result of the guerrilla warfare being waged by the National Liberation Front (FROLINAT) and of rumored coups, the president used further extreme measures that saw the random arrest and imprisonment of both civilian leaders and prominent military officers such as southern general Félix Malloum in 1973. National unrest and unwise policies such as the forcible reintroduction of the Sara initiation rituals called *yondo* contributed to the president's murder by the armed forces on 13 April 1975. General Félix Malloum, who succeeded as head of state, at first appeared more tolerant as he freed hundreds of political prisoners. But he, too, soon enacted oppressive and autocratic measures forbidding any type of political manifestation.

In the Congo, on the other hand, as Youlou attempted to curb the power of trade unions, a crippling general strike ensued, forcing him to resign the presidency in mid-August 1963.[24] A provisional government headed by Premier Alphonse Massamba-Débat followed. On 8 December 1963, a new Constitution paved the way for the rise of the prime minister to the presidency using an electoral college consisting of members of the National Assembly and local government officials.

Massamba-Débat created his own Marxist *Mouvement National de la Révolution* (MNR), which became the sole party in 1964 and the country's supreme organ in 1966.[25] Following a military coup on 3 July 1968, which brought to power Commander Marien Ngouabi as head of state, the Massamba-Débat Constitution was replaced by the Fundamental Act of 14 August 1968. Ngouabi abolished the previous party and established his own, the *Parti Congolais du Travail* (PCT), a Marxist-Leninist vanguard party. On 3 January 1970, a new Constitution was approved, and on 12 July 1973, another Constitution declared the Congo a "*république populaire*" under the banner of a single party—the PCT—which would be the only body to elect the president for a five-year term. The president would also serve as the chairman of the PCT's Central Committee.

Under mysterious circumstances, however, Ngouabi was assassinated on 18 March 1977, and Massamba-Débat was implicated, tried, and summarily executed. On 5 April 1977, Colonel Joachim Yhombi-Opango, from Fort Rousset in the north, was appointed head of state. A series of economic woes in February 1979, coupled with constant attacks from the left wing of the party accusing the president of not being a true Marxist but a pro-Western capitalist in disguise, forced Opango to resign suddenly in March 1979 and to hand over power to Mbochi (northern) colonel Dénis Sassou-Nguesso, chairman of the PCT. Sassou-Nguesso's ascent to power was followed by the promulgation of a socialist Constitution following the National Assembly elections. One of Sassou-Nguesso's first acts was to release Joachim Yhombi-Opango, who was, nevertheless, kept under house arrest, euphemistically termed "state protection." Subsequently, Sassou-Nguesso was elected president on 31 March 1979 and reelected president for five-year terms in 1984 and 1989. Three years into Sassou-Nguesso's tenure as president, 20 army officers were arrested after they purportedly staged a rebellion in Owando (center-north of the country), resulting, in 1988, in the death of its leader, Pierre Anga, who had eluded the police and the army for eight years. The officers arrested were all from the northern Kouyou ethnic group to which Ngouabi and Yhombi-Opango belonged. Again, ethnicity here seems to have played no role whatsoever.

In Chad, the civil war forced Malloum to relinquish power to Gukuni Wedei following his resignation in March 1979. Hisseine Habre defeated Gukuni in early June 1982 and remained the head of state until late 1990, when he was overthrown by Idris Deby. Chad experienced, in this period, not an ethnic civil war but an intraethnic and intrareligious war among Tubu and Zaghawa leaders. Under such conditions, talk of multiparty democracy meant nothing, notwithstanding pressures from the West.

A careful analysis of the post-1960 and pre-1990 period highlights several turning points in the history of the Congo and Chad that presaged the almost inevitable rise of the single-party state. Just as with many African leaders of the time, the argument of the crisis of the state and the nation was put forward by Youlou, Tombalbaye, and African politicians who ascended to power. Thus, the clashes that occurred in 1956 and 1959 in Congo gave impetus to Youlou's and his military successors' claim that only a single-party system could save the nation. In fact, one might point out that Youlou had already been encouraged by the power given to the state by the National Assembly in 1958. In that year, in an effort to crack down on the violence perpetrated by the Matsouanists, the assembly allowed the government to impose curfews, proscribe meetings where more than five persons were present, and institute a special court that could render the death penalty without appeal on those accused of inciting violence and political instability, including citizens who refused to pay taxes, like the Matsouanists. This served as a precedent for other steps to come. In Chad, the National Assembly that approved the one-party state in 1964 was 50 percent northern and 50 percent southern, with most Muslim politicians agreeing with the change.[26] Thus, the first Chadian president felt encouraged to issue autocratic decrees whenever he felt threatened.

To be sure, the hard economic realities of the postindependence era, particularly those of the 1970s, when, for example, Congo experienced a sharp fall in oil revenues and an increase in the inflation rate, contributed to the autocratic tendencies of the regime. Likewise, the Marxist-Leninist policies hurriedly put in place or advocated by labor unionists, students, and intellectuals prevented the leaders from following realistic economic policies and programs. These conditions whetted the appetite of the army, which, as elsewhere in Africa, was never prone to returning to either single-or multiparty democracy once it had taken over the reins of power. It must be said to its credit, however, that the Congolese army does not have a history of massive and repeated abuses and human rights violations against the citizens. In addition, the military coups in the country have been almost bloodless, while the civilian governments have never been as repressive as some others on the continent: at no time did Congolese jails burst at the seams with political prisoners, as was the case, for example, in Chad. Here, given the state of chronic economic crises, the hardships of the 1970s did not alter the situation.

While, on one hand, the ethnic factor was certainly present in the politics of the 1960s–1980s, at times, on the other hand, it was superseded or eclipsed by the intraregional hostilities, as was the case in the rivalries between the Sassou-Nguesso, Ngouabi, Yhombi-Opango, and Massamba-Débat. Yet, only for the relatively short interregnums did the Congolese people lose sight of their democratic aspirations. Since 1970, a groundswell of public opinion against the regimes and their autocratic posture had been growing. Labor unions, students, professionals, and even the army and the masses all had their grievances against the autocratic tendencies of the Marxist leaders. This explains the return to universal suffrage, which abandoned the electoral college in the presidential elections, the reintroduction of the distinction between party and state, and restoration of an elected National Assembly in 1973.

Unfortunately, in reality, these were only cosmetic structural changes to appease the opposition:

By scrapping the authoritarian 1970 constitution and replacing it with one that combined the principle of popular elections at the central and local government levels with strict party controls, lip service was paid to democratic procedures, the rural population again participated in the process of government (if only to a limited degree), and the PCT's authority remained intact.[27]

There is no doubt that, after 1977, the Congo drifted toward an autocratic regime, cemented by the rise to power of Colonel (later General) Denis Sassou-Nguesso. Although the process toward autocratic rule was initiated by a southern and a (Balali) Bakongo (Youlou), the north completed the task, thus reversing, just as in Chad, the rule of the majority Bakongo and Sara over the rest of the country, respectively.

As noted earlier, in Chad, the issue of autocracy and ethnicity was much more complex because the factor of ethnicity (mainly the rivalry between northern ethnic groups and the Sara) was intertwined with the problem of regional economic imbalance and the intrusion of religious differences, with Islam playing a disproportional role among northern politicians.

Although in postindependence Chad most of the civil service and the higher-ranking posts were occupied by southerners, mostly Sara, causing extreme resentment in the north, the Mangalme revolt of 1965 was sparked by increased taxation on cattle, while the spread of the rebellion in the prefectures such as the Biltine-Ennedi-Tibesti (BET) seems to have been caused or aggravated primarily by disrespect for Tubu traditions and by autocratic administration rather than ethnic hatred. Sara contempt for northerners was primarily a sentiment of revenge against the precolonial slavery the Tubu and Arabs had imposed on the south. Indeed, the Sara would have acted the same way had their southern fellow Moundang and others acted similarly. The major causes of conflicts were past slavery and the slave trade, which were carried out primarily on account of not ethnicity but religion. To be sure, the memories of the slave trade and the abuses by sultans were still fresh in the minds of the Sara even in the early 1960s. On Rabah, for example, Buijtenhuijs quotes a young civil servant who noted about his home region: "Rabah did not pass through Lere, neither did his soldiers. Nevertheless, the Moundang say that Rabah is [*sic*] a strong man. He grinds the Children in pillions and eats them."[28]

Similar remarks can be made about the Chadian civil war. If ethnic affiliation and ethnic dislike were the primary causes, the Sara would not have assassinated Tombalbaye, nor would Habre and Gukuni, both Tubu and Muslim, have fought against each other. By the same token, it is doubtful that Deby would have engineered a coup against his northern and kin Muslim, Habre, in 1990. Personal ambition, revenge motives, and unwise economic, cultural, and political decisions seem to outweigh any ethnic considerations or loyalties in the protracted Chadian conflict. In other words, it would be absurd to postulate that Sara army officers killed Tombalbaye in 1975 because of ethnicity—he was one of their own. They retained their ethnic solidarity. Their personal ambitions made them part ways with their coethnic president. Yet, it is true, as John Collier notes, that "Tombalbaye's failure to establish hiring and training policies geared to achieving greater ethnic and regional balance in public administration was one of his most serious shortcomings."[29] Unfortunately, his successors have not fared better either in this effort.

THE MOVE TOWARD MULTIPARTY DEMOCRACY (1989–1995)

As the winds of change toward multiparty democracy swept over most of Africa during the latter part of the 1980s, Sassou-Nguesso realized that soon the same thing would happen in the Congo. Thus, for the September 1989 National Assembly elections, he allowed 74 nonparty members out of 133 PCT candidates to run for the seats,[30] released 40 political prisoners, and announced that he was prepared (in light of the collapse of the socialist block in Eastern Europe) to abandon Marxism-Leninism. The country's economy had deteriorated beyond repair, despite IMF's intervention in 1986. His hands were sort of tied, as the amount of foreign debt had risen from $1.2 billion in 1980 to $4.7 billion in 1990, almost twice the country's GDP, leaving the Congo "totally bankrupt" by 1990.[31] Between 8 April and 7 June 1990, Nguesso consistently hinted his willingness to move toward allowing wider popular participation in the electoral process. He subsequently announced in July that a PCT congress would take place sometime in 1991 to plan for a multiparty system, although he let it be known that he opposed the notion of a National Conference, which the opposition was demanding, and vowed that no parties would be allowed until the approval of a new Constitution in February 1991.

At this point, his aim was to control the pace of democratization while strengthening the stand of his party and ensuring his personal victory if events were to lead too quickly to a multiparty system. As it turned out, events ran out of control, as opposition parties began to emerge ahead of his own timetable.[32] So, under pressure, the PCT held an extraordinary congress in December 1990, abandoned its Marxist-Leninist philosophy, and legalized multipartyism, while the assembly extended Sassou-Nguesso's presidential term to 1994.[33] However, what precipitated the change was a general strike by the PCT's Congolese Trade Unions—the *Confederation Syndicale du Congo* (CSC), led by Jean-Michel Bokamba-Yangouma—which paralyzed the country, especially Brazzaville, on 14 and 15 September. The labor unionists were attempting to disengage themselves from the grip of the PCT and sought higher wages, while demanding, at the same time, the introduction of multiparty democracy.[34]

As a result, on 25 February (till 10 June) 1991, the president convened a National Conference in Brazzaville, attended by 1,200 delegates from the 73 political parties, associations, professions, religious organizations, government and nongovernmental bodies, exiles, and even the army (20 delegates), under the chairmanship of the bishop of Owando, Msgr. Ernest N'Kombo.[35] Seven hundred delegates came from the opposition. Despite a brief, government-forced interval in March due to problems of representation and delegates' demands that the National Conference proclaim itself sovereign and a constituent assembly, the pace of dismantling the ancien régime was accelerated, with Sassou-Nguesso unable to stop it. Indeed, on 12 March, the National Conference declared itself sovereign and announced that the Constitution would be suspended and the National Assembly and local councils dissolved, while a 153-member Higher Council of the Republic, under the chairmanship of Msgr. N'Kombo, would oversee the drafting of a new Constitution and supervise implementation of the conference's resolutions. These measures were to lead to legislative and presidential elections.

In June, the president, retaining the title of commander of the armed forces, was replaced as head of state by a prime minister (Andre Milongo), a former World Bank administrator and leader of the *Union Pour la Démocracie et la République* (URD), to lead a transitional government, with the name of the country reverting to the Republic of the Congo. Soon thereafter, the political police and the director of the national police were disbanded and replaced, respectively. This was followed in July by the disbanding of the most feared Presidential Guard. Finally on 10 June, the National Assembly completed its work and ended with a wash-of-hands act symbolizing a reconciliation. (As if to add insult to injury to the president, in August the president's brother, Maurice Nguesso, was arrested over economic and fiscal scandals.) The reforms continued at full speed. A one-month-long strike in August–September 1991 by 7,000 civil servants in the Ministry of Interior threatened to disrupt the tempo of the democratic process.[36]

In December 1991, the Conseil Superieur de Communication (CSC) approved a draft Constitution, creating a National Assembly as well as a Senate, and introduced popular suffrage in presidential elections. A referendum of 15 March, with a 90 percent popular voter participation (the first time in 32 years), approved the draft Constitution by a 96.2 percent margin. The Constitution was very explicit in condemning, in the Preamble, ''state perpetrated injustice, to-

talitarianism, nepotism, ethnocentrism, regionalism, and social inequalities,''
while Article 42 outlawed discrimination based on ethnicity.[37]

Unfortunately, disturbances occurred in mid-January 1992, caused by the
president's supporters within the army, who demanded the reinstitution of the
military that had been removed in the interim on the basis of ethnic origins and
immediate disbursement of overdue salary. At one point, the army even requested that Prime Minister Milongo resign. This resulted in clashes between
the army and government supporters, out of which five deaths were reported.
Milongo did not resign but fired the secretary of state, as requested by the army,
and appointed an army favorite as defense minister. However, Milongo boldly
took for himself the title of supreme chief of the army.[38]

Municipal elections were held in May 1992, and Pascal Lissouba's *Union
Panafricaine pour la Démocratie Sociale* (UPADS) and Bernard Kolelas' *Mouvement Congolais pour la Démocratie et le Développement Intégrat* (MCDDI)
came out the winners, as announced on 4 June. The old PCT performed poorly
virtually everywhere in the country. The PCT and Sassou-Nguesso, however,
accused the government of massive voter fraud, although popular participation
had been very high (70 percent). On 24 June and 19 July 1992, the first and
second rounds of the long-awaited legislative elections took place, giving the
UPADS 39 of the 125 seats in the National Assembly, the MCDDI 29, and the
PCT 18. In the Senate contest held on 26 July, the UPADS won 23 seats out
of 60, and the MCDI 13.

Finally, on 2 August, the first round of the presidential elections involving a
dozen candidates took place, in which Lissouba, a former premier and a former
member of the PCT, received 36 percent of the vote, with Sassou-Nguesso
coming in a distant third. Consequently, Lissouba and Kolelas squared off on
16 August 1992. Lissouba was proclaimed the new president of the republic on
19 August, after capturing 60 percent of the vote cast.[39] The following month,
the new president appointed Bongho-Nouara, leader of a coalition of parties
supporting the new president, premier. On 8 September, Bongho-Nouara presented his new cabinet, once again regionally well balanced but dominated by
UPADS members. The president's coalition, labeled as the *Mouvance Présiden-
tielle* (Presidential Tendency), comprised some 50 parties, while the opposition
was made up of Sassou-Nguesso's Congolese Labor Party (PCT) and Kolelas'
MCDDI, a coalition named the Union of Democratic Renewal (URD),[40] joined
by an amalgam of some seven other parties. (The new URD, led by Kolelas,
should not be confused with Mikongo's older URD.)

From what we know now, however, ethnicity did play some role in the pres-
idential elections. For example, during the first presidential round, Kolelas car-
ried Lari-dominated Pool but hardly squeaked by as a winner in Brazzaville.
Both cities, although more diverse ethnically, are dominated by the Lari and by
Kolela's MCDDI. These two urban centers cast a high number of votes for
Milongo, leader of the *Union Pour la Démocratie et la République*, but not for
Lissouba. Lissouba won by a landslide in his region and in Nibolek (Niari,

Bouenza, and Lekoumo regions), where his UPADS dominates, and trounced his opponents in Kuilou (particularly in Pointe Noire, the region's capital). Jean-Pierre Thystere-Tchicaya, URD leader originally from Pointe Noire and a former PCT leader, came in second in Kouilou, receiving 28 percent of the vote, while Sassou-Nguesso carried "the sparsely populated" north,[41] especially the regions of Cuvette, Likouala, and Plateau, home of the PCT.[42] Former president Opango, from Cuvette, garnered only 27 percent of the vote on his own northern turf. In the runoff elections between Lissouba and Kolelas, however, the latter carried Brazzaville and Pool as well as Kouilou (by a narrow margin), but Lissouba won in the rest of the country.[43]

Sassou-Nguesso and the losers, alleging fraud, attempted to disrupt the results of the elections by withdrawing the PCT from Lissouba's coalition. The former president claimed that Lissouba had broken his pledge preceding the second round of the presidential elections to include more PCT members in the government. With the PCT joining the URD, the *Mouvance Presidentielle* was left with a minority in the National Assembly, resulting in a vote of no confidence for the government in October 1992. In an apparent smart, but undemocratic, move, the president, instead of asking the government to resign, dissolved the National Assembly altogether and scheduled new elections for 1993. At this point, the army stepped in and forced the two parties to agree on an interim government until such time when new elections would be held. World Bank administrator Claude Antoine Dacosta was chosen as the compromise candidate. The calm that followed led to the May 1993 first round of legislative elections, securing for the UPADS and its allies 62 of the 125 seats in the National Assembly, while the URD-PCT won 49 seats. Humiliated, Kolelas withdrew his UDCI from the second round, unwittingly giving the Presidential Tendency seven more votes in the assembly.

Again, in a brilliant move that would anger Sassou-Nguesso, Lissouba immediately appointed Yhombi-Opango, the former Congolese president whom Sassou-Nguesso had once imprisoned and released. In defiance, the MCDI appointed its own perfunctory cabinet, which the army rejected as it had accepted the results of the legislative elections. The atmosphere had now changed, and violence began to spread across the land, made worse by the fact that many of the political "barons," such as Kolelas, had their own militias, called ninjas. Sassou-Nguesso withdrew on 17 April to his Oyo village, 600 kilometers north of Brazzaville, followed by an army (security force) of 500 men, called cobras, posing a serious threat to peace and the stability of the country, threatening Lissouba's Zulus.[44] Sassou-Nguesso's threat prompted Lissouba to declare a state of emergency in mid-July 1993 and to dismiss the chief of the armed forces. Elsewhere, there were ethnic clashes incited by Kolelas and his party between his Lari ethnic group and the Babembe. The Babembe, through their ethnic son, Christophe Moukoueke, leader of the *Mouvance Presidentielle*, supported the president.[45] In June and July, further violent clashes occurred in Brazzaville between government supporters and opponents, causing 30 deaths.[46]

Thus, a curfew was imposed on Brazzaville on 16 July 1993. To underscore the seriousness of the situation, increased powers were given to regional *prefets* on arrests, confiscation of weaponry, and the disbanding of illegal assemblies, while foreigners were looked at with suspicion, and the media were subject to censorship.[47]

This was not the end of the violence, however. On 13 January 1994, opposition militias clashed with the army, resulting (since December 1993) in 115 people killed. An international mediation team made up of seven judges appointed by the Organization of African Unity, the European Community, France, and Gabon made an inquiry into the 3 May 1993 first round of legislative elections and pronounced eleven of them invalid, six in Brazzaville, two in the center, and three in the north. Since 1994, however, there has been sufficient peace for the Congolese people and their democratic experiment to move forward. On 6 August 1994, Christophe Moukoueke, representing the Presidential Tendency, and Bernard Kolelas, representing the opposition, rallied in front of the National Assembly house, hugged one another, and observed a minute of silence for those who died as a result of the clashes between their militias in Brazzaville in November and December. To cement this reconciliation, on 9 August 1994, Kolelas was rewarded with the position of mayor of Brazzaville.[48] At this point, the government feels so confident that it has started implementing a recovery program with assistance from the International Monetary Fund.[49]

In Chad, the move toward multiparty democracy did not begin until 1988, when the French and international agencies began pressuring Habre to liberalize the political system. Habre put in place a new Constitution in December 1989, which led to his endorsement as president for a seven-year term and to legislative elections in July 1990, contested by 436 candidates vying for the 123 National Assembly seats. Interestingly, however, even though the sole legal party was the president's party—the *Union Nationale pour l'Indépendance et Révolution* (UNIR), founded in 1988—many party stalwarts lost in the contest to candidates who were opposed to the regime.[50] Of course, Habre was ousted by Colonel Idris Deby, his former chief of staff, in November 1990. Thereafter, intense pressure from the Chadians and France was brought to bear on Deby to democratize the regime.

Following months of procrastination and accusations of alleged abuses of human rights, Deby finally convened the National Sovereign Conference in mid-January–April 1993, which was attended by some 800 delegates from all walks of life, but particularly from the dozen political parties that had been allowed to register in 1992. The conference appointed an interim prime minister (Sara M.D. and former minister of higher education Fidele Moungar) and established a *Conseil Superieur de Transition* (CST), led by former head of the Gouvernement d'Union Nationale Tchadinne (GUNT) Lol Mahamat Chowa, leader of an opposition party, the *Rassemblement pour la Démocratie et le Progrès*. It is interesting, however, that, to prevent the injection of ethnic and regional politics in the country, the law prescribed that no party would be legalized unless it had a minimum of 30 founding members, of whom at least 3 had to come from ten of Chad's fourteen prefectures.[51] After a vote of no confidence against Moungar's government by the Council of Ministers and the CST, engineered by the president's supporters in October 1993, Dr. Jean Alingue Bawoyeu was made premier. Moungar had enacted tough measures against abuses and massacres perpetrated by the security forces in Sara prefectures. Under the new Constitution, the presidential tenure is set for five years, the National Assembly is bicameral, while the administration is to be decentralized, and a constitutional court is to be created.

There are many questions regarding the Congolese experience in popular democracy, more so than the brief Chadian experience, that deserve answers. First, comes the issue of the roots of the democratic movement in the country. There is no doubt that the movement was primarily caused by internal factors, symbolized by the seemingly unending political oppression, the precarious economic conditions, and the evils associated with the single-party and autocratic regimes in Africa. It was not the effect of what happened in the Soviet bloc, although the tearing down of the Berlin Wall certainly emboldened the Congolese. Political oppression and hard economic times, most of which have been attributed, partly rightly, to the corruption, the mismanagement, and the nepotism of African autocrats such as Sassou-Nguesso, provided a fertile ground to the labor movement, just as was the case in Zambia. Without it, neither Youlou nor Sassou-Nguesso would have relinquished power in a single-party system that tolerated only monosyndicalism.[52]

One would be remiss, on the other hand, not to acknowledge that the West, particularly through France, both in the Congo and Chad, and its financial institutions such as the IMF and the European Community, played a major role in forcing the autocrats to liberalize the political system. It is difficult to prove, however, that such external pressures outweighed the impact of purely internal dynamics arising from the African desire not to be left out of the political process any longer.

Another intriguing question is why Sassou-Nguesso, throughout the process, including when the National Assembly proclaimed itself sovereign and stripped him and his party of power, did not call the army to stop the drift toward democratization. It would appear that Sassou-Nguesso learned from the recent experience on the continent, particularly that of other Francophone regimes, that what has been called the second African liberation could not be easily stopped. Second, it is also clear that the Congolese army (still dominated by the northern Kouyou) has often played an ambiguous role, at times defending the government, at times siding with the opposition, and on occasions forcing the two to find a political compromise. We might note here that Lissouba himself had appointed an army mediator (General N'Golo, at one point) in his dispute with his opponents.

Third, given the country's accelerated pace of change from 1991 to 1993 and its regional and relative ethnic polarization over the years, one would have expected a much higher level of ethnic violence and more incidents of ethnic-motivated deaths. There is no doubt that the campaigns and the electoral process were often influenced by the ethnic factor. The 1993 and 1994 clashes, especially in Brazzaville, where Kolelas' Lari ninjas destroyed the homes of the Nibolek,[53] and the reported kidnappings of opponents did have ethnic overtones. By the same token, however, there was cross-ethnic voting in the elections, which accounts, for example, for Lissouba's victory over Kolelas. One should also take note of the fact that several coalitions transcended ethnic boundaries and that the still predominantly northern government of southern Lissouba enjoyed strong support from many southern regions, particularly Niari, Bouenza, and Lekouma (which have a significant number of people from the Nibolek region). Also, the fact that the northern-based PCT allied itself with Kolela's Bakongo Lari and the Bakeke should not be overlooked. Finally, one ought not to forget that, as a means to deter exclusivist ethnic behavior, on 27 December 1990, the Congolese National Assembly stipulated that only parties with founders over 25 years of age from five different regions could be legalized in the country.[54]

CONCLUSION

It cannot be denied that the future of multiparty democracy in Africa is linked to the degree that the Africans are able to transcend strong ethnic loyalties for the common good and the nation. However, there is no conclusive evidence from the recent past that ethnicity has been the overriding or the primary feature in the elections in Congo and Chad. It is important to point out that in national elections, especially in Congo, candidates cannot win if their base is solely ethnic—the numbers to propel them to victory are not there. The second round of the presidential elections between Lissouba and Kolelas in that country proves the point. For example, Lissouba, who is from the south, was nevertheless able to sweep the north and carry the south handily (despite his narrow losses in Pool and Brazzaville). Indeed, the north did not attempt to boycott the elections because no northerner had come out victorious in the first round. It seems that the candidate's personality and experience, his proposed solutions to the country's problems, and his ability to engender confidence and a sense of fairness that transcends ethnic origin were the most important determinants of Lissouba's victory. For Chad, of course, the jury has been only partially seated: the world is still waiting to see whether or not the upcoming 1996 legislative electoral process will be Chadian and national or rather a contentious contest among the Sara, the Tubu, and the Zaghawa.

At present, it is difficult to imagine the Congolese going back to an autocratic, single-party regime, except if the military were to step in once again. When the army is left out of the equation, one of two scenarios is likely to occur in the near future: one in which the multiparty system would continue to make gains, leading to a truly democratic system, and another that would maintain the facade of multipartyism but fall under the control of a larger party, as was the case at the time the country acceded to independence in 1960. For Chad, the future is simply hard to predict, as military factions are still disturbing the peace, and no one knows how Deby would behave if he and his MPs were to lose. The rule of the gun could very easily return to Chad. Indeed, after a collapse of the effort to register voters 12 February–19 March 1995 (2.4 million were registered, but the results were declared void for alleged fraud),[55] the presidential and legislative elections were postponed first to April 1995 and then to April 1996. Three prime ministers have meanwhile attempted to lead a transitional government: Moungar (1993–1994), Kassire Koumakoye (May 1994 to April 1995), and Daniel Djimasta Koibla, Sara, member of Jean Alingue's party, the *Union pour la Démocratie et la République* (UDR) (1995–1996). Koibla, former minister in Hisseine Habre's cabinet and recently Deby's minister of interior, a successful organizer of the National Sovereign Conference, is a shrewd opposition politician, and many people expected him to lead the country to fair elections.[56] In fact, when he assumed power, one of the conditions he posed to the president and the *Conseil Supérieur de Transition* was that his would be the last provisional government before the April 1996 elections.[57]

Learning from past experience and errors, one should warn that both Congo and Chad have to guard against Africa's tendency to make policies or constitutional changes that revolve around an incumbent or a defeated leader, or what one would call Constitution-by-vengeance or retribution, as was about to happen in Zaire. Such Constitutions fail to address the national problem and are forced to adjust and change every time a new regime is installed, as we have seen in the Congo over the years. Obviously, the future of democracy in the Congo and Chad is also contingent upon the performance of the economy and the impact of the IMF programs. Although the economy should not be a *conditio sine qua non* for a country to move toward the institutionalization of democracy, as social scientists such as Samuel Huntington have claimed, a modicum of progress in living standards can only enhance the democratic process. The discovery of further oil deposits in Congo, in which the French Elf-Acquitaine Oil Society will have a major share,[58] and in Logone and Kanem in Chad[59] could bring renewed temptations for government to both dispense exorbitant salaries and embark on grandiose and wasteful programs, as has happened in Nigeria and Gabon. Finally, while Congolese trade unions will hopefully adopt realistic postures, in Chad the growing strength of the press, foreign pressure, and the rise of civil society could well have a moderating impact on the behavior of the military.

Overall, those who tend to give too much weight to ethnicity and its disruptive role should remember the convincing study done by James Wunsch, which seems to apply perfectly to the Congo and Chad:

It is important to note that the vast majority of Africans live at peace and in cooperation with their multi-ethnic neighbors. Ethnicity has only rarely grown into violence, and often when it has, as in Sudan, Nigeria, Rwanda, Uganda, and Burundi, it can be very clearly related to policies and constitutions constructed, and left by colonial powers: majorities (and in some cases the minorities) were given great advantage over other groups, and then placed in a constitutional structure which either sustained or worsened the situation.[60]

As a solution, just like elsewhere in Africa, what the Congolese and the Chadian people need is a strong, but a smaller, government that is able to tackle the massive problems the leaders have been unable to resolve over the past three decades. To the extent that this is done, "ethnicism" will be weakened. On the other hand, the issue of balanced regional development and a careful ethnic regional distribution designed to break up bloc ethnic voting can, more than anything else, curb the destructiveness of ethnically based behavior in the political arena. Given the small size of the country and its population and the smaller number of its ethnic groups, the Congo can find realistic solutions and long-range and fair regional and ethnic representation. A federalist solution does not seem to be appropriate to the Congo, and almost all Chadian leaders have rejected it since the 1960s. But, as Arthur Lewis put it years ago, a certain degree of power "devolution" from the center to the prefectures seems appropriate.[61]

Whichever solution the Congo and Chad adopt, however, some type of proportional representation, enshrined in the Constitution, might well work in both countries. Continuous cabinet reshuffling to achieve regional and ethnic parity is a tradition that has failed in the past and will continue to present problems as the Congolese and the Chadian people attempt to devise a multiparty democratic system that will preserve, as one of their Constitutions explicitly once said, "a government of the people, by the people, and for the people." Lissouba in the Congo is perhaps to be commended for contemplating a new Constitution *a la Sud Africaine* in 1997 providing power sharing between losers and winners and preventing violence.[62] There is no doubt that the winner-take-all tradition in Africa has been one of the causes of resentment and lawlessness.

Unlike in the Congo, in Chad, however, the role of a fundamentalist Islam, as in neighboring Sudan, could torpedo the future of democratization. Of the two, the Congo augurs for a smoother road to complete democratization, because the plethora of ethnic loyalties is more difficult to overcome in Chad than in the Congo, making the road toward democracy more problematic. As Clark notes on the Congo[63] and Cordell on Chad,[64] the country is 60 percent urbanized (30 percent for Chad), has a literacy rate of 62 percent (15 percent for Chad), and has a critical press and a well-developed civil society, although Chad is rapidly catching up with 300 new civil societies registered in 1994, from a mere 90 between 1963 and 1990,[65] and its *Union des Syndicats du Tchad* (UST) is also voicing more forcefully its concerns. Furthermore, it appears that "the statements of Congo's elites against ethnic violence have had some impact over the last few years."[66]

Finally, it must be said that for both Congo and Chad the role of France and some neighboring heads of state will be pivotal. In France, the *Quai d'Orsai* would support Deby only if moved to free democratic elections, while the Ministry of Cooperation under Mitterrand's presidency leaned toward Deby and would have liked to provide further financial assistance to see that the voter registration effort would be carried out by the National Electoral Commission (CENI) without flaws.[67]

In early 1996, among the potential presidential candidates, Deby was generally thought to have had the support of France, Gabon, Congo, and Sudan. Maurice Adoum el Bongo, who headed the National Conference, notwithstanding his age (he is 68 years old), was apparently the most popular (independent) candidate and reportedly had the support of Jacques Chirac and the Central African Republic's (CAR) president, Ange-Felix Patasse.[68] However, just before 2 June 1996, he (as well as Fidele Moungar) was disqualified from running due to alleged residence irregularities. Kassire Koumakoye, from Tandjile, was extremely popular in Mayo-Kebbi, the most populous prefecture, and had Kadhafi's support. The Kanembou people supported Lol Mahamat Chowa, although his friend, Abdoulaye Lamana, not very popular in his own prefecture—Chari-Baguirmi—was expected to run for the presidency. While Jean Alingue, a well-known politician who led the URD, was expected to be a formidable candidate, Colonel Abdelkerim Kamougue was quite popular in Moyen-Chari and the two Logones, and his chances to be a serious contender were expected to be good. Then there were familiar names whose supporters, some in France and some elsewhere, were attempting to put them on the ballot: Hisseine Habre and Gukuni Wedei. These two, however, did not run.

Eventually, fifteen candidates ran against Deby, allowing the president to garner 43.8 percent of the popular vote (with a 77 percent turnout) against the 12.39 percent that went to Kamougue, the strongest of the challengers. This forced a second round or runoff election, which pitted Deby against Kamougue on 10 July 1996. As expected, it resulted in a landslide victory for the president, who captured 69.09 percent of the vote. As expected, both times the opposition refused to accept the results, but the CENI declared the elections fair.[69] With the attendance of only seven African presidents, Deby took office on 8 August 1996. Just as in many other parts of Africa, therefore, the political fragmentation of the opposition resulted in the incumbent's victory. Legislative elections were planned for sometime before the end of the year.

NOTES

1. Ghia Nodia, "Nationalism and Democracy," *Journal of Democracy* 3, no. 4 (1992): 7.

2. Francis Fukuyama, "Comments on Nationalism and Democracy," in Larry Diamond and Marc F. Plattner, eds., *Nationalism, Ethnic Conflict and Democracy* (Baltimore and London: Johns Hopkins University Press, 1994), 23–28.

3. Marie Eliou, *La formation de la conscience nationale en République Populaire du Congo* (Paris: Edition Anthropos, 1977), 19–20.

4. Elikia M'Bokolo, *Noirs et blancs en Afrique équatoriale: Les sociétés cotières et la pénétration française (vers 1820–1874)* (Paris: Mouton, 1981), 157–67.

5. Jean-Michel Wagret, *Histoire et sociologie politiques de la republique populaire du Congo* (Paris: Librairie générale de droit et de jurisprudence, 1963; Paris: Pichon et Durand, 1963), 125.

6. Virginia Thompson and Richard Adloff, *Emerging States of French Equatorial Africa* (London: Oxford University Press, 1960), 477–80.

7. Virginia Thompson and Richard Adloff, *Historical Dictionary of the People's Republic of Congo* (Metuchen, NJ: Scarecrow Press, 1984), 29.

8. See Dennis Cordell, *Dar al-Kuti and the Last Years of the Trans-Saharan Slave Trade* (Madison: University of Wisconsin Press, 1985).

9. Robert Buijtenhuijs, *Frolinat et les révoltes populaires du Tchad, 1965–1975* (Paris: Mouton, 1978), 40–41.

10. Archives, Musée National du Tchad, W1, 11, 1924, 12 and 35.

11. Mario Azevedo, "Sara Demographic Instability as a Consequence of French Colonial Policy in Chad (1890–1940)," Ph.D. diss., Duke University, 1975, 141–240.

12. Samuel Decalo, *Historical Dictionary of Chad* (Metuchen, NJ: Scarecrow Press, 1987), 126.

13. Wagret, *Histoire et sociologie politiques*, 56–58.

14. Wagret, *Histoire et sociologie politiques*, 58–61.

15. Jacques Le Cornet, *L'histoire politique du Tchad de 1900 a 1962* (Paris: Pichon et Duran, 1963).

16. Virginia Thompson and Richard Adloff, *Conflict in Chad* (Berkeley, CA: Institute for International Studies, 1981), 434.

17. Rene Lemarchand, "The Politics of Sara Ethnicity: A Note on the Origins of the Civil War in Chad," *Cahiers d'Etudes Africaines* 80, nos. 20–24 (1980): 458.

18. Thompson and Adloff, *Conflict in Chad*, 436–37.

19. Thompson and Adloff, *Emerging States*, 484.

20. See Wagret, *Histoire et sociologie politiques*, 84.

21. Thompson and Adloff, *Emerging States*, 485–86.

22. Wagret, *Histoire et sociologie politiques*, 107.

23. Michael Kelley, *A State in Disarray: Conditions of Chad's Survival* (Boulder, CO: Westview Press, 1986), 11.

24. Pierre Engelbert, "Congo: Recent History," in *Africa: South of the Sahara* (London: Europa, 1994), 289.

25. *Afrique Contemporaine* 158 (2d trimester 1991): 58.

26. Bernard Lanne, "Les deux guerres civiles au Tchad," *Tchad: Anthologie de la guerre civile* (N'Djamena: Yamoko Koulro-Bezo, 1981), 55–56.

27. Thompson and Adloff, *Historical Dictionary*, 15.

28. Buijtenhuijs, *Frolinat et les revoltes populares du Tchad*, 40–41.

29. John Collier, "Historical Setting," in Thomas Collelo, ed., *Chad: A Country Study* (Washington, DC: U.S. Government Printing Office, 1993), 19.

30. *Afrique Contemporaine* 158 (2d trimester 1991): 58.

31. John Clark, "Elections, Leadership and Democracy in Congo," *Africa Today* 41, no. 3 (1993): 48.

32. *Jeune Afrique* 1554 (10–16 October 1990): 26–27; *Jeune Afrique* 1552 (22 September–2 October 1990): 27.

33. Engelbert, "Congo," 290.

34. *Jeune Afrique* 1564–65 (19 December 1990–1 January 1991): 17.

35. Patrick Girard, "Imperturbable Sassou-Nguesso," *Jeune Afrique* 1575 (6–12 March 1991): 16.

36. *Afrique Contemporaine* 158 (2d trimester 1991): 81.

37. *Afrique Contemporaine* 162 (2d trimester 1992): 35, 41.

38. Engelbert, "Congo," 290.

39. *Afrique Contemporaine* 163 (4th trimester 1992): 278.

40. *Africa Research Bulletin* (1–31 January 1993): 10847.

41. Clark, "Elections," 53.

42. *Africa Research Bulletin* (1–28 February 1995): 11753.

43. Clark, "Elections," 53.

44. *Africa Research Bulletin* (1–28 February 1995): 11753.

45. *Africa Research Bulletin* (1–31 January 1994): 11303.

46. *Africa Research Bulletin* (1–30 September 1993): 11153.

47. *Africa Research Bulletin* (1–31 July 1993): 11075.

48. *Africa Research Bulletin* (1–31 August 1994): 11551.

49. *Demos* 3, no. 3 (September 1994): 22.

50. Bernard Lanne, "Chad: Recent History," in *Africa: South of the Sahara* (London: Europa, 1995), 276.

51. Lanne, "Chad," 278.

52. Senne Andriamirado, "Congo en avant toutes!" *Jeune Afrique* 1551 (26 September–2 October 1990): 28.

53. *Africa Confidential* 35, no. 4 (1994): 5.

54. *Afrique Contemporaine* 158 (2d trimester 1991): 60.

55. *Africa Research Bulletin* (1–31 March 1995): 11785.

56. Geraldine Faes, "Pour qui roule Djimasta Koibla?" *Jeune Afrique* 1780 (16–22 February 1995): 36.

57. *Njamena Hebdo*, 20 April 1995, 4, 5, N'Djamena, Chad.

58. *Africa Research Bulletin* (16 June–15 July 1994): 11769.

59. See Geraldine Faes, "La France va-t-elle lâcher Deby?" *Jeune Afrique* 1780 (16–22 February 1995): 32.

60. James Wunsch, "Foundations of Centralization: The Colonial Experience and the African Context," in James S. Wunsch and Dele Olowu, eds., *The Failure of the Centralized State* (Boulder, CO: Westview Press, 1990), 35.

61. Arthur Lewis, *Politics in West Africa* (London: Allen and Unwin, 1965).

62. *Africa Research Bulletin* (1–30 June 1994): 11478.

63. Clark, "Elections," 60.

64. Cordell, *Dar al-Kuti*, 45.

65. William F. S. Miles, "Decolonization as Disintegration: The Disestablishment of the State in Chad," unpublished paper presented at the Brazzaville Conference, Boston University, 6–7 October 1994, 17.

66. Clark, "Elections," 60.

67. Faes, "La France va-t-elle lâcher Deby?" 32.

68. *Africa Research Bulletin* (1–31 March 1995): 11785.

69. See *Africa Research Bulletin* (1–31 May 1996): 12264; (1–30 June 1996): 12296–97; (1–31 July 1996): 12336.

Chapter 8

Civil Society, Democratization, and State Building in Kenya and Tanzania

JULIUS E. NYANG'ORO

INTRODUCTION

Africa has experienced significant changes in its political landscape since the beginning of the 1990s decade. Political changes in Africa are part of a global movement toward political liberalization. Not only have authoritarian regimes in Eastern Europe collapsed, but we have also witnessed almost universal liberalization of political systems in Latin America, especially in Brazil, Argentina, and Chile. These countries were better known for their "bureaucratic authoritarianism" in earlier decades than for their "democratic" practice.[1] In Africa, most of the authoritarian regimes—military or one-party systems—have liberalized, partly in response to popular protests but also as a result of international forces.

Given these developments, we can be hopeful that the crude authoritarianism of most states in Africa of the last three decades is a thing of the past and that politics on the continent will be practiced differently from now on. The initial basis for this hope is that even in the most authoritarian states of the past—Zaire, Togo, Malawi, and so on—the nature of the political discourse has fundamentally changed. In Zaire, for example, even though President Mobutu Sese Seko continues to manipulate the transition to pluralism in his country, he now must take into account an existing, legitimate opposition that is no longer operating exclusively underground. Mobutu's leadership is openly challenged, although the lives of opposition leaders are constantly in danger due to harassment by Mobutu's state agents.[2]

Similarly in Togo, despite President Eyadema's initial manipulation of the national conference and the apparent disarray in the ranks of the opposition, Togo's politics is now firmly being discussed in terms of pluralism and power sharing. The devaluation of the CFA (the common currency of French-speaking African countries) at the beginning of 1994 did not help matters, as the cost of living soared, and overall economic conditions have deteriorated. Worsening economic conditions forced some participants at Togo's national conference to concentrate more on economic survival rather than on political participation. The drive for increased political participation, however, has not been abandoned.

Malawi, perhaps the last bastion of authoritarianism in sub-Saharan Africa under Kamuzu Banda, finally held multiparty elections in May 1994, resulting in the defeat of Banda's Malawi Congress Party (MCP) and the election of Bakili Muluzi of the United Democratic Front (UDF) to the presidency. In one of his first acts as president, Muluzi declared that one of the big mansions that Banda had built for himself and his cronies would be turned into a parliament building, thus making better use of state resources. There was also talk of the Malawi government's instituting legal proceedings to recover money that Banda allegedly stole and stashed in foreign banks.[3] In mid-1995, Kamuzu Banda and his former right-hand man, John Tembo, faced murder charges in the deaths of four Malawi politicians in the early 1980s. Although the charges were eventually dropped for "lack of evidence," the fact that formerly powerful politicians could be brought to trial under such serious charges demonstrates that there is a genuine attempt to establish "the rule of law" in Malawi by the new regime.

These three examples should suffice as an indication that, in spite of continuing problems in these countries—problems in both the political and economic spheres—they have embarked on a path that will change the practice of politics in both the medium and long terms. This chapter is thus meant as a reflection on the significance of these broad changes with special emphasis on the countries of Kenya and Tanzania. A special emphasis is placed on the role of civil society in these countries, at both the formal and informal levels. Kenya and Tanzania present two interesting, contrasting experiences. Even though a generalization has been made that civil society in Anglophone Africa (which includes Kenya and Tanzania) is relatively stronger than in Francophone Africa,[4] it must be noted that there is also significant variation in the relative strength of civil society within Anglophone Africa. The argument presented in this chapter is that Kenyan civil society has been more active in the struggle for political liberalization than its counterpart in Tanzania. It is not clear, however, if recent advances that have allowed for a relatively more open political system in both countries are enduring enough to lead to effective state building. The state is defined as a set of institutions that provide a linkage between activities in the economic and political spheres of society. In the contemporary context of Africa's political economy, state building would entail, among other factors, the improvement of the relations among various groups in civil society and a correction of the fragmented economy. In the final analysis, this chapter is an examination of the "depth" of democratic change in these two countries. I use multipartyism in both countries as a starting point for the analysis.

BACKGROUND TO THE SWITCH TO MULTIPARTYISM:
KENYA AND TANZANIA

In December 1991, Kenya officially announced the repeal of the constitutional provision that had made the country a one-party state since 1982. The announcement by the Moi regime of this change followed the now much-publicized suspension of economic aid by Kenya's principal foreign donors—the United States, Britain, France, and the World Bank—at their consultative meeting in November 1991 in Paris. The donors gave the Moi regime six months to institute meaningful and substantive political and economic reforms before funds could be released. In the meantime, the U.S. government announced a travel advisory to Americans intending to visit Kenya during the peak tourist season in December. The reasons given for the travel advisory were that continuing political unrest posed physical dangers to foreigners visiting Kenya after an American tourist was killed by unknown assailants earlier in the year.[5] The combined effect of the aid suspension and the potential loss of revenue from the tourist industry—Kenya's largest earner of foreign exchange—was enough to make the Kenyan government take a second look at its commitment to one-party rule. Some political detainees were released, and Moi announced the arrest of Nicholas Biwott and the late Hezekiah Oyugi, respectively, former minister of energy and former permanent secretary in the Office of the President in charge of internal security.

Under normal circumstances, the dismissal and subsequent arrest of these two men would not raise an eyebrow; but these were not ordinary men in the political power structure in Kenya. Besides President Moi, Biwott and Oyugi were perceived to be the two most powerful people in the country. Biwott, through his business and ethnic ties to the president, was, for all intents and purposes, the "president's man." Oyugi, on the other hand, was privy to all state secrets, especially as they related to security and the human rights situation, which had been a point of contention with aid donors. Both Biwott and Oyugi had been implicated in the disappearance and subsequent murder of former foreign minister Robert Ouko in April 1990.[6] Thus, the arrest of Biwott and Oyugi was a major concession on President Moi's part to pressure from foreign donors. However, a few weeks after their arrest, the two men were released for "lack of evidence." Biwott remained in Parliament as a backbencher, while Oyugi was transferred to a new post as chairman of General Motors (Kenya). He died in London on 8 August 1992 of a brain ailment. The cause of his death is still surrounded in controversy, as are all deaths of prominent people in Kenya.[7]

At first glance it would seem that the decision to allow political pluralism and a multiparty system in Kenya was based on pressure from foreign donors, and, indeed, newspaper reports have suggested that to be the case.[8] While this argument may have some validity, I would like to suggest that the principal push for political reform was internally generated. I would argue that the seeds of opposition to one-party rule in Kenya were planted ironically by the Moi-led Kenya African Democratic Union (KADU) before independence in 1963. KADU's raison d'être was to voice the concerns of smaller ethnic groups in Kenya that did not seem to have influence within the Kenya African National Union (KANU)—the majority party. The merger of KANU and KADU in 1964 signaled the convergence of petty bourgeois interests that had found expression in the two parties before independence.[9] Kenya thus became a *de facto* one-party state in 1964.

From the very beginning, however, it was clear that the newly enlarged KANU was not a happy camp, as Oginga Odinga, leader of the opposition until his death in January 1994 and vice president under Kenya's first president, Jomo Kenyatta, was later to report in his autobiography, *Not Yet Uhuru* (1967).[10] Ajulu, among others, has characterized the conflict within KANU at that time as between a radical faction of the petty bourgeoisie (represented by people such as Odinga) and that of a traditional/embryonic bourgeoisie (represented by Kenyatta) with regard to the trajectory of Kenya's political and economic development. The formation of a new political party, the Kenya People's Union (KPU), in 1966 under the leadership of Odinga signaled the culmination of the rift between the two factions of the bourgeoisie. KPU was banned in 1969, and Kenya, for all practical purposes, remained a one-party state until December 1991.[11]

The point of emphasis, however, should be that throughout the postindependence period, there has been no consensus in Kenya on the desirability of a one-party system. Indeed, foreign pressure on the Moi government on the question of human rights has always been in reaction to internal struggles—by students, lawyers, politicians, clergy, and others. Thus, the massive riots by various segments of the population that took place in July 1990, primarily in the Central and Rift Valley Provinces in response to the banning of public meetings called to advocate political pluralism, must be seen as reflecting this long-standing tradition of opposition to one-partyism.[12] The call by the American ambassador to Kenya in 1990 and in subsequent months[13] for the release of political prisoners was based on evidence provided by, among others, members of the Kenya Law Society, whose leadership in the past few years has included people like Paul Muite, who until recently was vice chairman of the leading opposition party in Kenya, the Forum for the Restoration of Democracy—Kenya (FORD—Kenya). Paul Muite is a founding member of a new political party in Kenya known as SAFINA (the Ark).

While it would seem that the Moi government was reluctantly pushed to accept the introduction of a multiparty political system, the government in neighboring Tanzania seemed to have prepared itself for the inevitable change to multipartyism in deliberate fashion. Ironically, former president Julius Nyerere, one of the earliest proponents of one-partyism in Africa, seemed to have set the whole process of change in motion. In August 1990 in his farewell speech to the ruling Chama Cha Mapinduzi (CCM) National Executive Committee (NEC),

Table 8.1
Responses to the Question: Should There Be a Continuation of the One-Party System?

	Yes	No	No Response	No Opinion	Total
Tanzania Total	28,018.0	7,817.0	244.0	220.0	36,299
% of Total	77.2	21.5	0.6	0.6	100
Tanzania Mainland Total	25,725.0	6,118.0	238.0	200.0	32,275
% of Total	79.7	19.0	0.7	0.6	100
Tanzania Zanzibar Total	2,074.0	1,582.0	5.0	18.0	3,679
% of Total	56.4	43.0	0.1	0.5	100
Embassies Abroad Total	221.0	117.0	1.0	2.0	341
% of Total	64.8	34.3	0.3	0.6	100

Source: Nyalali Commission Report, vol. 1 (1992), 60.

which had just elected President Ali Hassan Mwinyi as its chairman to succeed the retiring ex-president, Nyerere argued that it was time to seriously think about adopting a multiparty system. He pointed to political changes occurring across the continent and cautioned that the best way to introduce a new system would be by gradualism with careful attention paid to the details of the transition to allow for minimal disruption and political conflict. He noted that further delay in consideration of the new proposal would only engender chaos, as had happened in other countries such as Kenya and Zaire.[14]

CCM heeded Nyerere's advice. President Ali Hassan Mwinyi appointed a commission in March 1991 headed by Chief Justice Francis Nyalali to assess the desirability and mechanics of change from one-partyism to multipartyism. The commission's members traveled across Tanzania and several foreign countries—including Zimbabwe, Zaire, Britain, and the United States—interviewing Tanzanians and foreigners alike on relevant issues connected with political transformation. It is interesting to note that, although the overwhelming majority of Tanzanians interviewed favored the continuation of a single-party system, the Nyalali Commission actually recommended the adoption of the multiparty system. Table 8.1 is a summary of views as compiled by the Nyalali Commission.

On the basis of the Nyalali Commission Report, which was presented to the president on 17 February 1992, two days later an extraordinary CCM National Conference unanimously passed a resolution formally opening the door to multiple political parties and repealed a clause in the country's Constitution that had given CCM monopoly over political activity in the country.[15] The CCM Conference, however, gave the following guidelines for the introduction of new parties:

1. New parties must be panterritorial with members on both sides of the union and should not be based on religion, regionalism, "tribe," race or creed.

2. They should be "genuine" parties formed by Tanzanians themselves and committed to protecting national gains.

3. Parties should respect and defend the principles of equality, justice, and human rights for all people.

4. Parties should accept and respect the principle of inviolability of the national borders of the United Republic of Tanzania and the territorial integrity of Zanzibar and all its islands.

5. Parties must advance their causes through the force of argument rather than argument of force.[16]

Underlying these guidelines is the anxiety prompted by some forces in Zanzibar pushing for more autonomy and possible withdrawal from the union. The "Zanzibar problem," as it has come to be known in Tanzania, has been raised by those who argue that the terms of the union between Tanganyika (mainland Tanzania) and Zanzibar in 1964 were inherently unfair to Zanzibar and that Zanzibar has remained a junior partner in the union despite the fact that Zanzibar had been a sovereign state until 26 April 1964. However, there is considerable opinion on the mainland that, if anything, Zanzibar, with slightly more than 500,000 people, has enjoyed a disproportionate influence in the union, as evidenced by the current union government. Ali Hassan Mwinyi, who was president of Tanzania from 1985 to 1995, is from Zanzibar, and so are many top government officials in various ministries and in embassies abroad. To be sure, the Zanzibar question is both a legal/constitutional question[17] and a political one.[18] As of July 1994, 60 members of Parliament (MPs), all backbenchers hailing from Tanzania mainland, supported a motion seeking implementation of a National Assembly (Parliament) resolution to create a Tanganyika government, with powers similar to the ones enjoyed by the Zanzibar government. It is widely believed in Tanzania that many senior officials in government from the mainland would support the Tanganyika motion but are reluctant to do so publicly for fear of losing their jobs, since the official position of the government is to maintain the union.[19] The debate on the union, however, has slightly subsided in the last year as a result of Nyerere's intervention. In a scathing pamphlet against those who favor dissolution of the union, Nyerere argued that any attempt at breaking the union will most likely lead to bloodshed, which most Tanzanians were not prepared to endure.[20] Arguably, the fact that the Zanzibar question is openly debated both within and outside Parliament is an indication that political liberalism has continued apace since 1990.

The Zanzibar question aside, Tanzania seems to have taken to multipartyism without much fanfare. By the end of June 1992, twelve parties besides CCM had been granted temporary registration, with even more parties seeking to be registered. By the middle of October 1992, the number of temporarily registered parties was over 20.[21] As of July 1994 a dozen or so parties were officially operating in Tanzania. One of the most viable of the opposition parties is the National Convention for Construction and Reform—Mageuzi (NCCR—Mageuzi), led by the human rights lawyer and activist Mabere Marando. In its first public rally in the coastal town of Tanga, NCCR—Mageuzi attracted a crowd of at least 10,000.[22] In March 1995, Augustine Mrema, former deputy prime minister and minister of home affairs, resigned from the ruling party CCM and from the government and joined NCCR—Mageuzi. NCCR—Mageuzi, in turn, nominated Mrema as its presidential candidate for elections in October 1995. Other opposition parties include the Union for Multi-Party Democracy (UMD), led by Chief Abdallah Fundikira, former justice minister in the first independence government in Tanganyika, and Chama Cha Demokrasia na Maendeleo (CHADEMA), led by Edwin Mtei, former governor of the Central Bank and minister of finance under Julius Nyerere.

On 29 October 1995, the first genuinely multiparty elections since independence were held in Tanzania, ending 34 years of one-party rule. The overwhelming winner of the elections was CCM, which gained 78.1 percent of the total seats in Parliament. Other parties gaining seats were Civic United Front, 10.2 percent; NCCR—Mageuzi, 6.9 percent; United Democratic Party, 1.5 percent; CHADEMA, 1.1 percent; and others, 2.2 percent. The significance of the large number of seats won by the Civic United Front (CUF) is that CUF won all the parliamentary seats in Pemba, the smaller island in Zanzibar and a hotbed for antiunion activities. Here lessons from Kenya could be instructive. Although the opposition in Kenya won more votes than the ruling KANU, in the December 1992 elections the opposition was badly split, thus allowing for the retaining of power by the Moi regime. In Tanzania, by contrast, the percentage of the seats for the combined opposition was only 21.9 percent.[23]

Arguably, how well civil society responds to the pressures and results of political liberalization determines the trajectory of democratic development in both countries. To be sure, we have had less than half a decade of multipartyism in both countries, and we may have to wait a few more years before a meaningful assessment of political change can be made. We have to guard against false optimism lest we became disillusioned by what we may see as too slow a change in the transition from authoritarianism.

CIVIL SOCIETY AND THE STRUGGLE FOR DEMOCRACY

The notion of civil society has gained currency in the contemporary discourse on democracy in Africa. In general political analysis, however, civil society as a concept is not particularly new. Patrick Chabal, among others, has suggested that civil society is now being introduced into the political analysis of Africa largely ''because the (over)emphasis on the role of the state has led to a definition of the political sphere as being virtually coterminous with the politics of the state.''[24] The crisis of the postcolonial state and the popular demand for less centralization have led the analysis of African politics to move away from "the state" as a primary focus to activities within civil society. Indeed, as numerous studies have shown, analyses of politics in Africa of the last decade or so had lagged behind "action on the ground" in the sense that for a significant portion of the population in African countries, the daily lives of individuals were conducted substantially in the vast area of activity away from the state that is understood to be "civil society." Thus, to most analysts of politics in Africa, the success of democracy on the continent is primarily (if not solely) dependent on how vigorously civil society is able to maintain its independence/autonomy from the state.[25]

Even though civil society as a concept is now widely used in the discourse on politics in Africa, it is still a concept that raises significant analytical and practical problems. A leading African intellectual, Samir Amin, for example, notes that it is difficult to discuss civil society outside the capitalist framework.[26] For Amin, the room for activity by civil society is predetermined by its function in relation to capital accumulation. Once there is a contradiction between civil society's activities and those of the need for capital accumulation, the former must be adjusted to suit the latter. Amin argues that, unless this inherent contradiction between forces of capital and those of the general "masses" who aspire to become "really" free is resolved, there cannot be real democracy. Liberal democracy, according to Amin, is thus limited by its incapacity to effectively challenge capitalist inequalities. Civil society in this context is not and cannot be dynamic enough to be the essential building block for democracy that is popular. Thus, if we follow Amin's argument to its logical conclusion, the basing of democratic hopes in Africa on "civil society," as understood in the bourgeois sense, leaves a lot to be desired.

Patrick Chabal quotes at length another leading Africanist scholar, J. F. Bayart, who is struggling to understand the concept of civil society in relation to Africa. I reproduce the quote here to emphasize the complexity that careful analysis of both the concept and phenomenon of civil society demands:

Though it is arguable that the concept of civil society is not applicable outside European history I shall define it provisionally as "society in its relation with the state . . . in so far as it is in confrontation with the state" or, more precisely, as the process by which society seeks to "breach" and counteract the simultaneous "totalisation" unleashed by the state. . . . The notion of civil society is thus an ambivalent (and not just conflictive), complex and dynamic relation between state and society. [Civil society] is not necessarily a discrete entity completely external to an equally discrete source of power. That much is obvious in the case of institutions or organizations which represent civil society within political society, such as parliaments, parties or trade unions. But it is equally true of the power structures themselves, these are by no means immune to the particularistic pulls of civil society. . . . Moreover, civil society is not necessarily embodied in a single, identifiable structure. It is by its very nature plural and covers all sorts of different practices; any unity there is requires human creativity. Finally, civil society is not merely the expression of dominated social groups. It encompasses not only popular modes of political action but also the claims of those socially dominant groups which are no less excluded from direct participation in political power.[27]

Of particular interest to me in the preceding quote is the recognition that civil society is not necessarily embodied in a single, identifiable structure and that it is not merely the expression of dominated social groups. It is a recognition that civil society as an arena is a complex place that reflects all the contradictions in society. The interests of capitalist, professional associations, nongovernmental organizations, trade groups, and so on are all represented in civil society, and thus access to the state by members of civil society may be differentiated relative to the power held by particular groups in society. This observation points to the danger that I see in the celebration and/or actual romanticization of civil society by Africanist scholars. The limitation of civil society as the midwife of democracy thus must be acknowledged.

This is not to suggest, however, that civil society, both as a concept and in its activities, is not useful to the understanding of contemporary Africa and the continuing opening up of the political and social space. As the French traveler Alexis de Tocqueville observed in relation to America in the last century, civil society is extremely important in defining the nature and extent of democracy in society. If we understand civil society to be a sphere of social interaction between economy and state, then there is an inverse relationship between the state's capacity to coerce the governed and the extent to which local/particularistic interests organize themselves to advance their objectives. The more the members of society organize themselves into groups to advance their particular interests, the less likely the state can function in an autonomous manner. As Joel Barkan has observed, in relation to Kenya and Nigeria, the proliferation of organized interests is a bulwark against unbridled state power. This autonomy is one of the key principles in the building of democracy.[28]

Yet, as I have noted, there is an inherent danger in the overcelebration of civil society as the basis for democratic change, given the relative strength of various groups in society. It needs to be pointed out that not all states are bad, and neither is the state always the enemy (cf. chapter 1). Historically, the state has played a positive role in political mediation between various groups in society and has also played a progressive role, especially in defense of capitalism vis-à-vis the reactionary forces of feudalism.[29] Thus, as we examine the role of the state in Africa, we need to specify the particular dynamic in which social forces are operating. The experience of most states in Africa, however, has been that of undermining democracy, thus allowing for the generalizations that we encounter about the positive nature of civil society. At this juncture, therefore, as the transition to more liberal politics in Africa continues and in spite of all the problems associated with the concept of civil society, activities within civil society are still a good measure of how "open" and "pluralistic" a political system is. Conversely, the "depth" of democratic change in Africa may be measured by the extent of its autonomy from the state.

CIVIL SOCIETY IN KENYA AND TANZANIA

In both Kenya and Tanzania, civil society has played an important role in pushing for pluralistic politics and the minimizing of state centrality in people's lives. State centrality in both countries was characterized by, among other things, the legal banning of oppositional parties and restricting political participation to KANU in Kenya and CCM in Tanzania. Given these formal restrictions to political activity, it is fair to say that, until recently in both countries, most of the opposition to the regimes in power was primarily informal. Participants in the opposition reflected the various interests in society: business and professional associations, the church, students, women's organizations, and so on.

In Kenya, two groups can be cited as having played an active role in opposing the Moi regime before 1991: the church and students, especially university students.[30] To a lesser extent, various women's organizations assumed an activist role in opposing the Moi regime, but this was after the lifting of the ban on multiparty politics in 1991, and most women's organizations actually concentrated on mobilizing women for political participation in the 1992 elections.[31] Thus, the church and students' activities still stand out in this regard. Two examples on the role of the church should suffice.

First, following the riots of July 1990, the Church of the Province of Kenya (CPK) (the Anglican Church) took issue with the government in terms of the causes of the riots. The CPK's clergy, especially Manases Kuria, then archbishop of Nairobi, Henry Okullu, then bishop of Maseno South in Nyanza Province, and the late Alexander Muge, bishop of Eldoret, demanded that the government face up to the economic and political needs of the people. Bishop Okullu specifically asked the government to resign to clear the way for a new beginning. Thus, in a Sunday sermon on 15 July 1990, Bishop Okullu asked the government to convene a constitutional assembly and called for a transitional government of national unity. Bishop Okullu justified his position by arguing:

Who has driven us to this ugly predicament, these temptations to go back to a state of backwardness which we could never have thought of? The blame must lie on the KANU Government which, in spite of all calls to arrange for a national convention, a dialogue with all the people and a democratic form of government, has insisted on going its own way.[32]

Bishop Okullu concluded his sermon by condemning the detention without trial of former cabinet ministers Kenneth Matiba and Charles Rubia, who had been picked up by the police for allegedly inciting people to riot. The two former ministers were not released until early 1992. Matiba in the meantime suffered a stroke and had to be flown to London for emergency medical treatment. He is now the leader of one of the opposition parties: FORD-Asili.

Second, the National Council of Churches of Kenya (NCCK) has been in the forefront over the years in opposition to the KANU politics of exclusion. Along with its constituent members, NCCK on various occasions called for the abolition of the queuing procedure, which had forced people at polling stations to queue behind their preferred candidate's picture or his or her representative, thus violating the principle of the secret ballot. This procedure was "exclusionary" because only those in support of the preferred KANU candidate would venture to the polling stations. Thus, exclusionary politics here was both by design and by default. As a result of the adoption of the queuing procedure, voter turnout in the 1988 general election fell precipitously to only 24.6 percent of those eligible, the lowest in Kenya's history.[33] In the period since allowing multiparty politics in Kenya, NCCK has produced educational materials urging people to exercise their constitutional right to vote, sometimes with a demonstrated preference for the opposition. As the NCCK further participated in the political process, including the attempt at reconciling the divergent opinions within FORD, its former general secretary Rev. Samuel Kobia was threatened with bodily harm. The speculation was that these threats had connection to the KANU regime.[34]

NCCK has continued to play a significant role in channeling political demands in the current phase of the transition by organizing a commission to study the causes and effects of the "ethnic" clashes that took place in the first half of 1992, accounting for several thousand deaths and the displacement of between 255,000 and 300,000 people, especially in the Rift Valley Province, which is President Moi's stronghold.[35] A parliamentary commission headed by Kennedy Kiliku, MP for Changamwe, to investigate the clashes, actually came to the same conclusion as the NCCK report. Both reports implicated high government officials, especially William Ole Ntimama, minister for local government, Ezekiel Barng'etuny, nominated MP, and Nicholas Biwott, MP and former minister of energy.[36] Thus, the role of the church in the struggle for pluralism and government accountability has been an extremely important one.

In Tanzania, it cannot be said with any certainty that the church has played any significant role in pushing for multipartyism. The Christian Council of Tanzania (CCT), for example, has not issued a major statement on the current changes. This, of course, is in marked contrast to NCCK's position in Kenya. Neither can one say that other organized groups in Tanzania have, over the years, been active in struggling against one-party rule. The apparent lack of opposition to one-party rule in Tanzania—formal and informal—can be explained, in part, by the success of Julius Nyerere in explaining and justifying one-partyism. But the data and the apparent intellectual force that Nyerere represented obscure one essential fact. CCM and its predecessors, Tanganyika African National Union (TANU) and the Afro-Shirazi Party (ASP), were very successful in carrying out their "corporatist" project, a point that has been argued elsewhere.[37] To elaborate on what is meant by corporatism here, I borrow James M. Malloy's characterization of corporatist regimes:

These regimes try to eliminate spontaneous interest articulation and establish a limited number of authoritatively recognized groups that interact with the governmental apparatus in defined and regularized ways. Moreover, the recognized groups in this type of regime are organized in vertical functional categories rather than horizontal class categories and are obliged to interact with the state through the designated leaders of authoritatively sanctioned interest associations. This mode of organizing state and society has been aptly termed "corporatism."[38]

CCM was relatively successful in achieving the corporatist project by making all organized groups (and secondary associations) part of the party structure. Thus, CCM had a youth league, a women's organization unit (UWT), a worker's unit (NUTA), and a grower's unit (USHIRIKA-Cooperatives). The key to holding these units together and subordinating them to CCM was the legal monopoly of power that the party had. By implication, the price of exclusion was too high for anybody who contemplated operating outside the party structure. In many ways, therefore, Tanzania was the classic case of state centralization, which left little room for dissent. It would be erroneous, however, to suggest that not belonging to CCM-sponsored activities or organizations meant one's life was in jeopardy, as was sometimes the case in Kenya. Rather, it meant that one could not hope to attain a high government post unless he or she was closely associated with CCM.

My contention is that the success with which CCM was able to organize itself in Tanzania without overt coercion, for the most part, created some social space in which individuals not aspiring to high government posts could actually live their daily lives without having to worry about government harassment. Furthermore, this social space actually created its own political culture, which had several elements, including a public cynicism against party operatives who were seen simply as political opportunists—an accusation raised by one leader of the opposition, Mabere Marando.[39] It is also now becoming apparent that CCM was not as entrenched in the regions and rural areas as previously thought, thus prompting the former secretary-general of the party, Horace Kolimba, to tour the country in a massive registration effort.[40] This leads to the conclusion that, despite CCM's legal monopoly of power, its reach in terms of creating fear among the citizens was limited. Goran Hyden's (1980) now classic study of politics in Tanzania was the first major exposition of the Tanzanian state's weakness in this regard, when he introduced the concept of the "uncaptured peasantry" in Tanzania.

So, in a contradictory way, CCM was actually successful in that politics of fear was not the norm and hence was the less passionate way with which people look at the issue of multipartyism in Tanzania. In contrast, those fighting for multipartyism in Kenya have suffered physical abuse at the hands of the regime. This has also engendered a "high-strung," passionate culture of opposition, including violence. As an example, some members of the two FORD factions were actually engaged in physical combat during the first elections for national party officeholders of FORD—Kenya. Followers of FORD—Asili had intended to disrupt FORD—Kenya elections until scores of them were arrested by the police for public disturbance.[41] Another example is the reaction of the followers of the unregistered Islamic Party of Kenya (IPK), who made the coastal city of Mombasa, the stronghold of Islam in Kenya, virtually ungovernable for about a week when the government refused to register the party allegedly because of its religious base and "exclusionist" tendencies.[42] In mid-1993 there were further disturbances on the Kenyan coast, thus continuing the tradition of violence in Kenyan politics. I would argue that the culture of intolerance has been dangerously nurtured in Kenyan politics as a result of the long-standing decision by the government to control every avenue of political life. Thus, the stone-throwing incidents at the FORD elections, the riots in Mombasa, and the so-called ethnic clashes in the Rift Valley Province are no accidents.

But perhaps the biggest obstacle to state building and democratization in Kenya is the problem associated with ethnicity and the use of ethnicity for political purposes. Much has been said about the colonial policy of divide-and-rule in Africa. The policy was based on favoring one ethnic group over others in terms of providing education or introducing development projects, which then would be the basis for one ethnic group's supporting the colonial enterprise. This, of course, had the ultimate effect of weakening the anticolonial struggle because the nationalists not only had to overcome the obstacles created by the colonial state but also had to deal with ethnic disunity among Africans.[43] In Kenya, the big ethnic divide was between the major and more numerous ethnic groups: Kikuyu and Luo, which formed the basis of the earlier KANU; and the smaller ethnic groups such as the Kalenjin, Jaasai, and Luhya. The smaller groups formed the basis of the earlier KADU. As we have seen, the two parties, KANU and KADU, merged under KANU at the time of independence. The fact that the initial politics of the predominant parties was essentially ethnic, the future of KANU, and, indeed, the reality of the post-1991 period have been heavily influenced by ethnic considerations.

In the aftermath of the new multiparty era in Kenya, all the major political parties, in spite of official denial, have used ethnicity as the primary basis for political mobilization. FORD—Kenya is heavily Luo-based; FORD—Asili is primarily Kikuyu, as is the Democratic Party. KANU now reflects the smaller ethnic groups, which in the later years of colonization and the early years of independence had allegiance to KADU. Even though previous analyses of Kenyan politics had attempted to move beyond ethnicity as a basis for political organization, it seems, however, that ethnicity as a mobilizing force is still a reality.[44] Githu Muigai has argued that "[in] the absence of other platforms upon which to base political appeal, ethnicity presents itself as the most natural basis of political organization, feeding as it does on pride and prejudice and on the 'herd instinct.' "[45]

Given the realities of ethnic politics not only in Kenya but in the rest of sub-Saharan Africa, it seems that, far from political liberalization's being a force to unite civil society across ethnic groups, it has actually provided an opportunity for ethnic leaders and politicians to revive and use ethnicity for narrow political ends. Thus, the failure of the Kenyan opposition to unite under one leader in the presidential ballot can largely be attributed to ethnic dynamics within the Democratic Party, FORD—Asili, and FORD—Kenya. Simple arithmetic tells us that the total number of votes for President Moi was 1,962,866, while the combined opposition received 3,437,458.[46] Clearly, if the opposition had united under one candidate, Moi would have been defeated. It follows, therefore, that for purposes of state building, ethnicity in Kenya has played a negative role and has been continuously used by leaders both in and out of government to create divisions among the population. Thus, even though civil society, which cuts across ethnic lines in Kenya, is fairly active and has played a significant role in bringing about political change, its efforts are still hampered by the reality of ethnic politics. In the case of Tanzania, however, ethnicity continues to be of less significance—and, indeed, almost irrelevant in terms of political mobilization.[47] Politicians in Tanzania still strive to make the whole country the basis of their appeal. Political tradition in postindependence Tanzania has been quite unkind to politicians who have attempted to use ethnicity as a basis for political mobilization. It is no accident, therefore, that Julius Nyerere's son ran as a candidate for NCCR—Mageuzi in Arusha region, while his father is from Mara region. Similarly, NCCR—Mageuzi has a very strong showing in the home district of CCM's presidential candidate, who won the election nationally in a landslide.

DEMOCRATIC CHANGE AND STATE BUILDING IN KENYA AND TANZANIA

The foregoing analysis was geared toward demonstrating the complexity of political change in the chosen case studies. Certainly, there is no straightforward answer to the question, How "deep" has democratic change in Africa been? The best one can do is make observations and raise questions that logically follow from the analysis.

There is no uniformity in the nature of change in African countries. Individual country experiences are dictating the nature of these changes in terms of who the principal operators are: churches, trade unions, nongovernmental organizations (NGOs), and so on. Civil society as a concept and as an arena for change is a complex phenomenon that requires desegregation at various levels. For our purposes, however, it is important that we acknowledge the potential that civil society has in advancing the democratic project but also recognize the danger of assuming that "civil society" as such will always play a progressive role in advancing democracy. Civil society's significance in our discourse is tied to autonomy, which society creates for itself vis-à-vis the state. Ethnicity, even though discarded as an important factor in contemporary politics, continues to show its resiliency and thus warrants more attention.

Finally, civil society should be understood at two levels. Both analytically and in terms of praxis, the relationship between the state and civil society is one of verticality: the state pushing for centralization while civil society is resisting. There is, however, the horizontal relationship among groups that constitute civil society. This relationship is complicated by the fact that while civil society may be united against the state, there is no necessary mutual interest horizontally, that is, within civil society itself. Thus, the political agenda for progressive forces is to ensure that civil society is subject to the democratic principles that it demands of the state; that is, how democratic is civil society? This is still an open question.

NOTES

1. Guillermo A. O'Donnell, *Modernization and Bureaucratic-Authoritarianism: Studies in South American Politics* (Berkeley, CA: Institute of International Studies, 1979).

2. *Herald* (Harare), 4 July 1995, 2.

3. *Daily News* (Dar es Salaam), 26 July 1994.

4. Richard Crook, "State, Society and Political Institutions in Côte d'Ivoire and Ghana," *IDS Bulletin* 21, no. 4 (October 1990): 24–34.

5. *New York Times*, November 1991.

6. Julius E. Nyang'oro, "The Quest for Pluralist Democracy in Kenya," *Trans-Africa Forum* 7, no. 3 (1990): 73–82.

7. *Society* (Nairobi), 24 August 1992.

8. *New York Times*, 4 December 1991.

9. Rok Ajulu, "Kenya: The Road to Democracy," *Review of African Political Economy* 53 (March 1992): 80.

10. Oginga Odinga, *Not Yet Uhuru* (London: Heinemann, 1967).

11. Ajulu, "Kenya," 79–87.

12. Nyang'oro, "The Quest for Pluralist Democracy in Kenya," 73–82; James N. Karioki, "University of Nairobi and the Demise of Democracy in Kenya," *Trans-Africa Forum* 7, no. 3 (1990): 83–93.

13. *Daily Nation*, July 1990, various issues.

14. *Daily News*, 15 August 1990.

15. *Daily News*, 20 February 1992.

16. *Tanzania Embassy Newsletter* (Washington, DC), March 1992, 1.

17. Issa G. Shivji, *Tanzania: The Legal Foundations of the Union* (Dar es Salaam: Dar es Salaam University Press, 1990); *Family Mirror*, Dar es Salaam, May 1992, 4.

18. *Africa Events* (June/July 1988): 14–27.

19. *Daily News*, 23 July 1994.

20. Julius K. Nyerere, *Our Leadership and the Destiny of Tanzania* (Harare: African Publishing Group, 1995; Swahili edition first published in 1994).

21. *Daily News* (Dar es Salaam), various issues, October 1992.

22. *Mfanyakazi*, 2 September 1992, 1.

23. Pamela R. Reeves and Keith Klein, *Republic in Transition: 1995 Elections in Tanzania and Zanzibar* (Report of the International Foundation for Election Systems [IFES] International Observer Delegation) (Washington, DC: IFES, 1995); see also Lisa Richey and Stefano Ponte, "The 1995 Tanzania Union Elections," *Review of African Political Economy* 23 (March 1996): 67.

24. Patrick Chabal, *Power in Africa: An Essay in Political Interpretation* (New York: St. Martin's, 1994), 82.

25. See for example, Joel D. Barkan, "Resurrecting Modernization Theory and the Emergence of Civil Society in Kenya and Nigeria," in David E. Apter and Carl G. Rosberg, eds., *Political Development and the New Realism in Sub-Saharan Africa* (Charlottesville: University Press of Virginia, 1994), 87–116.

26. Samir Amin, "Preface: The State and the Question of 'Development,' " in Peter Anyang' Nyong'o, ed., *Popular Struggles for Democracy in Africa* (London: United Nations University and Zed Press, 1987), 1–13.

27. Quoted in Chabal, *Power in Africa*, 83.

28. Barkan, "Resurrecting Modernization Theory," 109.

29. Manfred Bienfield, "Structural Adjustment and the Prospects for Democracy in Southern Africa," in David B. Moore and Gerald G. Schmitz, eds., *Debating Development Discourse: Institutional and Popular Perspectives* (New York: St. Martin's Press, 1995); see also Ellen Meiksins Wood, "The Uses and Abuses of 'Civil Society,' " in Ralph Miliband and Leo Panitch, eds., *Socialist Register* 1990: The Retreat of the Intellectuals (London: Merlin Press, 1990), 60–84.

30. Karioki, "University of Nairobi and the Demise of Democracy in Kenya."

31. Maria Nzomo, "Empowering Women for Democratic Change in Kenya: Which Way Forward?" in Ludgera Klemp, ed., *Empowerment of Women in the Process of Democratisation: Experiences of Kenya, Uganda and Tanzania* (Dar es Salaam: Friedrich Ebert Stiftung, 1994), 29–33.

32. *Daily Nation*, 16 July 1990, 1.

33. Joel D. Barkan, "Divergence and Convergence in Kenya and Tanzania: Pressures for Reform," in Joel D. Barkan, ed., *Beyond Capitalism vs. Socialism in Kenya and Tanzania* (Boulder, CO: Lynne Rienner, 1994), 28.

34. "Death Threat to NCCK Boss," *Target* (Nairobi) 361 (15 September 1992): 1–2.

35. Barkan, "Divergence and Convergence in Kenya and Tanzania," 38.

36. *Weekly Review*, 23 October 1992.

37. Julius E. Nyang'oro, "State Corporatism in Tanzania," in Julius E. Nyang'oro and Timothy M. Shaw, eds., *Corporatism in Africa: Comparative Analysis and Practice* (Boulder, CO: Westview Press, 1989), 67–82.

38. James M. Malloy, "Authoritarianism and Corporatism in Latin America: The Model Pattern," in James M. Malloy, ed., *Authoritarianism and Corporatism in Latin America* (Pittsburgh: University of Pittsburgh Press, 1977), 4.

39. *Mfanyakazi*, 2 September 1992, 1.

40. *Africa Events*, October/November 1992.

41. *Daily Nation*, 3 September 1992.

42. *Daily Nation*, 21 May 1992.

43. Ali A. Mazrui and Michael Tidy, *Nationalism and New States in Africa* (Portsmouth, NH: Heineman, 1984).

44. See, for example, Colin Leys, *Underdevelopment in Kenya: The Political Economy of Neocolonization* (London: Heinemann, 1975); Nicola Swainson, *The Development of Corporate Capitalism in Kenya* (Berkeley: University of California Press, 1980).

45. Githu Muigai, "Ethnicity and the Renewal of Competitive Politics in Kenya," in Harvey Glickman, ed., *Ethnic Conflict and Democratization in Africa* (Atlanta: ASA Press, 1995), 161–62.

46. International Republican Institute, *KENYA: The December 29, 1992 Elections* (Washington, DC: IRI, 1993).

47. Harvey Glickman, "Management of Ethnic Politics and Democratization in Tanzania," in Harvey Glickman, ed., *Ethnic Conflict and Democratization in Africa* (Atlanta: ASA Press, 1995), 289–309.

Chapter 9

Remaking the State: Assessing South Africa's Developmental Agenda

LARRY A. SWATUK

INTRODUCTION

Welcome to the "new" South Africa. Official rhetoric revolves around a heady language of "rebirth" and "reconciliation," of "Simunye—We are one!" and a leading role in a pending "African renaissance." Yet, the blitheness of this discourse masks a far more complex reality. To be sure, South Africa's "democracy" has moved beyond exclusion based on race toward a more inclusive dispensation. Getting this far has been more of a hard-won struggle than a miracle, though the world prefers to think of it as the latter. Successful state building involves much more than a political commitment to "good governance," whatever that may mean, and free market economics. In South Africa's case it involves, among other things, constructing and embarking on a developmental agenda whose central focus is the alleviation of poverty. The scale of human-made suffering in South Africa is appalling. In most cases, this suffering is a direct consequence of state policy. A complex political machinery was constructed to preserve white privilege. Whether this machine can be retooled and turned to more constructive enterprise is yet to be seen. It is also the central focus of this chapter.

RECONSTRUCTION AND DEVELOPMENT

In many daunting ways, the struggle continues. The Government of National Unity (GNU) inherits a form of state whose institutional structures were designed to marginalize and oppress the majority of people living within South Africa's territorial borders.[1] As a result, at least 32 percent of South Africans are unemployed; Africans themselves constitute 95 percent of South Africa's poor; between 12 and 14 million people are without access to safe water; and over 20 million live without adequate sanitation. In addition, "[i]nequality in access to jobs, services and economic resources as well as other pathways from poverty, such as education, skills training and health care continue to make it difficult for people to escape from poverty."[2]

According to recently released data from the United Nations Development Program (UNDP), South Africa remains one of the most unequal societies on earth. The top 10 percent of the population account for 47.3 percent of total income, whereas the bottom 10 percent account for 1.4 percent. When extended to the top 20 percent, share of total income rises to 63.3 percent. For the bottom 20 percent the comparable figure is a mere 3.3 percent.[3] The Gini coefficient for South Africa in 1993 was 58.4 (where a value of 0 equals perfectly equitable distribution, and a value of 100 equals perfect inequality), and an estimated 24 percent of the population lives on less than one dollar per day.[4]

The new government's challenge, therefore, is, first and foremost, to move from reconciliation at the level of the polity to reconstruction and development at the level of the socioeconomy. In recognition of this, the ANC's Reconstruction and Development Program (RDP) has become a symbol of both commitment and ideology of development for most South Africans.[5] GEAR, the government's Growth, Employment, and Redistribution strategy, is to be the means for realizing the primary goals of job creation, poverty reduction, and sustainable growth as articulated in the RDP.[6]

This is a formidable task. Moreover, there continues to be heated debate within South Africa about appropriate tactics. This debate mirrors arguments elsewhere about the role of the state in development and in the context of economic globalization.[7] Given the new South Africa's commitment to multiparty and participatory forms of democracy, and given its inheritance of a relatively robust civil society with a tradition of confrontation with the state, this is very much a public debate. It is also one that at times threatens to inhibit action in any direction.

In this chapter, I assess the likelihood that South Africa's state-makers will be able to move beyond what Southall terms the "double whammy."[8] On one hand, the GNU faces widespread popular, domestic pressure for democratization and development. These pressures demand commitment to state intervention and redistribution of resources. At the same time, state-makers face overwhelming pressure from global and national capital to liberalize the economy, pursue export-oriented niche development, and practice careful money management. These pressures suggest a policy of minimal state intervention in the economy. But such an approach to economic growth risks heightening domestic dissent as many popular demands go unmet. Whether both tasks—democratic development and sustainable economic growth—can be pursued simultaneously and successfully is a matter for extended discussion.[9]

The chapter proceeds as follows. In the first section, I examine South Africa's form of state, focusing on the rise and decline of a historic bloc arrayed around the tenets of apartheid capitalist development. The aim is to highlight the fact that South Africa's "negotiated revolution" left many factions of the old regime largely intact. These unresolved aspects of change, I argue, will haunt policy-makers and hamper meaningful transformation long into the next millennium.

In the second section, the chapter looks critically at state-building activities in South Africa and explores the likelihood that an ANC-led government can serve as the locus for a truly progressive, developmentally oriented, counter-hegemonic force in the twenty-first century. My conclusions are guardedly and perhaps naively optimistic: the record so far is mixed, but righting the wrongs of 300 years will take more than one term in office.

DEVELOPMENT AND STATE FORMATION: HEGEMONY AND CRISIS

Monopoly Capital and Development

While space does not permit a detailed analysis of the history of the apartheid state, two specific aspects of state building require elaboration: the nature of the historic bloc that emerged following the National Party's initial election victory in 1948 and the world economic crisis of the 1970s, from which this hegemonic bloc never recovered and which ultimately led to majority rule in 1994. As seen in the following review, South Africa's state form since independence in 1910 has been dominated by two distinctly different historic blocs, the first led by English mining capital, and the second by Afrikaner nationalist forces. Each historic bloc dissolved due to a combination of world order pressures that, in turn, initiated changes in the configuration of social forces within the state. At present, the ANC-led GNU is attempting to reconcile antagonistic elements within the state in order to achieve hegemony by consensus.

As is only too well known, South Africa's wealth derives primarily from monopoly capital's successful exploitation of the country's vast mineral resources, like gold, diamonds, titanium, uranium and coal. In the beginning this wealth accrued primarily to English colonialists, the battle for hegemony having been fought and won against early settlers known colloquially as Boers, which is Afrikaans for farmers, in the Anglo-Boer War of 1899–1902. Afrikaners, the descendants of Dutch and French Huguenot settlers, were, in the main, agro-pastoralists. Over time, mining developments resulted in massive social upheaval as indigenous peoples were coerced into wage labor, and a hitherto haphazard pattern of regional migration was routinized and bureaucratized. After 1910, when South Africa became a self-governing state, an ill-formed historic bloc emerged based primarily on race, with English mining and Afrikaans agricultural capital as predominant social forces in South Africa.

South Africa's primary commodity-producing economy was transformed by the Second World War. According to Dan O'Meara,

The government poured millions into the development of the local steel, chemical, textile and armaments industries. As Germany's submarine warfare sharply reduced the flow of imported manufactures, flourishing local industries expanded to take up the slack. This led to a far-ranging extension of South Africa's industrial base. . . . With its industries working at full capacity to meet wartime demand, its ports jammed with allied shipping on one of the world's crucial trade routes, its gold paying for much of the allied war effort, its farmers scrambling to produce the food for its army and for besieged Britain, South Africa's GNP grew by almost 70 percent in just six years between 1939 and 1945. . . . A founder member of the IMF, South Africa was listed among the world's 10 richest countries at the end of the war.[10]

Social Change, Apartheid, and Development

The war effort had a profound effect on South Africa's social relations of production. In macroeconomic terms, industry came to the forefront, displacing mining and agriculture in terms of its contribution to GDP. But industry also transformed the social geography of South Africa as thousands of Afrikaners and indigenous Africans became urbanized members of an industrial proletariat centered in the Transvaal. This transformation, in particular, the influx of so many blacks into urban areas, laid the groundwork for the Afrikaner-based National Party victory of 1948.

While Jan Smuts' United Party (UP) won an absolute majority of the votes cast, the UP was soundly defeated in the Transvaal and throughout rural, hence, Afrikaner-dominated, South Africa. The final tally was 79 seats for D. F. Malan's NP to 71 for the UP/Labor Party coalition. The election was fought primarily on the issue of race, specifically, the so-called black *oorstroming* (inundation) of the cities. But other, latent issues came to the fore, in particular, a general feeling among Afrikaners that the UP continued to represent the interests of big, English-speaking, business at the expense of entrenched Afrikaner agriculture and emergent Afrikaner industrial labor.

Apartheid became the driving force behind NP policy. According to O'Meara, while ''apartheid remained a fairly vague set of principles rather than a fully worked-out program,'' the slogan ''performed a double ideological function.''[11] On one hand, ''it gave expression to a very broad sentiment among most Afrikaners, regardless of social class, that the rapid urbanization of blacks during the 1930s and 1940s . . . threatened both their precarious places in the urban environment and their specific interests.''[12] On the other hand, the '' 'apartheid principle' . . . operated . . . to condense into a symbolic whole the divergent interests of each of the class forces within the nationalist alliance.''[13]

Over the next 40 years, the NP used the power of the state not merely to engage in what Adam and Moodley describe as ''grotesque Verwoerdian social engineering''[14] but to deliberately foster the development of Afrikaner industrial and finance capital. In this way, state building in South Africa resembled ongoing state capitalist projects elsewhere in the world; under the NP, South Africa during this period very much resembled a ''developmental state.'' However, the *idea* of the state, that is, that fiction out of which a sense of shared identity, of nationalism, might be constructed, encompassed only a privileged white minority. The *institutional basis* of the state—in other words, its capacity—was geared toward satisfying this unsustainable fiction: that South Africa was, indeed, a white republic. Thus, somewhat ironically, at a time when some states, such as the Asian NICs, were aggressively engaged in state building, South Africa's vast wealth served only to weaken the state.

Organic Crisis and State Strategy

The prolonged period of crisis in the world economy that began in the early 1970s and culminated in the dissolution of the neoliberal hegemonic bloc thrust South Africa into an organic crisis of its own. Davies and O'Meara suggest that South Africa's late-1970s-initiated policy of total strategy represented

a response to an organic crisis and attempt to reconstruct the political, ideological and economic conditions of stable capitalist rule. These policies did not simply emerge. They were produced out of deep political conflict within the ruling class and the consolidation under P. W. Botha of a new political alignment of class forces.[15]

Total strategy combined three elements: (1) development of a national security management system (NSMS), which, in effect, turned South Africa into a garrison state; (2) a domestic policy of WHAM—"winning of hearts and minds"—which sought, among other things, to make the homelands viable "states" in their own right, to extend political representation to coloreds and Indians through the creation of a tricameral legislature, and to create a black middle class whose interests would ultimately transcend race and come to recognize and embrace the "progressive" policies of P. W. Botha's government; and (3) a deliberate strategy of political, economic, and military destabilization of South Africa's neighbors.

By 1985, all these attempts had failed to strengthen the "state"; most dramatically, the defeat of the União Nacional para a Independência Total de Angola (UNITA) at Cuito Cuanavale despite South African military assistance signaled the death knell of regional destabilization (though Botha and his "hawks" would persist with this policy into the late 1980s, the appearance of dead South African soldiers turned white public opinion against such adventurism). This coincided with mass demonstrations, strikes, and stayaways domestically. South Africa, as suggested before, found itself in an organic crisis, the result of which is the Government of National Unity today.

As early as 1977, white business began to lobby for a more creative strategy. Both petty bourgeois and monopoly capital began to highlight the economic costs of apartheid and argue in favor of "reformed capitalism." This included a powerful lobby that favored abandoning several cornerstones of apartheid: restrictions on the mobility of African labor; job reservation laws; restrictions on black trade unions; and continuing strong state intervention in key areas of the economy. According to the Urban Foundation:

[O]nly by having this most responsible section of the urban black population on our side can the whites of South Africa be assured of containing on a long-term basis the irresponsible and political ambitions of those blacks who are influenced against their own real interests from within and without our borders.[16]

In essence, employers' organizations "were calling for a new hegemonic project."[17] Though P. W. Botha acceded to business' demands at 1979's Carleton Conference, popular domestic and more formal international pressure continued to mount. Internationally, the nine majority-ruled states of Southern Africa came together to form the Southern African Development Coordination Conference (SADCC). SADCC's main aim was to decrease member states' economic dependence upon, and political vulnerability to, South Africa.[18] Beyond the region, a combination of state and nonstate forces came together to press sanctions upon the apartheid regime. Each of these responses combined to materially and psychologically shore up domestic efforts for change. In combination with South Africa's worsening global economic position, these events created what O'Meara calls a "crisis of representation" within the ruling power bloc.

Yet, Botha's response was anything but enlightened. When he challenged the international community to "do your worst" in his classic 1985 "crossing the Rubicon" speech, he was virtually abandoned by all of the most powerful business and political factions within the historic bloc. As if to highlight the emerging two-track nature of South African "foreign" policy, shortly following Botha's speech representatives of Anglophone capital traveled to Lusaka for talks with the ANC.[19] This was followed by "the dramatic 1987 session with a range of Afrikaner intellectuals and opinion leaders in Dakar."[20] In August 1988, the Gencor-sponsored Consultative Business Movement was inaugurated and issued a challenge to South African business:

[t]o define the real nature of their own power, and to identify how they can best use this not inconsequential power to advance the society towards non-racial democracy.[21]

Consensus Seeking through Negotiation

P. W. Botha was formally replaced by F. W. De Klerk in February 1989. As the Mass Democratic Movement's defiance campaigns grew in strength, and as international pressure for change increased, it soon became clear to De Klerk that "we had to release Mandela."[22] Between Mandela's release on 2 February 1990 and the ANC walkout of negotiations in April 1991, the NP took a hard line. In particular, the NP sought to dictate the pace and content of negotiations, to conduct discussions at an elite level, that is, what came to be called "elite-pacting," and on a multiparty basis. In this way the NP hoped to achieve two things: (1) to isolate the ANC leadership from its more radical, populist base and (2) to wear it down with "endless highly technical negotiations."[23] This hard-line position was reaffirmed following the March 1992 whites-only referendum, which the NP organized in order to secure a mandate to negotiate a nonracial Constitution with the ANC.[24] According to O'Meara:

The President could have seized this opportunity to move ahead quickly. Instead he chose to interpret the vote as a mandate for a white veto in the new constitution. He stressed *ad nauseum* the NP "bottom line" that "power-sharing" and not majority rule was the only form of democracy acceptable to the NP. The ANC would have to accept this or no negotiations were possible.[25]

The result of such "obstinacy," O'Meara states, "was perhaps the most dangerous six months in South African history."[26] In April 1992 Chris Hani was assassinated; in May negotiations collapsed. This was followed by "Mandela's referendum," a "mass action" campaign that brought the country to a standstill. In June 1992, 43 ANC supporters were massacred in the Boiphatong squatter camp. This was followed in August by the killing of 50 ANC supporters by Ciskei soldiers near Bisho. At this point all actors took a step back. In September, the ANC and NP signed the "Minute of Understanding."

The agreement caused howls of rage from Inkatha Freedom Party Leader Mangosuthu Buthelezi who had become used to his privileged relationship with the NP. It "symbolised the end of all NP attempts to outmanoeuvre the ANC" and the beginning of real negotiations.[27]

From then on, the key buzzwords leading toward multiparty elections slated for April 1994 became "transformation through negotiation." Adam and Moodley explain: "[N]egotiations grant all major forces a stake in a historic compromise by which each party stands to gain more than it would lose by continuing the confrontation."[28] Indeed, all major forces did gain a stake.

The ANC obtained 62.7 percent of the vote, reassuringly short of the two-thirds necessary to write the permanent constitution alone; the NP got 20.4 percent, so six cabinet seats and a Deputy Presidency; and the IFP gained 10.5 percent of the national vote, and three seats in cabinet.[29]

The nearly mathematically perfect election results were due more to elite bargaining than serendipity, however. In order to "save the election process from complete collapse and produce results acceptable to the leaders of the ANC, NP and . . . IFP," party leaders sat together with the chairman of the Independent Electoral Commission, Judge Johann Kriegler, and "awarded" each other votes. According to Kriegler, "Let's not get overly squeamish about it. . . . [The parties] are in a power game with each other, and if they want to settle on the basis that they withdraw objections there's nothing wrong with it.''[30] We return to the implications of growing and/or persistent undemocratic tendencies later.

World Order and South African Forms of State

As should be clear by now, the "new" South Africa has a long and eventful history. Clearly, the GNU is not inheriting a blank slate on which to write history anew. The GNU inherits a strong state with a tradition of intervention in the economy and a predilection for social engineering. The "long global boom" facilitated this particular form of state building, just as the "world economic crisis" helped bring it—along with several other hegemonic projects, like communism in Eastern Europe and the Soviet Union and the Bretton Woods agreement—to a halt. Apartheid engineering empowered many people and created many vested interests; these interests will not easily be dislodged. In fact, by definition the Government of National *Unity* empowers many of those who most profited from apartheid.

In this way and as the *de facto* political party of business, the NP's attempt at reconstituting a historic bloc must be regarded as a success. South Africa's so-called negotiated revolution is akin to what Graf calls ''[t]his peculiarly late-twentieth century phenomenon of the democratic transition from above—in which, ironically, democratic reform is 'supplied by the very governments whose behaviour led to the demand for reform in the first place.' ''[31] Citing his own work on Nigeria, Graf states, "As once after colonialism, so nowadays after authoritarianism, a *successor elite*, both endogenous and exogenous, remains in power and ensures the continuity of the fundamental power constellation.''[32]

Yet, the democratic transition and popular forces' knowledge of the significant part they played in engendering the circumstances that made it inevitable, let alone possible, raise significant hopes on the part of the masses for meaningful, structural transformation. Will the ANC-led GNU be able to deliver? Evidence from other parts of the world suggests that it will not. Again, according to Graf:

Notwithstanding the success of popular mass movements in overturning authoritarian regimes in, e.g., Nicaragua or Iran, in Haiti or the Philippines, their role has generally been reduced to a mainly supportive or acclamatory one, particularly in the consolidation phase so beloved of many Western democratization theorists. The principal beneficiaries of the transitions in the Third World—as opposed to those in East and Central Europe—have been the external and internal elites.[33]

South Africa is not Nicaragua or Iran, however. To be sure, global and national pressures in support of neoliberal economic policy mark the new frontier of struggle. However, if South Africa is to overcome its legacy of racial exclusion and impoverishment, state-makers must neither lose sight of, nor underestimate the power of, those most marginalized under apartheid. At the same time, they must continue to take seriously the potential role in transformation to be played by the broad array of forces in civil society.

STATE BUILDING AND COUNTERHEGEMONIC MOVEMENTS

Doomsayers and Naysayers

There is no shortage of people willing to condemn the new government's behavior: from official policy to personal performance, the ANC in particular has come in for heavy criticism.[34] To be sure, a good deal of this criticism is deserved. Yet, much of it is criticism without construction. Detractors seem little inclined to seek answers to difficult questions, seemingly satisfied instead with keeping a running tally of mistakes. In this penultimate section I examine three aspects of state building in the "new" South Africa: (1) "nationalism" and symbolic manipulation, (2) economic policy and the relations of production, and (3) power sharing. In this discussion there are two fundamental questions to consider. First, has the ANC "abandoned the democratic revolution," or is it, in fact, engaged in a program of "structural reform"? Second, are these efforts sufficient for the construction of a durable historic bloc based on consensus? In the conclusion, I address the question, on the basis of the GNU's performance thus far, What can be said with any certainty about South Africa's prospects for sustainable, participatory development in the twenty-first century?

Legacies of "State Building" under Apartheid "Developmentalism"

As suggested earlier, the apartheid state was constructed upon an ideology based on the notion of siege, that is, the *laager* was under "total onslaught" and was to be defended at all costs. This type of nationalism was exclusivist in the extreme. South African state makers deliberately identified the "state" and the "nation" with race: if you were white, you were "inside," God-fearing, and protected; if not, you were "outside," God-forsaken, and to be protected from.[35]

Throughout the later 1970s and most of the 1980s this dualistic, largely negative construction of identity formed the basis for South Africa's nationally and regionally divisive policy of "total strategy." Forging "national unity" out of this legacy is difficult in the extreme. However, according to Weber, "[S]o contingent is the quality of nationalism that it can be created quite quickly by specific initiatives directed to that end, and just as quickly renounced by those who determine to do so."[36] This continues to be the hope of state-makers in South Africa today.

Standing in the way of the "new nationalism" are a number of apartheid-era structures inherited by the GNU. Most significantly, the commanding heights of the economy remain, for all intents and purposes, monopolistic and in white hands. Hiding behind the prevailing global discourse of ''the logic of market forces,'' monopoly capital is reluctant to participate actively in the transformation of the apartheid political economy. ''Production'' for ''accumulation'' and ''distribution,'' therefore, remains contested and problematic.

Second, the GNU inherits the bureaucracies of not only the apartheid state but the ill-functioning and-fated homelands as well. The ineptness and continuing corruption of this bureaucracy hamper delivery and fuel accusations of decreasing state capacity. Understandably, these bureaucratic problems are most acute at the provincial level.

Third, the GNU has taken aboard police forces and militaries that have been well-functioning and efficient symbols and tools of oppression for at least 45 years. Each of these institutions—the bureaucracy, the military, and the police—has developed practices based on near-endemic corruption and secrecy. At the same time, there are indications of deliberate destabilization of police activities by disaffected elements within the force. There also continues to be active resistance to integration of these formerly bitter enemies. Taken together, these factors inhibit policing and crime prevention.

In many ways, then, the ''new'' South Africa looks very much like the old: the army patrols the townships outside Richmond, a small rural town in Kwa-Zulu Natal; necklacing has returned to Soweto[37]; warlords, druglords and gangs sprout like deadly mushrooms around the decaying roots of Cape township life. Levels of both reported crime and corruption continue to rise. Self-help, from People against Gangsterism and Drugs (PAGAD)[38] in the Western Cape to private security firms and higher walls in the posh suburbs around Cape Town, Durban, and Johannesburg, is the order of the day. Delivery of basic goods and services remains problematic as taxpayers oppose the state at every turn, and funds disappear in the hands of inept and corrupt bureaucrats who continue to practice ''struggle bookkeeping.''

Several key questions immediately come to mind. How can unity be forged out of this deliberately engineered diversity? How can a sense of mutual cooperation be forged out of a legacy of understandably felt hatred and distrust? More practically, how can state institutions be reformed without sowing the seeds of future discontent? Most fundamentally, given South Africa's commitment to open, participatory democracy, in the absence of unity how can policies be forged that will simultaneously foster economic growth and satisfy all elements of civil society?

Manufacturing Unity, Retooling Identity

The manipulation of symbols is thought to be fundamental to the construction of national identity.[39] If the overarching image of the *swart gevaar*, the black peril, helped define and forge Afrikaner nationalism, then the new government's symbol of unity, that is, the *rainbow nation*, is hoped to do the same. Unlike the *swart gevaar*, the notion of a rainbow nation is inclusive and positive, with the colorful South African flag complementing this notion in brilliant fashion.

This classical liberal concept of unity through diversity is the focal point of every public event. Sport, as perhaps the most public event, has provided an important locus for those hoping to retool South Africans' collective identity along more inclusive and constructive lines. The rugby World Cup, hosted and won by South Africa in 1995, and soccer's African Cup of Nations, hosted and won by South Africa in 1996, were two such seminal events. Though the evidence is anecdotal, there is no denying the palpable sense of national unity that obtained during and long after these events. Beyond such public gatherings, however, sport continues to divide as much as it unites. Rugby and cricket are essentially white games; soccer, played on the dusty playing fields of the townships and in rural areas, remains the game for the masses. The divisiveness of public debate over Cape Town's Olympic bid, which revolved primarily around the issue of money well spent or better spent elsewhere, provided tangible proof of how riven South African society remains.

Madiba Nelson Mandela: simply the name evokes much emotion. Mandela himself is an important symbol of transformation and reconciliation in South African society. Despite clearly demonstrated "autocratic tendencies," there is no gainsaying Mandela's role as linchpin of the new democracy. The president is fully cognizant of this fact and has used his image as something of the "last twentieth-century hero" to good effect within and without the country. To be sure, there are problems inherent in such hero worship. For one, Mandela has stolen the thunder from many hardworking and unsung organizations in civil society. His decision to set up Mandela's Children's Fund has been so effective that NGOs working toward poverty alleviation have suffered as a result; funds that would normally have gone to them have been diverted toward Mandela's high-profile organization. Perhaps more importantly in the context of constructing a national identity, he has also stolen the thunder from hardworking and unsung members of his own government. "What happens when Madiba goes?" is an oft-heard refrain. Many have expressed dismay at the backroom way in which Thabo Mbeki has been made "crown prince" of South Africa. Yet the logic is impeccable: Mandela has taken deliberate steps to shift the focus from himself to his government. He has on numerous public occasions emphasized the small role he is playing in the "transformation." The simple fact of the matter, however, is that no one seems to be listening, so smitten are they with Mandela.

Unfortunately, the most effective symbol of unity to date is a negative one: the specter of illegal migration. Fears of South Africa's being inundated with drug smugglers, gun runners, and AIDS carriers from abroad have been heightened by dubious reports from right-wing think tanks and the media. The South African National Defense Force (SANDF), keen to find a meaningful role for itself in the postapartheid era, is only too happy to assist in enemy creation. The GNU has done very little to dispel this "threat," so desperate is it for a symbol of national unity.

Symbols of Substance

The ANC-led GNU has embarked on two very important symbolic projects, each of which will prove of lasting positive effect. The first is the Truth and Reconciliation Commission (TRC), chaired by Bishop Desmond Tutu. The second is the written national Constitution and the establishment of a Constitutional Court, whose fundamental task it is to see that it is upheld.

Many have questioned the sincerity of those applying for amnesty before the TRC. Some regard the TRC itself as an exercise in National Party bashing. Others lament the lack of cooperation by key figures and organizations, most notably, Mangosuthu Buthelezi and the IFP, senior members of the security forces, and former president P. W. Botha. Both big business and the Dutch Reformed Church, two important pillars of National Party strength, were less than forthcoming in their submissions.

The TRC, for all its shortcomings, is a necessary exercise in public healing. If nothing else, it deepens the historical record and broadens the historical narrative. When Bishop Tutu was asked in an interview if he was bothered by "four versions of South Africa's past," he responded, "Four versions . . . four . . . exist of the life of Christ. Which one would you have liked to chuck out?"[40] The process is not perfect, but it is more "truth" than South Africa has ever before heard or seen.

The Constitution, in contrast, is followed by much less fanfare and also less controversy, though it, too, is a contested document. The Constitution provides that government be structured at three levels: municipal, provincial, and national. The national structure is characterized by three branches of government: executive, legislative, and judicial. The Constitution, which was formally adopted on 8 May 1996 and ratified into law in February 1997, is a 137-page document that includes a lengthy Bill of Rights. These facts, in themselves, are not unusual. One innovative aspect, however, is the attempt to strengthen individual rights *through* group rights. At the 8 May 1996 adoption of the Constitution, President Mandela stated:

The individual rights and national self-determination of the South African people shall not be inhibited, but reinforced by the collective rights of communities.[41]

The inclusion of the notion "group rights," along with the decision to adopt a federal form of government, was part of the ANC's concessions to both the National Party and Inkatha, each of which was keen to preserve its "culture" and influence in its traditional bases of power. The Constitution stipulates that the state cannot discriminate against its citizens on the basis of ethnic or social origin, language, or religion. Moreover, it ensures the rights of citizens, individually and collectively as communities, to "enjoy their culture, practise their religion and use their language" and to form "associations and other organs of civil society."[42]

In Good's words, "the steps which have been taken towards a new openness in government seem most profound."[43] Good continues, quoting Etienne Mureinik:

"[P]robably the strongest theme" of the interim constitution is the aspiration to an "open and democratic society" based on freedom and equality. The principles governing the content of the final constitution instructed the Constitutional Assembly to provide for "freedom of information so that there can be open and accountable administration at all levels of government." Openness, he says, is what gives the South African constitution distinctiveness. It represents "an indispensable instrument of accountable and participatory government."

In support of the Constitution, government established the Constitutional Court. According to Constitutional Court judge Albie Sachs, the court "is an institution which plays a fundamental role in preserving our painfully won democracy and human rights." Sachs points out that South Africa's successful transition from a virtual police state to a *Rechtstaat*, a state based on the rule of law, is dependent, in part, on public perceptions. However, according to Sachs, the public is yet to perceive the importance of the change. This, in a circular way, inhibits transformation.

We seem to suffer from a fear of freedom, an unwillingness to explore the new spaces which we have opened up for ourselves. We remain baffled by the problems of living under the rule of law in a constitutional state. We are reluctant to slip out of the moulds of familiar political argument.

Although South Africa's Constitution provides for the rights of communities and the rights of individuals in a universalist way, it also stipulates that provinces may write their own Constitutions to "lay the foundation of the manner in which they will govern their citizens." Up to now, only KwaZulu Natal and the Western Cape have gone any distance toward this end. This is understandable, given that the Western Cape is controlled by the NP, and KwaZulu Natal by the IFP. Each party seeks to entrench its power in these areas and was disappointed that the Constitution did not confer more autonomy on the provinces. As a result, the NP is challenging the national Constitution by articulating in its draft provincial Constitution its intention to control aspects of government presently in national hands. The matter is presently with the Constitutional Court.

This tripartite struggle for political power is indicative of the difficulty of constructing a postapartheid historic bloc. While entrenched white interests are quite confident that they have successfully moved the ANC toward accepting a

neoliberal macroeconomic framework (see later), they remain determined to for-
tify this ideological victory by consolidating power in terms of geographical
space. If successful, could the Western Cape become a neowhite, neoliberal
laager? And KwaZulu Natal a Zulu "homeland"? In any event, the ANC has
taken a longer-term view to these problems, hoping to displace both the NP and
IFP through the ballot box over time.

Producing Consensus

Ironically, one of the biggest obstacles to a united approach to development
is the RDP. More specifically, it is the gradual shift in government policy away
from the people-centered ANC policy document toward a monopoly, capital-
friendly policy document known as GEAR, Growth, Employment, and Redistribution. Whereas the RDP document emphasized "growth through redistribution," GEAR emphasizes "growth with redistribution." GEAR is completely
compatible with business' own strategy document, *Growth for All*, which was
published by the South Africa Foundation, representing the 50 largest corporations in South Africa. With its emphasis on export-oriented development, privatization, deregulation, and "an appropriately valued currency," *Growth for
All* could have been written by a World Bank economist.[44]

Globalization, as fact and argument, becomes the overarching context within
which the GNU searches for a viable economic strategy. The leitmotif remains
that of "catch-up," only this time the image is reversed. To wit, "Few economies can afford to ignore this phenomenon, and South Africa is no exception.
Years of isolation and protectionism have left the country out of touch with
global standards. . . . The alternative is to be *left behind* as the globalization train
proceeds apace."[45] South Africa present, it seems, must be made to pay for the
sins of South Africa past.

Previous historic blocs have been heavily reliant on the foreign exchange
generated by the mining industry. Capital generated from the sale of gold, in
particular, helped fuel both South Africa's particular form of industrialization
and its efforts at social engineering. As a result, South Africa is the most industrialized—indeed, the only truly industrialized—country in sub-Saharan Africa, accounting for roughly 22 percent of continental GDP. While generating
great wealth and fostering an increasingly complex configuration of the social
forces of power in South Africa, this particular development path has left the
country extremely vulnerable to developments in the international division of
labor.

Though highly industrialized, the manufacturing sector is also highly dependent on imported inputs. In other words, it suffers from what might be called
"incomplete import substitution industrialization." The manufacturing sector is
a net consumer of foreign exchange, importing roughly four times as much as
it exports.[46] It is, therefore, extremely vulnerable to fluctuations in the availability of foreign exchange. As witnessed throughout the 1980s, capital flight and

declining revenues led to debilitating recession in the South African economy. Only the period between the fall of the Berlin Wall and the end of the Gulf War provided temporary respite from this condition, as investors bought gold as a hedge against uncertainty.

Presently, the price of gold wavers slightly above $300 per ounce. This means that, in spite of continuing industrial restructuring, involving, among other things, the shedding of labor and the upgrading of capital equipment, very few of South Africa's gold mines can turn a profit with the price of gold at such a low level. Not only does this condition hold out the possibility of massive layoffs in the mining sector, but, as already highlighted, the inability to generate foreign exchange in this sector has a dramatic wave (not a ripple!) effect throughout the economy.

These continuing structural difficulties have resulted in capital's call for a more open economy and less government intervention so that industry can take the necessary steps to become more competitive and therefore more profitable. In the main, this means mechanization and labor flexibility.

The unions, meanwhile, remain resistant to such innovation. In support of labor, COSATU and the SACP, in particular, point to government's ongoing inability to create jobs—despite promises and strategies articulated in the RDP—and the threat to existing jobs by GEAR-oriented development strategies.

Government, in turn, points to the progressive nature of its Basic Conditions of Employment Bill as evidence that it is acting in support of labor. However, this only serves to incite the ire of small business. Rules such as a living minimum wage, a 40-hour workweek, time and a half for work beyond 40 hours and double time on Sundays, and employers' need to provide after-hours transport to workers' places of residence are argued to be crippling to small businesses, which must cut costs in order to compete.

Where agriculture is concerned, government's commitment to World Trade Organization strictures regarding the lowering of tariffs and the phasing out of marketing boards, its support of regional trade regimes, and its intention to bring consumers' usage of water into line with its actual cost have all come under heavy criticism. Agriculture, like the manufacturing sector, is a traditionally highly subsidized and protected sector of the South African economy. Farmers fear for their futures under such liberalized conditions. At the same time, an estimated 3.5 million people who were dispossessed of their land during the apartheid era are looking to government for redress. While white farmers fear an arbitrary landgrab, the government has, in fact, budgeted R314 million for the acquisition of land on the basis of willing seller–willing buyer.[47]

An innovative approach by government for freeing up land for redistribution has been to enter into bilateral agreements with other SADC member states, facilitating the resettlement of white farmers farther north in Mozambique and Zambia.

Pressures in the townships have mainly come from those seeking jobs, housing, electricity, potable water, and sanitation facilities: all priority projects under the RDP. However, the same arguments obtain: big business fears government spending in these areas will fuel inflation and add to an already burgeoning budget deficit. In the meantime, people wait and watch.

Such are the legacies of the apartheid-era "developmental state." These and myriad other issues coalesce in the debate over macroeconomic policy, that is, whether GEAR is a viable development strategy or evidence of a "revolution betrayed." The plain fact of the matter is that government must play it both ways. As Cox points out, ruling groups face pressure from two directions: from within the state and from without. Dealing successfully with these different forces is largely a question of the social relations of production, that is, what kind of strategy of accumulation will facilitate the construction of a historic bloc through consensus at the domestic level while at the same time improving and stabilizing the state's position in the international world order.

It is folly for anyone to think that the ANC could withstand the collective pressure of the what Cox labels the "transnational managerial class," should it countenance a revolutionary approach to reconstruction and development.[48] At present, reform is its only option. Reform, in this instance, does not necessarily mean capitulation to neoliberalism. As Saul reminds us, such "false dichotomies" facilitate a "dialogue of the deaf" that "merely locks 'revolutionaries' and 'reformists' ever more tightly (and more self-righteously) into their own respective corners."[49] These issues are by no means settled. There are perhaps several "middle ways" to be explored. In the words of ANC MP Ben Turok, "[T]he state is not yet gelled."

Centers and Forms of Power

Though the state is not yet gelled, consolidation of forces is well under way. Power is being shared in the "new" South Africa in at least ten ways and at least two levels. Moreover, these categories are not mutually exclusive; they overlap in myriad ways. At the *political* level, power is being shared (1) between and among the ruling ANC; (2) between the ANC and its major alliance partners, COSATU and the SACP; (3) between the ANC and its main rivals, the NP and the IFP; (4) between the national government and the provinces; (5) among various institutions of the state; and (6) among governmental, nongovernmental, and community-based organizations. At the *economic* level, it is being shared (1) between the vested and well-entrenched interests of monopoly capital and the state, with established labor unions also participating; (2) between international capital and the state; (3) between international capital and South Africa's private sector; and (4) between the state and organs of civil society.

Clearly, space does not permit a full exploration of these linkages. However, it is important to look at the more important of these in at least a cursory way in order to get a sense of the emerging historic bloc in postapartheid South Africa.

Intra-ANC Struggles. The ANC elite is constantly fighting the urge to dictate policy to its members and to society at large. The organization recognizes the importance of pursuing transformation in an open and democratic way—after all, the party did come to power on populist shoulders. It continues to recognize the supportive strength of this mass base as well as its capacity for mobilization and disruption. At the same time the ANC needs to forge a united front within the party itself in order to impart a sense of composure, comfort, and direction in its rule. However, the ANC has always been an amalgam of interests and perspectives. Forging a united front in such a case is difficult, extant pressures facing the postapartheid state notwithstanding.

The bedrock of the ANC is presently showing many fissures. Three examples from the Eastern Cape will suffice. Following his expulsion from the party, Bantu Holomisa joined forces with disaffected NP MP Roelf Meyer to form their own political party, the United Democratic Movement. Holomisa has a powerful base in the Transkei and seeks to build on his popularity there. Second, the Eastern Cape ANC recently voiced its opposition to GEAR publicly, joining hands with its alliance partners, the SACP and COSATU. It also endorsed Winnie Madikizela-Mandela as its candidate for deputy president of the party in opposition to the national consensus candidate, Jacob Zuma. Third, the Transkei branch of the South African National Civics Organization (SANCO) has formally broken away from the ANC alliance in order that it may pursue its own, grassroots agenda. Each of these factors highlights the degree of disgruntlement felt at grassroots level: both Holomisa and Madikizela-Mandela are populists; SANCO is an amalgam of community-based organizations. That the Eastern Cape is a crucible for populist ferment is not surprising. It is also the second poorest province in the state (see later), so populist expression overlaps with perceived poverty and marginalization. This constitutes a deadly elixir the ANC cannot afford to let spread.

There has also been a series of high-level disagreements leading to ''redeployments'' of members unwilling to toe the party line. (Re)deployment as strategy has weakened the ANC at the center, facilitating and encouraging regional dissension. According to Thabo Masebe, ''[T]he deployment strategy of the movement has thus far not worked. The departure of key leaders and activists of the movement to government, the diplomatic service and the private sector . . . has left the main political body of the ANC in the hands of inexperienced members.''[50]

The long-running dispute between President Mandela and his former wife is suggestive of a different sort of split in the offing: between the conservative old guard and the radical and, at times, unpredictable ''young lions''; between the ''new authoritarian'' elite[51] and the increasingly marginalized masses. Though Mandela has attempted to intervene personally in a number of these disputes, it appears that the national core is content to pursue certain key, power-sharing arrangements and let others develop of their own accord. This issue will be revisited later under the ''National-Provincial'' heading.

Intraalliance Struggles: ANC/COSATU/SACP. There can be no denying the crucial role played by the unions in ending apartheid,[52] nor can one ignore the importance of the historical tie between the ANC and the SACP, perhaps best symbolized in the appointment of the late Joe Slovo as housing minister. Emerging tensions revolve around economic policy. The political question is whether the alliance serves the interests of all parties involved. Recently, Peter Mokaba, deputy minister of environmental affairs and tourism, called for the expulsion of SACP members from the tripartite alliance. At the same time, COSATU finds itself increasingly at odds with ANC policy but has tried to work within the alliance in order to facilitate debate,[53] the logic being, that it is better to be a small voice inside the halls of power than a big one shouting from outside. Yet, one might ask, is this the best strategy to confront the "Thatcherites"[54] among the ANC? Would a united COSATU/SACP voice unfettered by the need to bend to the desires of an overbearing ANC be more effective in putting forward and into effect labor's goals? Certainly, COSATU's 1.8 million members constitute a powerful political voice in the continuing struggle over development policy.

Intraelite Maneuvering: ANC/NP/IFP. Clearly, the ANC/NP "alliance" has played itself to an end. With the ANC holding 62 percent of the seats in Parliament and with the withdrawal of the NP from formal participation in the GNU, "collective decision making" is now nothing more than myth. Moreover, with the defection of Meyer, the retirement of F. W. De Klerk, and the election of conservative Marthinus van Schalkwyk as new leader of the NP, the party seems a spent force. Its obstinate unwillingness to confess to apartheid atrocities at the Truth and Reconciliation Commission is also thought to be hastening the NP's departure from public political relevance. In four municipal by-elections, the NP has been resoundingly defeated by Tony Leon's Democratic Party. These results provide empirical support to the growing impression that the moderate Afrikaans vote is swinging toward the Democratic Party. An October 1997 Idasa-conducted poll on the evolution of party support since 1994 shows national support for the NP to have fallen from 16 percent to 10 percent. Interestingly, it also shows support for the NP in its crucial support base in the Western Cape to have fallen from 53 percent to 28 percent. "Among Indian voters the drop had been from 49 percent to 21 percent, with only 18 months to go before the next general election."[55]

As for Inkatha, Mandela has played a very shrewd and careful political game in the co-opting of Buthelezi. Buthelezi is minister of home affairs and has been made acting president, on more than one occasion, in Mandela's absence. There is also speculation that Buthelezi will, in the future, be made a deputy president. To several observers, this behavior is "deeply mystifying" and undemocratic in the extreme.[56] To be sure, such "elite-pacting" is undemocratic; it is, however, entirely understandable, even laudable. Buthelezi's power is not based on material wealth; rather, it is geographical and "cultural," that is, his oft-iterated claim to be defending "Zulu nationalism" in the KwaZulu Natal region of South Africa. Buthelezi's power vis-à-vis nation building in South Africa is entirely negative; that is, it is the capacity to disrupt, if not completely derail, attempts at reconstruction and development. As terrorists well know, while achieving one's ends requires a great deal of power, preventing others from achieving their desired ends requires the exercise of considerably less.

The ANC, it seems to me, has taken a longer-term view of developments in KwaZulu Natal. In the short term, Buthelezi and the IFP must be placated for the sake of nation building, however contestable that notion may be. Instability in KwaZulu Natal would run like termites through the house of state, undermining much of the careful building the ANC leadership has done to bring consensus to development policy. In the longer term, the ANC seeks to build its strength in KwaZulu Natal—for example, through the elevation of Jacob Zuma to ANC deputy president, through land reform that will defuse the power of the chiefs through whom the IFP exercises much of its power—while simultaneously weakening Buthelezi's by drawing him inexorably into the national limelight. In the meantime, the IFP, lacking funds and a viable party platform, seems set to self-destruct.

National/Provincial Power Balancing. The provinces seem destined to become, over time, powerful centers of decision making in their own right. Given the diversity of needs, this gradual devolution of power seems appropriate. But just how this power will eventually be "devolved" is a matter of great concern and present political struggle. Under the Constitution, the provinces are accorded legislative competence over a wide array of functions. However, according to Southall,

[R]ather than these being original or exclusive, the constitution listed these powers as being concurrent with Parliament, and as subject to uniform norms and standards that may need to be applied throughout the Republic. It also made provincial taxation capacity dependent upon approval by Parliament, as well as providing for the latter to determine what "equitable" share of national revenues, and other special financial allocations, provinces should receive.[57]

Both the IFP and the NP are opposed to the overwhelming, intended dominance of the center, for obvious, highly political reasons. However, it must be noted that there is an emerging "politics of regions" centered on legitimate needs and grievances. As Southall aptly demonstrates, there are significant regional disparities *within* South Africa. For example, while the Western Cape has an estimated human development index (HDI) ranking of 0.76, an income per capita level of R4,188 and an unemployment rate of 13.3 percent, Northern Province has an HDI of 0.40, per capita income level of R725, and an unemployment rate of 24.8 percent.[58] Unfortunately, those provinces found to be lowest on the HDI scale—including also the Eastern Cape, the Northwest, and Northern Province—also face the greatest challenges: Bantustan reintegration, building a competent bureaucracy, attracting investment, and basic delivery of public goods, to name but four of the more prominent issues.

Coming to terms with these problems, while dependent on the national "purse," is sure to heighten interprovincial and provincial-national animosities, differences, and rivalries in the near future.

Institutional Development: Capacity, Delivery, Rivalry. Reorganization of the state has resulted in a series of fairly predictable and contradictory tendencies. For instance, in creating nine new provinces, the GNU simultaneously expanded the civil service while committing itself to the cutting of 300,000 civil service jobs over three years. Absorption was precipitated by the need to co-opt potentially disruptive elements within the state. At the same time, buyout packages have been offered for all those wishing to leave the civil service on a voluntary basis. Predictably, those taking the buyout thus far have been the most capable senior officials, many of whom are now reemployed by the state on a consultancy basis and at enormously inflated rates. Cost cutting and streamlining, therefore, have been undermined by this tendency. Capacity, too, has seriously been hampered.

Not surprisingly, delivery has suffered greatly. Several of the most prominent and important ministries—justice, safety and security, health, public service, and administration—have been wracked by corruption and mismanagement. Attempts to bring politicians into line and to make decision making more transparent and accountable have, for the most part, failed miserably. "Watchdog" organs like the office of the auditor general, the Office for Serious Economic Offences, and the ombudsperson suffer from a lack of funds and trained personnel.

There has been some attempt to farm out delivery to the private sector and to NGOs.[59] One positive example of successful delivery is the recently completed electrification scheme in the Western Cape township of Khayelitsha. South Africa's electricity supply parastatal, Eskom, in partnership with the French firm EDF Southern Africa has managed to electrify 43,000 homes, bringing power to 500,000 people. The project took two years to complete and employed a staff of 40.[60] Government, also, has recently passed the Not for Profit Organizations Bill, which abrogates the Fund Raising Act of 1978, which limited NGOs' abilities to raise money. It also made it mandatory that NGOs be registered with the state. The new law is said to introduce both flexibility and self-regulation into the NGO sector. Government is also in the process of establishing the National Development Agency, which is to be formally launched in July 1998. Part of the mandate of this agency will be to establish liaison with NGOs and to enter into "smart alliances with the poor and their organizations to influence government to give meaning to local economic development."[61]

Civil society in general and the NGO community in particular have been in something of a tailspin since the founding elections of 1994. Many of those long involved in NGO activity were drawn into government after the elections. At the same time, the deep well of international funds channeled through the NGOs in support of antiapartheid activities virtually dried up after April 1994. These funds, in almost every case, were redirected toward the ANC-dominated government. As a result, NGOs and community-based organizations (CBOs), like the various township-based civic associations, have suffered a two-tailed crisis: on one hand, how to raise funds, and, on the other hand, how to confront a government you worked so hard to empower with the facts of their failings.

Clearly, government and civil society must work together. But, in the words of Moses Mayekiso, former head of the South African National Civics Organization (SANCO),

civil society—comprising a whole range of autonomous grassroots organizations such as trade unions, township-based civic associations and rural village committees, women and youth organizations—must be built up, recruited for across party lines, and *empowered* in its own right.[62]

At the national level, there is a great deal of jockeying for position and resources among ministries and departments. Many of the most strategically important instruments of the state—for example, the military, police, development bank, foreign and finance ministries—are in a struggle over relevance and resources. Defense has seen its budget continue to shrink. Further retrenchments of the armed forces are forecast for 1998. Foreign affairs is increasingly disgruntled over two tendencies: on one hand, Mandela's penchant for unilateral decision taking, which harks back to the days of the role of the African "great man" in foreign policy making—hardly a strategy for state building in the twenty-first century—and, on the other hand, the growing impression that foreign affairs has become little more than a salesperson for Armscor, Denel, and South African military weaponry. There are also those who argue that while South African foreign policy is *made* by a small cabal of the "inner cabinet"— for example, Mandela, Mbeki, Pahad—it is *set* by the international financial institutions: in Peter Vale's words, the "business of foreign policy is business."[63]

South Africa Incorporated. Over the course of the 1990s and as South Africa gets nearer to the elections of 1999, there has been a quiet shift in the discourse. Save for the ongoing public debate over GEAR and neoliberalism, politics is less about confronting global capital and more about accommodating state policy to it; in Cox's terms, it is increasingly concerned with problem solving, less so with critique. This should be clear from the preceding discussion: focus, capacity, delivery; the devolution of power from the center to the provinces, to NGOs, to the civics, to the private sector; providing business with opportunities to "compete" successfully in the international market so that South Africa will not "fall behind" but can "catch up" with other late-developing Third World states; pursuing black economic empowerment through grants to small business, affirmative action, and skills training. Such is the language of development; such are the strategies of accumulation; and such is the nature of bloc formation in the "new South Africa." Is this enough to deliver South Africa safely and securely into the twenty-first century? Many say it is. But many more say it is not. What, then, are South Africa's prospects for the next millennium?

CONCLUSIONS: SOUTH AFRICA IN THE TWENTY-FIRST CENTURY

At the outset of this chapter, the question was asked, Can South African state-makers get beyond the "double whammy"? In other words, can they success-fully pursue the consolidation of democracy and development domestically while successfully dealing simultaneously with the overwhelming demands of globalization and a neoliberal world order? It seems to me that, based on the foregoing analysis, the only realistic answer to this question is "perhaps." As is only too clear from the discussion, there are as many obstacles as there are opportunities for reconstruction and development in the "new" South Africa. In this final section, I put forward five imperatives for the consolidation of (popular) democracy and (people-centered) development in twenty-first-century South Africa.

Dangerous Discourse

South Africa is a deeply divided society, but unity is emerging at the top. This "unity" hinges on the shared discourse of neoliberalism. For new converts, like Peter Mokaba—he of "one settler, one bullet" fame—"the market" in mix with "good government" appears as a magic formula, the careful application of which will act as a panacea for all South Africa's ills. Internalizing these received ideas results in rewards and favors from the "purveyors and surveyors" of global capitalism. According to Moore,

It is as if the days of "political" development and modernization have returned to the international development agencies' agenda, with the same uncomfortable but inevitable mix of calls for democracy *and* order. "Get your governments right" is the advice, and development will follow. If the state can clear the path, the wonders of economic lib-eralism will be able to manifest themselves. Fail, and we will leave you to your "tribal butchery."[64]

This is a dangerous formula. South Africa's state makers, in particular, the ANC leadership, even if they are not "socialist," must step back from this ideological abyss and reflect very hard on the language, the policies, and the expected results of neoliberalism. In other words, they should consider the source. If they do, they will find that such an approach to "development" is system-maintaining; as such, it is concerned with problem solving, not trans-formation; it is therefore designed to preserve the present world order; and it requires a good deal of willful blindness on the part of those who imagine that the system is not in need of fundamental change.

In the case of South Africa, the question should be asked, In terms of system maintenance, is late-twentieth-century South Africa something you wish to pre-serve for the twenty-first century? For those who feel inclined to say yes, let me add this qualifier: Soweto, Alexandra, Cato Manor, Cape Flats, Khayelitsha. If still unconvinced, then this: the number one cause of death among children under five in South Africa is diarrhea. Or this: out of an estimated total population of 40.6 million, fully half exist without adequate sanitation facilities. These are not "problem-solving" issues; South Africa's state form requires fundamental change. In the absence of meaningful change, Vice President Thabo Mbeki warns of the possibility of race riots within three to five years' time.[65] This, unfortunately, is not an empty threat.

Strengths as Weaknesses, Weaknesses as Strengths

As this chapter has demonstrated, the present attempt at state building reveals as many strengths as weaknesses. This dichotomy is most apparent at three levels: economy, society, and government. I take each of these in turn as a means to discussing my hypothesized five developmental imperatives.

The Economy. In terms of *strengths*, South Africa's economy is highly developed, diversified, and industrialized. Its infrastructure is well developed, and there are moderately good backward and forward linkages throughout the various sectors of the economy. It is Africa's "economic powerhouse," accounting for approximately 22 percent of continental GDP. Its economy is approximately the size of Finland's. These are no small achievements. Indeed, they provide a firm basis on which to reconstruct a society more centrally and sustainably concerned with development as "social production," not simply "physical production."

However, as discussed earlier, South Africa's economy suffers from structural crisis. As the world economy continues to change, South Africa's industrialists have been little inclined to change with it. There continues to be a "propensity to import," rather than active engagement in import substitution. In the mining industry, there continues to be an overreliance on primary commodity production with minimal mineral beneficiation. There is acute dependence on sales of gold as prime provider of foreign exchange. While gold continues to slip in value, and South Africa's mines become ever more expensive to operate, there is a lack of creative thinking regarding ways out of the crisis. Indeed, for a powerful multinational like Anglo American, the preferred "solution" seems to be diversification out of South Africa, not out of minerals.[66] Given the alarming skewness of wealth generated by apartheid-oriented, primary commodity-dependent development, South Africans should be actively engaged in reinvesting profits in South Africa, not sending them out of the country or wasting them in luxury consumption. The persistence of South Africa's economic malaise is not so much a problem of production as it is a problem of investment.[67]

Yet, among South Africa's "cell-phone elite," this situation gives rise to double denial: on one hand, given the veneer of successful developmental mimicry, a denial that there is, in fact, a problem, and on the other hand, a denial that past practice has in any way contributed to the present crisis.

The *first developmental imperative*, then, is that business and industry must be made to actively participate in reconstruction and development. It is very unfortunate that capital should have so readily denied its fundamental role in apartheid engineering. Capitalists should, in fact, be ashamed of their submission to the Truth and Reconciliation Commission. The mooted "reparations tax" that the captains of industry were so quick to shoot down should, in fact, form the basis for business' participation in what might be called "South Africa 21." Government could, in fact, mildly coerce these reluctant revolutionaries along with quid pro quo: for example, if you actively participate and voluntarily contribute, there will be various tax breaks, government supports, and so on to come your way; if you do not participate "voluntarily," you will be made to pay, and you will forfeit proffered incentives.

The Society. Postapartheid South Africa is an active and relatively participative democracy. There is a robust civil society that boasts skills, organizational capacity, and self-awareness. There is an active and powerful trade union movement with a long tradition of participation in politics. At the same time, there is impressive, demonstrated capacity for the spontaneous organization of social movements in response to the myriad problems facing South Africa's marginalized millions. There is an increasing tendency for civil associations to link up with less well formed CBOs in the townships and rural areas in support of developmental activities. Unlike most other parts of Africa, social forces in South Africa are predisposed toward "voice"—that is, political participation—rather than "exit."

To be sure, the impressive strength and diversity of South African society constitute an important nexus for social production. At the same time, this array of social forces constitutes a potential breeding ground for division and populist revolt. In terms of division, cracks are already showing at various points in the social foundation, for example, between organized labor and business; between unionized and nonunionized workers; between white farmers and the landless and land-hungry.

In terms of populist forces, numerous community self-help organizations—like PAGAD—show a marked tendency toward vigilantism. There is also the vast army of unemployed youth who are ripe for mobilization. This same group shows a ready intolerance of "foreigners" and an increasing propensity for anomic violence. While prone toward clientelism and instrumentalism—for example, the township warlord as guarantor of one's context for survival—this is not to say that over time they will not come to understand the collective strength of their numbers and their shared goals. In the past, so-called black-on-black violence was tolerated, even encouraged as constitutive of system maintenance. Today it is neither tolerable nor racially contained.

The *second developmental imperative* is that organized forces within civil society must resist the temptation of co-optation by the government. COSATU and the SACP must resist the temptation to seek instrumental rewards through corporatist arrangements, for these rewards, in the context of neoliberalism, will be fleeting and retractable. Rather, they must work outside government toward raising the level of consciousness and politicization of the marginals and the less well organized. They can do this by actively participating in rural and township development projects. Progressive forces within civil society must not lose sight of the possibilities for transformation that exist in the present situation. Change is possible.

The *third developmental imperative* is that the ANC leadership must not lose sight of its roots. As Hein Marais aptly points out, "[t]he exigencies of the anti-apartheid struggle have left a situation where populism will thrive mainly in or on the outskirts of the ANC. It has no other viable political residence."[68] Leadership must not lose sight of the double-edged nature of civil society: as force for development and as force for social breakdown. The ANC must resist the temptation to stifle dissent or to interpret dissent as "weakness." It seems to me that civil society in South Africa is a valuable resource in the reconstruction and development process and a "voice" not to be suppressed. This is especially so given the neopopulist nature of society–government relations that exists in present-day South Africa.

The ANC-Led Government. When majority rule came to most other African states, state-makers faced a double bind. Their economies continued to be tied in a fundamentally unequal way to the global economy. They also came to power with very few skilled personnel, certainly too few to manage the state in the manner of a determined developmental elite. In terms of human resources, South Africa faces no such difficulty. While there are a continuing brain drain and skills drain of disaffected whites out of government, the GNU is blessed with a battery of highly skilled and articulate state-makers. This group is racially mixed, so it brings a diversity of perspectives and opinions to the process of state building. These people are also not far enough beyond "the struggle" to forget how close South Africa came to a violent implosion. They are also not far enough from the struggle to forget what it was that they were fighting for.

The ANC-led government benefits from an unusual condition whereby those in exile spent much of their time productively, acquiring both intellectual and practical skills from universities and other institutions around the world. Those who chose to stay and fight acquired an acute sense of the relationship between idealism and realism. They were very much concerned with the practical side of grassroots activities and activism. Together, this constitutes a formidable human resource where state-building activities are concerned.

However, the ANC leadership shows a tendency, domestically, toward obstinance bordering on arrogance regarding questions of developmental direction and government policy. Yet, at the same time, it demonstrates a loathful obsequiousness toward the international community, in particular, the United States, the European Union, and the international financial institutions. Granted, state-makers in the "new" South Africa are enamored of this global attention. Many also feel fortunate that the policies and suggestions emanating from the centers of global capital jibe so closely with their own individually instrumentalist tendencies toward self-enrichment. It is as if many among the new elite suffer from the reverse of anorexia nervosa: when they look into the mirror, they see a reflection that is fat and healthy, rather than the reality, which tends toward emaciation.

This leads me to my *fourth developmental imperative*: the ANC leadership must look to its own history first in devising a sustainable developmental agenda. If those sitting at the top of the commanding height of Ben Turok's appropriately named "skyscraper economy" wish to imagine that South Africa is the United States or Germany, that is their prerogative. But it must be remembered that successful late-developers like the Asian tigers mimicked Western production processes, *not* their consumption habits.

This leads to my *fifth developmental imperative*: in pursuit of "catch-up" development, state-makers must look East, not West, for assistance. This is not to say that South Africa should attempt to mimic Asian development paths. As has already been pointed out, the prosperity generated by the postwar boom was utilized in fundamentally different ways in South Africa and the NICs. While Asians were busy with state-led import substitution industrialization and the production of manufactures for export, South Africa's state-makers were manufacturing little more than hatred and vast inequality in the state and the region. As a result, their development trajectories diverged inexorably.

Rather, what I am suggesting is that South African state-makers exploit the very real (developmental and sociological) philosophical differences that exist between the three emerging global regions, particularly, that between the United States and Japan. As Stallings and Streeck so clearly demonstrate, "Struggles among the United States, Europe and Japan over trade policy, as well as between the United States and Japan over development policy, highlight a new willingness of Japan and Europe to challenge the United States."[69] This "rift" has been labeled the end of the Washington consensus.

Recently, Japan has shown a new willingness to become actively involved in development issues. This has been nurtured along by a growing global awareness that the NICs and Japan have been successfully pursuing "growth *with* redistribution." Recent data from both the World Bank and the UNDP reveal that among Asian late-developers income inequalities are smaller, and the incidence of poverty is less severe than in both Europe and the United States.

It is often argued that, with the end of the Cold War and the demise of the Soviet Union, there is only one paradigm for development, and it is a neoliberal one. This false dichotomy serves to limit choice by blocking out creative thinking in those parts of the world sorely in need of both. Compounding the problem in South Africa is the continuing fascination with all things American. To be sure, for many South Africans there is a cultural affinity with the United States that crosses color lines. At the same time, Asian culture, as opposed to Asian commodities, is more mystifying and seems to be less easily packaged and sold around the world, particularly in a "McWorld" where English is the emerging lingua franca.

However, if South African state-makers are serious about transformation, they must resist "Uncle Sam" and actively pursue other options for development. Just as much of the Third World played the two cold warriors off each other, so now must South Africa play (Far) East against West. To reiterate a point, the aim here is to increase options for state building and not to merely mimic Asian strategies.

Humanity's Burden

This chapter is centrally concerned with the role of the state in development. In particular, it has focused on prospects and probabilities for South African reconstruction and development in the twenty-first century. It has argued in support of an active, interventionist state, citing both historical (e.g., the emergence of the British liberal state) and contemporary (the Asian late-developers) examples where possible. Some years ago Basil Davidson depicted the state in Africa as the "black man's burden." Granted, he was focusing on a particular form of state, but his characterization performed a disservice to African state-makers. For, at the end of the twentieth century, the "state" is not the black man's burden; it is humanity's burden. While there are trends toward "new regionalisms" and examples of peoples the world over living "postnationalist" lives, the fact remains that we have not yet devised a more inclusive form of social organization to meaningfully challenge the hegemony of "the state." But this is not to say that states are all the same; nor is it to say that states are some kind of immutable, objective reality. As I have argued throughout this chapter, and in contrast to World Bank and UNDP characterizations, states vary and change. They are social constructions, and as such they can be deconstructed, unmade, and made again.

So the "problem" of the state is a universal one, but "solutions" vary in time and space. Moreover, there is no "final solution"; changes in world order and at the level of the society raise new challenges for state-makers seeking hegemony and continuity. In my analysis of the state-building activities of the ANC-led GNU, I have tried to emphasize the changing forms of state and how particular events provide opportunities for fundamental restructuring. I have urged resistance to pressures from a transnational managerial elite and the necessity of creative thinking throughout state and civil society. I remain optimistic that the ANC-led GNU can, indeed, pursue a transformative, structural, reform-oriented developmental agenda. While the temptation toward co-optation is worrying, I am confident of the emergence of a "determined" developmental elite from the complex of social forces that makes contemporary South Africa such a vibrant and vexing state form. If there is "always something new out of

Africa,'' then there must be something new out of South Africa; if not, the twenty-first century seems too terrifying to contemplate.

NOTES

1. Peter Vale, "Regional Security in Southern Africa," *Alternatives* 21 (1996).

2. Government of South Africa, Department of Water Affairs and Forestry, "White Paper on National Water Policy for South Africa," April 1997.

3. UNDP, *Human Development Report 1997* (New York: Oxford University Press, 1997), 222–23.

4. UNDP, *Human Development Report*, 76.

5. African National Congress (ANC), *The Reconstruction and Development Program* (Johannesburg: Umanyano Press, 1994).

6. Government of South Africa, *Growth, Employment, and Redistribution: A Macroeconomic Strategy* (Pretoria: Department of Finance, 1996).

7. Gary Gereffi and Donald L. Wyman, eds., *Manufacturing Miracles: Paths of Industrialization in Latin America and East Asia* (Princeton, NJ: Princeton University Press, 1990); William D. Graf, "Democratization 'for' the Third World: Critique of a Hegemonic Project," special issue of *Canadian Journal of Development Studies* entitled *Governance, Democracy, and Human Rights*, ed. Nasir Islam and David R. Morrison (1996); Nigel Harris, *The End of the Third World: Newly Industrializing Countries and the Decline of an Ideology* (Harmondsworth: Penguin, 1986); Overseas Economic Cooperation Fund (OECF), "Issues Related to a World Bank's Approach to Structural Adjustment: Proposal from a Major Partner," OECF Occasional Paper No. 1, October, 1991; Barbara Stallings, ed., *Global Change, Regional Response: The New International Context of Development* (Cambridge: Cambridge University Press, 1995); UNDP, *Human Development Report*; World Bank, *The East Asian Miracle: Economic Growth and Public Policy* (Washington, DC: World Bank, 1993; World Bank, *World Development Report 1997: The State in a Changing World* (New York: Cambridge University Press, 1997).

8. Roger Southall, "Beyond the 'Double Whammy': The New South Africa in the New World Order," *Third World Quarterly* 15, no. 1 (1994).

9. Cf. Stephen Gelb, "South Africa's Post-Apartheid Political Economy," in Larry A. Swatuk and David R. Black, eds., *Bridging the Rift: The New South Africa in Africa* (Boulder, CO: Westview Press, 1997); Joan M. Nelson and Stephanie J. Eglinton, *Global Goals, Contentious Means: Issues of Multiple Aid Conditionality* (London: ODC, 1993).

10. Dan O'Meara, *Forty Lost Years: The Apartheid State and the Politics of the National Party, 1948–1994* (Johannesburg: Ravan, 1996), 21.

11. O'Meara, *Forty Lost Years*, 64.

12. O'Meara, *Forty Lost Years*, 64–65.

13. O'Meara, *Forty Lost Years*, 65.

14. Heribert Adam and Kogila Moodley, *The Negotiated Revolution: Society and Politics in Post-Apartheid South Africa* (Johannesburg: Jonathan Ball, 1993), 1.

15. Rob Davies and Dan O'Meara, "The State of Analysis of the Southern African Region: Issues Raised by South African Strategy," *Review of African Political Economy* 29 (July 1984): 68.

16. O'Meara, *Forty Lost Years*, 184–85.

17. O'Meara, *Forty Lost Years*, 184.

18. Larry A. Swatuk, *"Of Growth Poles" and "Backwaters": The New South Africa in Africa* (Toronto: York University, Center for International and Strategic Studies, 1995).

19. O'Meara, *Forty Lost Years*, 331.

20. John S. Saul, *Recolonization and Resistance in Southern Africa in the 1990s* (Trenton, NJ: African World Press, 1993), 109.

21. O'Meara, *Forty Lost Years*, 387.

22. O'Meara, *Forty Lost Years*, 401.

23. Saul, *Recolonization and Resistance*, 109.

24. Adam and Moodley, *The Negotiated Revolution*, 2.

25. O'Meara, *Forty Lost Years*, 410.

26. O'Meara, *Forty Lost Years*, 411.

27. O'Meara, *Forty Lost Years*, 412.

28. Adam and Moodley, *The Negotiated Revolution*, 3.

29. Kenneth Good, "Accountable to Themselves: Predominance in Southern Africa," *Journal of Modern African Studies*, prepublication draft, 36, n. 92; cf. Kenneth Good, *Realizing Democracy in Botswana, Namibia, and South Africa* (Pretoria: Africa Institute of South Africa, 1997), 114–18; Roger Southall, "Regionalization and Differentiation in South Africa: Some Policy Implications for Canadian Aid," in Larry A. Swatuk and David R. Black, eds., *Canada and Southern Africa after Apartheid: Foreign Aid and Civil Society* (Halifax: Center for Foreign Policy Studies, 1996).

30. Quoted in Good, "Accountable to Themselves," 36.

31. Graf, "Democratization 'for' the Third World," 43; he is quoting Robert Bates, "The Impulse to Reform in Africa," in Jennifer Widner, ed., *Economic Change and Political Liberalization in Africa* (Baltimore: Johns Hopkins University Press, 1994), 25.

32. Graf, "Democratization," 43.

33. Graf, "Democratization," 43.

34. Good, *Realizing Democracy*; Good, "Accountable to Themselves."

35. R. B. J. Walker, *Inside/Outside: International Relations as Political Theory* (Cambridge: Cambridge University Press, 1993).

36. Ralph Pettman, *State and Class: A Sociology of International Affairs* (London: Croom Helm, 1979), 119.

37. According to a report by Lungile Madywabe: "Appalled by the necklacing of an alleged gang member three weeks ago, ANC branches in Soweto hastily organized mass meetings across the township last week to gauge public sentiment on crime. To their surprise, well-attended mass meetings produced bristling views on how to deal with thugs. Not only was the community unconcerned by the brutal killing . . . angry residents recommended far more horrid measures for dealing with criminals in the area." See "Soweto Bays for More of the Same after Necklacing of Suspected Thug," *Sunday Independent*, 9 November 1997.

38. People against Gangsterism and Drugs (PAGAD) is a Muslim-dominated, community-based organization formed to combat gang rule in the Cape Flats of the Western Cape. With no small touch of irony, gang leaders themselves came together to form CORE, the anti-PAGAD Community Outreach Forum. Their claim, as members of CORE, was that they have "reformed" themselves. For an overview, see Stefaans Brummer, "Pagad, Gangs Mix It Up with Politics," *Mail and Guardian*, 9–15 May 1997.

39. Benedict Anderson, *Imagined Communities: Reflections on the Origin and Spread of Nationalism* (London: Verso, 1983); Pettman, *State and Class*, 117–28.

40. See Antjie Krog, "Unto the Third or Fourth Generation," *Mail and Guardian*,

13–19 June 1997; Frank Ferrari's interview with TRC chair Bishop Desmond Tutu, "South Africa May Not Have the Blueprint for Peace, But We're Trying," *Sunday Independent*, 12 October 1997.

41. In John Stremlau (with the cooperation of Helen Zille), *A House No Longer Divided: Progress and Prospects for Democratic Peace in South Africa*, Report to the Carnegie Commission on Preventing Deadly Conflict (New York: Carnegie Commission, July 1997), 13.

42. In Stremlau, *A House*, 16.

43. Good, *Realizing Democracy*, 90.

44. Herbert Jauch, "Economics after Apartheid," *Canadian Dimension* (August–September 1997): 26.

45. *Mail and Guardian* (Johannesburg), 21–27 November 1997.

46. O'Meara, *Forty Lost Years*, 173.

47. However, as of April 1997, the Land Reform Pilot Program had disbursed less than R20 million of this allotment. "The program, which consists of 195 projects, was set up in early 1995 as a way to 'kickstart' efforts to give land to 39,000 households. . . . Officials cite lack of resources, lack of experience in implementing land reform, cumbersome bureaucratic procedures and other reasons for the slow pace" (Jim Day, "Land Redistribution Flops Badly," *Mail and Guardian*, 11–17 April 1997).

48. According to Robert Cox, this group has "attained a clearly distinctive class consciousness . . . though they do not identify themselves as such. . . . Being a member of a class does not mean submerging conflicts of interests with other class members—indeed, it is of the essence of a capitalist class that rivalries exist among capitalists. What it does mean is awareness of a common concern to maintain the system that enables the class to remain dominant. Various institutions have performed the function of articulating strategies in this common concern: the Trilateral Commission, the OECD, the IMF, and the World Bank all serve as foci for generating the policy consensus for the maintenance and defense of the system" (Robert Cox, *Production, Power, and World Order: Social Forces in the Making of History* [Cambridge: Cambridge University Press, 1987]).

49. Saul, *Recolonization and Resistance*, 145.

50. See Thabo Masebe, "Grassroots Challenge Betrays the Culture and Traditions of the ANC," *Sunday Independent*, 12 October 1997.

51. The term is from Good: "The new authoritarianism, built on predominance and power sharing among the elites, backed by corporate power and the 'patriotic bourgeoisie,' has potentially greater permanency than apartheid" (Good, "Accountable to Themselves," 47).

52. Saul, *Recolonization and Resistance*, 106–10.

53. Jauch, "Economics after Apartheid," 27.

54. See Jeremy Cronin and Blade Nzimande, "ANC Thatcherites Want a Party of Black Bosses," *Mail and Guardian*, 10–16 October 1997.

55. See Marion Edmunds, "Weighing up a Weak Opposition," *Mail and Guardian*, 23–29 May 1997; Adrian Hadland, "Defeat in Boksburg Hastens the NP's Slide," *Sunday Independent*, 19 October 1997. The four municipalities are Boksburg, Kempton Park, Witbank, and Margate.

56. Good, "Accountable to Themselves," 38–40.

57. Southall, "Regionalization and Differentiation in South Africa," 68.

58. These statistics are from a Development Bank of South Africa study cited in Southall, "Regionalization and Differentiation in South Africa," 72. In global terms,

Western Cape's HDI is classified as "medium human development"—in spite of the mass poverty of the townships!—comparable to Lithuania (.762) or Croatia (.760). Northern Cape, in contrast, would be classified as "low human development" on a par with former Zaire (.381), Nigeria (.390), and the Comoros Islands (.412). (See UNDP, *Human Development Report 1997*, 148.)

59. Which is entirely in line with World Bank thinking about less and better government. See chapter 5 of World Bank, *World Development Report 1997*.

60. See John Spira, "Cape Electrification 'Miracle' Could Spread throughout SA," *Sunday Independent*, 14 September 1997. EDF stands for *Electricité de France*.

61. The quotation is from Phumzile Mlambo-Nqcuka, the deputy minister of trade and industry. See "Government Challenges NGOs to Help Empowerment," *Sunday Independent*, 21 September 1997.

62. In Saul, *Recolonization and Resistance*, 113.

63. Peter Vale, "Backwaters and Bypasses: South Africa and 'Its' Region," in Swatuk and Black, *Bridging the Rift*.

64. David Moore, "Reading Americans on Democracy in Africa: From the CIA to 'Good Governance,' " *European Journal of Developmental Research* 8, no. 1 (June 1996): 124.

65. See editorial, "Mbeki's Warning on Poverty Is a Matter of Survival for All of Us," *Sunday Independent*, 2 November 1997.

66. See Larry A. Swatuk, "The Nexus of Sovereignty and Regionalism in Post-Apartheid Southern Africa," in Mark E. Denham and Mark O. Lombardi, eds., *Perspectives on Third World Sovereignty: The Postmodern Paradox*, (London: Macmillan, 1996).

67. See Patrick Bond, *Commanding Heights and Community Control. New Economics for a New South Africa* (Johannesburg: Ravan, 1991).

68. See Hein Marais, "The Problem Is Business, Not Big Bad Winnie and the Populists," *Sunday Independent*, 23 November 1997.

69. Barbara Stallings and Wolfgang Streeck, "Capitalisms in Conflict? The United States, Europe, and Japan in the Post-Cold War World," in *Global Change, Regional Response: The New International Context of Development* (Cambridge: Cambridge University Press, 1995), 87.

Chapter 10

Ethiopia: Missed Opportunities for Peaceful Democratic Process

MOHAMMED HASSEN

First and foremost, I believe only a successful democratization process will save Ethiopia from a vicious cycle of misery and destruction. I do not believe for a moment that the Tigrai People's Liberation Front (TPLF) and the organization it has created, the Ethiopian Peoples' Revolutionary Democratic Forces (EPRDF), which monopolizes the transitional government of Ethiopia, are so wise that they alone can plan and shape the democratization process and decide the destiny of 56 million people. Together with other opposition organizations, the EPRDF leaders can play a very decisive role in addressing the crucial issue of our time—the democratization of Ethiopia—thus securing their place in history. Second, following the collapse[1] of the Ethiopian state in 1991, democratization has become all the more indispensable for state building and institutional sources of its legitimacy. Democratization means "a highly complex process involving successive stages of transition, endurance and consolidation. This process ultimately leads to both institutionalization and consolidation of structures and conditions conducive to structural transformation"[2] and could change the Ethiopian state from being dominated by one ethnic group into the state of all its citizens. Only such a profound transformation will reconstitute the Ethiopian state into a legitimate sovereign authority, "[t]he accepted source of identity and the arena of politics, . . . the decision-making center of government,"[3] and the institution that maintains law and order and enhances societal cohesion.

Third and most important, I sincerely believe in the freedom, liberty, fraternity, and unity of the peoples of Ethiopia. As an optimist who believes in the unity of free people in a free country, I have an undying dream that one day the Oromo, the Amhara, and Tigrai, and other peoples of Ethiopia will be able to establish a democratic federal system. To me only a genuine federal arrangement offers better prospect for the future of Ethiopia.

In essence a federal arrangement is one of partnership, established and regulated by a covenant [consent], whose internal relationships reflect the special kind of sharing that must prevail among the partners, based on a mutual recognition of the integrity of each partner and the attempt to foster a special unity among them.[4]

The strength of federal arrangement is that it combines self-rule (which satisfies the aspiration of oppressed nations and nationalities) and shared rule[5] (which takes into consideration the geography, demography, culture, history, and, above all, economic interdependence of the peoples of that country). A federal arrangement cannot work if it is designed and imposed by the leadership of a single party, as the leaders of the TPLF's halfhearted, futile attempt clearly demonstrate. The TPLF leaders not only lack legitimacy to design and implement a federal arrangement in Ethiopia but also risk misapplication of the concept of federalism itself.[6] Federal arrangement works when it is designed by the people and their representatives and implemented with their freely expressed consent for its purpose and framework. The new system will, in effect, be a universally designed agreement to establish a new body politic "in such a way that all reaffirm their fundamental equality and retain their basic rights."[7] The road to a democratic, federal Ethiopia is a long and difficult one, but it must start before the looming dictatorship blocks all the paths to the promised land. The aim of this chapter is to show what went wrong with the democratic experiment in Ethiopia and suggest what should be done to correct it.

From 1941 to 1994 Ethiopia missed a number of opportunities to transform or modernize its economic and political institutions that would have created factors conducive to democracy, such as higher rates of literacy and education, urbanization, strong mass media, tolerant political culture, and, above all, wealth, which would "provide the resources needed to mitigate the tensions produced by political conduct."[8] Today, Ethiopia is the second poorest country in Africa and one of the least developed countries in the world. In the past half century, the Ethiopian ruling elites distinguished themselves by their progressive impoverishment of their country and by their fear of democracy. "The Ethiopian elite is one of the least democratically-minded interest groups inside or outside of Ethiopia; it does not respect nor have faith in the abilities of ordinary Ethiopians to make wise political decisions."[9] The elites proved incapable of devising solutions to the burning economic, political, social, and cultural issues of the day.

I know of no society in Africa where the dignity and humanity of individuals have been so thoroughly squashed or obliterated to the same extent as is the case with Ethiopian peasants and poor, uneducated men, women and children.[10]

Instead of solving economic and political problems of the country, the Ethiopian ruling elites have created complex problems that are now tearing the social fabric of Ethiopia. The story is too long to be narrated in a short chapter such as this one. I focus on only a few points, which highlight missed opportunities in the past half century.

In 1941 Ethiopia had a window of opportunity to lessen the burden of the conquered and colonized peoples of southern Ethiopia in general and the Oromo in particular. The Oromo, like other peoples of southern Ethiopia, were conquered and incorporated into the Ethiopian empire during and after the 1880s. After their conquest, the Oromo lost not only their sovereignty but also their rights and human dignity as they became landless, rightless, second-class colonial subjects who were insulted, abused, and dehumanized in all ways great and small. During the short-lived fascist occupation of Ethiopia (1936–1941), the Italians destroyed the twin pillars of Ethiopian colonialism in southern Ethiopia, namely, the *Gabbar* system (serfdom) and slavery. The Italians not only destroyed the old social order but also built extensive roads and started limited literacy programs in a number of languages, including the Oromo language, which was used on the radio as well as in the court system all over Oromia, Oromo territory within Ethiopia. After his restoration to power in 1941, Emperor Haile Selassie (1930–1974) had a good opportunity to right the old wrongs and build a state on the basis of equality among the peoples of Ethiopia. On the contrary, the first thing the emperor did after his return to power was to stop the Oromo-language radio program of the Italian period and ban the use of that language in the court system as well as for educational purposes. In 1942 not only did Haile Selassie's regime ban literature in the Oromo language, "but most of what was already available was collected and destroyed."[11] As a result of this policy, the Oromo language, which is one of the major African languages, until recently lacked "developed literature and has less printed materials than any language with a comparable number of speakers."[12] Other languages in southern Ethiopia did not enjoy a better position than the Oromo language. I focus on the Oromo language for one purpose alone: to show that from 1942 to 1974, the Oromo language was banned from being used for preaching, teaching, and production of literature. In the words of Paul Baxter:

Oromo was denied any official status and it was not permissible to publish, preach, teach or broadcast in Oromo. In court or before an official an Oromo had to speak Amharic or use an interpreter. Even a case between two Oromo, before an Oromo speaking magistrate had to be heard in Amharinya. I sat through a mission service at which the preacher and all the congregation were Oromo but at which the sermons as well as the service was given first in Amharinya, which few of the congregation understood at all, and then translated into Oromo.[13]

The period from 1942 to 1990 was the time when the program of Amharization[14] and de-Oromoization was intensified, through the educational system, cultural institutions, and governmental bureaucracy.

The school was designed to inculcate Ethiopian patriotism in Oromo children by stripping them of their language, their culture and identity. It remains the belief of Amhara rulers and elites that to be an Ethiopian, one has to cease to be an Oromo. The two things were/are seen as incompatible.[15]

In the school nothing positive was taught about the Oromo as a people, their history, culture, and way of life. On the contrary, like other colonial systems in Africa, there was a systematic attempt to break the Oromo in body, soul, and spirit so as to dehumanize and reduce them to the condition of helplessness and dejection. In short, successive Ethiopian elites "sought not only to destroy the Oromo people's pride in their achievements but also needed to keep them chained with no faith in themselves, their history, and national identity."[16] This was the fate of the Oromo, who constitute 40 to 50 percent of the population of Ethiopia. Other peoples of southern Ethiopia suffered similar fate. This was because Haile Selassie's regime followed a policy of assimilation as the mode of integration into the Ethiopian system. Those who were assimilated or Amharized ceased to be themselves. It did not dawn on Emperor Haile Selassie and his ruling elite that one could be an Oromo, Somali, or Walayeta but still remain a loyal Ethiopian. I write all this not to exaggerate the failures of Haile Selassie's regime but just to show that during his long reign, Ethiopia lost a good opportunity of creating an Ethiopian nation, Ethiopian culture, Ethiopian languages, and Ethiopian history that generates a common feeling and reflects both the past achievements and future aspirations. What is projected as the identity of the Ethiopian nation—national culture, national language, national religion, national dress, national symbols (the monarchy, the church, the flag, national anthem)[17]— is simply that of the Amhara-Tigrai nations. The modern Ethiopian state was not brought about by natural growth of unity of peoples but, on the contrary, through brutal conquest. Up to 1991, the Ethiopian state was the *state of* the ruling Amhara elites. "[M]ost Amharas . . . suffered as much, if not more oppression, degradation and grinding poverty as the rest of the population at the hands of ruthless Amhara . . . despots."[18] The Amhara elite, which numbered probably less than 5 percent of Shawan Amhara population, co-opted the Tigraian elite and assimilated the elites of the conquered peoples of southern Ethiopia and transformed itself into the ruling elite. This elite expropriated Ethiopian nationalism because their leader, Menilek, the king of Shawa and later the emperor of Ethiopia (1889–1913), created the modern Ethiopian empire, institutionalizing the monopoly of power in the hands of the elite of the Amhara of Shawa. In other words, after the creation of the modern Ethiopian empire during and after the 1880s, the Shawan Amhara elites dominated the political, military, economic, cultural, religious, and social life of the Ethiopian state. Their institutions became the institutions of the Ethiopian state, which was owned, controlled, and dominated by the same elites up to 1991. Since the nationalism of the ruling elites became Ethiopian nationalism, there is no Ethiopian nationalism based on collective pride of all the peoples of Ethiopia. This does not mean that there is no Ethiopian nationalism. Indeed, there is an Ethiopian nationalism, but today it is undermined by the existence of rival nationalisms. There are Amhara,

Tigrai, Eritrean, Ogaden Somali, Oromo, and Sidama nationalisms. Even the old Abyssinian nationalism, which was based on Christianity, the Orthodox church, the monarchy, and Amhara-Tigrai solidarity, is now a history, with the Amharas and Tigrai fighting among themselves ironically in the name of Ethiopian nationalism but in reality for the control and domination of the Ethiopian state. Given all these, where is a single Ethiopian nationalism based on collective pride of all the peoples of Ethiopia? Yet the ruling Shawan Amhara elites up to 1991 not only managed to mask their governmental nationalism as "Ethiopian nationalism" but also projected their own interest as national interest and their own survival as the survival of Ethiopia.

During the 1960s, the regime of Emperor Haile Selassie had ample opportunity to carry out a land reform program and encourage the development of a tolerant political culture. His regime not only failed in both respects but unwittingly transformed a peaceful, self-help association into a Pan-Oromo national movement that gave birth to Oromo nationalism. This was the Matcha-Tulama Association (1963–1967), which developed in three stages: first, the failure to integrate the assimilated Christian Oromo into the Ethiopian political processes; second, the realization of the assimilated Oromo that they were badly treated and discriminated against by the ruling Amhara elites; and third, the events of 1966, which suddenly politicized the movement and resulted in the rise of Oromo nationalism. For the first time, the new ideology of Oromo nationalism became an instrument for mobilizing the Oromo of various regions in their name and interest.

The development of the Matcha-Tulama Association exposed one major weakness of the Ethiopian political process that is often overlooked in the discussion on Ethiopia. This is the intense anti-Oromo prejudice within the Amhara ruling circle. During the 1940s and the 1950s only few Oromo were educated. Those lucky ones had all the necessary criteria to integrate them into the heart and the soul of the Ethiopian system.[19] They were mainly Christians, were culturally Amharized, and spoke Amharic. They were ardent Ethiopian nationalists and loyal to the emperor. Yet they were not treated as equals by the Amhara ruling elites.

The life of assimilated Oromos was often peripheral. In spite of their total submission to "pressures for their 'cultural suicide' and to the dominance of the Amhara over non-Amhara peoples in all aspects of life," they were seldom treated as equals by the Amhara. The Amharization of the Oromo and other groups was attempted "without integrating them as equals or allowing them to share power in any meaningful way." As the "Amhara mask" they wore was often too transparent, assimilated Oromos rarely reached decision-making positions within the Ethiopian bureaucracy. Despite the hard efforts they were making to sound like a native speaker, and the change of their personal names to Amharic ones, their pronunciation of some of the Amharic words often exposed their ethnic origins. Hence, they usually were confined to middle and lower rungs of the bureaucracy, and were expected to act as zombies carrying out orders from their Amhara superiors.[20]

The reality of Shawan Amhara political domination was first succinctly expressed in a manifesto produced during the 1960 failed coup. The manifesto, which was not broadcast during 1960, appears to have inspired Walleligne Makomnen's 1969 paper "on the question of nationalities in Ethiopia."[21] The manifesto, among other points, stated:

Ethiopia is all its districts and people. . . . Today the name Ethiopia applies only to ruling ethnic group [i.e., Amhara]. Ethiopian culture is the culture of the same group. When one speaks about religion, Ethiopia is presented as the land of the believers of only one religion [i.e., Christianity]. Whenever the issue of language is raised, the existence of all languages [except Amharic] is denied. In today's Ethiopia, the cultures, religions, and languages of our people are to be destroyed and replaced by those of the ruling group.[22]

The manifesto went on, stating that Ethiopia belongs to all its people, who should have the opportunity to participate in the affairs of their country. Career opportunities should be open to all Ethiopians. Public officials must be elected by the people. Tenancy must be abolished. Landless farmers must have their own land. The criteria for owning land should be nothing but to be an Ethiopian citizen.[23] The authors of the manifesto not only expressed the prevailing inequalities within the Ethiopian society but also raised the thorny issue of "land to the tiller," which became the binding revolutionary slogan for the Ethiopian student movements both at home and abroad. After the failed coup of 1960, Emperor Haile Selassie had a wonderful opportunity to implement land reform and liberalize his administration. Instead, his policy not only intensified the landlessness of the peasantry but also entrenched his authoritarian rule. Lack of foresightedness, initiative, vision, and timely reform was and still is the hallmark of the Ethiopian political culture.

If some politically conscious Oromo military officers were unhappy about the landlessness, rightlessness, and cultural oppression of their people before the 1960 coup, they were alarmed by the turn of events. After the failed coup, the government of Selassie followed a secret policy of controlling and limiting the promotion of high-ranking officers of Oromo origin. This policy angered many high-ranking officers, including Colonel Alemu Qitessa, one of the two key founding members of the Matcha-Tulama Association.[24] The other key founding member was Haile Mariam Gamada, a widely recognized expert on Oromo history. He was outraged not only by the oppression to which the Oromo were subjected but also by the treatment of Oromo history in Ethiopian historiography. The aims and objectives of the association were to build schools and spread literacy; to build clinics and hospitals; to build roads; to build churches for Christians and mosques for Muslims; and to help the disabled and unemployed.[25] Interestingly, Haile Mariam Gamada coined the name of the association and produced its logo, the *oda* (sycamore tree).[26] The name of the association symbolized the unity of two major Oromo confederacies, the Matcha and Tulama, while its logo, the oda, was the symbol of self-administration.[27] "Traditionally the Oromo believed Oda to be the most sacred of trees, the shade of which was the source of peace, the center of religion, and the office of government—the meeting group for the democratically elected Gada leaders.''[28] The symbolic meaning behind the association was the unity of all Oromo and their return to the Gada political system.

The Matcha-Tulama Association (hereafter, the association), had a policy-making board of thirteen men, including four military officers, two lawyers, government officials, and businessmen. They were all highly successful men who were well respected among the Oromo. They were the most privileged elements of the Oromo society. This privileged social element who the first Pan-Oromo national movement. They returned to their root in reaction to unbridled policy of Amharization,[29] not to mention their realization of the legal, economic, political, social, and cultural policies that affected the Oromo. In other words, the conflict between the ruling Amhara elites and the educated Oromo within the Ethiopian establishment forced the latter toward the Oromo issue. It is not idle to speculate that, had the ruling Amhara elites been wise enough to share meaningful power with the professional Oromo elites, they would have delayed the rise of political nationalism among the Oromo. On the contrary, after 1960, the ruling Amhara elites hastened the politicization of the educated Oromo. It has been rightly said:

When the educated professionals find themselves unable to gain admission to posts commensurate with their degrees and talents, they tend to turn away also from the metropolitan culture of the dominant ethnic group and return to their ''own'' culture, the culture of the once despised subject ethnic group. Exclusion breeds failed assimilation, and reawakens an ethnic consciousness among the professional elites, at exactly the moment when the intellectuals are beginning to explore the historic roots of the community.[30]

The personal histories of many of the individuals who played pivotal roles in the Matcha-Tulama Association are the best examples for what has just been said. Several military officers from the rank of brigadier general to the private soldier, civilian officials, professional elites, and business and religious leaders joined the association as a consequence of their disillusionment with the Ethiopian government policy toward themselves and their people. They joined the association for various reasons, but, by joining it, they elevated the status and transformed the image of the association. Most of all, they provided the association with their skills, knowledge, organizational capacities, and leadership qualities, and in the process they transformed what started as a self-help organization into a Pan-Oromo movement with huge membership and branch offices all over Oromia. The classic example among those who were disillusioned with the government policy and joined the association was General Taddesse Biru. The general was a deeply religious man, an ardent Ethiopian nationalist, and loyal supporter of Emperor Haile Selassie. In fact, he was instrumental in foiling

the 1960 coup. He was married to an Amhara woman, very fluent in Amharic
(he could not speak the Oromo language), and passed as an Amhara. To all
intents and purposes, he was a completely Amharized Oromo who regarded the
Matcha-Tulama Association as a "tribal" organization. When he was approached and invited to join the Association by Colonel Alemu Qitessa (the
president), his response was that he could not join it because that organization
was involved in tribal politics.[31] However, as the chairman of the National Literacy Campaign, General Taddesse agreed to cooperate with the association in
its mission of spreading literacy among the Oromo. The general was very active
in the National Literacy Campaign, which was conducted entirely in the Amharic
language. The goal of the campaign was to spread literacy among Amharic
speakers as well as literacy and Amharic language among non-Amharic speakers. General Taddesse, who believed in the double mission of the literacy campaign, enthusiastically supported the Matcha-Tulama Association's literacy
program. This alarmed Prime Minister Akelilu Habte Wolde, who assumed General Taddesse to be an Amhara and therefore confided in him the educational
policy of the Ethiopian government in these terms:

It is good to say learn. However, you must know who to teach. In terms of education,
we have left behind the Oromo at least by a century. If you think in terms of teaching
the Oromo, remember they are vast (an ocean whose wave could flood us).[32]

In other words, the prime minister told General Taddesse Biru to curtail the
literacy campaign among the Oromo. It is interesting to note that in the 1960s,
the Ethiopian government feared that if the large Oromo population was taught
even in Amharic, they would endanger the Amhara hold on power. General
Taddesse could not believe what he had heard from the mouth of the Ethiopian
prime minister. He was shocked and rudely awakened by the blatant discrimination directed against the Oromo. It became painfully evident to General Taddesse Biru that the central focus of the Ethiopian prime minister and his
dominant aim were to curb the rising national feeling of the Oromo. The arro-
gant Amhara ruling elites, whose identities were never questioned and who had
never known cultural subjugation and loss of land and rights to their fellow
countrymen, were insensitive to the ethnic feelings of non-Amhara almost to
the point of stupidity. They had a unique capacity to turn even an ardent Ethiopian nationalist and a deeply religious and loyal officer into an equally ardent
Oromo nationalist. To his credit General Taddesse Biru believed in the unity
and equality and equal treatment of all Ethiopians. For that purpose, he decided
to join the Matcha-Tulama Association (which he had refused to join earlier)
and used it as a platform for his goal of the unity, equality, and equal treatment
of all Ethiopians. In this he was encouraged by the bylaws and the day-to-day
activities of the association. Although a Pan-Oromo movement, the goal of the
association was to end national oppression in Ethiopia. It was open to all Ethiopians. For this purpose members of the oppressed nations and nationalities were

invited to join and gladly joined the association. They included the Adare, the Afar, Bella Shangul, the Gamo, the Gimira, Issa, Kulo Konta, the Sidama, and the Walyeta.[33] Twenty-six non-Oromo individuals held responsible positions within the various committees of the association.[34] From this perspective, it is fair to say that the association was the first organization that brought together the oppressed nationalities of southern Ethiopia who, like the Oromo, were exposed to national oppression, economic exploitation, and cultural domination.

When General Taddesse Biru joined the association, he wanted to use its platform for his goal of spreading literacy, while the leaders of the association wanted to use his name, his fame, his charismatic personality, and, above all, his standing within the government and his closeness to the emperor and the prime minister for the purpose of protecting and expanding the activities of the association. The leaders of the association unwittingly traded the calm, grass-roots activities of the organization for high-stake publicity, which attracted the envy, jealousy, and, above all, the fear of the Amhara ruling elites, who were eager and ready to destroy the association together with its leaders. Soon after the general joined the association, Prime Minister Akelilu Habte Wolde, to his horror, found out that, after all, Taddesse Biru was not an Amhara. He wanted to control the damage done by confiding to him the educational policy of the government, by physical elimination of the general himself.[35] At that time, General Taddesse Biru was assistant police commissioner and the chairman of the National Literacy Campaign.[36] When he joined it, the association had twelve subcommittees, among which the subcommittee for education, history, and regional branch offices were the three most important. General Taddesse Biru served as the chairman of Subcommittees for Education and Regional Branch Offices. He was the most important figure, the guiding spirit, and the dynamic and energetic leader who feared for his life and rapidly politicized the movement. General Taddesse and other militant and radical members of the association knew what was coming, and they wanted to ignite the fire of Oromo nationalism before the destruction of the movement.

By 1966, the association had offices all over the Oromo regions of Ethiopia. It attracted tens of thousands of members from different corners of Oromia. It also attracted Oromo students from Addis Ababa University, including Lieutenant Mamo Mazamir, Ibssa Gutama, Barro Tumsa, Yohannes Lata, Mekonnen Gallan,[37] and Taha Ali. With the exception of Mamo Mazamir, who was hanged by the government in 1967, the rest were founding members of the Oromo Liberation Front in 1974. (Many others whose names are not listed here were members of the association and later became founding members of the OLF.) Except for the martyred Barro Tumsa, the rest are still prominent members of the same organization. This establishes a solid link between the transition from the Matcha-Tulama Association to the OLF. Among the university students who joined the association and radicalized the youth wing of the movement was Lieutenant Mamo Mazamir, who considered the writing of Oromo history as the precondition for correcting the distorted image of, and revolutionizing, the

Oromo masses. He made writing Oromo history and production of literature in Afaan Oromoo (the Oromo language) the ideological battleground for the movement. Since not much Oromo history was taught in the Ethiopian educational system, and the little that was taught was greatly distorted, Mamo believed that the association had to write Oromo history. That task was left to him and Haile Mariam Gamada, a man with encyclopedic knowledge of Oromo history. It is interesting to note in passing that the association's concern with writing Oromo history, to a large extent, was a reaction to the Ethiopian historiographic treatment of the Oromo. Lieutenant Mamo Mazamir wrote "History of the Oromo," which was confiscated by the government when his house was searched in 1967. In addition to history, the document Mamo prepared included a plan for a new government, a new Constitution, and distribution of land among the landless tenants.[38] This was too much for the ruling Amhara elites, and Mamo Mazamir was hanged for producing that document.[39]

What transformed the association from being a self-help organization in the administrative region of Shawa, to the Pan-Oromo movement all over Oromia was the public meeting held on 15 May 1966 in Arsi at a place called Itayaa. There thousands of Oromo from the Arsi region and the leadership of the association from Addis Ababa (both Muslims and Christians) met and discussed how they were all subjected to harsh economic exploitation and political oppression. It was the beginning of coordinated and united Oromo activities.[40] It was the beginning of the realization of the importance of unity, and those who were at the meeting vowed never to be divided again. They even went beyond religious taboo, and Muslims ate meat slaughtered by Christians, and the Christians also ate meat slaughtered by Muslims. This was an unheard-of event in Ethiopia, which outraged the Amhara ruling elites. The meeting was addressed in Afaan Oromoo, the language that was proscribed from being used in public in Ethiopia.[41] All subsequent meetings were addressed in the same language. Dramas written in Afaan Oromoo by Mamo Mazamir, that brilliant young officer of boundless energy, were shown at subsequent meetings. At huge mass meetings fierce oratory, dramas, poems, and prayers in Afaan Oromoo all combined to move the Oromo into tears of anger against the Ethiopian system. The Oromo became conscious of their deprivation and their treatment as second-class subjects and expressed their determination to be free and equal with the rest of the population of Ethiopia.

It is important to note here that the leaders of the Matcha-Tulama Association emphasized the various Oromo commonalities such as language, culture, the Gada system, historical experience, and political ideals, while toning down other local, regional, and religious differences, which Haile Selassie's regime exaggerated in order to weaken Oromo unity. In other words, the leadership of the association cultivated Oromo national consciousness, which led to the development of Oromo nationalism in the 1960s. This realization persuaded the ruling Amhara elites to destroy the Matcha-Tulama movement sooner rather than later. The leaders of the association appealed to the emperor for justice but to no avail. Then the leadership of the association under the direction and influence of General Taddesse Biru decided to assassinate the emperor and capture the state power. Through planted informers in the movement, the emperor knew all about the poorly planned and badly coordinated plot, which was to take effect on 5 November 1967. Shortly thereafter, on 17 November, the government, using as a pretext a bomb explosion at a cinema hall in Addis Ababa, which was planted by its own agents,[42] imprisoned over 100 leaders and key members of the association, which it dissolved. The government won a short-term Pyrrhic victory. But within seven short years (i.e., 1974) its policy unwittingly transformed Oromo politics beyond recognition. The Oromo demand for equality within Ethiopia was transformed into Oromo demand for self-determination in Oromia. Oromo demand for literacy in Amharic language and using Geez script was transformed into demand for literacy in the Oromo language in Latin alphabet; in short, the Ethiopian government's unwarranted policy of destroying a peaceful Oromo movement produced Oromo elites' rejection of Ethiopian identity itself.

The 1974 revolution offered Ethiopia yet another good opportunity not only to heal the old wounds, to redress the old injustice, to right the old wrongs but also to democratize itself and bring about a meaningful devolution of power in that country. However, unfortunately, that opportunity was missed when the young army officers, who illegally seized power, aborted the popular revolution and stopped all attempts at democratizing the country. For seventeen years Ethiopia suffered under an incredible military dictatorship whose historic mission was nothing but destruction. It is believed that more than 2 million Ethiopian peasants lost their lives between 1974 and 1991, not to mention millions who were internally displaced or thousands of educated Ethiopians who were scattered as refugees to all corners of the globe. When the authors of sorrow and destruction were overthrown in May 1991, it was with a sigh of relief, a time of joy, and a moment of hope for all the peoples of Ethiopia.

Those who would disagree, as I do, with many of the measures that the TPLF/EPRDF leaders took in the past must give credit to their boldness, political courage, military strategy, and formidable contribution to the destruction of the military dictatorship. However, that victory will be meaningless until the peoples of Ethiopia enjoy the blessing of a truly democratic government. Democracy is a form of government,[43] as well as a political system,[44] that was never given an opportunity to flourish in Ethiopia. In Ethiopia power was never based on the will of the people; it was always obtained through, and maintained by, force. This is true of the current rulers of Ethiopia. The culture of the ruling elites, which emphasizes hierarchy, authority, and centralization, not only is less conducive to democracy but also aborts the institutionalization of democratic organizations, as the following discussion shows. The Ethiopian ruling elites (past and present) have not realized that democracy is people's rule, which empowers them to solve their own problems. Democracy gives people possibilities to make their own decisions on issues ranging from building clinics in villages to participating in the future of their country. However, sadly, there is a strong determination on the part of the EPRDF leadership to view democracy as an instrument for transforming the transitional period into a permanent monopoly of state power. That is not democracy but a new form of dictatorship. It is already too obvious that the EPRDF does not accept the fact that the dominant role it played in defeating the former military dictatorship does not entitle it to the monopoly of state power in Ethiopia. The contradiction between the EPRDF's achievement of the past and its ambition to remain in power permanently in the name of democracy aborted the democratization process in Ethiopia.[45]

In July 1991, a National Conference was convened in Addis Ababa at which "some thirty-one political movements signed a Transitional Charter, which created a Council of Representatives with eighty-seven members and established the Transitional Government of Ethiopia (TGE)."[46] The TGE was "billed as a coalition government representing three main interests: the Oromo interest, the Amhara interest and the Tigrean interest with others . . . being considered important but secondary."[47] The coalition government was strictly a government of ethnic politics that aspired to be transformed into a government of national politics at a later date.[48]

However, from the very beginning, the EPRDF leadership emphasized ethnic politics, for the purpose of disorienting possible rival organizations. According to one observer of the Ethiopian political scene, for the Tigraian elites, who control the Ethiopian state since 1991, ethnic politics "is a master-stroke. It decimates their opponents in Addis Ababa and leaves the center exclusively to them."[49] This means that the EPRDF leaders use ethnic politics "to divide Ethiopia into strangely shaped ethnic regions, the equivalent of the South African homelands."[50]

As early as 1991, it was already clear that the EPRDF leadership did not want to realize that the measure of a democratic government is the extent to which it allows opposition groups to organize and contend for power. Since 1991, the only sort of liberty that was manifest under the transitional government was the liberty of the EPRDF forces to destroy the liberty of others. Democracy cannot be established by destroying organizations. In fact, democracy "cannot be imposed by force. Rather, it is based on largely voluntary compliance with a set of rules of the political game."[51] The chief function of the transitional government should have been to protect and preserve the rights of individuals and organizations rather than render those rights nonexistent. If the transitional government continues with its policy of controlling or emasculating or destroying opposition groups, the experiment with democracy would be stillborn. According to Tecola Hagos, the former supporter of the EPRDF leadership and now its bitter critic, "[W]hat remained in power since 1991 is an illegitimate power structure, a reestablishment of feudalism and autocracy dressed in new symbols with the descendants of yesterday's feudal warlords as the main actors in this sickening Ethiopian political tragedy."[52] If Hagos' claim of a reestablish-

ment of feudalism in Ethiopia is an exaggeration, overwhelming evidence presented later supports his hard-hitting argument about the restoration of autocracy
in Ethiopia. When one organization monopolizes the power and the resources
of the state as the EPRDF does, it discourages openness and accountability and
encourages the use and abuse of power. As early as 1991 the transitional government used coercion and outright violence and suppression "in its battle
against those who challenge it."[53]

Since 1991, the EPRDF forces have been summarily assimilated into the
Ethiopian state as the embodiment of the new order, thus giving birth to a new
political class. The new political class not only insists that all opposition groups
totally disarm, so that it will have absolute monopoly over the arsenal of destruction, but has already used authoritarian methods to advance its irresistible
drive toward the creation of a one-party state. The length to which the tunnel
vision of the new political class interests can go is already depressing. First, the
EPRDF, which is a formidable military organization, has become the state unto
itself. EPRDF soldiers have become a national army. It has created its police
force. Its security apparatus is said to be as large as that of the regime it has
replaced. Worst of all, it has rehired the assassin squad used by the dictator
Mengistu Haile Mariam for the purpose of eliminating those suspected of opposing the regime. Once again individuals have started "disappearing"—a euphemism for secret killings. Furthermore, "former confidants and officials of
Mengistu, individuals from the old bureaucratic establishment, have effectively
penetrated the power structure of the EPRDF and have succeeded in creating
walls around the leaders of the EPRDF."[54] It appears that the TPLF/EPRDF
leaders use the former military regime's oppressive machinery of the state more
subtly and efficiently. They are slowly, but surely, becoming more intolerant of
any opinion other than their own. They have almost done away with the principles of tolerance and peaceful existence enshrined in the National Charter of
1991. Although the charter is not a perfect document, it is a centerpiece to the
human rights and democratic rights of Ethiopians and "laid down the protocol
for the relationships between members who attended the [July 1991] Conference
and adopted the Charter."[55] The EPRDF leaders not only ignore the human
rights and democratic rights of Ethiopians enshrined in the charter but also
illegally expelled members from the Council of Representatives. For instance,
in 1991,

[t]here were twenty-one ethnic political organizations that formed the TGE. As of October
1993, there are not more than seven of the Liberation Movement's founding members
of the Charter, which means that the coalition government has collapsed.[56]

The EPRDF leaders not only monopolize the government-controlled mass
media but also use state resources to create front organizations. Since 1991, the
so-called Peoples Democratic Organizations (PDOs) have mushroomed all over
the country. As in war, in the race to multiply front organizations, the first

casualty is truth itself. From all available evidence the front organizations have no power. They are under the firm grip of TPLF control. Indications are that innocent members of the front organizations who raise embarrassing questions are summarily dealt with. Interestingly, the kind of people who join front organizations are those who are attracted and strengthened by material rewards as well as the protection and political cover that the EPRDF gives them. Because submission to the EPRDF is necessary, joining the PDO has become a safety net. To refuse to join the PDO means disloyalty to the new political class, which entails exclusion from a leadership role, expulsion from jobs, and outright imprisonment. Ironically, PDOs have so far failed to win the cooperation, much less the trust and confidence, of the people whose interest they are supposed to serve. Winning the minds and the hearts of the people is much more difficult than creating front organizations. In the face of strong opposition by various organizations and rejection by the vast majority of the peoples of Ethiopia, the new political class relies heavily on the instrument of despotic power that it monopolizes.

We must realize that strong opposition organizations and democracy are "like Siamese twins—one cannot survive without the other." If all viable opposition groups are destroyed, swallowed up, or emasculated by the EPRDF, a euphemism for one dominant organization, what will be established in Ethiopia behind the facade of democracy will be the dictatorship of the TPLF, pure and simple. Today, being the supporters of the OLF or several other independent organizations is increasingly untenable in Ethiopia. Supporters are subjected to poisonous propaganda directed at the organizations they support. They are constantly harassed, imprisoned, and killed. What is not in doubt is that the establishment of a one-party dictatorship will have a far greater negative impact on the Ethiopian political landscape than anything we have seen since 1991. Although the EPRDF forces loom large in relation to other organizations in Ethiopia, they have limited capacity to contain popular resistance. The EPRDF forces, which inherited most of the Soviet arsenal from Mengistu's days, may temporarily defeat organizations such as the OLF. However, organizations that have the support of the people cannot be destroyed. This explains why three years after the EPRDF government claimed that it had eliminated the OLF as a military force, that organization's guerrilla army is more active today than it was six months ago. Under this circumstance, the real test for the EPRDF leadership is not to militarily defeat opposition organizations but to liberate its forces from the need to destroy and open their minds to the advantages of generous peace with rival organizations. It has been said that before making war, make sure your enemy is weak, but if you want peace, it is better that your adversary is strong.

It must be stated clearly that the opposition organizations, too, have a responsibility in promoting democracy in Ethiopia. They have to make a decisive choice for peace over war. The real test for the opposition organizations is not military confrontation but dialogue with the EPRDF leadership. They have to stop paying only lip service to peace in Ethiopia. They have to abandon the policy of attempting to overthrow the regime in power by defeating it on the battlefield. I believe the violent cycle of overthrowing a government in power undermines the prospect for stability and democracy in Ethiopia. Stable democracy requires political order, and political order does not spring up organically. It is made up by the people and their organizations. Ethiopian political leaders in and out of the country must make the decisive choice for peace over military confrontation, which is crucial in the end by its breadth of understanding, imagination, insight into the complex problems of the country, and responsibility to the future of all the peoples of that country. Meanwhile, other negative factors are also disturbing. There has been an alarming increase in hatred in and outside Ethiopia.[57] I do not remember any time in my life when so much hatred has engulfed the mind, the body, and the soul of educated Ethiopians. Hatred is the cancer that eats the vital organs of any society. It pollutes the mind, and the pollution of the mind is inseparable from the pollution of the human spirit; and the protection of human life is inseparable from the preservation of the generous human spirit.

Although the transitional government bears special blame for intensifying hatred, it alone is not responsible for the whole atmosphere. Educated Ethiopians in general and the supporters of the former Amhara ruling elites in particular have not stopped looking back in anger and forward in fear. They have not yet started looking around in awareness. Hence, they have not done much to inform and refine public discourse on democracy and the issue of human rights violations in Ethiopia. On the whole, until the overthrow of military dictatorship in May 1991, the supporters of the former ruling elites were generally oblivious to the suffering of the people. For instance, they were silent when the former military government literally rained bombs on Eritrea. They were silent when the same regime deliberately starved probably a million peasants in Tigrai and northern Ethiopia in 1984/1985.[58] They were totally silent when the same regime, through the so-called villagization program, uprooted over 8 million Oromo peasants and regrouped them in protected villages, where their movements were controlled, and their labor and produce were monopolized by the state.[59] The same supporters of the former ruling elites, who shouted loud about Eritrea's separation from Ethiopia in 1993, were totally silent about the concentration camps in Oromia, namely, at Hurso in Hararghe, Dedessa in Wallaga, and Blatta in Sidamo.[60] As the educated sector of the society, Ethiopian intellectuals have surprisingly not advocated for the human and democratic rights of all the peoples of Ethiopia. When they do, they usually address only the human rights violations of one particular ethnic group.[61] The Ethiopian elite, which "lives in a cocoon of self-delusion, and is absorbed in a limited world,"[62] have failed to reach the obvious conclusion: the human rights violations directed against one individual or a particular ethnic group are violations directed against all the peoples of that country. Until educated Ethiopians can marshal the moral courage to identify the problem as the existence of an undemocratic political culture rooted in the monopolization of state power by either the Amhara or Tigraian elite, Ethiopia will continue to be misruled by dictators who will preside over the slow-motion disintegration of that country.

Let us face it, the TPLF is not the first organization to establish autocracy in Ethiopia. From the time of Emperor Menilek (1889–1913) up to now, Ethiopia has failed to produce a single government that considered its subjects as citizens,[63] a single government that held itself accountable to its subjects, a single government that upheld the human rights of its subjects, a single government that respected its own laws, a single government that tolerated even loyal opposition, a single government that did not survive by the sword, a single government that did not plunder the peasantry, a single government that established a state based on the equality of all Ethiopians, and, above all, a single government that was not dominated either by the Amhara or Tigraian elite. Instead of the Shawan Amhara elite that dominated the Ethiopian political landscape for a century, now it is the Tigraian elite who regained "political ground lost in the last one hundred years, i.e., since the death of Yohannes IV [in 1889]."[64]

The EPRDF leadership . . . failed to understand that the chronic illness of the political structure of Ethiopia was not the lack of personalities, but a more fundamental defect in the structure of the Ethiopian government which had failed repeatedly to meet the dynamic changes inherent in a growing population and expanding empire.[65]

The failure of democracy to take root in the Ethiopian political culture enabled self-made Ethiopian leaders to slaughter and smother their subjects, trying to convince the survivors that their real enemy was and still is those who oppose the government of the day. It is precisely for this reason that the new Ethiopian rulers who loudly shout about democracy and human rights one day, the next day massacre innocent people for no other reason than participation in peaceful demonstration.[66] In Ethiopia governments have changed. Leaders have changed. But the abuse and misuse of power remain constant. Abuse of power has been at the very center of the dialectic of crisis and change sweeping Ethiopia. The former military regime not only grossly abused power but also bequeathed to the TPLF/EPRDF the authoritarian inheritance of Ethiopian politics. The authoritarian aspect of the new rulers was "initially hidden from view, because they displayed a considerable capacity for producing promising rhetoric about democracy."[67] It is ironic that while the 1991 Transitional Charter recognizes the human rights and democratic rights of Ethiopians, the transitional government did not allow the people to support organizations such as the Oromo Liberation Front (OLF) or the Islamic Front for the Liberation of Oromia (IFLO). Hence, the need to form the Oromo People's Democratic Organization (OPDO), in whose name other Oromo organizations are systematically undermined. Interestingly, in 1991 the EPRDF leaders staked their claim to legitimacy on their ability to facilitate the transition to democracy. So in 1991 the transitional period started with a fine promise of democracy. For a while in 1991, it appeared as if a tolerant political culture was developing in Ethiopia. That was the time when various organizations, including the EPRDF, the OLF, the IFLO, and other organizations, worked together without recourse to armed conflict. That window of opportunity (which was closed soon) raised hopes for the establishment of a democratic system—a system that would promote human rights, lead to economic development and increased welfare, ensure peace and stability in Ethiopia while fostering cooperation and mutual understanding among the peoples of that country. Then the thing called democracy was an inspiring idea. But within a year it quickly lost its way through the arrogance of power.

What went wrong? Several answers could be given, but three are very crucial. The first is the EPRDF's leaders' failure to realize that democracy is much more than window dressing. Opposition organizations did not help either. The second is the EPRDF's attempt at liquidating opposition groups. The existence of two separate armies complicated the situation. The third is EPRDF's manipulation of the elections of 1992, 1994, and 1995. The EPRDF's leaders failed to realize that democracy as a form of government is responsive to the preferences of its citizens:

Such responsiveness requires that citizens must have opportunities to (1) formulate their preferences, (2) signify their preferences to their fellow citizens and the government by individual and collective action, and (3) have their preferences weighed equally in the conduct of the government. These three opportunities, in turn, are dependent on the following institutional guarantees.

1. freedom to form and join organizations

2. freedom of expression

3. right to vote

4. eligibility for public office

5. right of political leaders to compete for support [and] . . . for votes

6. alternative source of information

7. free and fair elections

8. institutions for making government policies depend on votes and other expressions of preference.[68]

These conditions "cover three main dimensions of political democracy, namely competition, participation, and civil and political liberties,"[69] none of which exist in Ethiopia. The EPRDF leadership encouraged the formation of small parties, which they could control, manipulate, and dominate. Consequently, "by the summer of 1992, the number of registered political parties had grown to more than two hundred, but only a couple of handfuls had significant numbers."[70] Organizations such as the OLF and the All Amhara People's Organization (AAPO), which in any democratic election could pose formidable political challenge to the EPRDF leadership, were deliberately marginalized and effectively suppressed. These organizations were prevented from emerging as a political force, which was "an affront to the development of democracy in Ethiopia."[71] In other words, organizations such as the AAPO, the IFLO, and the OLF were not given meaningful opportunities to participate in the political life of Ethiopia. What is more, since 1993, freedom of expression has been under attack in Ethiopia.

The abuse inflicted by the current Ethiopian government against free speech and free press is not limited to only written or spoken criticisms, but goes much deeper in its far reaching, neurotic restrictions. In exactly the same manner as the former brutal government of Mengistu dealt with dissenting voices, imagined or otherwise, the current Ethiopian government has detained a very popular singer, Elfinesh Keno, because her songs, which praise Oromo culture and heritage, are believed by the government to be seditious.[72]

It is interesting to note that the OLF and the TPLF cooperated in the 1980s. However, the cooperation was transformed into conflict when the TPLF tried and failed to bring the OLF under its wing. Then in 1990, the TPLF created the Oromo Peoples Democratization Organization (OPDO), with which it wanted to replace the OLF. Although the OLF participated in both the London and Addis Ababa conferences of May and July 1991, respectively, coauthored the Transitional Charter, and joined the TGE, the TPLF/EPRDF leadership appeared not to have changed its policy of destroying the political and military capacity of the OLF. The source of conflict appears to have been the existence of two armies and the rise of Oromo nationalism.

Even after the formation of the TGE during the summer of 1991, there was no attempt to integrate the OLF army and the EPRDF soldiers into a single national force. The failure to integrate the two armies was a major problem that deepened suspicion between the two organizations. The EPRDF leadership, which had at its disposal overwhelming military superiority, decided on a short-cut route to victory. Instead of making every effort to integrate the OLF army into a national force, it opted to destroy it militarily on the battlefield. That was a tragic mistake. The war between the two organizations, which started during the summer of 1992, is still in progress, though with much less intensity. There will not be any winner in this conflict. The real losers will be the peoples of Ethiopia. No shortcut leads to permanent peace in Oromia except through protracted negotiation and integration of forces.

Although protonationalism developed among the Oromo in the 1960s, modern Oromo nationalism consolidated itself with the formation of the OLF in 1974. Even after 1974 nationalism remained a minority movement among the Oromo. This was because the Ethiopian military regime was able to contain Oromo nationalism and to isolate the OLF from people and limit it to small areas of Hararghe, Bale, and Wallaga. The military regime's policies of resettlement, villagization, and collectivization were undertaken mainly for the purpose of containing Oromo nationalism and isolating the OLF from its mass base.

The OLF was part of the TGE up to 1992. During this short period, OLF cadres and soldiers were openly operating in every corner of Oromia. This provided unprecedented opportunity for the transformation of Oromo nationalism from a movement of small groups to a mass movement. The rapid development of Oromo nationalism since 1991 was partly a response to the TPLF/EPRDF soldiers' occupation of Oromia, partly to the collapse of the Ethiopian state,[73] and, above all, to the Oromo organizations' activities. These organizations include the OLF, the IFLO, the OPDO, United Oromo People's Liberation Front (UOPLF), and the Oromo ABO Liberation Front (OALF). All these organizations are the manifestation of Oromo nationalism. Even the OPDO, which was formed by the TPLF in 1990, is beginning to take on a life of its own as an autonomous Oromo nationalist organization. The Oromo organizations may not agree on several issues, but they have all contributed to the transformation of Oromo nationalism from a small movement to a mass movement. In this, the OLF played a very decisive role. Although the OLF is militarily, politically, and organizationally weak, inept, and ineffective, its contribution to the consolidation of Oromo nationalism is formidable.[74] Interestingly, the EPRDF military attack on the OLF is also an attack on Oromo nationalism. This is because, by attempting to destroy the military and political capacity of the OLF, the EPRDF leadership hopes to weaken and contain Oromo nationalism. Strangely, the attack on the OLF was launched after that organization expressed its commitment to the democratization of Ethiopia. After 1991, the OLF was subtly changing its policy of independent Oromia to that of autonomous Oromia within Ethiopia. The purpose was to enable the Oromo to decide their destiny, administer themselves, and be their own masters in their own areas. "The one word I heard on the lips of every Oromo—man, woman, and child—was bilisummaa—FREEDOM."[75] From this perspective the attack on an independent Oromo organization that does not receive its marching orders from the TPLF/EPRDF is not only an attack on Oromo nationalism but also a clear assault on the right of the Oromo people to have their own independent organization. The attempt to destroy the OLF today is a cruel revenge of history. The TPLF, which attempted and failed to bring the OLF under its wing from 1984 to 1990, is now using the cover of the EPRDF and the governmental resources at its disposal to militarily destroy the organization that has the support of the overwhelming majority of the Oromo.[76] The attempt to destroy the OLF angers not only the Oromo but all who have concern for the future of democracy in that country. The attack on an independent organization is the greatest setback to the hopes and ideals of peaceful democratic change in Ethiopia since the overthrow of the military dictatorship in May 1991. Democracy cannot be built by militarily destroying an organization that expresses the profound aspirations of a given national group. Trust cannot be built between the rulers and the people, whose leadership is destroyed, whose property is confiscated, and who are treated as if they were under foreign military occupation.[77]

Democracy is not a magical solution for all the problems of Ethiopia once and for all. What democracy does is enable the people to establish mechanisms and institutions with which to manage and regulate societal conflict. What this means is that the democratization process gives the people valuable experience during the challenging journey from centralized misrule to federal self-administration. The road to that end is long and difficult. It is a process of history making that will face many challenges and frustrations. Nevertheless, the immediate change of direction from dependence on bullets for governance to the ballot box for self-administration must, at the very minimum, include the freedom to freely organize and contend for power.

What did the transitional government of Ethiopia do in that respect? It prevented independent organizations from freely organizing and contending for power in 1992. Consequently, Ethiopia's first multiparty elections for the district and regional councils in June 1992 "were turned into a single-party exercise."[78] The EPRDF leaders learned an important lesson from the 1992 election, which is that they can manipulate any election without provoking an outrage and condemnation from the Western powers that support them politically, financially, and morally.

In any free and fair election in Ethiopia, the TPLF/EPRDF would lose. It would lose because the TPLF, which has established the Tigraian ethnic domination over Ethiopia, represents about 10 percent of the population of Ethiopia, while Oromo organizations represent 40 to 50 percent of the population of Ethiopia. To preempt the prospect of losing a democratic election in Oromia, the TPLF forced the OLF to withdraw from the June 1992 election. Consequently,

Ethiopia's leaders blew a golden opportunity to set their country on a new course. . . . The promise of a chance to choose their leaders and manage their own affairs had aroused great popular excitement for this thing called Democracy. Millions of Ethiopians registered to vote, often despite huge obstacles, because they believed that this time it was going to be different. What they got was more of the same: broken promises, betrayed hopes and yet another permutation of age-old imperial intrigue.[79]

Because of well-documented, widespread irregularities in the electoral process, the closure of over 140 campaign offices, and the imprisonment and killings of cadres, the OLF boycotted the elections and was forced to withdraw from the transitional government.[80]

Consequently, a great opportunity for peace was wasted and armed conflict between EPRDF and the other organizations, particularly with the OLF and the Oromo people, has become more intensive. In addition to the many lives it costs every day, the conflict is also seriously affecting agricultural activities in many parts of the Oromo country which hitherto has more or less been the breadbasket of Ethiopia.[81]

In the name of democracy, men and women, young and old, are killed, and hundreds are tortured in many prisons in Oromia.[82] In the name of democracy, the EPRDF leadership appointed the Constitution Drafting Commission. This was "solely designed to keep in power the current leaders through an indirect voting system of a primitive parliamentary election process."[83] After the Constitution was drafted by the commission, which was "simply the alter ego of the ruling power,"[84] there was an election for the 548 members of the Constituent Assembly, which was "boycotted by all opposition political groups rendering the entire election exercise meaningless."[85] In December 1994, the Constituent Assembly ratified the new Constitution. According to one legal scholar, "The most striking feature of the Constitution is . . . the absence of separation of power and minimal checks and balances between the legislative, the executive and the judiciary."[86] The whole exercise of Constitution drafting, election, and ratification was designed

[f]or the sole purpose of legitimizing the predetermined ascendance of Meles Zenawi as Prime Minister. The Prime Minister is the head of government, Chairman of the Council of Ministers and the Commander-in-Chief of the armed forces. . . . This means a single political organization could stay in power for twenty–thirty years or even until the Second Coming.[87]

The EPRDF leaders know fully well that "a government that cannot be voted out of office is not accountable, thus not democratic."[88] The EPRDF leaders who "have been consistently deceitful"[89] about the collapse of democratization in Ethiopia used the transition period to perpetuate their power structure permanently.

The period of transition was intended as a time for the establishment of democratic institutions and for keeping the government in check, giving it powers to carry out only temporary measures. It was not meant as a scheme to gain time and create excuses for legitimacy in an inherently defective quasi-Stalinist system of political power structure.[90]

The EPRDF Constitution, which was drafted and ratified at the cost of more than 50 million Ethiopian bir, may not bring about a democratic form of government and social change in Ethiopia because of the absence of popular support for the drafting of the Constitution. Like previous Ethiopian Constitutions, it will remain on paper. The reason for this is quite obvious. It was a Constitution single-handedly produced by one organization and its partners. Independent organizations, which represent probably 80 percent of the population, were not party to the drafting of this Constitution. It lost legitimacy before it was even ratified. This proves once again that a constitutional drafting exercise by itself cannot create a democratic government or end authoritarian rule. It is sad to note in passing that this is neither the way to establish a new federal democratic order nor the way to create trust and confidence in the new Constitution. In the words of Professor Marina Ottaway, a constitution drafted only by the parties allied with the government, while opposition movements remain outside the process, cannot lead to democracy. . . . Unless the great majority of organizations participate in the process and accept the results, adopting a constitution and holding elections will remain a useless exercise.[91]

Since 1955, the Ethiopian ruling elites have artfully drafted four Constitutions.[92] But they forgot to realize that

[i]t is an even greater art to bring the constituency to endow the constitution with legitimacy. Constitutional legitimacy involves consent. It is certainly not a commitment that can be coerced into obedience to a particular regime. Consensual legitimacy is utterly necessary for a constitution to have real meaning to last. The very fact that although rule can be imposed by force, constitutions can exist as meaningful documents only by consent, means that constitutional documents cannot be treated in the abstract divorced from the power systems of which they are part and the political cultures from which they grow and to which they must respond.[93]

The EPRDF regime, desirous of preserving as much of the Abyssinian control of Oromo politics as possible, reluctantly recognized the geographical identity of Oromia and accepted the use of the Latin alphabet for the Oromo language, both of which have been implemented by the OLF since 1974. Both of these developments are positive, for which the EPRDF leadership should be commended. However, the same leadership failed to include major organizations such as the OLF, IFLO, AAPO, and many others in the drafting of the federal Constitution. Thus, once again Ethiopia missed an opportunity of drafting a Constitution endowed with legitimacy based on consent. Another opportunity to democratize Ethiopia and build its institutions has been lost. It is too painful to conclude that "every political and economic idea that was tried by the Ethiopian governments over the last fifty years did not solve Ethiopia's political and economic problems."[94]

CONCLUSION

A good part of this chapter is critical of the EPRDF leadership's activities since 1991. This is because it is "[t]he party responsible for the current political and economic problems facing Ethiopia."[95] However, it is never too late for the EPRDF leaders to change course and stop the slide toward a one-party dictatorship.

If the EPRDF leaders are serious about democracy and the future of Ethiopia, they have to change course and give meaning, substance, and purpose to their rhetoric of "Federal Republic of Ethiopia." To do this, first, they have to realize that "federal principles grow out of the idea that free people can freely enter into lasting yet limited political Associations to achieve common ends and protect certain rights while preserving their respective integrities."[96] Today, the Oromo, like other national groups in Ethiopia, do not regard themselves as free people, and therefore they cannot freely enter into political associations to establish a Federal Republic of Ethiopia. To do that, they have first to gain their freedom through peaceful self-determination. Second, the EPRDF leaders should realize that the challenge for them is not to use their formidable military muscle for abusing power, dominating people, destroying rival organizations, and waging war in Oromia. I believe the war in Oromia should end not on the battlefield but on the negotiating table. Battlefield victory deepens the wound of defeat and shame, thus fueling future conflict, while resolution of conflict at a negotiating table heals the old wounds and redresses the old injustice. Third, the EPRDF leaders must realize that asserting Oromo national identity and demanding equality and genuine participation in administering themselves in Oromia within Ethiopia are not reckless narrow nationalism but a legitimate and necessary measure of self-determination. "Like the people of Tigrai and Eritrea, the Oromo have a legitimate right to decide their own destiny. It is their own business to decide about their future and no one will decide it for them."[97]

The challenge for the Oromo is to act as responsibly as possible and contribute their share to the establishment of a democratic federal system in Ethiopia. The leaders of Oromo organizations must make their stand on one cardinal issue crystal-clear. This is whether they want to establish an independent Oromia, separate from Ethiopia, or an autonomous Oromia within Ethiopia. They have to choose either one or the other but not mix both. I believe autonomous Oromia within Ethiopia is much more beneficial to the Oromo and other peoples of Ethiopia than an independent and separate Oromia. If Oromo leaders, especially the leaders of the OLF, opt for autonomous Oromia, they have to be willing and ready to integrate their army into the Ethiopian national army through negotiation. Under federal arrangement, Oromia will have its own police force and militia. Oromo leaders must also be willing and ready to transform their organizations from guerrilla movements into political parties. Such transformation will enhance the prospects for democratization of Ethiopia. Democracy will not only uplift the crushed humanity of the Oromo and revitalize their stagnant economy but also enhance their strategic significance in the future of Ethiopia. Hence, the democratization of Ethiopia will be of greatest benefit to the Oromo. The challenge for the leaders of the EPRDF is to realize that, together with the OLF and the leaders of other organizations, they stand on the threshold of history— the democratization of Ethiopia. Together, they can build a better future for the people of Ethiopia. Separately, they can destroy each other and the country. The peril lies in aborting the experiment with democracy before it is established. Building a democratic federal structure is an experiment in joint human endeavor for living together, for settling conflicts rationally through dialogue, a genuine search for mutual benefit characterized by the spirit of give-and-take, tolerance, concession, and compromise. For this to happen, the EPRDF leaders must accept the principle that the voice of the people determines the choice of the people. Organizations learn by mistakes. Much of the responsibility for aborting the recent democratic experiment in Ethiopia lies with the EPRDF leadership, which was so eager to dine on the fruits of its military victory. Alone, the EPRDF leadership has the military power to destroy the hope for a federal democratic future in Ethiopia. Together with other organizations, the EPRDF leadership can establish a federal democratic system in Ethiopia. Ethiopia can be at peace with itself only by establishing a federal democratic order that upholds the political, economic, cultural, and religious rights of its various national groups. If the EPRDF leadership acts with enlightened moderation, it needs our support and deserves it. Above all, it will create trust and confidence—the precondition for building a democratic system. Trust and confidence between organizations and the people they represent are the two greatest assets to the ideals and values of federalism in Ethiopia. It is not military victory that will bring about the desired federalism but, rather, determined efforts by all organizations; trust and confidence will begin loosening the grip of hatred, mistrust, and suspicion among people and prepare the necessary climate for building a democratic system the only way it can be built—by the people from the bottom up. By cooperating with other organizations (on the basis of equality) the EPRDF leaders can give a new hope for a democratic experiment, as well as inspiration and purpose for the future of the peoples of Ethiopia.

To begin the democratization process in earnest, the necessary political climate must be created in which the leaders of all organizations in and outside the country feel that they are part of the political process. The tasks they face are daunting. It is hoped that they will face them bravely, with an air of optimism, hope, and confidence and bring to the joint endeavor the understanding that democracy is not only an investment in the future but also the best choice for the country that wants economic development and the progress of free human spirit. If democracy fails in Ethiopia, the losers will be all the peoples of that country. If it succeeds, it will have a strong impact on the countries of the Horn of Africa, all of which are suffering from the lack of democracy.[98] "Democracy's strength" lies in the fact that it is the only practical way for the Amharas, the Oromo, the Tigraians, and other people of Ethiopia to live together as they did in the past instead of killing each other and destroying their future.

I believe no serious person expects miracles from the EPRDF leadership alone. But everyone with even a modicum of concern for the future of Ethiopia should urge the EPRDF leadership to open up the political system so that all organizations in and out of the country can participate in the political process of their own future. There is nothing magic about admitting mistakes and changing course. Monopolization of power, under whatever guise, has not only failed to solve problems but created new ones. The magic is what all political forces working together can achieve for the future of Ethiopia, bringing it back to the important position it once held and still deserves in today's Africa. In democratization, harmony, and cooperation among the various political forces lies the future of Ethiopia.[99]

NOTES

1. Edmond Keller, "Remaking the Ethiopian State," in I. William Zartman, ed., *Collapsed States: The Disintegration and Restoration of Legitimate Authority* (Boulder, CO: Lynne Rienner, 1995), 125.

2. Mahmood Monshipouri, *Democratization, Liberalization and Human Rights in the Third World* (Boulder, CO: Lynne Rienner, 1995), 16.

3. I. William Zartman, "Introduction: Posing the Problem of State Collapse," in Zartman, *Collapsed States*, 5.

4. Daniel J. Elazar, Exploring Federalism (Tuscaloosa: University of Alabama Press, 1987), 5.

5. Elazar, *Exploring Federalism*, 5.

6. Tecola W. Hagos, *Democratization: Ethiopia (1991–1994) A Personal View* (Cambridge, MA: Khepera, 1995), 27.

7. Hagos, *Democratization*, 4.

8. Georg Sorenson, *Democracy and Democratization: Dilemmas in World Politics* (Boulder, CO: Westview Press, 1993), 26.

9. Hagos, *Democratization*, 48.

10. Hagos, *Democratization*, 4.

11. Mekuria Bulcha, "The Language Policies of Ethiopian Regimes and the History of Written Afaan Oromo: 1844–1994," *Journal of Oromo Studies* 1, no. 2 (Winter 1991): 99–100.

12. Bulcha, "The Language Policies of Ethiopian Regimes," 91.

13. P. T. W. Baxter, "Ethiopia's Unacknowledged Problem: The Oromo," *African Affairs* 77, no. 308 (1978): 288.

14. Bulcha, "The Language Policies of Ethiopian Regimes," 99.

15. Bulcha, "The Language Policies of Ethiopian Regimes," 101.

16. Mohammed Hassen, *The Oromo of Ethiopia: A History, 1570–1860* (Cambridge: Cambridge University Press, 1990), 3.

17. Mohammed Hassen, "Why Did It Take So Long for the Oromo to Be Politically Mobilized?" in Bichaka Fayissa, ed., *Proceedings of the Conference on the Oromo Nation*, held at York University, Toronto, Canada, 4–5 August 1990 (Murfreesboro: Middle Tennessee State University, 1991), 7.

18. Hagos, *Democratization*, 27.

19. Dawit Wolde Giorgis, *Red Tears: War, Famine and Revolution in Ethiopia* (Trenton, NJ: Red Sea Press, 1989), 117.

20. Bulcha, "The Language Policies of Ethiopian Regimes," 104.

21. Compare Walleligne's article, "On the Question of Nationalities," *Struggle* (1969): 4–7 with the content of the manifesto.

22. Olana Zoga, *Gezatena Gezot Matcha-Tulama Association* (Addis Ababa: n.p., 1993), 10.

23. Zoga, *Gezatena Gezot*, 10–11.

24. Zoga, *Gezatena Gezot*, 12. On 24 July 1995, at the Oromo Studies Association Conference, which was held in Washington, D.C., Colonel Alemu Qitessa stated bluntly that Haile Selassie's government followed a secret policy not only of controlling and limiting the promotion of high-ranking Oromo officers but also of reducing the number of Oromo soldiers in the military.

25. Zoga, *Gezatena Gezot*, 16.

26. Zoga, *Gezatena Gezot*, 18.

27. Zoga, *Gezatena Gezot*, 19.

28. Hassen, *The Oromo of Ethiopia*, 14.

29. Bulcha, "The Language Policies of Ethiopian Regimes," 102–5.

30. Anthony D. Smith, "Nationalism, Ethnic Separatism and the Intelligentsia," in Colin H. Williams, ed., *National Separatism* (Vancouver: University of British Columbia Press, 1982), 31.

31. Zoga, *Gezatena Gezot*, 24.

32. Zoga, *Gezatena Gezot*, 24–25.

33. Zoga, *Gezatena Gezot*, 75–77.

34. Zoga, *Gezatena Gezot*, 29.

35. Zoga, *Gezatena Gezot*, 28.

36. Zoga, *Gezatena Gezot*, 28.

37. Zoga, *Gezatena Gezot*, 89.

38. Zoga, *Gezatena Gezot*, 249.

39. Zoga, *Gezatena Gezot*, 161, 163, 249.

40. Zoga, *Gezatena Gezot*, 161, 163, 249.

41. John Markakis, *National and Class Conflict in the Horn of Africa* (Cambridge: Cambridge University Press, 1987), 260.

42. Zoga, *Gezatena Gezot*, 138–49. See also Baxter, "Ethiopia's Unacknowledged Problem," 291.

43. Sorenson, *Democracy and Democratization*, 3.

44. Sorenson, *Democracy and Democratization*, 12.

45. Hagos, *Democratization*, 15.

46. Keller, "Remaking the Ethiopian State," 133.

47. Hagos, *Democratization*, 97.

48. Hagos, *Democratization*, 97.

49. Makau Wa Mutua, "The New Oligarchy," *Africa Report* (September–October 1993): 31.

50. Marina Ottaway, "Democratization in Collapsed States," in I. William Zartman, ed., *Collapsed State* (Boulder, CO: Lynne Rienner, 1995), 238.

51. Ottaway, "Democratization in Collapsed States," 235.

52. Hagos, *Democratization*, 5.

53. See, for instance, "Ethiopia 1992: Human Rights Records," *The Oromo Commentary* 2, no. 2 (December 1992): 27–30.

54. Hagos, *Democratization*, 95.

55. Hagos, *Democratization*, 13.

56. Hagos, *Democratization*, 97.

57. See, for instance, "Hate on the Rise," *Ethiopia* 1, no. 4 (October 1992): 1–2. This document is published and distributed by Barry Goss from Cairo, Egypt. See also Hagos, *Democratization*, 138.

58. See, for instance, Jason Clay and Bonnie Holcomb, *Politics and the Ethiopian Famine, 1984–1985* (Cambridge, MA: Cultural Survival, 1985), chapters 4–9 and 191–95.

59. See, for instance, Jason Clay, Sandra Steingraber, and Peter Niggli, *The Spoils of Famine: Ethiopian Famine Policy and Peasant Agriculture* (Cambridge, MA: Cultural

Survival, 1988), chapters 4–10. See also Robert D. Kaplan, *Surrender or Starve: The Wars behind the Famine* (Boulder, CO: Westview Press, 1988), 1–10.

60. It is estimated that more than 90 percent of the over 20,000 so-called OLF prisoners of war were innocent people who were detained by the TPLF/EPRDF government in three concentration camps in 1992/1993. There was no protest against such gross human rights violation by educated Ethiopians.

61. See, for instance, *Ethiopian Register* (July 1994): 15–16, 29–32.

62. Hagos, *Democratization*, 124.

63. Hagos, *Democratization*, vii.

64. Hagos, *Democratization*, 9.

65. Hagos, *Democratization*, 126.

66. For instance, on 25 March 1992, while 30,000 people were demonstrating in the town of Watar, Hararghe, EPRDF soldiers killed 92 people and wounded over 300, who later died in hospital. See *The Massacre of Innocent Civilians by the EPRDF* (Addis Ababa: OLF Publication, 27 March 1992), 1.

67. *Oromo Bulletin* 1, no. 3 (July 1992): 1–2.

68. Sorenson, *Democracy and Democratization*, 12.

69. Sorenson, *Democracy and Democratization*, 12.

70. Keller, "Remaking the Ethiopian State," 133.

71. Hagos, *Democratization*, 85.

72. Hagos, *Democratization*, 135–36.

73. Keller, "Remaking the Ethiopian State," 125.

74. Hassen, "Why Did It Take So Long?" 13.

75. Ronald Ward, "Pilgrimage in Oromia-Madda Walaabuu," *Qunnamtii Oromia* 3, no. 1 (September 1992): 15.

76. Mohammed Hassen, "Eritrean Independence and Democracy in the Horn of Africa," in Amare Tekle, ed., *Eritrea and Ethiopia from Conflict to Cooperation* (Lawrenceville: Red Sea Press, 1994), 103–4.

77. Hassen, "Eritrean Independence," 103–4.

78. Ottaway, "Democratization in Collapsed States," 238–39.

79. Gilbert D. Kulick, "Ethiopia's Hollow Election Observing the Forms," *Foreign Service Journal* (September 1992): 41–45.

80. "Memorandum of Why the OLF Is Forced to Withdraw from the Election," *Oromo Bulletin* 1, no. 2 (June 1992): 1–10.

81. Mekuria Bulcha, "Sailing against the Winds of Change and EPRDF Politics vs. Regional and International Developments," *The Oromo Commentary* 2, no. 2 (December 1992): 1–3.

82. See for instance, *Quinnamtii Oromia* 3, no. 1 (December 1992): 1–3.

83. Hagos, *Democratization*, 39.

84. Hagos, *Democratization*, 34.

85. Hagos, *Democratization*, 38.

86. Hagos, *Democratization*, 47.

87. Hagos, *Democratization*, 49.

88. Ottaway, "Democratization in Collapsed States," 248.

89. Hagos, *Democratization*, 99.

90. Hagos, *Democratization*, 127.

91. Marina Ottaway, Testimony prepared for presentation to the House of Foreign Relations Subcommittee on African Affairs Hearing, March 1993.

92. The Constitution of 1955, the draft Constitution of 1974, the Constitution of 1987, and the draft Constitution of 1994.

93. Elazar, *Exploring Federalism*, 164.

94. Hagos, *Democratization*, 4.

95. Hagos, *Democratization*, 244.

96. Elazar, *Exploring Federalism*, 33.

97. Mohammed Hassen, "Eritrean Independence," 106.

98. Hassen, "Eritrean Independence," 107–8.

99. Hassen, *The Oromo of Ethiopia*, 200.

Chapter 11

Somalia: Problems and Prospects for Democratization

HUSSEIN M. ADAM

INTRODUCTION

The pervasive and explosive crisis confronting several African states goes beyond the need to adopt cosmetic democratic reforms. In a deeper sense, it represents historical structural factors—a mismatch between the colonial/neocolonial state and African civil societies. The end of the Cold War has reduced, even severely limited, in some cases, the opportunities for states "suspended" over their civil societies, extracting military, technical, and financial resources from competing external powers. Somalia became the perfect historical instrument for the implosion of this basic contradiction precisely because the Cold War had facilitated the creation of an exceedingly heavy military state over a decentralized, relatively democratic civil society surviving on meager resources.

Unlike the rest of Africa, during the 1960s, Somalia seemed to represent a "nation" in search of a "state."[1] Colonial partitions had dismembered the Somali-speaking people into British, Italian, and French (Djibouti) Somalilands; at the same time a portion of the Somali population fell under Emperor Menelik's Ethiopia (the so-called Ogaden), and another portion became part of British-ruled Kenya—the Northern Frontier District or NFD. British Somaliland obtained independence on 26 June 1960 and voluntarily joined Italian Somaliland to form the United Republic of Somalia on 1 July 1960. The young and fragile republic embarked on struggles to unite with the remaining three Somali territories. Somali nationalism was still in its infancy, and yet the Somali Republic manifested an aggressive brand of national consciousness.

Even though the potential for irredentism in Africa is relatively high, postindependent Somalia turned out to be the only consistent irredentist state. In 1963,

Somalia encouraged and supported an uprising in Kenya's NFD. In 1964, the Ethiopian army attacked several Somali border posts to dissuade Somalia from supporting a guerrilla uprising within the Ogaden. The relatively pro-Western Somali parliamentary regime turned to the USSR to increase its army from 3,000 to 10,000. On 21 October 1969, Somali military commander Mohamed Siyad Barre overthrew the "artificial democracy" (multiparty parliamentary regime) and instituted a military and personal rule dictatorship with Soviet support. He increased the army to 37,000 and sought to reclaim the Ogaden in a major 1977 war with Ethiopia. The Soviets backed Ethiopia as he broke with them and came under U.S. patronage. Paradoxically, he continued to augment the army to 120,000 by 1982 and directed it to wage wars against Somalia's civil society.

Ironically, what began as the search to establish a state corresponding to the greater Somali nation ended with the total collapse of the existing Somali state in January 1991. As of May 1991, the former British Somaliland (northern Somalia) declared the formation of a self-declared Republic of Somaliland. With regard to democratization possibilities, the de facto Republic of Somaliland seems to evolve toward its own brand of consociational democracy discussed later. If southern Somalia succeeds in restoring some form of state, it will most probably be based on a power-sharing formula—only this time power sharing among "strongmen" in control of fractured parts of the country, rather than a genuine consociational system.

CLANS AND SOURCES OF CLAN CONFLICTS

The Somali population of 8 to 10 million is made up of six major clan-families (Hawiye, Darod, Isaq, Dir, Digil, Mirifle); each one is subdivided into six or more clans, and each clan is subdivided into subclans and subsubclans, all the way down to lineages and extended families. Within the series of concentric and interconnected circles, with kaleidoscopic and diffuse attachments, the most stable subunit is the lineage segment, consisting of close kinsmen who together pay and receive blood compensation in cases involving homicide. In general, the Somali people share a common language (Somali), religion (Islam), physical characteristics, and pastoral and agropastoral customs and traditions.[2]

Clanism is the Somali version of the generic problem of ethnicity or tribalism: it represents primordial cleavages and cultural fragmentation within Somali society. After World War II, politicized clanism among Somalis favored nationalism and a Greater Somalia concept. At other times, clanism has assumed a negative aspect—the abandonment of objectivity when clan and local/parochial interests must prevail. Clan consciousness is partly a product of elite manipulation, the co-optation and corruption of politicians claiming clan leadership,[3] but at times the elite themselves are manipulated by politicized clanism.

On the other hand, aspects of clan consciousness, transcending elite-manipulated false consciousness, reflect a plea for social justice and against exploitative relations among ethnic groups. Uneven class formation has led certain groups to utilize clan formation as embryonic "trade unions." In such cases, affirmative, action-type policies are the best way to overcome discrimination against clans and groups. Clan consciousness tends to rise during periods of extreme scarcities—drought, famine, wars. Clan conflicts are also instigated by memories of past wars for resources or for naked prestige. However, such disputes take place mostly between neighboring clans, and intricate mechanisms have been evolved for conflict resolution, for clan territory is often extensive and sometimes even noncontiguous. By far the greatest damages brought about by clan conflicts spread over large geographic areas have resulted from elite manipulation of clan consciousness.

During the early years of the Somali civilian-dominated state, clan politics did not lead to violent conflicts and civil wars. Political parties tried to channel it into relatively peaceful competition. Unfortunately, greed and corruption among the emerging elites led to confusion and political paralysis. They could not even agree on a script for the Somali language, let alone take resolute measures to transform rural life and the economy. The system, derived from the Italian Constitution, manifested its "false democracy" essence during elections when parties multiplied, as organizations and clans splintered; and following elections, there was a rush to join the leading party in order to obtain ministerial positions and other official perquisites. The parliamentary and ministerial edifice, built on sand, was bound to collapse as a result of the hostile encounter with the "hard" institution within the state—the Somali National Army.

THE PROBLEMATIC VIOLENT TRANSITION

At first, the Siyad military regime seemed destined to strengthen the young Somali state. The military regime, unencumbered by the delays and costs entailed in a parliamentary process, mobilized resources for the implementation of various socioeconomic programs. The regime conducted campaigns against urban and rural illiteracy (after scripting the Somali language), expanded health and education services, resettled drought victims, and encouraged self-help community projects. The era of somewhat creative sociocultural experiments lasted until the year of the Ogaden War with Ethiopia, 1977–1978. Even before that date, Siyad began consolidating personal power and establishing a brutal autocratic regime. After 1977, the regime became more openly self-centered and vindictive; the opposition began to rise and, finding no room for political protest and dialogue, took up arms and began military operations in and out of Somali–Ethiopian border areas.

Siyad's Machiavellian personal rulership allowed him to manipulate the people and the potential opposition for several years; however, in the long run it facilitated the disintegration of the National Army and a plethora of other military security organizations as corporate entities. He went on to institute Latin American-style, state-sponsored, urban terroristic activities, but these only served to augment the external clan-based opposition groups while alienating most of the people from the regime. Once the armed opposition to his regime grew, Siyad singled out the northern region, inhabited by the Isaq clan-family, for extraordinary punishment. This treatment helped to strengthen the pro-secession sentiment that manifested itself during 1991 and after. After dropping "socialism" as rationalizing rhetorics, Siyad adopted clanism—a crude attempt to impose a clan hegemony over a basically decentralized and egalitarian civil society. This poisoning of clan relations laid the basis for the state collapse and savage civil wars that ensued. Thus, governance that was not simply bad but brutal as well helped to ignite the basic historical contradiction between the postcolonial state and Somali civil society.

Military, technical, and financial foreign assistance played a key role in pro-longing the life of Siyad's regime. When the United States and other donors stopped aid in 1989/1990, the regime collapsed soon after, in 1991. However, international intervention to craft/restore a post-Siyad new order missed several windows of opportunity: in 1978, when Siyad was obliged to rely on the United States; in 1980, when his army attacked a Majerteyn clan whose elite had gone to Ethiopia to start a rebellion; in 1988, when the civil war erupted in the north; and during the immediate post-Siyad period (1991). Unfortunately, citing se-curity reasons, diplomats and the UN staff evacuated Somalia in 1991. Media attention to the civil war-induced famine in the Bay region led President Bush to intervene under the UN-mandated Operation Restore Hope (ORH) in Decem-ber 1992 with 36,000 U.S. troops, to be followed in May 1993 by the United Nations Operations in Somalia (UNOSOM) with 28,000 troops.

Siyad's clan persecutions obliged the opposition to utilize their own clans as organizational bases for armed resistance. The first clan-based armed opposition group seemed to have stumbled into existence. After failing in an anti-Siyad coup attempt in 1978, Colonel Abdullahi Yusuf fled to Ethiopia, where he es-tablished the Somali Salvation Democratic Front (SSDF). The front attracted support mostly from his subclan of the Majerteen clan (another part of the Darod clan-family that spawned Siyad). The SSDF, following a burst of cross-border activities, atrophied as a result of heavy reliance on foreign funding from Libya, Abdullahi Yusuf's dictatorial leadership, and Siyad's ability to appease most of the Majerteens as fellow cousins within the Darod clan-family. Eventually, with funds and clan appeals, he was able to entice the bulk of SSDF fighters to return from Ethiopia and participate in his genocidal wars against the Isaq in the north and later against the Hawiye in the south, including Mogadishu. Following Si-yad's fall, the SSDF has claimed control of the Bari, Nugal, and parts of Mudug (northeast) regions of Somalia, under the contested leadership of General Mo-hammed Abshir. Since the aborted SSDF Congress of mid-1994, Colonel Ab-dullahi Yusuf has challenged General Abshir's leadership; so far, violent conflicts have not erupted among the subclan supporters of the two self-declared SSDF chairmen!

The major opposition clan grouping was the Somali National Movement

(SNM), which derived its main support from the Isaq clan-family of the north. The SNM was established in London early in 1981 but soon decided to move its operations to the Ethiopian Somali towns and villages close to the border with former British Somaliland. It is alleged that Qadhafi disliked SNM leaders and would not finance their movement; they were obliged to raise funds among the Somali Isaq communities in Saudi Arabia and the Gulf, in other Arab states, in East Africa, and in Western countries. This decentralized method of fundraising gave the movement relative independence: it also enhanced accountability to its numerous supporters. The SNM evolved protodemocratic procedures. Between 1981 and 1991 it held about six congresses, during which it periodically elected leaders and evolved policies. In 1988, the SNM conducted several raids and a major military operation in northern Somalia following a peace accord between Ethiopia and Somalia that removed Ethiopian restraints on SNM operations. They were able to block Siyad's huge army barricaded in towns and bases for the next two years. The SNM played an indirect role in the formation of the United Somali Congress (USC), an armed movement based on the Hawiye clan-family that inhabits the central regions of the country, including Mogadishu. A combination of uncoordinated wars waged by armed, clan-based opposition factions led to the overthrow of the heavily armed Siyad dictatorship in 1991, pushing the Somali political pendulum from tyranny to anarchy.

PROBLEMS AND PROSPECTS FOR DEMOCRATIZATION

In spite of Somalia's violent transition from tyranny toward anarchy, there is a growing strength in Somali civil society—essentially, because the entire state has collapsed.[4] In the north and practically in most areas of the country that did not require the intervention of foreign troops, the role of "traditional elders" (both secular and religious) has been both visible and positive. Women leaders have also been active, and women and children constituted a majority in demonstrations for disarmament and peace. Throughout the crisis, professionals, especially doctors and nurses who stayed in the country, have served as positive role models. Teachers have begun to revive rudimentary forms of schooling in urban areas.

As an aspect of civil society strength, the private sector has become revitalized. Gone were the so-called socialistic restrictions imposed by the dictatorship. The thriving, small-scale, private sector (in both the north and the south, including Mogadishu) has moved far ahead of embryonic regulatory authorities. In most parts of Africa, the state pulls or constrains civil society; in Somalia the embryonic state is challenged to keep up with a dynamic, small, private sector. In 1988 there were eighteen Somali voluntary development organizations (VDOs); now the number of such organizations has grown, and they need help from international VDOs to enhance the nonprofit private sector.

There is a palpable spirit of anticentralism, an atmosphere favoring local autonomy, regionalism, and federalism—and, in the north, self-determination and secession. As a corollary, there is a preference for locally controlled police forces over a large standing central army. In Somaliland and, to some extent, in northeast Somalia, there are embryonic manifestations of consociational democratic mechanisms involving consensus, proportionality, and avoidance of winner-take-all situations. Somali irredentism has collapsed with Siyad, and in its place one finds broad cooperation and relative harmony between Somalia and Ethiopia. There is also a vibrant emerging free press—about six papers in Hargeisa and over sixteen in Mogadishu. Printed in Somalia, they are produced by computers and mimeograph machines.

Operation Restore Hope and the United Nations have assisted in rebuilding Somalia's infrastructure, including ports, airports, roads, and bridges. Operation Restore Hope undertook a number of transitional measures, such as providing food for famine-stricken zones. Food aid needed to be carefully targeted: as food-for-work to strengthen the voluntary sector, the purchase of locally produced food to help monetize the economy and strengthen local markets; however, vulnerable groups had to receive food through nongovernmental organizations (NGOs)/VDO-supported local health and maternity services. This targeted food strategy sometimes fell short in practice, resulting in distorted Somali food markets. Somalia needs assistance to evolve a public sector that is accountable to local taxpayers. Foreign aid helped facilitate corruption in the previous regime: the country needs assistance to get back on its own feet, without being put on the dole.

It is useful to provide at least a rough, working definition of democracy to offer suggestive comparisons with evolving Somali political developments. Larry Diamond et al. in *Democracy in Developing Countries: Africa*[5] provide a useful definition containing three main conditions: (1) competition among individuals and organized groups that is both meaningful and extensive; (2) a high level of political participation in the selection of leaders and policies through regular and fair elections; and (3) an adequate level of civil and political liberties. As of 1994, the northern Republic of Somaliland has begun to meet some of these conditions within its embryonic political processes and institutions. Lapses have already occurred, given the armed conflicts with opposing groups in 1995. Southern Somalia is still groping to achieve reconciliations to ensure peaceful political cooperation. The five-month (June–October 1993) war between General Aidid and the U.S./United Nations served to considerably delay this process, which had begun to pick up some momentum as of early June 1993, when his branch of the USC within the Somali National Alliance (SNA) met with his old friend Colonel Abdullahi Yusuf heading an SSDF delegation. This reconciliation conference, held in Mogadishu (up till then a hostile venue for the SSDF), issued its peace and cooperation declaration on 4 June 1993. On 5 June, UNOSOM had provoked the USC-SNA militia into the deadly encounter over the Mogadishu radio station that led to the death of about 40 Pakistani UN soldiers.[6]

The decentralized, clan-based, armed groups that engaged Siyad's formidable army viewed themselves as part of Africa's movement toward democracy, often called Africa's second struggle for independence. However, none of them anticipated the serious problems that would follow the military overthrow of Siyad. The war between Aidid's and Ali Mahdi's USC faction over the control of state power turned Mogadishu into another Beirut, thereby ensuring complete state collapse. The northern SNM considered Ali Mahdi's "crowning" himself interim president as another instance of southern political arrogance, the straw that broke the camel's back: in May 1991, they established the breakaway Republic of Somaliland, creating an Eritrea-type problem.[7] Siyad left Mogadishu, but, unlike Mengistu, he did not leave the country until Aidid's forces finally chased him out in May 1992. Meanwhile, adopting lessons from the *Resistência Nacional Mozambicana*'s (RENAMO) (Mozambique) terrorist book, his forces continued to engage in spoiler raids aimed at further destabilizing Mogadishu. These raids and counterraids went through the Digil-Mirifle territories around Baidoa. Most of these clans, especially the Rahanwin, were badly affected. They launched their own liberation movement, the Somali Democratic Movement (SDM). Unfortunately, they were not armed enough to withstand the onslaughts. Siyad's forces, in particular, raided their camels, cattle, sheep, goats, and crops forcing thousands to flee deep into forests and mountains. Production ceased, and a terrible famine ensued, terrible enough to launch Operation Restore Hope. The civil wars have obliged most Somali factions to launch their own clan-based protopolitical organizations. The first five are the relatively older ones; each name is linked to its group's approximate clan affiliation:

1. Somali National Movement (SNM, Isaq, Republic of Somaliland)

2. Somali Salvation Democratic Front (SSDF, Majerteyn, Darod)

3. United Somali Congress (USC-SNA), Aidid, Habar Gedir, and other Hawiye clans)

4. United Somali Congress (USC, Ali Mahdi, Abgal, and other Hawiye clans)

5. Somali Patriotic Movement (SPM-SNA), Omar Jess, Ogaden, Darod)

6. Somali Patriotic Movement (SPM, General Gabiyo, Ogaden, and other Darod clans; recently, however, the two seem to have reunited as an Ogaden grouping under Jess)

7. Somali Democratic Movement (SDM, Digil-Mirifle/Rahanwin)

8. Southern Somali National Movement (SSNM-SNA) Dir clans, previously aligned to the northern SNM)

9. United Somali Front (USF, Issa clan)

10. United Somali Party (USP, Dulbahante and Warsangeli, Darod clans)

11. Somali Democratic Alliance (SDA, Gadabursi clan)

12. Somali National Democratic Union (SNDU, other Darod clans)

13. Somali National Front (SNF, former President Siyad's Marehan organization, Darod)

14. Somali National Union (SNU, based on the ancient urban dwellers outside the clan system)

15. Somali African Muki Organization (SAMO, based on the so-called Bantu Somali sedentary farmers)

Practically all the clan and social groupings in the society have formed a political organization. So far only the members of the Somali castes—Tumal, Midgan, Yibir—have not yet formed one. Those in Ethiopia have already done so: the Gabooye Democratic Front ("Gabooye" is a generic name for members of Somali traditional castes).

Given the scope and intensity of the civil wars, it would be unrealistic to expect the pro-democracy movement to regain its previous optimism and momentum in a short time. For the southern third of the country, the so-called Triangle of Death, thousands of foreign troops had to deliver relief to save lives and to ensure that productive activities would resume their previous levels, for two-thirds of the country includes Somaliland, local committees utilizing traditional law, *xeer*-maintained law and order. Today these areas are ready to embark on reconstruction, provided they get relevant assistance. The priority is to turn swords into camel bells, to ensure peace and stability. To turn clan conflicts into peaceful competition would constitute a significant step in Somali political development. Present indications are that political development will not lead inevitably to centralized authority or to the old unitary state. There will be need for coordination, planning, and maximization of scarce resources but within a decentralized and somewhat fragmented state. The political posturing of the past four years has a deadly serious aspect: the need to establish institutions and structures that do not facilitate the dominance of one clan group over others. Historically, Somali clans have been involved in their own unique forms of political development, which "at bottom, means men's cultivation of forms for public power and authority that enable them to meet external challenges and internal needs. Ethnic groups are proving that nations do not have a monopoly on political development."[8] Somali clans have not only promoted political development but also shown themselves adept in the past with the intricacies of constitutionalism.

The current situation is one in which, with the full collapse of the state, Somalis have been obliged to rely on traditional *xeer*. A similar situation occurred in the sixteenth century, when the Islamic state of Adal collapsed.[9] From its coastal capital of Zeila, its famous leader, Ahmed Gurey, waged several successful wars against the Christian Abyssinian kingdom. In 1542 his highland enemies defeated his armies, leading to the decline and collapse of Adal.[10] Oral traditions record the recurrent wars, famine, chaos, and banditry (*shifta*) that followed. A common response to the decline of public law was to revive and revitalize the *xeer*. The Isse clan (Dir clan-family) in particular produced an elaborate Constitution, *Xeer Cisse*.[11] The Constitution bound together six subclans—three related by blood kinship and three "adopted" subclans. Having lived under the pluralistic state of Adal, they decided to transcend the concept of kinship based solely on "blood." Although blood kinship is pervasive, Somali genealogies also indicate examples of kinship by "contract" and through "fictitious" stories of origin. All the six subclans came to constitute the Issa clan through this legal instrument—all of it composed in poetic style to assist memorization. It was decided that the traditional clan leader, the *Ugaas* (other Somalis use *Suldan* or *Boqor*), would be chosen from the numerically smallest subclan of the six, which happens to be of the three "adopted" subclans in the original contract. The leader is first among equals. The Constitution provides detailed provisions concerning choosing the right *Ugaas* as well as dethronement. A nonthreatening subclan was given, through the *Ugaas*, special prestige, recognition, and responsibility in adjudicating claims and disputes objectively and fairly. It is claimed that this specially crafted social contract carried the Isse through the chaos and turmoil of the sixteenth century and continues to minimize and resolve intra-Isse conflicts. The *Ugaas*, like other Somali traditional leaders, presides over the decision-making body or assembly, the *shir* (open to all adult males of the clan). Since the decision taken would bind the whole *shir*, including opponents, the good leader seeks to accommodate the opposition along consociational practices to avoid pressures that might later divide the group. Above all, given the cultural obsession with pride, every effort would therefore be made to avoid a loss of face.

Reconciliations legitimate and facilitate political cooperation. Northerners have taken a grassroots approach to the process. Traditional secular and religious (local) elites, modern elites, representatives of nongovernmental organizations, and ordinary citizens have participated in peace and reconciliation conferences held in virtually all the main towns: Berbera, Burao, Sheikh, Hargeisa, Erigavo, and Borama. Elders play a leading role, and, in their wisdom, Siyad's wars brought conflicts to civil society, and unless these are healed, there will be no mutual trust necessary to reestablish state organs. This approach has won the support of most of non-Isaq clans, and the SNM was therefore able to transform Somaliland from a clan to a multiclan or territorial project. Somaliland relies on the territorial basis of the British colonial borders, thereby including a heterogeneous grouping of at least four non-Isaq clans as well as numerous Isaq clans. It is not simply based on Isaq claims to clan homogeneity.

Following the 1992 conflict between two Isaq clans—the Issa Muse and the Habar Yunis—the Sheikh reconciliation *shir* went further in traditional practices: group marriages to demonstrate good faith were undertaken between the two ex-warring clans. In Mogadishu, grassroots meetings have appeared late and in sporadic fashion. Otherwise, the field has been dominated by elite-level reconciliation meetings sponsored by foreign powers. In 1991, the Italian and Egyptian governments organized two conferences in Djibouti. General Aidid and his allies refused to attend because they detected attempts to legitimate Ali Mahdi's "coronation." The UNOSOM-sponsored January 1993 Addis Ababa conference brought in all the fifteen political factions listed earlier (the SNM attending only as observers). They could agree only on a cease-fire, which was hardly implemented. The March 1993 Addis Ababa meeting included representatives of civil society and agreed on a basic outline of transitional authority. Following Aidid's ordeal, an Addis Ababa III Conference took place (December 1993), but nothing much was achieved. The Egyptians called a Cairo meeting early in 1994, but Aidid and his allies once again boycotted this meeting.

SNM and Somaliland constitutional practices up to 1994 involve leadership rotation and electoral participation within a relatively bottom-up approach; in the south, faction leaders hold power without electoral legitimacy. Relatively speaking, the SNM has proved to be the most democratic of the various insurgency movements. At its 1981 founding in London, it elected Ahmed Jiumale from the Habar Awal clan as its first chairman. It raised its funds in a decentralized manner from local and expatriate members of Isaq clans and subclans. This saved them from coming under the control of Colonel Gadhafy, who funded the SSDF. It continued to hold elections regularly, according to its Constitution. Sheikh Yusuf Madar (also Habar Awal) won the next election; the third election was alleged to have been stolen by its military wing, headed by Colonel Abdulkadr Korsar of the Habar Yunis clan. "However, the dominance of the military faction did not endure and, without any great acrimony or bloodshed, SNM again changed its leadership. A new civilian group was installed at the 1984 Congress."[12] Korsar was replaced by the charismatic Ahmed Mohamud "Silanyo" from the Habar Jeclo clan, who had the distinction of being the only one who served two terms. In 1990, the SNM elected Abdurahman Tuur (Habar Yunis) as chairman, who served as the first president of Somaliland.

The SNM Central Committee was made up of seats allocated according to traditional proportionality involving the eight "sons" of the clan-family founder, Sheikh Isaq constituting therefore the main clan branches of the Isaq: Toljaclo, Ayub, Arab, Habar Awal (Saad Muse and Isa Muse), Garhajis (Habar Yunis and Idagale), Muse, Sanbul and Imran (constituting the Habar Jeclo alliance). The SNM Central Committee was enlarged early in 1991 to include, on a proportional basis, representatives of non-Isaq clans in order to serve as the Parliament or National Assembly of the Somaliland Republic. Membership became pruned and refined enough to constitute a 75-member House of Elders (*Guurti*) and a 75-member House of Representatives, a total of 150 for the northern Parliament. (This may be the first time in postcolonial Africa that traditional elders were given such power and prestige.) The House of Elders will handle clan conflicts and will strive to ensure reconciliations and peace. It would also scrutinize legislation to see to it that it does not violate Islamic principles. There is also talk about forming an Administrative Council of Elders as an advisory body to help the administrative, day-to-day handling of clan conflicts.

The British colonial administration of Somaliland left records and precedents that were used to arrive at Isaq/non-Isaq proportionality. The 1960 elections conducted under the British utilized winner-take-all electoral districts. The British tried, however, to organize electoral districts in such a way so as to ensure an outcome that reflected clan proportionality. Out of the 33 parliamentary seats for the territory, Isaqs won 21 seats, and non-Isaqs won 12 seats (a rough proportion of two to one). The Somali National League (SNL) and United National Front (UNF), representing Isaq-led and-supported political parties, polled 54 and 34 percent of the popular vote; the non-Isaq USP polled 12 percent. Current Somaliland president Ibrahim Mohamed Egal, as head of the SNL, became first northern premier on 26 June 1960, just before unification on 1 July. The Gadabursi who hosted the Borama reconciliation and constitutional conference that ended in May 1993 asked for the formula to be slightly revised to give them more seats. Isaq clans volunteered to lose seven seats, which were added to their ratio. The Habar Yunis have expressed dissatisfaction with their eight seats and have pushed for further reforms. To make their demands felt, they have boycotted sessions of the new Parliament. Their anger is part of the current northern armed conflicts, though, to a large extent, the fire was ignited by elite manipulation—the few that are pro-federation with General Aidid and the many that are pro-independence. The current clan composition of members is as follows:

Habar Awal	16
Garhajis (Habar Yunis & Idagale)	16
Arab	13
Ayub	6
Toljaclo	4
Habar Jeclo and Allied Class	33
Subtotal for Isaq	88
Dulbahante (Darod)	23
Gadabursi (Dir)	21
Warsangeli (Darod)	9
Isse (Dir)	9
Subtotal for Non-Isaq	62
Total	150

The Borama Peace and Reconciliation Conference lasted from January to May 1993. The length itself represents an indigenous rhythm. At first, it set out to reconcile clan differences; then it laid out constitutional guidelines: there will be a president, vice president, and assembly constituting two houses, and the court system will function independently of the government. Then the 150-body assembly served as the electoral body to elect the president (Egal by 99 votes) and Abdurahman Au-Ali from Borama as the vice president. The incumbent president Abdurahman Tuur and former foreign minister Umar Arte also ran but lost. This transitional government was given till May 1995 to prepare for a referendum and to establish a commission to prepare a draft Constitution. The current emergency has facilitated extending President Egal's term for eighteen months. Somaliland's major problem is that no country has so far recognized it. A Supreme Court has been established, and the rule of law has begun to be exercised in that two groups of citizens are currently in the process of suing the administration for violations of contracts. Political parties will be allowed in the next phase; however, groups are able to informally organize clan and subclan groupings as political lobbies and to participate in indirect elections. Freedom of expression and freedom of the press thrive, through a relatively crude press. Publications criticize the government through poems, proverbs, and cartoons.

With the hope that the rule of law can be made uniform and predictable in Somaliland, a group called Lawyers for Civil Rights in Hargeisa aims to supplement the use of customary law and *Shari'a* by presenting to the government proposed legal codes that are also based on useful precedents from Somalian and British law.[13]

At least in the short run, the current emergency does not provide a conducive environment for the further development of democratic institutions.

As early as January 1993, UNOSOM wanted to pressure Somali elites to set up a juridical Somali state, oblivious of the fact that such pressures contributed to the prolongation of the civil wars. The 15–27 March 1993 Addis Ababa Conference resisted pressure to form a centralized state and adopted a regional autonomy approach based on Somalia's eighteen regions (actually, thirteen not counting the five northern regions), each of which is to establish a regional administrative council, police forces, and judiciaries, as well as district councils, leading Somalia observers to comment that the conference decided to turn Somalia into eighteen Somalilands! Avoiding the issue of forming an immediate national government, Addis II recommended the formation of a Transitional National Council (TNC) of three representatives (including one woman) from each region, five additional seats for Mogadishu, and one representative from each of the fifteen political factions (a total of 74 members). UNOSOM finally backed this regional autonomy approach and speeded up the process, especially after it freed its energies from the General Aidid debacle. As of January 1994, UNOSOM had assisted in the formation of 53 district councils out of 81 (excluding Somaliland) and eight out of thirteen regional councils (again, excluding Somaliland).[14]

In 1986, Somalia, Ethiopia, Sudan, Kenya, Uganda, and Djibouti established the Intergovernmental Authority on Drought and Development (IGADD), headquartered in Djibouti. The Organization of African Unity (OAU) and President Clinton asked Ethiopian president Meles Zenawi and IGADD to play the leading role in promoting Somali peace and reconciliation. In March, at the Nairobi IGADD Summit (Eritrea is now a member), the East African leaders invited President Egal and all the factional leaders. Egal continued to participate as an observer. The other factions engaged in intensive informal consultations ending in a formal agreement. They agreed to hold a formal National Conference in Mogadishu in May 1994 to elect a president, several vice presidents, and a prime minister and formally launch the TNC. The northern SNM was invited, and General Aidid and former president Abdirahman Tuur recently met in Addis

Ababa and agreed to work out federal arrangements for Somaliland. President Egal and his government have condemned such talks as violating Somaliland's constitutional status and procedures. This incident does, however, indicate the emergence of elite politics and maneuvers in line with the pledge to abandon the logic of force for the ethic of dialogue. For some time, the leaders entertained the notion of a Council of Presidents involving a series of rotating presidents, but they seem to have dropped this idea, at least for the time being. Any co-ordinating body that will serve as a transitional government will have to be based on the principle of a multiclan grand coalition.

Professor Arthur Lewis in his thought-provoking book *Politics in West Africa* first recommended that Africans drop the winner-take-all electoral principle and form grand coalitions as a more realistic way to operate African governments:

One can alter the constitutional rules for forming a government: for example, instead of the President sending for the leader of the largest party to form a Cabinet, the rule may tell him to send for the leader of every party which has received more than 20 percent of the votes, and divide the cabinet seats between them, or such of them as will co-operate. . . . To write the coalition idea into the rules of forming a government in place of the present government versus opposition idea would itself be quite a step forward.[15]

From ideas such as those of Arthur Lewis, Lijphart, and other European po-litical scientists had been formulated a "consociational" theory of democracy that seeks to avoid the pitfalls of the majoritarian, winner-take-all model.[16] So-mali studies scholar and political scientist David Laitin has argued that Somalia is in an excellent position to evolve its own unique version.[17] Somaliland has until recently taken steps toward a consociational or power-sharing democracy. The facilitating conditions are there: no clan-family or clan can hope to domi-nate/impose a hegemony (Siyad tried, using the huge national army, which has since evaporated, and there are no plans to establish another one). The clans have recognized leaders who have, at least in the past, cooperated with one another. Traditional Somali society endorses the principle of proportionality, as discussed earlier. It is also tolerant of the use of a mutual veto for any group that considers a proposed measure vital to its survival and well-being. Segmental autonomy to allow each group sufficient resources may be achieved through the principle of territorial regional autonomy/federalism, which has already been formally endorsed. Many Somali clans are territorially concentrated, while in multiclan regions the principle of proportional power sharing may be applied. This is one way the new authorities may be able to avoid instituting costly, difficult to manage, direct preferential policies.[18] Civil service, commissions, committees, and other bureaucratic appointments will be implemented on the basis of merit criteria and proportionality. Consociation practices would facilitate clan organizations and clan competition, and would, hopefully, discourage vi-olent clan conflicts.

A number of enabling factors need to be mentioned. Somalia's emerging consociational democracy needs to put a premium on the emerging private sector in order to reduce conflicts by keeping the public sector relatively small, lean, and efficient. There is an excessive reliance on the unleashed private sector to transform rural life and the economy. Clan competition within the private sector does not seem to give rise to the tensions one finds in the public sector. A vibrant, small-scale private sector has mushroomed unhindered by the nationalizations, the parastatals, the price controls, and the rentier-state regulations of the Siyad military dictatorship. A great deal of the emerging private sector is in the hands of women, most of whom have played remarkably constructive roles during the catastrophe. UNOSOM has attempted to establish local police forces that would be accountable to district and regional bodies. Somalia's more democratic future will be better safeguarded if the present consensus not to establish a new central army is maintained. A nonprofit sector led by indigenous Somali nongovernmental organizations has developed and needs nondependency assistance from international nongovernmental organizations (INGOs). State collapse and the civil wars have given Somalia the opportunity to rely on remarkable forms of self-reliance that need to be built on to produce a post–Cold War society that is relatively free from neocolonial dependencies.

For serious, long-term socioeconomic development, Somalia, like its neighbors, will have to rely on an emerging Horn of Africa common market. Relations with Ethiopia, Djibouti, and Eritrea are excellent, and relations with Kenya have improved considerably during the past few months. Earlier on, General Aidid had accused Kenya of supporting pro-Siyad forces. The old Somali irredentist policy has been thoroughly discredited because Siyad had converted it into a tool of his attempted Darod domination. When he failed in his military attempt to join the "Ogaden" into Somalia, he turned to using Ogadenis to "colonize" northern Somalia. During the 1960s, Somali irredentism was popular because the five-pointed star seemed to offer something for many of Somalia's clan.[19] What is journalistically termed the "Ogaden" is actually a vast territory containing several clans besides the Ogadenis. The Gadabursi and Issa in the western half of Somaliland have clansmen in Djibouti and even larger populations in what is today Ethiopia's Region Five. Sizable Isaq populations occupy the Haud and Reserve Area of Region Five. The Ogaden, other Darod, and Hawiye clans as well as numerous smaller clans occupy the rest of Region Five. Northern Kenya has Darod, Hawiye, Dir, and other clans. This is why Somali irredentism was widely popular until Siyad discredited it by turning it into a Darod affair. Another reason for good Ethiopia–Somali relations is that most of the key leaders in Somalia/Somaliland launched their movements from within Ethiopia and received Ethiopian support.

CONCLUSION

The challenge for Somali political development is to transcend violent clan conflicts toward peaceful clan competition. Clans cannot simply be wished away; the current situation represents a basic realism that clans exist, and they need to be harnessed and gradually modified to promote positive political developments.[20] Siyad's Machiavellianism considered clan organization illegal while he surreptitiously armed clans to wage savage wars. Clan consciousness is sometimes based on self-identification, on a "subjective belief in common descent," which, as the Isse clan example shows, is sometimes based on a mutual defense "contract" rather than on an objective blood relationship.

Elite—government and opposition elites—manipulations provide the major source of clan conflicts.[21] Colonial elites first introduced this practice within a centralized state, leaving a divide-and-rule legacy to be exploited by the postindependence elite. Military dictator Siyad carried the practice to outrageous levels through the provision of abundant modern arms and the adoption of terror as state policy aimed at achieving Marehan (Darod) hegemony. Armed opposition groups used defensive clanism and military bases in Ethiopia to overthrow the viciously clanist regime. Clanism operates in a defensive manner for those struggling for social justice and equality—the elite and masses are bound together by consciousness of shared oppression, which is significantly different from forms of "false consciousness" artificially manufactured by a cynical elite. Under peripheral capitalism, uneven class formation produces a unique dialectic of class and clan. Historical memories and environmental pressures (disasters) facilitate clanism as a group phenomenon.

In the post–Cold War period, with its rhetorics of a new democratic world order, democratic governance is increasingly advocated as the basis for international economic and social assistance. Somalia, north and south, needs priority assistance to conduct urgent voluntary mass disarmament. The United Nations seems to have conducted significant demobilization in Mozambique, while it has lagged terribly behind in Somalia and Somaliland. The youthful clan militias with guns need training programs and various other incentives to be able to reenter civil society without their arms. After careful screening, some of them could be recruited as part of the new, locally accountable police forces. In the south, the political situation continues to pose dangers of violent clan conflicts, especially in the Kismayu area. More than half of the political factional leaders, including Mohamed Farah Aidid (USC-SNA), Abdullahi Yusuf (SSDF), Umar Jess (SPM-SNA), Abdi Warsame (SSNM), and Umar Masala (SNF), were senior military officers in Siyad's army. Due to the clan factor, today none of them can conquer Somalia militarily. To create a government, they need to reconcile their differences and create multiclan coalitions along consociational lines. This would prove to be an "authoritarian" or "strong-men consociationalism," requiring the eventual introduction of the electoral principle, leadership rotation, and the rule of law for the transition to evolve toward consociational democracy. Perhaps the post–Cold War democratic order would serve as incentive for such a transformation. The Republic of Somaliland, on the other hand, despite recent setbacks, is groping toward "power-sharing, decision-making through consensus, respect for autonomy, and acceptance of differences."[22]

Somaliland faced clan conflicts during 1991–1992. Its political culture—a resurrection and modernization of traditional values and practices—assumes the inevitability of political conflicts and the possibility of managing them without dictatorship or violence. The new regime proved resilient, even though at this early stage, clan self-determination is relatively more important than individual human rights and the respect for detailed observance of democratic procedures. Today, Somaliland is facing the greatest challenge so far. Hard-liner opposition members decided to circumvent the Borama Conference constitutional process and agree to abandon the independence proclamation in favor of an unspecified "Somali Federation" with General Aidid's coalition. Former Somaliland president Abdirahman Tuur and finance minister Ismail Buube signed federal agreements with General Aidid. They were joined by former police commander Jama Mohamed Ghalib, who, until 1995, served as an influential member of the Somaliland National Assembly.

Egal's term was to expire in May 1995, but he has been able to exploit the crisis to ask the National Assembly for an additional eighteen months. The Somaliland official "hard-liners" have been bolstered by the recent importation of 25,000 tons of newly printed Somaliland currency. Meanwhile, the "federalist hard-liners" have been encouraged by UNOSOM funding for Somali "reunification," a pet project of the International Community; in reality such funds have been used to destabilize Somaliland by promoting fighting and armed rebellion against the government of President Egal. Many northern elites believe that even if the current crisis were to bring down Egal's administration, a restored peace and political order will still be established on the basis of Somaliland's embryonic consociational democracy.

The short-and medium-term prospects for democratization in southern Somalia are bleak; in Somaliland, after a promising start along consociational or power-sharing lines, a question mark has been raised by recent clashes.

NOTES

1. David Laitin and Said S. Samatar, *Somalia: Nation in Search of a State* (Boulder, CO: Westview Press, 1987).

2. I. M. Lewis, *A Modern History of Somalia: Nation and State in the Horn of Africa* (Boulder, CO: Westview Press, 1988).

3. John S. Saul, *The State and Revolution in Eastern Africa* (New York: Monthly Review Press, 1979), 391–423.

4. Naomi Chazan, Robert Mortimer, J. Ravenhill, and D. Rothchild, *Politics and Society in Contemporary Africa* (Boulder, CO: Lynne Rienner, 1988).

5. Larry Diamond, Juan Ling, and Seymour M. Lipset, *Democracy in Developing Countries*, vol. 2, *Africa* (Boulder, CO: Lynne Rienner, 1988), xvi.

6. John Drysdale, *Whatever Happened to Somalia? A Tale of Tragic Blunders* (London: HAAN Associates, 1994).

7. Donald Rothchild and Victor A. Olorunsola, *State versus Ethnic Claims: African Policy Dilemmas* (Boulder, CO: Westview Press, 1983).

8. Cynthia H. Enloe, *Ethnic Conflict and Political Development* (New York: University Press of America, 1986), 14.

9. Harold D. Nelson, *Area Handbook for Somalia* (Washington, DC: GPO for Foreign Area Studies, American University, 1982).

10. Touval Saadia, *Somali Nationalism: International Politics and the Drive for Unity in the Horn of Africa* (Cambridge: Harvard University Press, 1963).

11. Ali Moussa Iye, *Le Verdict De L'arbre* (Dubai: International Printing Press, 1991).

12. Ahmed I. Samatar, *Socialist Somalia: Rhetoric and Reality* (London: Zed Books, 1988).

13. Leah Leatherbee and Dale Bricker, *Consensus and Dissent: Prospects for Human Rights and Democracy in the Horn of Africa* (New York: Fund for Peace, January 1994).

14. *Horn of Africa Bulletin* (HAB) 6 (January–February 1994): 16.

15. Arthur Lewis, *Politics in West Africa* (London: Allen and Unwin, 1965).

16. A. Lijphart, *Democracy in Plural Societies: A Comparative Exploration* (New Haven, CT: Yale University Press, 1977).

17. David Laitin, "A Consociational Democracy for Somalia," *Horn of Africa* 13, nos. 1, 2 (January–March, April–June 1990): 62–68.

18. Donald L. Horowitz, *Ethnic Groups in Conflict* (Berkeley: University of California Press, 1985).

19. John Drysdale, *The Somali Dispute* (New York: Praeger, 1964).

20. Larry Diamond, "Review Article: Ethnicity and Ethnic Conflict," *Journal of Modern African Studies 25*, no. 1 (1987): 117–28.

21. Marie Bongartz, *The Civil War in Somalia* (Uppsala: Current African Issue II, Nordiska Afrikainstitute, 1991). See also Archie Mafeje, "The Ideology of 'Tribalism,' " *The Journal of Modern African Studies* 9, no. 2 (August 1971): 253–61; Mohamed H. Mukhtar, "The Emergence and Role of Political Parties in the Inter-River Region of Somalia from 1947 to 1960," in Annarita Puglielli, ed., *Proceedings of the Third International Congress of Somali Studies, May 1986, at the University of Rome* (Rome: Il Pensiero Scientifico Editore, 1988).

22. Leatherbee and Bricker, *Consensus and Dissent*.

Selected Bibliography

Adam, Heribert and Kogila Moodley. *The Negotiated Revolution: Society and Politics in Post-Apartheid South Africa*. Johannesburg: Jonathan Ball, 1993.

African National Congress (ANC). *The Reconstruction and Development Programme*. Johannesburg: Umanyano Press, 1994.

Agbese, Pita O. "Sanitizing Democracy in Nigeria." *TransAfrica Forum* 9, no. 1 (Spring 1992).

Ajulu, Rok. "Kenya: The Road to Democracy." *Review of African Political Economy* 53 (March 1992).

Ake, Claude. "Rethinking African Democracy." In Larry Diamond and Marc F. Plattner, eds., *The Global Resurgence of Democracy*. Baltimore: Johns Hopkins University Press, 1993, 70–82.

————, ed. *Political Economy of Nigeria*. London: Longman, 1985.

Amin, Samir. *Neo-Colonialism in West Africa*. New York: Monthly Review Press, 1973.

Ansah, J. Frimpong. *The Vampire State in Africa: The Political Economy of Decline*. Trenton, NJ: Africa World Press, 1992.

Awoonor, Kofi. *The Ghana Revolution: Background Account from a Personal Perspective*. New York: Oases, 1984.

Ayaode, John A. A. "State without Citizens: An Emerging African Phenomenon." In Donald Rothchild and Naomi Chazan, eds., *The Precarious Balance: State and Society in Africa*. Boulder, CO: Westview Press, 1988, 100–118.

Bakary, Tessy. "Elite Transformation and Political Succession." In I. William Zartman and Christopher Delgado, eds., *The Political Economy of Ivory Coast*. New York: Praeger, 1984, 38–46.

Barkan, Joel. "The Rise and Fall of a Governance Realm in Kenya." In Goran Hyden and Michael Bratton, eds., *Governance and Politics in Africa*. Boulder, CO: Lynne Rienner, 1992, 167–92.

————. "Divergence and Convergence in Kenya and Tanzania: Pressures for Reform."

In Joel D. Barkan, ed., *Beyond Capitalism vs. Socialism in Kenya and Tanzania.* Boulder, CO: Lynne Rienner, 1994.

Baxter, P. T. W. "Ethiopia's Unacknowledged Problem: The Oromo." *African Affairs* 77, no. 308 (1978): 283–296.

Bayart, Jean-François. "Civil Society in Africa." In Patrick Chabal, ed., *Political Domination in Africa: Reflections on the Limits of Power.* Cambridge: Cambridge University Press, 1986.

Boahen, Albert Adu. *The Ghanaian Sphinx: Reflections on the Contemporary History of Ghana, 1972–1987.* Accra: Ghana Academy of Arts and Sciences, 1989.

Callaghy, Thomas. "The State as Lame Leviathan: The Patrimonial Administrative State in Africa." In Zaki Ergas, ed., *The African State in Transition.* New York: St. Martin's Press, 1987, 87–116.

Callaghy, Thomas M. and John Ravenhill, eds. *Hemmed In: Responses to Africa's Economic Decline.* New York: Columbia University Press, 1993.

Clark, John. "Elections, Leadership and Democracy in Congo." *Africa Today* 41, no. 3 (1992): 41–60.

Collelo, Thomas, ed. *Chad: A Country Study.* Washington, DC: U.S. Government Printing Office, 1993.

Crook, Richard C. "Patrimonialism, Administrative Effectiveness and Economic Development in Côte d'Ivoire." *African Affairs* 88, no. 351 (April 1989): 205–28.

Daddieh, Cyril Kofie. "Ivory Coast." In Timothy M. Shaw and Olajide Aluko, eds., *The Political Economy of African Foreign Policy: Comparative Analysis.* New York: St. Martin's Press, 1984, 122–44.

———. "The Management of Educational Crises in Côte d'Ivoire." *The Journal of Modern African Studies* 26, no. 4 (1988): 639–59.

Decalo, Samuel. *Historical Dictionary of Chad.* Metuchen, NJ: Scarecrow Press, 1987.

Diamond, Larry. "Three Paradoxes of Democracy." In Larry Diamond and Marc F. Plattner, eds., *The Global Resurgence of Democracy.* Baltimore: Johns Hopkins University Press, 1993.

Drysdale, John. *Whatever Happened to Somalia? A Tale of Tragic Blunders.* London: HAAN Associates, 1994.

Engedayehn, Walle. "Ethiopia: Democracy and the Politics of Ethnicity." *Africa Today* 40, no. 2 (2d quarter 1993): 29–52.

Engelbert, Pierre. "Congo: Recent History." In *Africa: South of the Sahara.* London: Europa, 1994.

Friedman, Steven. "South Africa's Reluctant Transition." *Journal of Democracy* 4, no. 2 (April 1993), 56–70.

Glickman, Harvey, ed. *Ethnic Conflict and Democratization in Africa.* Atlanta: ASA Press, 1995.

Good, Kenneth. *Realizing Democracy in Botswana, Namibia, and South Africa.* Pretoria: Africa Institute of South Africa, 1997.

Gyimah-Boadi, E. "Economic Recovery and Politics in the PNDC's Ghana." *Journal of Commonwealth and Comparative Politics* 27, no. 3 (1990): 328–43.

———. "Ghana's Uncertain Political Opening." *Journal of Democracy* 5, no. 2 (1994): 75–86.

———, ed., *Ghana under PNDC Rule.* Dakar: Codesria Books, 1993.

Handloff, Robert E., ed. *Côte d'Ivoire: A Country Study.* Washington, DC: Federal Research Division, Library of Congress, 1991.

Hassen, Mohammed. *The Oromo of Ethiopia: A History, 1570–1860*. Cambridge: Cambridge University Press, 1990.

Horowitz, Donald. "Democracy in Divided Societies." *Journal of Democracy* 4, no. 4 (1993): 18–38.

Houphouët-Boigny, Félix. "Black Africa and the French Union." *Foreign Affairs* 35, no. 4 (July 1957): 593–99.

Huntington, Samuel. "Will More Countries Become Democratic?" *Political Science Quarterly* 99, no. 2 (1984): 193–218.

Huq, M. M. *The Political Economy of Ghana, the First 25 Years*. London: Macmillan, 1989.

Hutchful, Eboe. "New Elements in Militarism: Ethiopia, Ghana and Burkina." *International Journal* 41, no. 4 (1986): 802–830.

Hyden, Goran. "Governance in the Study of Politics." In Goran Hyden and Michael Bratton, eds., *Governance and Politics in Africa*. Boulder, CO: Lynne Rienner, 1992.

Ihonvbere, Julius O. *Nigeria: The Politics of Adjustment and Democracy*. New Brunswick, NJ: Transaction, 1994.

———. "Closer Integration in Global Economy Vital for Africa." *IMF Survey* 24, no. 14 (17 July 1995): 217–20.

Jackson, Robert H. and Carl G. Rosberg, Jr. "Why Africa's Weak States Persist: The Empirical and Juridical in Statehood." *World Politics* 35 (October 1982): 1–24.

Keller, Edmond. "Remaking the Ethiopian State." In I. William Zartman, ed., *Collapsed States: The Disintegration and Restoration of Legitimate Authority*. Boulder, CO: Lynne Rienner, 1995.

Kulick, Gilbert D. "Ethiopia's Hollow Election Observing the Forms." *Foreign Service Journal* (September 1992): 41–45.

Laitin, David. "A Consociational Democracy for Somalia." *Horn of Africa* 13, nos. 1, 2 (January–March, April–June 1980).

Laitin, David and Said S. Samatar. *Somalia: Nation in Search of a State*. Boulder, CO: Westview Press, 1987.

Lijphart, Arend. *Democracy in Plural Societies: A Comparative Exploration*. New Haven, CT: Yale University Press, 1977.

———. "Majority Rule in Theory and Practice: The Tenacity of a Flawed Paradigm." *International Social Science Journal* 129 (August 1991): 483–93.

Lindblom, Charles E. "The Market as Prison." *Journal of Politics* 44, no. 2 (May 1982): 324–36.

Loxley, John and David Seddon. "Stranglehold on Africa." *Review of African Political Economy* 62 (1994): 485–93.

Macpherson, Crawford B. *Democratic Theory*. Oxford: Clarendon Press, 1973.

Mamdani, Mahmood. "Peasants and Democracy." *New Left Review* 156 (March/April 1986): 37–49.

Mengisteab, Kidane. "Responses of Afro-Marxist States to the Crisis of Socialism: A Preliminary Assessment." *Third World Quarterly* 13, no. 1 (1992): 77–87.

Nelson, Harold D. *Area Handbook for Somalia*. Washington, DC: Government Printing Office for Foreign Area Studies, American University, 1982.

Nyang'oro, Julius E. "The Quest for Pluralist Democracy in Kenya." *Trans-Africa Forum* 7, no. 3 (1990): 73–82.

Nyang'oro, Julius E. and Timothy M. Shaw, eds. *Corporatism in Africa: Comparative Analysis and Practice.* Boulder, CO: Westview Press, 1989.

Nyerere, Julius K. *Our Leadership and the Destiny of Tanzania.* Harare: African Publishing Group, 1995.

Nyong'o, Peter Anyang'. "Democratization Processes in Africa," *Review of African Political Economy* 54 (1992): 97–102.

———, ed. *Popular Struggles for Democracy in Africa.* London: United Nations University and Zed Press, 1987.

Nzomo, Maria. "Empowering Women for Democratic Change in Kenya: Which Way Forward?" In Ludgera Klemp, ed., *Empowerment of Women in the Process of Democratisation: Experiences of Kenya, Uganda and Tanzania.* Dar es Salaam: Friedrich Ebert Stiftung, 1994, 29–33.

Nzouankeu, Jacques-Mariel. "The African Attitude to Democracy." *International Social Science Journal* 128 (May 1991): 373–85.

O'Meara, Dan. *Forty Lost Years: The Apartheid State and the Politics of the National Party, 1948–1994.* Johannesburg: Ravan, 1996.

Ottaway, Marina. "Democratization in Collapsed States." In I. William Zartman, ed., *Collapsed States: The Disintegration and Restoration of Legitimate Authority.* Boulder, CO and London: Lynne Rienner, 1995.

Owusu, Maxwell. "Democracy and Africa—A View from the Village," *The Journal of Modern African Studies* 30, no. 3 (1992): 369–96.

Price, Robert M. "Neo-Colonialism and Ghana's Economic Decline: A Critical Assessment." *Canadian Journal of African Studies* 18, no. 1 (1984): 163–93.

Rothchild, Donald and E. Gyimah-Boadi. "Populism in Ghana and Burkina Faso." *Current History* 88, no. 538 (May 1989): 221–24, 241–46.

Sandbrook, Richard. "Liberal Democracy in Africa: A Socialist-Revisionist Perspective." *Canadian Journal of African Studies* 22, no. 2 (1988): 240–67.

Sartori, Giovanni. "Rethinking Democracy: Bad Polity and Bad Politics." *International Social Science Journal* 129 (August 1991): 437–50.

Saul, John S. *Recolonization and Resistance in Southern Africa in the 1990s.* Trenton, NJ: African World Press, 1993.

———. "Globalism, Socialism and Democracy in the South African Transition." In Ralph Miliband and Leo Panitch, eds., *Socialist Register 1994.* London: Merlin Press, 1994.

Scarritt, James R. "Communal Conflict and Contention for Power in Africa South of the Sahara." In Ted Robert Gurr, ed., *Minorities at Risk: A Global View of Ethnopolitical Conflicts.* Washington, DC: U.S. Institute of Peace Press, 1993, 252–89.

Shaw, Timothy M. "The South in the 'New World (Dis)Order': Towards a Political Economy of Third World Foreign Policy in the 1990s." *Third World Quarterly* 15, no. 1 (1994): 17–30.

Shivji, Issa. "The Democracy Debate in Africa: Tanzania." *Review of African Political Economy* 50 (March 1991): 79–91.

Shivji, Issa, ed. *State and Constitutionalism: An African Debate on Democracy.* Harare: SAPES, 1991.

Sisk, Timothy D. *Democratization in South Africa: The Elusive Social Contract.* Princeton, NJ: Princeton University Press, 1995.

Sklar, Richard. "Developmental Democracy." *Comparative Studies in Society and History* 23, no. 4 (1987): 686–714.

Southall, Roger. "Beyond the 'Double Whammy': The New South Africa in the New World Order." *Third World Quarterly* 15, no. 1 (1994): 121–137.

Swatuk, Larry A. "The Nexus of Sovereignty and Regionalism in Post-Apartheid Southern Africa." In Mark E. Denham and Mark O. Lombardi, eds., *Perspectives on Third World Sovereignty: The Postmodern Paradox.* London: Macmillan, 1996.

Swatuk, Larry A. and Black, David R., eds. *Bridging the Rift: The New South Africa in Africa.* Boulder, CO: Westview Press, 1997.

Szeftel, Morris. " 'Negotiated Elections' in South Africa: 1994." *Review of African Political Economy* 61 (1994): 457–470.

Thompson, Virginia and Richard Adloff. *Historical Dictionary of the People's Republic of Congo.* Metuchen, NJ: Scarecrow Press, 1984.

UNICEF. *Ghana: Adjustment Policies and Programs to Protect Children and Other Vulnerable Groups.* Accra: UNICEF, November 1986.

Vines, Alex. *"No Democracy without Money": The Road to Peace in Mozambique (1982–1992).* London: Catholic Institute for International Relations, 1994.

Widner, Jennifer A. "The Rise of Civic Associations among Farmers in Côte d'Ivoire." In John Harbeson, Donald Rothchild, and Naomi Chazan, eds., *Civil Society and the State in Africa.* Boulder, CO: Lynne Rienner, 1994, 191–215.

Wood, Ellen Meiksins. "The Uses and Abuses of 'Civil Society.' " In Ralph Miliband and Leo Panitch, eds., *Socialist Register 1990: The Retreat of the Intellectuals.* London: Merlin Press, 1990.

Young, Crawford. *The African Colonial State in Comparative Perspective.* New Haven, CT, and London: Yale University Press, 1994.

———, ed. *The Rising Tide of Cultural Pluralism.* Madison: University of Wisconsin Press, 1993.

Zolberg, Aristide R. "The Specter of Anarchy: African States Verging on Dissolution." *Dissent* 39 (Summer 1992): 303–11.

Index

About the Contributors

HUSSEIN M. ADAM is an Associate Professor of Politics in the Political Science Department at the College of the Holy Cross. His articles have appeared in numerous international journals, including *Journal of Islamic Studies, Review of African Political Economy, African Affairs, Peace Review—The International Quarterly of World Peace*, and *Radical America*.

MARIO J. AZEVEDO is Chair and Frank Porter Graham Professor in the Department of African-American and African Studies, the University of North Carolina at Charlotte. He is author of several books and articles on Southern Africa and Francophone Equatorial Africa.

CYRIL DADDIEH is Director of the Program in Black Studies and Associate Professor of Political Science at Providence College. He taught previously at Salisbury State University. He has also served as a DuPont Visiting Scholar at Mary Baldwin College and a Rotary International Teaching Ambassador at the Legon Center for International Affairs (LECIA) of the University of Ghana. His most recent publications include "Universities and Political Protest in Africa: The Case of Côte d'Ivoire," "South Africa and Francophone African Relations," "Democratization and the Grassroots: The Case of Jomoro District Assembly, Ghana," and *Education and Democracy in Africa: Preliminary Thoughts on a Neglected Linkage*.

E. GYIMAH-BOADI is Head of the Governance Program at the Institute of Economic Affairs in Accra, Ghana, as well as Professor in the Department of Political Science at the University of Ghana-Legon. He previously held faculty positions at the University of Swaziland, American University, Dartmouth College, and SAIS. His recent publications include "Ghana's Encouraging Elections: The Challenges Ahead" and "Civil Society in Africa," both in the *Journal of Democracy*. He is coauthor of "The Politics of Economic Renewal in Africa" in *Agenda for Africa's Economic Renewal*.

MOHAMMED HASSEN is an Associate Professor of History at Georgia State University, Atlanta. He is the author of *The Oromo of Ethiopia: A History, 1570–1860*. He has also published more than a dozen articles, many book chapters, and numerous book reviews. He was the president of the Oromo Studies Association from 1994 to 1996.

JULIUS O. IHONVBERE is Professor of Government at the University of Texas at Austin. He is currently Program Officer in the Governance and Civil Society Unit of the Ford Foundation in New York. His articles have appeared in numerous international journals, including *Africa Today*, *The Journal of Modern African Studies*, *International Politics*, *Asian and African Studies*, *World Development*, and *The Journal of Political and Military Sociology*. His recent books have included *Nigeria: The Politics of Adjustment and Democracy*; *Economic Crisis, Civil Society and Democratization: The Case of Zambia*; and *Nigeria: The Illusions of Power* (with Timothy Shaw).

KIDANE MENGISTEAB is Professor and Chair of the Department of Political Science and Geography at Old Dominion University. He is the author of *Ethiopia: Failure of Land Reform and Agricultural Crisis* and *Globalization and Autocentricity in Africa's Development in the 21st Century* and coeditor of *Beyond Economic Liberalization in Africa*. Among his current research interests is the relationship between globalization and democracy.

JULIUS E. NYANG'ORO is Professor and Chair of African and Afro-American Studies at the University of North Carolina, Chapel Hill. Among his numerous previous publications are *The State and Capitalist Development in Africa* and *Discourses on Democracy*. He is currently working on a number of projects related to the question of political transition in Africa.

MARINA OTTAWAY is Senior Associate and Codirector, Democracy Project at the Carnegie Endowment for International Peace and Adjunct Professor of African Studies at the School for Advance International Studies, Johns Hopkins University. She has held teaching positions at the University of Addis Ababa, the University of Zambia, the American University in Cairo, and the University of the Witwatersrand in South Africa. Her publications include *South Africa: The Struggle for a New Order*, *Democratization and Ethnic Nationalism*, and an edited volume, *Democracy in Africa: The Hard Road Ahead*.

JOHN S. SAUL is a member of the editorial collective of Southern Africa Report in Toronto and also teaches political science at York University there.

He taught for almost a decade in Africa and, since the 1960s, has written or edited a dozen books and innumerable articles on political developments on that continent (including the forthcoming *South Africa: Apartheid and After*. He is currently preparing a large-scale, analytical history, *Thirty Years War for Southern African Liberation, 1960–1990*.

LARRY A. SWATUK is a Lecturer in the Department of Political and Administrative Studies at the University of Botswana. He is the author of, among other things, *Between Choice in a Hard Place: Contenting Theories of International Relations* and coeditor of *Bridging the Rift: The New South Africa in Africa*.